EXPERIMENTAL
ABNORMAL PSYCHOLOGY

MONOGRAPHS IN PSYCHOLOGY
An International Series

EXPERIMENTAL ABNORMAL PSYCHOLOGY

B. V. Zeigarnik

Moscow State University
Moscow, USSR

Translated by Timothy C. Brock

Psychology Department
The Ohio State University
Columbus, Ohio

PLENUM PRESS • NEW YORK—LONDON • 1972

Blyuma Vul'fovna Zeigarnik is Professor of Psychology at Moscow State University. She was graduated in 1927 from the University of Berlin. For many years Professor Zeigarnik has been the director of the Psychological Laboratory of the Moscow Institute of Psychiatry of the Ministry of Public Health of the RSFSR. She lectures on general and abnormal psychology. Her recent research has been concerned with the pathology of thought and personality.

The original Russian text, published by Moscow University Press in Moscow in 1969, has been revised and corrected by the author for the present edition. The English translation is published under an agreement with Mezhdunarodnaya Kniga, the Soviet book Export Agency.

Зейгарник Блюма Вульфовна

VVEDENIE V PATOPSIKHOLOGIYU
ВВЕДЕНИЕ В ПАТОПСИХОЛОГИЮ

Library of Congress Catalog Card Number 70-167678

ISBN 0-306-30543-7

© 1972 Plenum Press, New York
A Division of Plenum Publishing Corporation
227 West 17th Street, New York, N.Y. 10011

United Kingdom edition published by Plenum Press, London
A Division of Plenum Publishing Company, Ltd.
Davis House (4th Floor), 8 Scrubs Lane, Harlesden, NW10 6SE, London, England

Printed in the United States of America

Foreword

In recent years psychology has considerably expanded and enriched its relations with medical practice, first and foremost with psychiatry. This orientation toward experimental abnormal psychology has been closely tied to the practical tasks of psychiatry: differential diagnosis, establishment of the structure and extent of impairment, and the dynamics of mental disorders as affected by treatment, etc.

Experimental abnormal psychology has been no less important for the theoretical problems of psychology and psychiatry. The study of pathological changes in mental processes helps in dealing with questions about the structure and formation of mental activity. The research findings of abnormal psychology also have important implications for overcoming biologizing tendencies in the interpretation of human psychology.

The present book does not try to provide an exhaustive exposition of all divisions of abnormal psychology. It introduces the reader only to those problems which at the present time seem to be best worked out experimentally: the breakdown of intellectual capacity, thought disorders, the methodology of setting up an experiment in the psychiatric clinic, and certain questions relating to motivational disturbances and psychological growth and decay.

Some rewritten sections from the author's earlier book, "The Pathology of Thinking," have been included.

The present volume is intended for psychology students, for psychologists, and for physicians working in psychiatry.

Research in experimental psychology by the author and her colleagues constitutes the factual basis for the book's theses. This research was carried out in the Laboratory of Experimental Abnormal Psychology of the Moscow Institute of Psychiatry, which for many years has been the core program of the School of Psychology at Moscow State University.

I am sincerely grateful to the staff of the Institute and especially to my colleagues at the Laboratory. I would also like to express my gratitude to the physicians and psychologists at the Gannushkin Psychoneurological Hospital Number 4 for their unceasing assistance.

B. V. Z.

Contents

Chapter 1

Subject Matter and Tasks
of Abnormal Psychology

The subject matter of abnormal psychology is mental disturbances
resulting from brain disease. Whereas general psychology deals
with the characteristics of mental structure and development, abnormal psychology studies the structure and mechanisms of different forms of mental deterioration. Thus, for example, if general psychology studies the principles according to which thinking
is shaped and takes place, then abnormal psychology deals with
the principles and forms of disturbances in thinking.

As a division of general psychology, abnormal psychology proceeds from its theoretical assumptions and deals with the solution
of problems posed in clinical psychiatric practice.

Abnormal psychology is located at the juncture of two sciences:
psychiatry and psychology. Hence, the findings of abnormal psychology are significant for the theoretical and practical questions
of both disciplines.

The study of psychological change is one of the important
means for analyzing the structure of normal mental activity and
for developing a general psychological theory. The research findings of abnormal psychology are just as important for the theoretical and practical problems of psychiatry.

It should be noted that familiarization with the ideas and findings of modern psychology is necessary for every physician no
matter what his specialty. The physician deals not only with the

1

sick organism but also with the sick man who is reacting continu-
ally to the situation caused by his illness. The physician must
know how to thoroughly understand the patient's personality, the
peculiarities of his character, experiences, and needs, and, by
doing so, choose the appropriate strategy in relating to him. He
must know how to mobilize the personality of the patient in the
struggle with disease and to get the patient to relate adequately to
his own illness. Excessive overanxiousness about his health as
well as a careless attitude by the patient towards his illness must
be skillfully corrected by the physician. The effectiveness of the
treatment depends to a great extent on the attitudes of the patient
himself.

The findings of psychology are necessary too for the development of medicine as a science. Different branches of psychology
can be taken advantage of depending upon the particular clinical
field. For example, in pediatrics, the findings of child psychology
are applicable, such as assumptions about the principal activity of
the child at various developmental stages (the works of A. V. Zaporozhets, D. V. Él'konin, L. I. Bozhovich, and the research of J.
Piaget); the oculist can benefit from information about the properties of visual activity (works of A. A. Yarbus); the therapist can
use findings from work on interoception, such as data on sublimi-
nal sensation (B. G. Anan'ev, G. V. Gershuni, A. N. Leont'ev) and
so forth.

In 1966 the Ministry of Public Health of the USSR introduced
the teaching of medical psychology into the medical schools because knowledge of psychology was considered necessary for every
medical specialization.

Psychology has an especially great significance for psychiatry and neurology. The findings of psychology are essential for
analyzing the origin and course of mental illness and the structure
of psychopathological symptoms. In investigating different psychological disorders, psychiatry has always used psychological concepts and naturally these concepts have continued to be those of
the current empirical, or so-called, functional psychology.

Soviet psychologists (L. S. Vygotskii, P. Ya. Gal'perin, A. V.
Zaporozhets, A. N. Leont'ev, A. R. Luriya, S. L. Rubinshtein) pro-
ceed from different methodological assumptions in their research.
On the basis of the general propositions of the Marxist-Leninist

theory of reflection and the Sechenov-Pavlov teachings on the reflex nature of the mind, Soviet psychologists rejected division of
the mind into separate innate functions and maintained that different forms of mental activity develop in the course of life as a function of upbringing and training. A child is not born with "little
functions" of thought and memory, which expand during growth and
decline with brain disease; thought and memory are in fact different forms of activity that are shaped during ontogenesis.

These principles, founded on concrete research, may provide
the basic explanation of many abnormal symptoms and syndromes.
However, one must distinguish the subject matter of abnormal
psychology from that of general psychopathology as a division of
psychiatry. Although these topics may coincide in some respects,
nevertheless, we think that their present stage of development allows a certain demarcation.

General psychopathology, as a division of medicine, studies
the most typical symptoms and syndromes of disease conditions.
General psychopathology, which covers both the genesis and etiology of mental illness, is broader than abnormal psychology, which
investigates the structure of a particular form of mental disorder
and compares the mechanisms of deterioration with the norm. The
latter must assess psychopathological phenomena in terms of contemporary psychological concepts.

As a division of psychology, abnormal psychology proceeds
from its basic premises: the principle of determinism and the
principle of growth. What do these principles require? Rather
than binding us to the study of an individual's isolated responses
to a stimulus, they require qualitative examination of the content
of his mental activity, i.e., an analysis of changes in his actions,
behavior, and cognitions. As S. L. Rubinshtein showed, the correct philosophical definition of determinism means that an external cause does not directly determine a person's responses; it
acts through internal conditions. "An external influence," as
stated in his book "Being and Consciousness," "has a given psychological effect only as it is reflected through the subject's psychological state, through his system of accumulated thoughts and
feelings" (page 226). Applying this to concrete research in abnormal psychology means that it is necessary to proceed from studying the breakdown of separate functions to the study of changes of

different forms of the patient's activity, including changes of personality orientation and motives.

The tenets of Soviet materialist psychology concerning the genesis of mental processes lead to the same conclusion. The very formation of these processes is impossible without the contribution of motivational ingredients. A. N. Leont'ev, in showing that mental processes are formed during the course of life, emphasized that this formation takes place in the process of mastering a world of objects and phenomena created by man. He shows that biologically inherited properties constitute only one (albeit a very important one) of the formative conditions of mental functions. The basic formative condition is indeed the mastery of the world of objects and phenomena created by mankind. In addition, Leont'ev emphasizes that this learning is an active process; to open the world of objects to a child the child must actively work with these objects and phenomena. This learning takes place in interaction with other people. The child is "brought into this world by the people around him and they guide him in this world."

Therefore the most important condition for learning to master the environment is the availability of relations with other people. Complex mental activity is socially conditioned from the very beginning; it forms in the course of mastering the environment in interaction with other people with whom the child has definite relationships. These relationships are determined by concrete historical conditions but, once established, they themselves determine the person's behavior and actions. The social needs, motives and interests which arise in the process of mastering the environment form the child's personality. With the development of human society, ways of satisfying these needs are, as Karl Marx put it, "more and more humanized." New, more sophisticated, needs appear while the old ones undergo differentiation and transformation.

In destroying the mental behavior of the person, disease frequently changes the peronality component of that behavior — a fact well known to psychiatrists. All psychiatric texts and monographs include detailed and exceptionally faithful and vivid descriptions of personality disorders typical for patients with different nosologies. However, psychopathological analysis still treats the symptom as basically a disturbance of a mental function or the symptom is even explained by positing disorder of physiological processes.

Meanwhile, it is clear from the aforementioned theoretical principles of materialist psychology that analysis of a psychopathological phenomenon must take into account the patient's personality disturbance and changes in his attitudes, needs, and interests. Therefore investigation of personality disorders is worthwhile, both practically and methodologically. The correct solution of this problem will be possible only when it is based on the principles of determinism and growth in the dialectical-materialistic sense. The fact that abnormal psychology is oriented towards studying personality disorders changes the formulation of certain specific research questions. These questions will be discussed in future chapters.

A further problem of great promise confronting the comparatively young borderline field of abnormal psychology is the development of adequate techniques which might insure objective interpretation and analysis of psychopathological phenomena in the scientific terms of materialist psychology. The refinement of procedures and the standardization of individual techniques constitute the subject matter of concrete research in abnormal psychology. Further development of this division of abnormal psychology goes beyond questions about procedural rules; it acquires a certain methodological significance, opening new possibilities for the analysis of the qualitative structure of psychopathological symptoms and syndromes.

The practical uses of the psychology experiment in the psychiatric clinic are quite varied. The experiment must not be carried out in isolation from clinical tasks and it must be geared to the concrete questions of clinical practice.

What then are the sorts of problems that can be posed to psychological research?

1. In the first place, the psychology experiment can be used for differential diagnostic purposes.

It is self-evident that diagnosis cannot be established on the basis of some laboratory studies; rather it must be based on comprehensive clinical inquiry. However, psychology laboratories have accumulated experimental facts characterizing disorder of mental processes in different kinds of illness. Therefore the findings of experimental psychology can serve as supplementary material in the establishment of a diagnosis. So, for example, in the clinical analysis of a patient's condition, it is sometimes necessary to separate an asthenic condition of organic nature from schizophrenic inertia. The discovery of retarded mental processes, with poor memory and recall for stimuli, and the demonstration of a relationship between these disorders and exhaustion testifies to the existence of organic disease, while, at the same time, unproductive thinking in the absence of asthenia and with good memory is more often observed in schizophrenia.

2. The analysis of the structure of a defect, independently of differential diagnosis, may be a problem for psychological experimentation. Such an analysis of the structure of disturbed mental processes can turn out to be extremely important in describing new forms of disease or ones that have been little studied.

3. A further task for experimental psychology is the establishment of degrees of mental impairment. This problem acquires special urgency in the analysis of disease processes, for example, in following up on the effectiveness of a course of treatment.

The establishment of the degree and dynamics of mental impairment is also necessary in the work of expert consultants in the industrial, forensic, and military fitness areas.

The enumerated tasks are not the only ones for research in experimental psychology. In the process of clinical work other specific questions can also arise which require a competent psychologist (experimental analysis of individual psychopathological phenomena, for example, hallucinations, delirium, and the characteristic reactions during pharmacological testing). Here we have only touched upon the most essential tasks.

Chapter 2

Historical Outline

At the close of the 19th century, psychology gradually lost its character as a speculative science and the experimental method began to penetrate its investigations. It is customary to consider Wundt's laboratory of physiological psychology, organized in 1879 in Leipzig, as the first laboratory of experimental psychology. The experimental methods of Wundt and his students also penetrated clinical psychiatry (the psychiatric clinic of Kraepelin); at the same time experimental psychology laboratories were also opened in the psychiatric clinics of Russia.

The history of experimental psychology is linked with the development of psychiatry and neurology. Even in the last century the "Medical Psychology" of R. Lotze (1852) and the "Medical Psychology" of D. T'yuk (1892) had already been published. However these works, as N. S. Lebedinskii and V. N. Myasishchev rightly noted, were no more than "sketches of the psychiatry of the authors' era."

During the 1920's works appeared on medical psychology by well-known foreign psychiatrists: E. Krechmer's "Medical Psychology" treated problems of breakdown and growth from a constitutional position that is unacceptable to us; P. Janet's "Medical Psychology" dwelt on the problems of psychotherapy.

The development of medical psychology in the Soviet Union was distinguished by the presence of a solid natural science tradition. Laboratories of experimental psychology existed in major psychoneurological institutions, even in the prerevolutionary period. In his day Sechenov attached great significance to the rap-

prochement of psychology and psychiatry. In his letter to M. A.
Bokova in 1876, he indicated that he was setting about the creation
of medical psychology, which he called his "Swan Song." Writing
of psychology, he said that "it is that science which has clearly become the basis of psychiatry just as physiology is the basis of
pathology of the body."[1]

Russia's first clinical laboratory of experimental psychology
was opened by Bechterev in 1885 in Kazan. Subsequently similar
laboratories were opened in psychoneurological clinics in Petersburg, Moscow, Kharkov, Yur'ev and other cities. Among the first
experimental investigators were M. K. Valitskaya, V. P. Vorotyn-
skii, L. S. Krainskii, P. V. Zaborskii, V. F. Chizh, and others.
The research orientation of psychology laboratories in psychiatric
clinics withstood the idealistic trend of psychological science at
that time.

It was no accident that professors of psychiatry took part in
discussions at the end of 1894 at the meetings of the Moscow Psychological Association and in the journal "Problems of Philosophy
and Psychology" (1894, November). Countering a proposal of N. N.
Lange's about the desirability of opening psychological laboratories
at some Russian universities, the professors of psychiatry S. S.
Korsakov and V. F. Chizh reported that such laboratories already
existed and spoke out against the underestimation and hushing up
of laboratories of "empirical psychology" in medical institutions.

A large amount of experimental psychology research was carried out in the clinic of mental and neural disease of the Military-
Medical Academy under the direction of V. M. Bekhterev. His col-
laborators and students did experimental studies of the properties
of association, concentration (attention), and intellectual efficiency
in various mental illnesses (schizophrenia, manic-depressive
psychosis, progressive paralysis, epilepsy, etc.).

In stating certain fundamental views about the techniques of
experimental psychology, Bekhterev emphasized that experimental
study of patients is a necessary supplement to and extension of
clinical observations.

---

[1]Cited in the book by Kaganov "Philosophy of I. M. Sechenov," Moscow, 1948,
  page 101.

Bekhterev and F. D. Vladychko specially devised a number of fundamental recommendations and concrete procedural techniques for objective investigation of the mentally ill. Among the huge number of methods used by the Bekhterev school, the most widely employed were the word association experiment, the technique of defining and comparing concepts, the proof reading test for the study of attention, calculating tasks for recording the dynamics of patients' capacity for work, etc. Among the experimental investigations of the Bekhterev school, those of major importance were M. I. Astvatsaturov's studies of speech, K. N. Povarnin's work on attention, and V. V. Abramov's research on creativity in the mentally ill.

Bekhterev considered it absolutely necessary to try out clinical methods beforehand on a large number of mentally normal subjects of varying education and age. And so, almost all of the experimental investigations of the Bekhterev school studied groups of normal and mentally ill subjects with comparatively homogeneous educational backgrounds. Thus, for example, L. S. Pavlovska compared the free associations, judgments, and reasoning of healthy subjects and those suffering from paralytic imbecility; she also compared the reasoning ability of normals, idiots (oligophrenia), and schizophrenics. Another of Bekhterev's students, L. S. Gutman, compared the properties of the association process, attention span, and curves of intellectual work capacity in normals and mentally ill during different phases of manic-depressive psychosis.

An observation of Bekhterev's deserves special attention: experimentation enabled him to penetrate more deeply into the qualitative features of the intellectual activity of the mentally ill, and to sometimes discover lawful relationships which could not be revealed by mere clinical observation. So, for example, the speed of word association in patients suffering from manic agitation turns out to be, for the most part, slowed down in comparison with the norm and not accelerated at all. In both phases of the illness, manic and depressive, which are so contrasting, experimentation revealed many common features.

A. F. Lazurskii, also a student of Bekhterev's, played a prominent role in shaping the direction of Russian experimental psychology. He was convinced that psychology must be just like natural sciences in that all its conclusions must be based on the study of concrete facts. The psychology laboratory set up by Lazurskii in the Psychoneurological Institute founded by Bekhterev, turned into one of the most important centers of Russian scientific psychology.

Lazurskii was an innovator in experimental procedure: he expanded the boundaries of experimentation in psychology by applying it to the normal conditions of everyday life; and he made concrete forms of activity and complex personality manifestations the topics of experimental study. In his foreword to Lazurskii's book, "General Experimental Psychology," L. S. Vygotskii wrote that Lazurskii belongs to those researchers who embarked upon the transformation of empirical psychology into a science.

Lazurskii proposed a system of experimental procedures which was labeled "naturalistic experimentation" and which occupies, as it were, an intermediate position between observation and experiment. In the beginning his techniques were applied to children but later they were carried over into clinical psychiatry.

The essential condition of the naturalistic experiment, distinguishing it from the laboratory experiment, is that the subject must not suspect that he is being experimented upon. This avoids the premeditation of responses which often hampers the determination of individual differences in the laboratory experiment. In the naturalistic experiment, just as in any experiment, it is possible to confront the subject with certain previously studied conditions which elicit a given process or reaction. It is this possibility to arbitrarily elicit mental processes and to direct them one way or another, that constitutes a big step forward in comparison with ordinary observation.

In research with the naturalistic experiment, influence is exerted by conditions under which the focal activity takes place just the same as it is observed naturally. For example, it is established beforehand in what kind of play a particular character trait of a child is especially striking. Then, with the aim of studying the manifestation of this trait in different children, the latter are involved in similar play. During the play activity the investigator watches for the appearance of just this character trait in the children. The path of research led from simple observation, through the discrimination of typical traits and individual manifestations thereof, to the creation of an experimental situation, an experimental lesson or game.

The psychiatric clinic of S. S. Korsakov in Moscow was a second center for the development of clinical psychology. In 1886 the second psychology laboratory in Russia was set up in this clinic under the leadership of A. A. Tokarskii. Like all exponents of progressive trends in psychiatry, Korsakov believed that knowledge of the fundamentals of psychology provides the groundwork for correct understanding of mental breakdowns; it was no accident that he began to teach his course on psychiatry with an account of the fundamentals of psychology. The followers of Korsakov, V. P. Serbskii, A. N. Bernshtein, and others, adhered to similar traditions.

Without dissociating mental activity from physiological processes, but also without reducing it to the latter, Korsakov proceeded in his lectures from the materialist viewpoint of I. M. Sechenov; he propounded the idea that "the neural mechanism, constituting the substrate of a mental phenomenon, functions as a type of reflex act."

The publications which issued from Korsakov's clinic made a valuable contribution to psychological science. Among such studies one must include first and foremost the writings of Korsakov himself. Of his writings, "Psychology of Microcephaly" and "Medical-Psychological Studies of One Form of Memory Disorder" included interesting analyses of the structure of imbecility. The clinical observations and views in these writings summed up to the idea that disturbances of intellectual activity are not reducable to the breakdown of separate abilities but that the question properly concerns complex forms of disturbance of all rational goal-directed activity.

The works of A. A. Tokarskii constituted another valuable contribution to psychology. In his work "On Stupidity," Tokarskii analyzed dementia and imbecility.

A. M. Bernshtein's book describing procedures in experimental psychology appeared in 1911; in the same year F. G. Rybakov published his excellently designed "Atlas of Psychological Research on Personality." Interest in experimental psychology was also shown by the fact that a number of meetings of the Moscow Association of Psychiatrists were devoted to familiarization with research techniques. Articles on the experimental study of patients appeared in a journal called "Neuropathology and Psychiatry."

Thus, on the eve of the Great October Revolution, abnormal psychology had achieved indisputable success in Russia and had begun to assume the character of an experimental discipline – experimental abnormal psychology. A network of psychology laboratories was created in the clinics and experimental techniques for studying pathological conditions were worked out; the leading psychiatrists and neuropathologists (V. M. Bekhterev, S. S. Korsakov, V. P. Serbskii, G. I. Rossolimo, and V. A. Gilyarovskii) worked in close cooperation with psychologists.

The development of abnormal psychology after the Great October Revolution went hand in hand with the general development of psychology as a science founded on Marxism-Leninism. That the struggle with idealism affected research in abnormal psychology too was evident in attempts to analyze abnormal states from a materialist point of view and to develop and perfect objective research techniques.

The ideas of the eminent Soviet psychologist L. S. Vygotskii played a major role in establishing abnormal psychology as a distinct discipline. His ideas, which were developed later on in general psychology by his pupils and coworkers (A. N. Leont'ev, A. R. Luriya, and P. Ya. Gal'perin), were the following: 1) the human brain is equipped with principles of functional organization that are different from those of the animal brain; 2) the development of higher mental processes is not predetermined solely by the morphological structure of the brain; mental processes do not come into existence only with the maturation of brain structure; they take shape in the course of life as a result of training and upbringing and the acquisition of human experience; 3) lesions in some areas of the cortex have different implications at different stages of mental growth. These propositions determined to a great extent the direction of research in abnormal and neuropsychology.

Vygotskii himself pioneered the study of thought deterioration with his own experimental investigations. Studies of cognitive disorder and speech deterioration constitute one of the most extensively developed branches of abnormal psychology, both here and abroad.

Intensive research in experimental psychology has been carried out for several decades at Leningrad's Bekhterev Brain Insti-

tute under the leadership of V. N. Myasishchev. Following in the
Bekhterev tradition, Myasishchev strove to combine psychiatry
and psychology and to introduce objective methods of studying
patients into the psychiatric clinics. His students and coworkers
attempted to develop methods for objectively recording emotional
components of human mental activity. As an objective indicator
they used the individual's electrodermal characteristics (EKG) as
registered by a galvanometer; studies with EKG were conducted
on various kinds of mental activity in different groups of mentally
ill.

A number of studies, done in the psychology branch of the
Leningrad Brain Institute, investigated emotional-volitional processes in patients with various illnesses (manic-depressive psychosis, progressive paralysis, hysteria, etc.). These studies
utilized topics from Kurt Lewin's school: the effect of success
on level of aspiration in hysterics; recall for finished and unfinished tasks in schizophrenics, manic-depressives and others. In
these studies an operational principle was found for overcoming
Lewin's formalism. The studies were aimed at analyzing the
structure of the patients' work activity, that is, how the patients'
attitude toward work affected their competence. On the basis of
these studies, Myasishchev proposed that disturbance in the ability to work must be regarded as a basic manifestation of mental
illness and that a work-fitness indicator can serve as one of the
criteria of the patient's mental condition. The writings of the
Leningrad School of abnormal psychologists of that period still
retain their topicality and their substantive and methodological
significance.

At the same period, a series of major studies was carried
out in the psychology laboratory of the Central Research Institute
for Performance Assessment, an institute founded for the first
time in the world in the USSR. Besides dealing with general questions of fitness evaluation and the placement of patients suffering
from somatic illness, staff members of that laboratory took part
in evaluating the work capacity and the job placement of the mentally ill. The publications of this laboratory dealt with the properties of intellectual activity in patients with brain trauma and the
characteristics of mental activity and work capacity in epileptics
and schizophrenics. The significance of this series of studies
transcends the narrow scope of fitness assessment. While ana-

lyzing disturbances in work capacity the staff members of the
assessment center devoted much attention to studying different
forms of mental activity (V. M. Kogan, É. A. Korobkova). Kogan's
conclusion is of special interest since it was based on a large
body of factual material. He concluded that in some organic brain
diseases the basic mental disorder, which reduces the patient's
ability to work, is a narrowing of his scope of attention, his inability to take into account several changing environmental influences
occurring at one time.

During World War II abnormal psychologists took part in rehabilitation work in neurosurgical hospitals. The subject matter
of abnormal psychology became mental disorders occasioned by
brain injury. A number of studies dealt with the rehabilitation of
motor and speech impairment and the restoration of ability to work
in disabled veterans.

In the following years scientific research and practical work
in abnormal psychology began to be curtailed. This happened notwithstanding the indisputably fruitful influence which the session
of the two academies in 1950 exerted on the development of psychiatric and psychological ideas. The curtailment was due to the
successive consistent adoption of the reflex principle to explain
mental events, first in the session itself and then, in the subsequent years errors were made in interpreting the subject matter
of psychology. Owing to the erroneous interpretation of certain
statements of I. P. Pavlov, the view was disseminated that psychology was supposedly concerned with the description of subjective
phenomena and that for causal explanation, it was necessary to
look only to the physiology of higher nervous activity. As a result
of these false views, psychological research in psychiatry began
to be replaced by physiological research.

As we know, these views were criticized at the 1962 All-Union
Conference on Philosophical Issues in the Physiology of Higher
Nervous Activity and Psychology. This conference, which was
convened by the Academy of Sciences of the USSR, the Academy
of Medicine of the USSR, and the Academy of Pedagogical Sciences
of the RSFSR, resolved to condemn biologizing tendencies in the
science of man.

The resolution noted that, after the 1950 session, "the wide
dissemination of a negative attitude toward psychology entailed

practical harm and methodological error as some scholars tried
to reduce the subject matter of psychology to the physiology of
higher nervous activity." Measures for the development of medical psychology were discussed at this conference together with
other problems. Decisions were taken to expand the network of
abnormal psychology laboratories and to introduce the teaching
of medical psychology into the medical schools. Abnormal psychology laboratories conducting intensive research were reopened
in many research institutes of psychiatry and in institutions offer-
ing psychoneurological services.

One of the chief problems in abnormal psychology is disintegration of thinking. Work on this problem is being pursued in
various directions: the laboratory of the Moscow Institute of Psychiatry is studying personality changes in the structure of thought
disorders; the laboratory of the Institute of Psychiatry of the
Academy of Medicine is working on a connection between thought
disorder and the process of converting knowledge into action. Another line of research (pursued by the laboratory of the Moscow
Institute of Psychiatry under the Ministry of Public Health of the
RSFSR) is directed at the classification and psychological analysis
of personality disturbances observed in clinical psychiatry. These
studies are being pursued in various directions: experimental investigations of personality reactions; the psychological analysis of
clinical accounts of personality deterioration; and the analysis of
so-called "internal evidence of disease" in various mental illnesses. Studies of the deterioration of skills in older mental patients are being performed within the framework of continued
study of the issue raised by Vygotskii concerning the relationship
between mental growth and decay.

Research in abnormal psychology has made noteworthy progress in the psychiatric clinics of Tiflis. Using D. I. Uznadze's
theory, a number of Georgian psychologists and psychiatrists are
studying disorders of set in different mental illnesses.

Research in abnormal psychology recently expanded considerably in the professional practice of forensic psychiatrists and industrial experts.

Utilization of the methods and findings of experimental abnormal psychology has made special progress in the psychoneurological institutions for children. Methods are being devised to facili-

tate early diagnosis of mental retardation; the complexities of
childhood imbecility and dementia are being analyzed to find additional diagnostic signs and symptoms; Vygotskii's principle about
the "next developmental area" is being used to work out procedures for the "teaching experiment" so as to reveal important
predictors of training readiness in children.

Along with the research done by the abnormal psychologists
themselves, the number of comprehensive studies in clinical psychology is increasing. At the same time too there is a vigorous
effort to develop and standardize the research procedures which
have been published in a number of methodological writings and
texts. In 1956 the Moscow Institute of Psychiatry published a
statement on methodology entitled "Experimental Psychological
Research on Patients in Psychoneurological Institutions." This
statement set forth the tasks and theoretical premises of psychological experimentation in the clinic. In 1958 another methodological statement was published by I. N. Dukel'skaya and É. A. Korobkova: "Appraisal of Industrial Disease and Job Placement of Schizophrenics." This statement summarizes the findings of clinical research on the industrial performance of patients. It is shown that
with the right attitude toward work and with a certain critical review of his condition, the patient could be placed. Industrial adjustment depends on the totality of clinical-industrial factors, the
most significant of which is the extent to which favorable mutual
relations have been established in the work group. An especially
important factor in the patient's adjustment is thought to be the
realization that he is playing a meaningful role in the work group,
his positive "social self-concept."

In recent years the number of publications describing methods
of experimental abnormal psychology has increased. M. N. Kononova's "Guide to Psychological Research on Mentally Ill Children"
came out in 1961. In 1962 S. Ya. Rubinshtein's text was published
which described applied techniques in detail and interpreted experimental findings.

The rapid growth of research and practice in experimental
abnormal psychology is evident too in the fact that the professional associations, psychologists as well as psychiatrists and
neuropathologists, have divisions which coordinate research in
abnormal psychology. At the All-Union Psychology Conventions
in 1959 and 1963, reports by abnormal psychologists were widely

represented. They focused on the following problems: 1) the implications of psychology for medical practice; 2) the problem of adjustment; and 3) the pathology of thinking. A similar program took place at the All-Union Convention of Neuropathologists and Psychiatrists in 1963.

A special symposium, "Abnormal psychology and psychological processes" was organized for the 18th World Congress of Psychology held in 1966 in Moscow. The reports given at the symposium showed the relevance of research on mental pathology for the theoretical issues of general psychology.

The growth of a young corps of professional workers in experimental abnormal psychology has become especially noticeable recently. This development is facilitated by the decision of a portion of the students at the School of Psychology at the Moscow and Leningrad State Universities to specialize in abnormal psychology. These students complete course work and diploma theses with a clinical psychiatric foundation, while also becoming proficient in the procedures of experimental research with the mentally ill. Upon graduating, psychologists with this speciality are sent to work in psychiatric hospitals where they conduct independent research. Young physician-psychiatrists and defectologists monitor psychological experimentation in the individual psychoneurological institutions.

The network of experimental abnormal psychology laboratories is growing not only in scientific institutions but also in service establishments — in hospitals and health centers.

To raise the qualifications of abnormal psychologists, the Moscow Research Institute of Psychiatry under the Ministry of Public Health of the RSFSR, in cooperation with the School of Psychology of Moscow University, recently undertook a series of organizational measures. During 1960-65 two seminars for abnormal psychologists were set up, one for examining methods, and the other for exchanging experiences with young staff members working in the outlying districts. Some of the most prominent psychiatrists and psychologists of the country participated in these lectures. Thus, experimental abnormal psychology is now developing in our country as a field of knowledge with its own subject matter, its own practical applications, its own methods, and its own personnel.

Chapter 3

Fundamentals of Experimental Design
in Abnormal Psychology

The basic method of abnormal psychology, like that of any other
area in psychology, is the experiment. Since the methods of research in abnormal psychology are derived from the basic theoretical principles of general psychology, the selection of specific
techniques is a technical problem that involves the principles of
methodology as well. Therefore, to understand the special features of experimentation in abnormal psychology, a few words
about the research methods of general psychology would be in
order.

The experimental method is not the only avenue to knowledge
in psychology, but it has become the dominant one as psychology
developed into an exact science and it has come to be associated
with the general theoretical propositions of psychology.

As is known, rationalist psychologists tended to discriminate
separate abilities of the human mind, where each one processes
external information in its own way. Formerly psychology was
little more than a speculative description of the functions of these
abilities.

Speculative description of the individual's internal world was
characteristic of the rationalist psychologists: even today this approach is typical of the proponents of the so-called "verstehen"
psychology (Spranger and Dielthei). While denying the breakdown
of the mind into separate processes or functions but accepting the
indivisible unity of mental life, representatives of this school be-

lieve that even though natural events must be explained, mental events can only be understood. The views of "verstehen" psychology are reflected in the notions of existentialist psychologists. In practice, this means that psychologists must confine themselves solely to observing and recording the patient's behavior, utterances, and his self-examination; they renounce experimentation and hence the possibility of manipulating the conditions and activities which determine the course of a given process. In sum, existentialist psychologists may describe a phenomenon but not penetrate to its essential nature.

Empirical psychology, which replaced rationalism, brought with it a different conception of research methods. With the development of empirical psychology, the experimental method (Wundt, Ebbinghaus, Titchener) began to establish itself and was then used by neurologists and psychiatrists. Psychology laboratories were opened in the major clinics of V. M. Bekhterev in Leningrad, E. Kraepelin in Germany, and S. S. Korsakov in Moscow. Various procedural principles were used in the laboratories: let us examine them briefly.

Quantitative measurement of mental processes, a method based on Wundtian psychology, prevailed in the clinics for a long time. The view that mental processes are innate functions which change only quantitatively during development resulted in consideration of the feasibility of a "measurement" psychology. Experimental research on mental processes was reduced to establishing the quantitative features of separate mental acts.

Quantitative measurement of ability was the foundation of the methodology of psychological research in psychiatric and neurological clinics. The study of deterioration of any function consisted in determining its quantitative deviation from the "norm."

In 1910 one of the most prominent neural pathologists, G. I. Rossolimo, developed an experimental method which, in his view, made it possible to establish the level of separate mental functions, a sort of psychological profile. Rossolimo thought that various pathological states of the brain evoked specific typical "profiles of psychodynamic change." This method was predicated upon the empiricist assumption concerning the existence of innate, isolated abilities. This was an erroneous theory and, just like the simplistic quantitative analysis of mental disturbances, it could not be adopted in clinical practice. But the attempt itself, to bring psychology closer to the solution of clinical problems, was progressive for that period.

Quantitative measurement of individual mental functions found its most extreme expression in the Binet-Simon test researches which were focused at first on ascertaining intellectual level. These tests were predicated on the assumption that the intellectual capacities of the child are predetermined by hereditary factors and are little influenced by training and upbringing. Each child has his own predetermined, more or less constant, age-related intellectual coefficient (I.Q.).

The problems set to children required definite knowledge and skills for their solution but, at best, they made it possible to assess the quantity of acquired knowledge and not the structure or the qualitative features of intellectual activity.

Research based on such tests does not permit prediction of the child's future development. Meanwhile, such tests have been used in some countries, to "stream" children into those who are supposedly gifted from birth and others in whom retardation of intellectual development is declared to be equally dependent on innate factors. We in this country also used tests in the so-called pedagogical studies of school children. But they were justifiably condemned as pseudoscientific in a resolution of the Central Committee of the All-Union Communist Party (Bolsheviks) on July 4, 1936.

Test techniques continued to dominate the work of foreign clinical psychologists. In numerous recent monographs and articles on the experimental study of patients, just such tests have been mentioned, including those aimed at estimating I.Q. (the Wechsler-Bellevue and others).

Research on patients by means of tests does not allow taking into account the individual features of intellectual activity, the qualitative aspects of disturbance, or the possibility, so vital to the solution of clinical problems, of compensation.

Test research produces only end-results, while the work processes of the subject, his relationship to the task, the motives inducing him to choose this or that course of action, his personality orientations, his desires – in short, all the multifarious qualitative properties of his activities – remain hidden.

Along with this purely quantitative approach, there is a tendency noticeable in foreign abnormal psychology to use techniques
directed only at manifestations of the patient's emotional experiences. Exponents of this approach use the so-called "projective"
techniques in their research. The tasks do not envisage any particular means of solution. In contrast to tests, which require completion of the task according to definite specifications, the projective technique uses any particular problem only as an occasion for
the subject to exhibit his feelings and the peculiarities of his personality and character. In a specific application, the subject must
describe pictures that are sometimes realistic ("thematic apperception test," abbreviated as TAT) and sometimes devoid of meaningful content. An example of the latter is the so-called "ink-blot"
test of Rorschach, which consists of various symmetrically arranged configurations of quite fantastic shapes. The realistic pictures consist of depictions of activity or poses of figures. The
subject has to describe the picture and relate everything that comes
to mind (what the pictures remind him of, what he thinks of them,
what he is feeling). The experimenter records his utterances.

Thus, the projective technique appears to be essentially the
opposite of testing because, in terms of the author's intent, it appears to facilitate qualitative assessment of the subject's behavior.
Testing only permits judgment about the results of task performance, while the projective technique, by its nature, excludes the
whole problem of right and wrong answers. The investigator using
the projective technique is not concerned with errors or correct
answers, but rather with the personality-responses of the subject
and with the nature of the associations that are elicited by the test.
The authors feel that in projective testing, a certain identification
of the subject with the depicted figures occurs. According to the
French psychologist Ombredane, "personality is reflected with
this technique, as an object on a screen" (hence, the name "projective"). The technique is frequently called "the clinical approach to the mind of the healthy individual."

However if we analyze the kinds of personal experiences and
orientations in question, then it turns out that the investigators
are frequently trying to use this technique to uncover the "uncon-
scious-latent" motives and desires of the patient. Individual features of the patient's perception (for example, does he see the ob-

jects as moving or stationary, in describing Rorschach tables; does
he pay attention to the broad features of the drawings or to minor
details, etc.) are taken to be indicators of personality traits. Thus,
this technique, in contrast to quantitative measurement of separate
functions, is thought to afford qualitative analysis of the personality as a whole. The rational element, contained in the projective
approach, must be made use of. But some of the schemes suggested so far for interpreting the subject's responses seem sup-
positious and ill-founded.

The principles of experimental research are quite different
in Soviet psychology. The doctrine of materialist psychology, that
mental processes do not consist of innate abilities but of the kinds
of activities which take shape in the course of life, implies that
psychological experimentation must study mental disorders as disturbances of activity. Experimentation must be directed at qualitative analysis of different forms of mental impairment and at the
discovery of the underlying mechanisms. If we are talking about
cognitive disturbances then the experimental techniques should
show how certain cognitive processes, which took shape in the
patient during his everyday life, break down and how his acquisition of new associations is being modified and in what way his using the system of old associations and past experience is being
distorted. Since any mental process has a certain movement and
direction, one should construct experimental research in a way
which reflects disturbances of these parameters. Therefore, experimental data should characterize mental deterioration not only
quantitatively but qualitatively as well.

Of course it goes without saying that the experimental findings must be reliable and that statistical treatment must be used
where appropriate, but quantitative analysis should not replace,
either partially or wholly, qualitative characterization of the data.
Quantitative analysis presupposes thorough psychological description of the facts. Before embarking on measurement, one must
establish what is being measured.

One should agree with A. N. Leont'ev's remark (in his article
''Some long-term problems of Soviet psychology'') that there is no
need to force a convergence between scientifically valid experiments ''which facilitate qualitative assessment and the so-called
tests of intellectual giftedness whose use was justifiably condemned

not only here but in many other countries as well."[1] Consequently the basic principle of constructing a psychology experiment is qualitative analysis of the characteristics of the patient's mental processes rather than isolated quantitative measurement. It is important not only with what difficulty or to what extent the patient comprehends and completes the task but also how he comprehended it and what caused his errors and difficulties (it must be emphasized that the analysis of mistakes made by the patient while completing experimental tasks, is exceedingly interesting and indicative in evaluating his mental activity).

In other words, research in the clinic can be compared to a "functional probe," the technique widely used in medicine whereby the activity of any organ is tested. The role of a "functional probe" in the psychology experiment can be played by experimental tasks that can actualize the intellectual operations used by the individual in his everyday life. The abnormal psychology experiment must be a model of the everyday situation which can actualize not only the patient's mental functions but also his attitudes, orientations, and the goals on which specific motives are based. In other words, the experimental situation must facilitate the study of the activity of the sick individual.

One must examine another feature of the abnormal psychology experiment: its design must help to discover not only structural changes but also forms of mental activity which have remained intact. This type of approach is especially pertinent to the rehabilitation of impaired functions.

By 1948 A. R. Luriya had expressed the view that successful restoration of complex mental functions depends on the extent to which the rehabilitation can rely upon intact components. He emphasized that the restoration of disturbed forms of mental activity must attempt to rebuild functional systems. The work of many Soviet authors proved the fruitfulness of such an approach. Research on rehabilitation mechanisms in motor impairment arising from gunshot wounds in World War II indicated that a decisive role is played during rehabilitative work therapy by the mobilization of functioning orientations which have remained intact (S. G. Geller-

---

[1]A. N. Leont'ev, "Some long-term problems of Soviet psychology," Problems of Psychology, 1967, Vol. 6, p. 14.

shtein, A. V. Zaporozhets, A. N. Leont'ev, S. Ya. Rubinshtein). Psychologists who worked with speech disorders came to a similar conclusion.

É. S. Baine, in his monograph "Aphasia and Ways of Overcoming It," writes that recovery from aphasic disturbances hinges on actuating the intact components, developing them, and gradually "building up their capacity" for replacing the defective functions (page 223). Rebuilding of a defective function goes hand in hand with the development of an intact function. V. M. Kogan has put this problem in even wider perspective: in his monograph "Restoration of Speech in Aphasia," he convincingly shows that restoration must be based on the resuscitation of skills that have remained intact. The author is completely right in emphasizing that rehabilitation (here, speech rehabilitation) must actualize an entire system of associations and personal attitudes, even though pathologically affected. Hence, Kogan proposes that rehabilitation elicit the conscious attitude on the part of the patient to the semantic content of a world in its relation to an object. His views concern the restoration of functions which can be said to be rather circumscribed – speech and praxis. But these views can be applied with even greater justification to the rehabilitation of more complicated forms of mental activity, to the rehabilitation of lost intellectual efficiency (the patient's singlemindedness and energy). In these cases the question concerning preserved potentialities becomes especially acute (for example, in deciding about the patient's fitness for work and the feasibility of continued study, etc.).

For an experiment to be able to answer these complicated questions, for it to be able to show what components of the patient's mental activity are preserved, it must not be directed solely at revealing and analyzing the end products of behavior. Experimental design must allow us to take into account how the patient looks for solutions. Most of all it must enable the experimenter to intervene in the strategy of the experiment to discover how the patient perceives his "help," whether or not he can take advantage of it. But designing experiments according to rigidly standardized tests does not let us detect preserved components.

It is necessary to mention again a number of features which distinguish the clinical experiment from one using healthy individuals, that is, addressed to issues in general psychology. The

basic distinction here is that we must always take into account the
patient's unique adjustment as determined by his pathological condition. The presence of delirium, agitation, or inhibition may require an experimenter to design his experiment differently and
occasionally to change it while it is going on. For all their individual differences, healthy subjects try to carry out instructions,
they "accept" the task, whereas the mentally ill sometimes not
only do not try to complete the task, but incorrectly interpret it
or resist the instructions. For example, in doing a verbal association experiment with a healthy individual, the experimenter
tells him beforehand that he must listen to words as they are pronounced and the subject actively cooperates. However in carrying out the same experiment with a negativistic patient an opposite
effect often occurs: he actively refuses to listen. In such instances
the experimenter has to run the experiment in a roundabout way:
he pronounces the words quite incidentally and records the patient's reactions. Frequently one has to experiment with a patient
who interprets the test situation in a delusional fashion, for example, he believes that the experimenter is using hypnosis or rays
on him. Of course, when the patient has such an attitude toward
the experimenter it affects the way he carries out the task; he
frequently does it wrong on purpose, delays answering, and so on.
In such instances, the design of the experiment must also be modified.

There is still another feature which distinguishes experimental design in the clinic from the usual psychology experiment: the
diversity and multiplicity of techniques employed. This can be
explained as follows: mental deterioration is a process that never
affects just one level but always several. In actuality, it doesn't
happen that one patient's processes of synthesis and analysis are
the only ones disturbed while in another, purposefulness of personality is the impaired function. The execution of any experimental
task permits assessing different kinds of mental impairment.
Nevertheless, not every technique can insure determination of
a given kind or of the degree of impairment with equal clarity and
reliability.

Very often a change in the instructions, or any situational nu-
ance whatsoever, alters the nature of the experimental evidence.
For example, when an experimenter stresses the importance of
his own evaluation in an experiment on verbal recall and repro-

duction, the results are more likely to reflect the subject's concern about his performance than about his mnemonic processes. One has to compare the results from different variations of an experiment since in work with a sick individual frequent alterations are often introduced throughout the test (if only because of the changing condition of the patient). There are additional reasons for such a comparison. In carrying out a given task, the patient not only does it correctly or incorrectly but work on the task frequently makes him aware of his deficiency and he strives to find a way of compensating for it and to find reliable guidelines for correction. Opportunities for doing this vary with the task. Frequently it so happens that a patient who can tackle a more difficult task correctly, fails to solve an easier one. An understanding of the nature of such a phenomenon can be gained only by comparing data from different tasks.

Finally, in conclusion: the patient's mental disturbance is often unstable. Amelioration of his condition is accompanied by the disappearance of certain peculiarities of his cognitive behavior, while others persist. Thus the nature of the observed disturbances can change artifactually. Therefore, comparing the results from different variations of a given method which is used repeatedly, provides the basis for judgment about the nature, quality, and dynamics of cognitive impairment. Hence the reasonableness and justification behind the stipulation that research on mental deterioration not be limited to any single procedure but employ a variety of techniques.

In the study of defective children it is especially important to focus experimental techniques on uncovering the qualitative characteristics of mental disturbance. Any degree of psychological underdevelopment or disease is always attended by further, albeit retarded or distorted, development. The psychology experiment must not be limited to establishing the structure of a single level of the young patient's mental processes; it should primarily be aimed at ascertaining his potential condition.

It is well known that this was first advocated in the 1930's by L. S. Vygotskii in his doctrine on the "area of developmental readiness." In his book "The Problem of Training and Intellectual Growth During School Years," he writes "the capacity of the child for intellectual growth can be determined at the very least by explaining two of his levels: the level of actual development and the area of developmental readiness." Vygotskii means those potentialities of the child, which do not appear independently as the effects of certain conditions, but which can be realized with adult assistance. The child's skill at transferring problem-solving techniques acquired with adult assistance to independent activity is the chief mark of intellectual growth. Hence the child's mental growth is characterized less by his actual level and more by his level of developmental readiness. The decisive factor is "the discrepancy between the level of problem-solving attainable with guidance (with adult aid) and the level attainable independently" (page 477).

We have discussed Vygotskii's well-known doctrine in some detail because it defines a principle of experimental design that is applicable to defective children. Test research done by foreign psychologists can, at best, reveal only the "actual" (Vygotskii's terminology) level of the child's mental growth and that only quantitatively, while the child's potentiality remains hidden. But without such prognostication of the child's future development, many problems, for example, choosing a special training school, can't be effectively solved. Experimental research into the psychoneurology of children must be conducted with due regard for Vygotskii's position and it must be designed along the lines of a training experiment.

This type of research is used by A. Ya. Ivanova, who gives children problems which they have not hitherto encountered. As the children carry out these tasks, the experimenter extends them different kinds of help in a strictly standardized fashion. How the child takes to this assistance is recorded and, in this way, the assistance itself is included in the structure of the experiment. To achieve standardized assistance, Ivanova modified several generally accepted procedures of abnormal psychology research such as object classification, Koos's method, the classification of geometric figures, and a series of successive pictures. The stages of assistance are carefully regulated and recorded by the author, and both quantitative gradations and qualitative characteristics are taken into account. Ivanova's use of the training experiment has enabled her to differentiate between different kinds of abnormal development. The training-experiment technique was also used by N. I. Nepomnyashchaya, who studied the development of counting skill in intellectually retarded children. Nepomnyashchaya proceeded from P. Ya. Gal'perin's theoretical views on the stepwise formation of intellectual activity; he showed that retarded children experienced difficulty in short-cutting primitively developed behavior: it has to be overcome with special effort and over a long period. If attainment of short-cut mechanisms could be managed through special training, then it was possible, within certain limits, to overcome the defect in such children.

A system of measured prompting was used by P. G. Natadze to form aesthetic concepts in healthy children. By means of an elaborate procedure, Natadze was able to reveal different developmental levels. The training experiment, based on Vygotskii's thesis on the "area of developmental readiness," reveals the child's potentialities and, in so doing, serves as a device for studying the structure and degree of mental loss in abnormal children, which is most helpful when these children have to be assigned to special schools.

Chapter 4

Disturbances in Intellectual Capacity

Psychological disorders in the mentally ill are diverse in nature.
As a rule psychological research has examined cognitive disorganization (mainly of thought processes), while only a few studies
dealt with disturbances associated with personality changes. It
must be said, however, that mental disorders cannot be fully analyzed in terms of cognitive and personality parameters. It is a
mistake to reduce the entire diversity of mental disorders to alterations in the organization of intellectual operations or to motivational disturbances.

Psychology experiments have failed to show how conceptual
organization is affected in a number of mental cases: the patients
comprehended the task, which required synthesis and generalization; their associations were adequate; and even their relationship
to the experimental situation was unaffected. But at the same time
their inability to maintain a correct behavioral approach to concrete tasks led to mistakes. In such cases, we are faced with disturbed mental work capacity.

This problem has been studied more extensively by research
psychologists at the Institute for Performance Assessment; they
have shown the diversity of fundamental determinants of disturbed
capacity for work in mental patients. As long ago as 1936 V. M.
Kogan stated that the chief cause of reduced fitness in many mental patients is a shrinkage of the scope of attention, that is,
an inability to respond to several environmental influences simultaneously. Performance assessment led to the identification of
those functional difficulties which preserved the basic habits and
skills necessary for short-term mental operations; this group of

psychologists was accordingly encouraged to seek out special experimental research techniques.

The problem of disturbed work capacity was investigated by E. A. Korobkova. In her presentation at the 18th World Congress of Psychology she defined work capacity as "the ability to engage in long-term systematic activity of a socially useful nature" (page 163). She classified disorders of work capacity according to whether the disorder affected purposefulness, volition, control and regulation of effort, or behavioral dynamics.

In the present chapter we intend to sidestep disturbances in work capacity in the wide sense in order to discuss disorders of mental efficiency which seem to result from exhaustion (fatigability). According to E. A. Korobkova's scheme, these disorders are most akin to dynamic disturbances in the affective-volitional area. Intellectual operations based on habits acquired in earlier activity often remain intact while in the meantime the patient is unable to execute a number of intellectual functions demanding long-term steady exertion.

Several manifestations of the exhaustion of such patients often make it seem as if separate processes have been disturbed. The exhaustion can be manifested as a memory disturbance and as in-

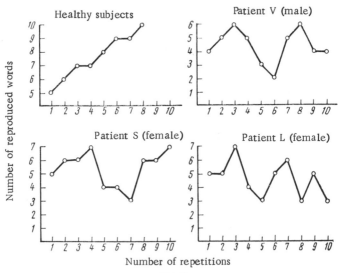

Fig. 1

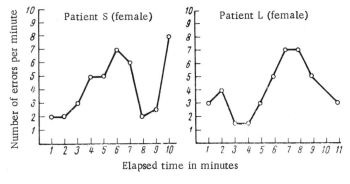

Fig. 2

stability of attention. If such patients have to learn 10 words by heart and we draw a curve depicting the quantity of reproduced words we find that the curve looks broken (Fig. 1).

Similar results were obtained in studying patients with Kraepelin's test. The technique consists of printing a pair of numbers to be added on a blank sheet. The experimenter tabulates the number of additions done in a minute and the number of errors.[1] The curve which depicts the number of errors is similarly broken, evidence for discontinuity and lability in the patient's performance (Fig. 2).

Similar instability was observed both in complex kinds of mental activity and in elementary phenomena, for example, in the timing of sensory-motor responses. The timing characteristics of sensory-motor responses were obtained using Shulte's technique, "locating numbers in tables." The patient was successively exposed to five tables (60 × 60 centimeters) on which the numbers from 1 to 25 were located haphazardly. The patient had to indicate and name the numbers in order. This technique shows the rapidity of the eye's orienting and seeking movements.

In a dissertation at the Psychology Laboratory of the Moscow Institute of Psychiatry, V. I. Vasil'eva established the following facts in a study of mental disturbances in vascular patients. Total time for finding all the numbers on the tables was clearly retarded

---

[1]For more detailed description of this as well as subsequent techniques see S. Ya. Rubinshtein, "Techniques of Experimental Abnormal Psychology," Moscow, 1962.

in the vascular patients in comparison with a group of healthy subjects. However, detailed analysis of the time for each separate seeking response shows that the overall retardation is explainable by the occurrence of isolated seeking responses that were excessively long, together with others of normal speed.

As a rule, while the patients are trying to find numbers at normal speed, they loose track of order, that is, they look at a number but don't see it. And they sometimes declare that a particular number isn't even in the table. In other words, the overall delay in completing the task turns out to be due to extreme heterogeneity in the timing of individual responses. Vasil'yeva suggests that this heterogeneity in seeking responses may be due to a temporary inhibitory state arising in the cerebral cortex when the visual analyzer is under stress.

In addition, data obtained in studies of patient's visual-motor coordination yielded an equally sensitive indicator of changes in their sensory-motor responses. These studies were conducted by our colleague, S. Ya. Rubinshtein, who used her own technique: the subject has to learn to figure out how to press on a rubber bulb with such finesse that a preassigned movement is carried out under visual control. An ink-record of the movement was obtained on a kymograph tape.[2] It was found that the data curve looked jerky and irregular for patients whose clinical characteristics showed disturbances due to arteriosclerosis. These patients correctly accomplished the assigned movement with respect to force and speed, but their pressing was incorrect.

The writer has shown that disturbance of afferent neural connections of the cerebral cortex evidently causes the obtained desensitization in the correction mechanism. Rubinshtein is persuaded that the irregular jerky character of the curve is essentially due to the fact that the correcting impulses are incorrectly delayed and that their strength is disproportionate to external conditions.

This discontinuity of mental processes and dynamic instability are linked, it seems, with fluctuating cortical tonus. This often leads to the disturbance of higher forms of intellectual activity; it

---

[2]A detailed description of this method is given in S. Ya. Rubinshtein's "Techniques of Experimental Abnormal Psychology."

can lead to judgmental inconsistency. The characteristic feature of this disturbance was instability in completing tasks. The generalization level was not essentially impaired, the patients correctly grasped the instructions; they did a good job of analyzing and synthesizing the material; and they understood the metaphorical meaning of proverbs and metaphors. However, the patients could not maintain adequate reasoning. While they carried out the experimental task, the patients could not maintain the correct approach over a long time period; correct ways of carrying out the task were mixed with incorrect ones.

Let us discuss in somewhat more detail the tactics used by these patients while working on a "classification of objects" problem. In this task the subject is shown a number of objects (things, cards) which he has to sort into separate groups on the basis of some general attribute. This method was first used by K. Goldstein in his work on aphasia: the patient had to sort real objects according to what they were made of. The psychological difficulty here is that a "general" classification rule (the kind of material a thing is made of) was often contradictory to the customary concrete associations between the objects (for example, according to the role of material composition, a pen might be grouped with a spoon; but the functional connection between pen and book interferred with such a grouping). Consequently, to classify in terms of a general attribute, concrete links between objects have to be suppressed and classification according to an abstract principle has to prevail. Later on the technique was modified (L. S. Vygotskii, G. V. Birenbaum, B. V. Zeigarnik); instead of real objects themselves, drawings were shown to the subjects on cards. Apart from purely technical ease, this method makes possible a large variety of sorting rules; the objects can have unusual shades of color; they can take on usual shapes, etc.

One of the variations of this technique consists in presenting the subject with a set of 70 cards with drawings of a wide variety of objects: domestic animals, wild animals, instruments, people from different occupations, furniture of various kinds, fruits, vegetables, trees, etc. The instructions require allocating the cards into several groups so that each group contains cards that are similar according to the defining attribute.

The selection of cards permits several kinds of classification (according to the material composition, or the function of the ob-

ject: furniture, instruments, etc.). Without going into a rundown
of all possible types of classification, suffice it to say that whatever may be the substantive distinctions among groups, the task
itself requires comparing and detecting only elementary similarities and differences between objects as well as the ability to de-
duce the general attribute which underlines their heterogeneity.
This task accordingly provides a means of showing the level of the
generalization process and of learning whether the subject con-
structs groups only on the basis of partial concrete associations
or whether he rises to the level of abstract generalization (and is
influenced by this level throughout the entire experiment). The
experiment that has been described also permits assessment of
task-completion tactics. Does the patient group objects initially
on the basis of partial attributes, while rising only gradually to
higher degrees of generalization (for example, does he initially
group just birds together, then birds and animals, and only at the
end group these objects with persons, thus constructing the class
"living beings")? Or does he immediately construct the class
according to the more general attribute ("living beings," "plants,"
"inanimate nature")? Does he manage the task independently or
rely on the help of the experimenter?

The design of this experiment is loose and "dynamic"; the
experimenter not only observes which associations the subjects
use in forming groups, but he actively intervenes, helping or
"hindering" the subject by eliciting correct solutions from him,
or "provoking" errors. If the experiment is properly conducted
it reveals not only the subject's level of generalization but also
his attitude toward his mistakes. The experiment shows whether
the subject notices errors, whether he corrects them, or whether,
in spite of the experimenter's indications, he persists in making
incorrect classifications.

Different kinds of mental fluctuations were revealed with this
method: the abstract nature of task performance was interrupted
by responses to situational order. So, for example, a certain patient working on "object classification" separates out the right
group of persons (blacksmith, physician, child), then he begins to
isolate a group of plants and here he separates out flowers to which
he adds a beetle, with the justification that "a beetle is always
found on flowers." In exactly the same fashion, having isolated
a class for furniture, he adds a bottle and a glass, saying "they

are in the cupboard." When the experimenter says "think that over," he takes the glass away from the furniture group, saying "it is dishware," and then, without prompting, takes the beetle away from the flower group, adding it to the animal group, and explains "fish and birds can go here too for they are all living things." This example shows that cognitive fluctuations in patients were manifested as alternations of abstract and situational solutions. Task completion at an abstract level did not appear to be a persistent work mode.

In other patients erroneous solutions were due to forgetfulness. Thus, having isolated a class correctly according to a general attribute, these patients began to isolate an analogous class. For example, patient K separated out a "plant" group of vegetables, flowers, and fruits, but then he began to isolate still another group for plants. Such designation of groups of the same kind are extremely typical. Similar erroneous acts and judgments occasionally occur in carrying out other tactical maneuvers, for example, in establishing analogies.

Often the correct and adequate execution of a task is interrupted suddenly by the onset of affective fluctuations. A little mistake, together with an ill-advised comment about it by the experimenter, can disorganize correct completion of the task.

Fluctuations in mental work capacity led to incorrect solutions and to incorrect judgments. However, the latter arose only periodically and did not show that the patient's intellectual processes were permanently impaired or that synthesizing functions had been destroyed. Other errors in the patient's thinking occurred because individual correct judgments were not pursued to the proper conclusion; they were broken up, separate stages were forgotten and never consolidated into one orderly chain of reasoning. Such disturbances cannot be explained as disorders of the conceptual system for they have a dynamic quality: the patients correctly plan the course of reasoning and, for a while, the sequence is completed within the limits of the previously established program; however, the patient is unable to maintain the program, despite adequate planning, and it is easily disrupted.

One should note that fluctuations in the intellectual performance of patients are not found in all experimental tasks. They can fail to occur even in complex tasks that involve single acts.

However they have been found most of all in the solution of multi-event problems which require reasoning and the retention of several attributes. The findings of V. M. Kogan's research certainly show this. Kogan found that in cerebrovascular diseases, perceptual capacity was constricted and this led to difficulties when several attributes had to be combined.

When the illness is of mild severity such judgmental inconsistencies can be corrected. Frequently it is enough for the experimenter to ask the patient what he is doing or simply to express surprise at his behavior, that is, to draw the patient's attention to his mistakes so that he corrects them, easily and by himself.

It should be noted that fluctuations in the patient's performance occurred as a result of the slightest changes in conditions of work. This is illustrated by the following findings from research using the technique "matching phrases and proverbs." A number of patients who had correctly determined the metaphorical meaning of proverbs made glaring mistakes when they had to match them with appropriate phrases (we showed this in our article especially concerned with the understanding of metaphorical meaning). For example, one of the patients who understood and correctly explained the proverb "all that glitters is not gold" matched it with an inappropriate phrase "gold is heavier than iron," but then he immediately corrected his mistake and was embarrassed that he made it. Another patient, having correctly explained the proverb "you can't back out once you've begun," matched it with the phrase "things must not be put off till tomorrow."

Especially sharp fluctuations of performance level have been observed in tasks requiring that the trend of thought be maintained for a long time together with constant inhibition of irrelevant associations. These fluctuations in intellectual performance of our patients, which could be observed during one and the same experiment, reached a peak toward the end of the experiment. In some instances, where the patient's condition improved, these fluctuations disappeared.

In analyzing the nature of fluctuations in the level of intellectual performance, the original question was their dependence upon task complexity. However, our findings show that the irregularity of patient's intellectual performance was due neither to the complexity of the material nor to difficulties in organizing it. As we said above, the obtained fluctuations were often observed even during execution of the most elementary tasks such as retention and reproduction of ten words or finding numbers in Shulte's tables.

All these findings demonstrate that intellectual instability does not depend on how complicated the tasks are. Any kind of activity can be within reach of a patient for any length of time and for a while it will be done with more or less difficulty. One and the same experiment can sometimes elicit a high level of performance from the patient, in which his reasoning is sustained in a logical fashion, and sometimes judgmental inconsistency will be obtained.

It seems to us that these facts have fundamental importance. They indicate that intellectual instability in the performance of very diverse tasks constitutes a manifestation of a more general disturbance — instability in intellectual work capac-ity. The instability in intellectual work capacity causes the same patients to appear sometimes as integrated persons, who think and behave satisfactorily, and sometimes as individuals bereft of pur-pose. Such disturbances are most frequently encountered in pa-tients suffering from the early phases of cerebrovascular disease.

Such fluctuations are evidently the main manifestation of the quick onset of neural exhaustion. This propensity to exhaustion is unique; it must be distinguished from the usual exhaustion ob-servable in the healthy individual. In the latter, slowdown of work tempo and rise in the number of errors comes toward the end of the experiment; this is indicated in experiments with healthy sub-jects (adults and children). Hence, if the subject is tired, he will do classification of objects more slowly, but he will do it ade-quately. But the propensity to neural exhaustion of our patients leads to a temporary change in the quality itself of their cognitive performance.

We may assume that a process of defensive inhibition lies at the basis of such neural fatigability. I. P. Pavlov repeatedly wrote that conditioning required that neural processes have a definite strength. Brain diseases lead to a functional weakening in cortical dynamics and to a reduction in cortical tone which is manifested in the spreading inhibition labeled "defensive" by Pavlov. This inhibited state has a functional character; it appears to be tran-

sient, but, all the same, it leads to a temporary weakening of
cerebral work capacity, which, as we have already said, makes it
look like separate functions have been disturbed.

A number of clinical symptoms which look like disturbances
of separate mental processes are in fact differently formed manifestations of disorders in work capacity. Thus, when patients com-
plain that they forget what they have read or to do their errands, it
often looks like a memory disorder; when patients notice that incidental, insignificant stimuli (a nearby conversation, a softly playing radio) interfere with their work, it looks like their attention is
scattered. In reality, all these symptoms reflect one disorder,
namely, that exhaustion of cortical neural dynamics sets in too
easily and affects intellectual competence.

Work capacity can be disturbed by rapid satiation which, in
appearance, is close to exhaustion, but which has quite a different
psychological structure. This notion was introduced by the German psychologist Kurt Lewin to indicate a condition in which the
individual's desire to continue an action that he has begun is exhausted while, at the same time, the situation forces him to keep
on. In these conditions, according to the findings of Lewin's co-
worker A. Karsten, changes occur in the activity of the subject:
"variations" arise. Thus, if the subject had to carry out a monotonous task, for example, line tracing, this action was interrupted
by "behavioral variations." The subjects were distracted from
the objective; they did other things, some totally irrelevant (they
began to whistle or to sing; the external aspects of their activity
changed – the lines were drawn too large or too small, and their
configuration was changed). Karsten regarded these variations as
symptoms indicating that satiation was setting in, that is, they constituted a force interfering with the purposefulness of the behavior.

Satiation is unrelated to fatigue. Much has been written concerning the relationships between susceptibility to fatigue, work
capacity, and illness. The first to address this question was
Kraepelin, who established the significance of such factors as
trainability and susceptibility to fatigue in assessing personality competence. Kraepelin and his followers showed that any work
can be divided into several phases: getting oriented to the task,
ability to practice, and fatigability. Satiation symptoms cannot be
reduced however to Kraepelin's factors. As the early works of

V. N. Myasishchev and his colleagues, E. E. Plotnikov and R. I. Meyerovich, have shown, the exhaustion effect belongs to those mental phenomena which stem from the individual's attitude toward work that still has to be done. Karsten herself showed this. When the meaning of the task was changed (for example, if there were new instructions to the effect that the experiment was about the subject's stamina), the "behavioral variation" disappeared. Karsten's research showed that exhaustion symptoms ("variations," concurrent actions) did not arise immediately in healthy subjects. They only appeared after a more or less prolonged time interval.

In certain forms of illness the exhaustion syndrome set in rather quickly as shown by É. A. Korobkova's research on neurotics, R. I. Meyerovich's on progressive paralytics, and our own studies of asthenics with diverse etiologies.

We will return again in Chapter 6 to the problems of satiation and personality relationships. Here we only wish to indicate that the onset of satiation should be included among the factors which disrupt human work capacity.

Fluctuations of intellectual work capacity can arise due to a disturbance of quite a different function, namely, the tendency to extreme use of mediation. Actually there was no personality impairment in patients who displayed reduced intellectual competence. They noticed their mistakes and tried to compensate for them. But there sometimes arose an excessive urge to behave and act in a mediated or indirect fashion. This was especially clear in an experiment on mediated memory using the "pictogram technique": the patients had to remember words with the help of conventional symbols. The patients are excessively concerned with finding the conventional symbol; they show all kinds of fear that the "drawn symbol would not remind them of the word"; and the verbal reproduction itself turned out to be incomplete and undifferentiated (with healthy individuals such mediation via symbols improves verbal reproduction).

The mediation of any action is, in itself, an adequate feature of behavior in a healthy individual. Even though the active mediation diverts some of the subject's effort, mediation does not impair either the integrity of his learning nor the logical flow of judgments and conclusions. But the efforts of our patients are so sharply concentrated on compensatory techniques and on the constant search for "crutches" that perceptual integrity and the harmonious flow of intellectual process are disturbed. Increased striving by the patient to mediate and correct his behavior hampers the completion of intellectual work and gives it a discontinuous flavor.

The question of work-capacity disorder is very important for solving practical problems, both clinical and pedagogical. Frequently the child's lack of progress or productivity is explicable not in terms of a poor level of knowledge or loss of skill or lack of dedication, but simply in terms of an alteration in cortical neural dynamics that causes a reduction in competence (work capacity can be restored by therapeutic or corrective-pedagogical intervention). Behavioral adequacy is disturbed due to the transitory onset of fluctuations in tonic activity. This problem also has definite theoretical relevance. A more detailed analysis of alterations in work capacity will facilitate getting at the especially complex problems of the relationship between cortical activity and the structure of action and of the relationship between mental activity and the regulation of behavior.

Chapter 5

Disturbances of Thinking

Disturbances of thinking constitute some of the most frequently encountered symptoms of mental diseases. Clinical manifestations of thinking disorders are extremely diverse; some of them are considered typical for a given kind of disease. In diagnosing a disease, clinicians are frequently influenced by the presence of a particular kind of thinking disturbance. Therefore, in all psychiatric texts and monographs, dealing with the most diverse clinical problems, we find statements about thought disorder; many articles on the disorganization of cognitive activity are to be found as well in the psychological literature. However, there is no single principle to determine the basis for analyzing these disorders; this comes about because, in describing and analyzing disturbances of thinking, researchers proceeded from different psychological theories of thinking and with different methodological biases.

The study of thinking is one of the most developed areas in psychological science; it was always a central problem and, indeed, it is here that the various original theoretical positions of investigators are most clearly revealed. If the 1930's and 1940's saw interest in the problem of thinking and consciousness decline somewhat due to the distraction of depth psychology, then, in subsequent years, studies of the psychology of thought have been on the increase again. In line with technical advances, psychology has been trying out the cybernetic approach. Even though this approach to thinking enriched psychology considerably, it brought with it incorrect views regarding the nature of human thinking. A number of foreign scholars (Newell, Shaw, et al.) made statements according to which thinking can be reduced to elementary information processes, to symbol manipulations. A computer program for problem solution began to be promulgated as a theory of thinking. Hence, a new problem arises today, namely, how to bring out the specifically human element in guiding research on problem solving.

O. K. Tikhomirov has studied creative thinking in humans; his research, based on a large amount of experimental evidence, showed that not only is it "impossible to regard a machine program as a theory of human thought, but it is also impossible to cast the real nature of human thinking in terms of a system of cybernetic concepts."[1]

Study of the specifically human element in the thinking process has become the paramount task. Analysis of different kinds of thought pathology has led to a very rich collection of data which justifies acknowledging the unique naturo of human thinking. The findings of experimental psychology convincingly show that thinking should be approached as one kind of activity (L. S. Vygotskii, P. Ya. Gal'perin, A. N. Leont'ev, S. L. Rubinshtein). As already noted, the analysis of thought disorder has been carried out in terms of the prevailing conceptions of contemporary psychology. The Würzburg school made the problem of thinking an object of psychological study early in the 1920's. The associationist psychology, which had prevailed until that time, did not deal with the problem of analyzing cognitive activity. Thinking was reduced to specification of associations. Only sensations and their copies (ideas, images) were thought to be real.

Psychological analysis of thinking consisted in classifying the laws of association, whereby complex ideas or images are created out of elementary ones. One of the founders of associationist psychology, A. Baine, assigned to associations the fundamental role in thinking. Wundt's introduction of the experimental method to psychology was undoubtedly an advance in the history of psychology. However, the research done by Wundt and his followers was based on associationist principles. G. Ebbinghaus, G. Muller, T. Zigen, the major exponents of the experimental psychology of that era, thought that the laws of association were universal. Thus,

---

[1]O. K. Tikhomirov, The cognitive value of simulating creative thinking in a computer, "Contributions to the Polish-Soviet Symposium," Moscow, Izd. Akad. Nauk SSSR, 1967, page 50.

concepts, judgments, and conclusions were characterized as associations of ideas. "A judgment," said Zigen, "is a higher degree of development of an object-association" (page 273). Other proponents of experimental associationist psychology felt that thinking was reduceable to the actualization of associations.

The problem of the reproduction of ideas became the cornerstone of the associationist theory of thinking. Thinking itself began to be labeled reproduction. Thinking was frequently construed as a derivation from other mental functions: memory and attention. Such conceptions were the basis for the research done in the psychology laboratory at the psychiatric clinic of the important German psychiatrist, E. Kraepelin.

To a great extent, the views of associationism determined the course of research on the psychopathology of thinking. Disturbances of thinking were inferred from disturbances of other functions. An attempt was made to show that at the basis of thought disorder was disorder of the so-called intellectual prerequisites: memory and attention. For example, disturbances in the cognitive activity of epileptics was explained as the disturbance of combinations of basic abilities (E. Kraepelin, K. Heilbronner, M. Ya. Sereiskii). Other writers thought that intellectual activity of epileptics was impaired due to extreme instability of attention (V. P. Osipov). A number of investigators mentioned memory impairment as the cause of disordered thinking in epileptics (G. I. Bershtein).

To explain the nature of cognitive disorder in senile patients, writers pointed to disturbance in the ability to retain what has been perceived. The nature of thinking disturbances here was reduced to disorder of memory (V. A. Gilyarovskii, M. O. Gurevich, C. G. Zhislin, et al.). To explain cognitive disturbance in connection with brain trauma, a number of writers (P. Ya. Golant, M. O. Gurevich, V. A. Gilyarovskii, R. S. Povitskaya) were inclined to believe that intellectual disturbances set in because attention has been disrupted.

The views of the Würzburg school also exerted a major influence on the study of psychopathological thinking. As is known, the representatives of the Würzburg school (Kulpe, Ach, Salz, et al.) stated that thinking is not reduceable to associative processes, that it has its own special characteristics and that these characteris-

tics cannot be reduced to the graphic content of sensations and perception. The chief mechanism of thought is the determining tendency; it stems from conceptual representations of goals and it is
not consciously perceived by the person himself. In this fashion
the Würzburg psychologists were the first to enunciate concepts
regarding goals and tasks; however, the mechanism of thinking,
the determining tendency, is contrasted with knowledge via sensations. Thinking is proclaimed an act of "pure" thought, uncon-
nected with prior experience or knowledge. Relying on the views
of Brentano and Husserl regarding intention, the Würzburg psychologists divorced thinking from sense knowledge.

As a result a number of German psychiatrists thought that an
insufficiency in the "primary endowment of mental structure"
caused schizophrenia. According to Berze, who exposited this
theory most clearly, such a primary structure is the "tone of consciousness" (the activeness of the "ego") and, in schizophrenia,
"tone" turns out to be disturbed ("hypotonia of consciousness").
"Hypotonia of consciousness" is thought of not only as an intuitive
construct; it determines all psychopathological symptoms, including thought disturbances.

The views of Gruhle are close to this characterization. He
defines thought disturbance in schizophrenia as a disturbance of
"intensity," with disturbance of personality strength as the underlying factor. Beringer agreed with this view and stated his view
that weakness of "the intentional arc" is the cause of thought disorder in schizophrenia; Stranskii attributed it to "intrapsychic
ataxia."

Thus thought disorders were treated as secondary, as the
manifestations of disturbances of a particular strength and intensity of the mind. In his article on the psychology of schizophrenia
(in the 9th volume of Bumke's "Handbook"), Gruhle metaphoric-
ally stated a position which determined the course of research on
schizophrenic thinking for a long time: The machine remains intact in the schizophrenic and his memory and attention are unim-
paired; however he cannot synthesize separate conclusions, each
of which is correct.

A similar interpretation of thinking as a special kind of
"spiritual activity" was expressed especially by Jaspers: intellect was contrasted with thinking. At the same time as thinking

was defined by him as a manifestation of intrapsychic activity, intellect was regarded as an aggregate of abilities: memory, attention, and speech entered in as the "prerequisites of intellect." This subdividing has penetrated even our own psychology. For example, in Gurevich and Sereiskii's textbook of psychiatry, we read: "the thinking processes, functionally speaking, are closely related to the nature of the intellect; nevertheless these two concepts are not identical. When the intellect is undisturbed, as pathology shows, marked disturbances of thinking may nevertheless exist. Thinking represents intellect in action, a manifestation of intrapsychic activity; by using the intellectual powers, the thinking processes embrace the active components of intention, attention, affective tendency, and purposive orientation. Hence, in contrast to intellect, which is stable within certain limits and capable of only slow variation (in the direction of development or impoverishment), the thinking processes are dynamic: they change in accordance with various factors even in normal conditions, and show especially marked, but not irreparable disturbance during pathological states. These changes in either direction (disintegration or reintegration) may take place suddenly, or in steps" (pages 39-40). Many investigators have noted the simultaneous existence in a patient of an intact intellect and impaired thought processes.

This distinction between intellect and thinking resulted in attempts of investigators to seek a separate genesis for the disturbances of thinking in gross forms of organic disease and in schizophrenia. The disturbance of the cognitive processes arising in severe organic disease – for example, after trauma – were defined as disturbances of the intellect, or of the "prerequisites of the intellect"; the disturbances of the higher cognitive processes in schizophrenia, on the other hand, were interpreted as disturbances of "real" thinking.

The notion of a distinction between intellect and thinking, and the reduction of the latter to some special essence, were widely employed to characterize the mental activity of schizophrenics. Investigators of schizophrenia began to isolate a certain "basic disturbance" (Grundstörung) from which all peculiarities of mental changes were derived. In so doing, they pointed out that the incomprehensibility and oddity of the thought and behavior of these patients cannot be explained. These views were based on the notions of the "verstehen" psychology of Dielthei and Spranger, according to which, as we have already noted, mental processes cannot be explained.

The view was particularly widely held that the "basic disturbance" of the schizophrenic patient was his autism, which was held to be responsible for the disintegration of his intellectual activity. The problem of autistic intelligence was raised by the German psychiatrist E. Bleuler. We shall now discuss in some detail his monograph, which is specifically concerned with autistic thinking.

Bleuler contrasted concrete thought, which reflects the outside world, with autistic thinking, which depends neither on the outside world nor on logical principles, but which is determined instead by "affective demands." "Affective demands" were defined as the seeking of satisfaction and the avoidance of unpleasant experience.

Bleuler expressed this contrast in the following words: "logical thought, corresponding to reality, is the intellectual reproduction of the associations which reality presents to us." Autistic thought, however, is controlled by desires and has nothing to do with logic or with reality. Bleuler contrasts logical and autistic thought in accordance with their genesis. He writes: "The weakening of the logical thought processes leads to the predominance of the autistic; this is all the more understandable since logical thought, which operates with the aid of memory images, must be acquired by means of experience, whereas autistic thought processes operate solely by inborn mechanisms."

The conceptualization of Bleuler has a certain historical value: in contrast to the formal intellectualistic psychology and psychopathology of his time, he stressed the affective basis of thought processes or, more precisely, the fact that the direction of thought is dependent on human needs. The fact that Bleuler stressed the role of affective desires in thinking, and the fact that he associated the intellect with needs and desires (even though he confined his examination to one need, and to its biological level at that), constitute, in our opinion, an achievement rather than a failing of his book. Our principle objection to his concept of autistic thought is that it unjustifiably divides the real from the affectively based thought processes. Although he correctly points out that the former reflect the outside world and are regulated by it, he isolates this principal form of thought from emotions, desires, and needs.

Bleuler's attempt to subdivide the single process of rational cognition into two genetically and structurally different forms of intellectual activity and to introduce to psychopathological terminology, the concept of autistic thinking (intelligence, independent of the outside world) seems false.

The writings of Gestalt psychology exerted a major influence on the study of thinking. In the works of W. Köhler, M. Wertheimer, and K. Dunker, thinking is thought of as a sudden "understanding" of the situation, unprepared by previous experience and knowledge. The activity of thinking consists in restructuring separate parts (configurations) of the problem situation; a new "whole," a "new Gestalt," is formed. The separate elements of the problem situation are perceived in new relationships to one another, depending on the new "Gestalt." The restructuring itself occurs thanks to a suddenly grasped "insight."

In spite of the fact that Gestalt psychologists such as Dunker and Maier raised the issue about the productivity of thinking, they could not discover its specific mechanisms; they analyzed thinking either by means of principles borrowed from perception or deduced this mechanism from the phenomena of consciousness; an object outside of consciousness did not exist for the Gestalt psychologists.

It is necessary to state that the principles of Gestalt psychology, as applied to thinking, have had little influence on research in abnormal psychology. Only particular problems, of a more methodological nature, were useful.

Soviet psychology succeeded in overcoming the conceptualization of thinking either as an innately (imminently) formed process or as an act arising from the linking up of associations. One of the fundamental theses of Soviet psychology (L. S. Vygotskii, P. Ya. Gal'perin, A. P. Leont'ev, S. L. Rubinshtein) is that thought is the process whereby the person masters a system of functions and knowledges that are the products of sociohistorical development.

Soviet psychology defines thinking as the generalized and mediated reflection of reality, intimately connected with sensory perception of the world and with practical human activity.

In describing the dialectical way of perceiving the objective world, V. I. Lenin wrote: "The dialectical road to the recognition of truth, to the recognition of objective reality, runs from living contemplation to abstract thought, and from these to practical activity."[1]

Rational cognition is not limited to the reflection of the unique or the particular, but it also reflects the most essential interrelationships of reality. The process of cognition is characterized not only by the transfer from the sensory to the rational, but also by the fact that it must revert once again to practical activity.

This process, which reflects the outside world most completely, becomes possible only through the existence of language, which, in Marx' words, is the "very essence of thought."[2]

These general principles of Marxist-Leninist theory form the basis of the views of Soviet psychologists on the nature of mental processes, including thinking. Thinking is a special form of human behavior which developes in the course of practical experience, as man is faced with the necessity of solving problems.

To understand the nature of the processes involved in thinking, it is very important to investigate their genesis. Mental properties are formed in the course of ontogenetic development. Vygotskii's investigations aimed to refute the view that mental processes, including thinking, are internal mental properties or self-contained mental functions. He repeatedly postulated that mental processes arise during group behavior and during social intercourse. He said that activity which is at the outset shared by two people, becomes a part of the individual's behavior repertory.

The view that mental activity is formed from external activity was developed most logically by A. N. Leont'ev and P. Ya. Gal'-perin. In his writings, Gal'perin points out that any process of assimilation begins with a concrete action with objects. Later on there is less external action with objects and the operation is carried over into external speech, and, finally, into speech "to oneself," "mentally." Thanks to this it is abstracted from concrete objective conditions and it acquires a more generalized character. There occurs, in the words of the author, a specific "contraction of the process," so that it becomes automatized and changed into a dynamic stereotype.

---

[1]V. I. Lenin, "Complete Collected Works," Vol. 29, pages 152-153.
[2]See K. Marx and F. Engels, "Collected Works," Vol. 3, page 448.

Leont'ev calls this factor the factor of formation of the mechanism of the corresponding mental function, and goes on to say that many links of the process become unnecessary, are not reinforced, become inhibited, and disappear. Together with this contraction of the process, a reinforcement of the corresponding reflex connections of the "reduced system" takes place. A. V. Zaporozhets cites this point of view on the basis of the experimental study of the formation of voluntary movements in the child.

It should be noted that the understanding of mental processes as processes developing from external activity is also found in the writings of a number of progressive psychologists outside the Soviet Union (J. Piaget, A. Wallon).

The views developed by Soviet psychologists – namely, that theoretical activity develops from external activity, and that mental properties, both general and special, are the product of ontogenetic development – are based on the doctrines of I. M. Sechenov and I. P. Pavlov on the reflex nature of mental activity. In his "Elements of Thought," Sechenov states that thought begins with the formation of ideas about an object and then passes directly into the "extrasensory region." Sechenov shows that abstract concepts are formed under the influence of real transactions. In his book "Elements of Thought" he states: "The transfer of thought from the experimental region to the extrasensory takes place by means of prolonged analysis, prolonged synthesis, and prolonged generalization. In this sense, it is the natural continuation of the preceding phase of development, using the same methods and, consequently, the same intellectual processes" (pages 251-252).

The view held by Soviet psychologists that thinking is an activity which develops from practical experience and arises in the course of the life of an individual, rests on the teaching of Pavlov. Thinking is based upon conditioned-reflex activity and develops as a result of individual experience. Hence, by postulating the reflex nature of thinking, Soviet psychologists reject the principles of idealistic, empirical psychology, which regards thinking as an inborn faculty or function, which only increases quantitatively in the course of development.

The psychological investigation of the origin and development of thinking, as S. L. Rubinshtein point out, consists of the discovery of its principles as an analytic synthetic activity.

The discovery of the reflex nature of all these processes, even in the most elementary acts, revealed their multistage structure. In Sechenov's words, "the idea of a mental act as a process must be held as fundamental" (page 252). Even the most elementary human mental processes, such as feeling and perception, are processes in the sense that they take place in time and possess somewhat variable dynamics. All human intellectual activity is characterized by such processes.

Intellectual activity consists not only of the ability to perceive and be aware of surrounding events, but also the ability to act in conformity with a set purpose. Thinking is an active, goal-directed process, directed toward the solution of a definite problem.

The findings of Soviet psychology have shown that thinking is an activity that depends on a system of concepts, is directed at problem solving, and is subordinated to the goal of assessing the conditions under which a task can be accomplished. To carry out the task successfully it is necessary to keep the goal constantly in mind, to realize a program of operations, and to check task execution against the expected results. This checking permits correction of all these operations.

These views of Soviet psychology on the structure of thinking must form the basis for analyzing different kinds of thought pathology. The thought disturbances, encountered in psychiatric practice, are diverse in nature: it is difficult to fit them into a strict classificatory scheme. However, we can talk about certain parameters which may serve as rubrics for the different variations of thought distortions observed in the mentally ill.

On the basis of numerous studies accumulated in the Psychology Laboratory of the Moscow Institute of Psychiatry, it is possible to differentiate three kinds of pathology and thinking: (1) operational disorders, (2) dynamic disruptions, and (3) disturbances in purposiveness.

The cognitive properties of each individual patient rarely fall into definite categories representing one type (or subtype) of intellectual disturbance. Complex combinations of different types of disturbance are often observed in the structure of the pathologically affected thinking of the individual patient. For example, in some cases, a disturbance of generalization is combined with a disturbance of purposiveness, while in others it may be found together with various subtypes of disturbances of generalization.

1. OPERATIONAL DISORDERS

Thinking, as a generalized and indirect reflection of the outside world, is manifested in practical life as the assimilation and utilization of knowledge, as the acquisition and application of new methods of intellectual activity. This assimilation is accomplished not as the simple accumulation of facts, but rather as a process of synthesis, generalization, and abstraction. Thought depends on a certain system of concepts which makes it possible to reflect action in generalizations and abstractions.

S. L. Rubinshtein correctly indicated in his book "Thinking and Ways to Study It" that generalization stems from an analysis which reveals basic relationships. Intellectual operations with concepts must imply a different attitude toward an object, one in which the opportunity is allowed of establishing different relationships between objects. It must be possible to establish connections between the concepts as well. Meanwhile, the systems of connections established and generalized in previous experience are not now annulled, for the formation of a generalization proceeds not only by means of the newly created generalization of single objects, but also by means of the generalization of previous generalizations. Vygotskii often returned to this point, that is, the principle of Lenin which stated that intellectual operations with concepts enabled man to take a long view of the impressions and ideas directly received by the sense organs so that, when he reverts to practical activity, he obtains an even fuller and more detailed reflection of objective reality.

Generalization is cast in a language system that transmits mankind's experience and facilitates extrapolation from individual impressions. In certain pathological mental conditions (for example, intellectual retardedness and some kinds of organic dementia) patients lose the ability to engage in generalization and abstraction.

Investigations of the intellectual operations of patients with different brain diseases have shown that disturbances of the operational side of thinking may assume various forms. Notwithstanding their great variety, they may be grouped into two types: (a) a lowering of the level of generalization; and (b) a distortion of the process of generalization. We shall describe the most general characteristics of this disturbance, illustrating them with typical examples.

Lowering of the Level of Generalization

The ability to work with general attributes is characteristic of analytic and synthesizing thought.

The lowering of the level of generalization implies that the patient's judgments are dominated by direct ideas of objects and phenomena; operations with general signs are replaced by the establishment of concrete connections between objects. During the performance of an experimental task such patients are unable to select from the full assortment of signs those which disclose the concept most fully. Hence, in tests where these intellectual operations are clearly involved, concrete-situational intrusions are most frequently observed. This kind of thought pathology shows up especially well in the object-classification test, a short description of which was given in Chapter 4.

In that experiment one such patient refused to place a cat and dog in the same group "because they fight." Another patient would not group together a fox and a beetle because "the fox lives in the forest while the beetle flies." The special signs "lives in the forest" and "flies" determine the patient's reasoning to a greater degree than did the general sign "animals."

With a well-marked lowering of the level of generalization, the patients were generally incapable of performing the classification test. It seemed to them that the objects differed so much in accordance with their concrete properties that they could not be grouped together. Even the table and chair could not be grouped together because "you sit on a chair but you work and eat on a table." One patient refused to group together a key and a pair of scissors, because they are different: "this is a key and these are scissors; what can they possibly have in common?" In some cases the patients formed a large number of small groups on the basis of an extremely concrete link between them, for example: key and lock, pen and pen holder, thread and needle, exercise book and pencil. Sometimes the subjects grouped together objects as elements of a theme (telling some story about the objects), but produced no classification. One such grouping, for example, consisted of an egg, a spoon, and a knife; another, an exercise book, a pen, and a pencil; a third, a key, a lock and a cupboard; a fourth, a tie, a glove, a thread, and a needle, etc. The subject explained his choices as follows: "He came home from work, ate an egg with the spoon, cut a slice of bread, and then did some work, took an exercise book, pen, and pencil, ... " Erroneous solutions of this type are called concrete-situation combinations.

Such solutions were found principally in oligophrenics (95% of these patients) and in epileptic patients who have had the condition since childhood (86%). Solutions of this type are also observed in a high proportion (70%) of patients with severe forms of encephalitis.

As a rule, the mental states of these patients showed no psychotic symptoms (delusions, hallucination, disturbances of consciousness, etc.); a general intellectual deterioration merely predominated.

These patients could perform a simple task correctly if its conditions were firmly delineated in advance. Subsequent changes in the conditions evoked confusion and erroneous behavior. Although they readily followed the hospital routine, performed relief duties, and generally aided the staff, they often came into conflict with their surroundings, did not understand jokes, and engaged in arguments with other mentally defective patients.

Sometimes the objects were sorted in such a way that only the two nearest objects were grouped together. For example, a table was grouped with a sofa ("you have to sit at the table"), exercise book ("perhaps to write something"), pencil ("you write with a pencil or a pen and there isn't a pen here"). The patients made no attempts at classification.

All these examples indicate that the operation of classification, which is based both on the detection of the dominant property of an object and an abstraction from a large number of other concrete properties and attributes of objects, gives rise to difficulty, forcing many types of mental patients to resort to grouping on the basis of concrete situations.

Similar results were obtained in this group of patients when they performed the test using the technique "exclusion of objects" which is also used to study generalization strategies and consists in the following.

The subject is given cards on each of which are drawn four objects, chosen so that three of them are related to each other while the fourth does not match the rest. The subject is asked to say which of the four is superfluous. For example, he may be shown a card with pictures of a protractor, scales, a clock, and spectacles, in which case the spectacles must be the exception because the first three articles are measuring devices.

The psychological essence of this method is that the subject must first understand the conditions governing the entire operation. Only when the subject has found the principle of generalization joining the three objects can he exclude the fourth.

This method also demonstrates whether or not the subject can find the correct work formula to justify his chosen principle of selection. It also allows one to note if and when the subject changes from one method of solution to another. Here are some examples of how that task is carried out. Patient K, when shown as objects, a thermometer, a watch, scales, and a pair of spectacles, exclaimed that the thermometer ought to be excluded because "only a sick person needs it." A patient from the same group suggested grouping together the watch, the thermometer, and the spectacles, because "if a man is nearsighted, he will look at the thermometer and the watch through his spectacles."

When presented with four objects of which three bore some relation to sources of artificial light (a kerosene lamp, a candle, and an electric flashlight) and one to natural light (the sun), the patients often chose the kerosene lamp as superfluous, explaining that nowadays it is no longer necessary, for "even in the most remote places electricity is available." Other patients excluded the candle for the same reason.

Typical examples of responses of this type are given in Table 1. We may see that the patients employed properties of the object and formed associations between them which were valueless for performance of the test.

Sometimes, immediately upon attaining an understanding of the instructions, the patients would protest: "There is nothing superfluous here, all the objects are necessary." For example, patient D when shown pictures of a boot, a slipper, a shoe, and a foot exclaimed: "Excuse me, nothing is superfluous here. This

Table 1. Typical Replies of Patients with Lowered Levels of Generalization in the Exclusion-of-the-Superfluous-Object Test

Pictures presented	Patient	Patient's responses
Kerosene lamp, candle, electric flashlight, sun	K (oligophrenia)	You must take away the candle. You don't need it if you have a flashlight.
	D (epilepsy)	You don't need the candle, it soon burns down so that it is useless, you may fall asleep, and then it may flare up again.
	S (epilepsy)	You don't need the kerosene lamp, for electricity is available everywhere now. You can take away the candle, too. No, you had better keep the candle in case the electricity supply breaks down. This often happens where I live, and so we keep a stock of candles.
	K-n (epilepsy)	If it is daytime you must take away the sun, for it is light without it, but if it is night, then . . . (the patient is lost in thought).
		In any case there is no sun at night . . .
		No, that is wrong, in the daytime you must take away the candle and leave the sun, but at night you don't need the sun.
Scales, watch, thermometer, spectacles	K-n (epilepsy)	The thermometer is unnecessary. There isn't a doctor here, or a hospital. The scales are superfluous. They are needed in a shop when things have to be weighed.
	S-v (oligophrenia)	Take away the thermometer; it is only needed in the hospital.
	R-v (epilepsy)	I don't know, everything is necessary – the watch for the time, the thermometer for measuring the temperature. Perhaps the spectacles, if the man can see well, but if he is nearsighted, he will need them. Scales are not always necessary, but they are useful in business.

is a man's foot, and you can put a slipper, a boot, a shoe, or a sock on it . . . of course there is no sock here . . . if it had been a woman's foot, the slipper would have fitted . . . and perhaps if her foot had been lame, the boot . . . . I think the shoe would fit a

man's foot." When the experimenter suggested eliminating the
foot, since it is a part of the body while the other three objects
are articles of footwear, the patient burst out laughing: "You must
be joking, how on earth can you take away the foot? If a man had
no feet, why would he need footwear."

The patients approached the pictures of the objects from the
point of view of their practical utility, and they could not perform
the theoretical operation which the test required.

The impossibility of performing the test on the level of generalization and the inability to abstract from the individual concrete
properties of objects were due to the fact that the patients could
not grasp the conventions of the test. This inability to understand
the conventions was particularly prominent during the test requiring the interpretation of proverbs and metaphors.

As we know, proverbs constitute a type of folklore in which a
generalization or conclusion is transmitted through the image of
an individual fact, or event, a concrete situation. The true meaning of the problem becomes clear only if a person can abstract
from the concrete facts mentioned in the proverb, and when the
concrete, isolated events acquire the character of a generalization.
It is only by the satisfaction of this condition that the gist of the
proverb can be transferred to similar situations. This transfer is
similar in its mechanism to the transfer of the method of solving
one problem to another, as is seen especially clearly when phrases
are matched with proverbs. In discussing the problem of transfer,
S. L. Rubinshtein remarks that "at the basis of transfer lies generalization, and generalization results from analysis, coupled with
synthesis" (page 75).

We now consider two variations of this technique.

Variant A. Explanation of Proverbs and Meta-
phors. The subject is given proverbs and metaphors and is asked
to explain them. The proverbs chosen are common and not too complicated. In addition, the subject is asked to think, either of some
examples of everyday life to which the particular saying applies,
or to point out the similarity or difference between two other proverbs. If the subject's interpretation of a proverb is not clear to
the experimenter, he is asked to write a short story to illustrate
its meaning. The experiment proceeds in the form of a conversa-

tion, in which the experimenter plays a very active role. By asking appropriate questions he can verify the accuracy and depth of the patient's comprehension of the metaphorical meaning and elucidate the difficulties which may arise. For this reason the questions must be put carefully to the subject.

The severest disturbance of intellectual activity which this test may reveal is the complete inability to understand the metaphorical meaning, in which case the subject renders a literal interpretation of the proverb or metaphor. However, the ability to correctly interpret proverbs does not necessarily indicate the subject's level of generalization. Some proverbs may be so familiar to the subject that a correct interpretation of them means no more than that the subject already knows their meaning; in these cases no generalization of new material has taken place. A far more demonstrative method is that which requires the matching of phrases and proverbs.

Variant B. Matching Phrases and Proverbs. The subject is given a series of proverbs written in tabular form and cards on which certain phrases are written; some of these phrases may have nothing to do with the meanings of the proverbs, but may contain words reminiscent of the proverbs. The subject is asked to arrange the phrases and proverbs by meaning, so that each proverb is matched by only one phrase. Several series of proverbs and phrases are presented, graded in difficulty. By way of illustration we show the first and easiest of the series. Proverbs: 1) You cannot hide an awl in a sack; 2) Strike the iron while it is hot; 3) All that glitters is not gold; 4) Take care of the pennies and the pounds will take care of themselves; 5) As the ale is drawn so it must be drunk. Phrases: 1) Gold is heavier than iron; 2) The cobbler mended the boots with an awl; 3) Everything that looks good isn't good; 4) What goes up must come down; 5) The blacksmith worked all day today; 6) By combined efforts all difficulties can be overcome; 7) The truth cannot be concealed; 8) Don't put things off until tomorrow.

This variant of the method differs in certain respects from Variant A. The understanding of the metaphorical meaning of a proverb is facilitated by the fact that although the subject may have only a confused understanding of the meaning, the phrase acts as a prompting device. The phrases provoke a difficulty of another sort,

however. The chances of slipping into an approximately similar
meaning are increased, for some words duplicated in the phrases
and proverbs may easily provoke uncritical matching in cases
where the metaphorical meaning is not completely clear. Thus
the critical factor here is not the ability to understand the abstraction, but rather the ability to inhibit what does not correspond to
the meaning of the proverbs. The implementation of both variants
will thus reveal not only the subject's general level of abstraction,
but also the extent of its stability.

Both Soviet and foreign authors have investigated the understanding of metaphors. The work of Piaget and Vygotskii demonstrated the connection between the understanding of metaphors and
the level of conceptual development.

Difficulty in understanding the metaphorical meaning of expressions depends not only on the lowered level of generalization
but on such other possible factors as a negativistic attitude of the
patient and possible changes in the dynamics of his thinking, and
it may depend on the content of his knowledge. All these factors
will be discussed in the following chapters; at this stage we shall
merely mention that the patients who could not distinguish a generic
sign in an experiment on the classification of objects frequently
could not understand the metaphorical meaning of proverbs.
"Strike the iron while it is hot" means, according to one patient,
that "iron must not be forged when it is cold." Another patient
said: "There is no such thing as an iron hand. If you mean an
artificial limb, that is made of wood and not of iron." Another
patient, given the proverb, "Sit on your own sledge" ("Know where
you belong"), said: "Why should I sit on somebody else's sledge?
Why should I, it is unpleasant to sit on a strange sledge." The experimenter tried to explain that this proverb can apply to other situations than those concerning sledges. The patient disagreed:
"How did it come about that somebody sat on a strange sledge?
Was he perhaps deep in thought, thus absentmindedly setting off
with the wrong sledge?" Experimenter: "Now, if a man was doing something that wasn't his own affair, could you use this proverb?" Patient: "No, you couldn't, in one case it is 'affair' and in
the other it is 'sledge'." Only with great difficulty could the metaphorical meaning in some cases be explained to the patient; however, when the next problem was presented to the same patient he
again refused to consider anything other than its literal meaning.

Lowering of the level of generalization is also found in research on patients' processes of secondary generalization or mediation. This technique is called the "pictogram task."

The subject is required to remember fourteen words. As an
aid to memorization he is instructed to think of something which
will help him to reproduce the required words in the future, and
to draw it on paper. He is forbidden to take notes or to jot down
letters as mnemonic devices. The subject is told that the quality
of the drawing is immaterial. There is no time limit for the test.

The method was first suggested by Luria for investigating the
use of drawings as aids in memorization. It was later used with
slight variations to study intellectual processes. The experiment
is conducted in such a way that while the subject assumes that it
is only memory that is being investigated, the experiment is in
fact mainly concerned with studying the general nature of his intellectual processes.

The task of creating a conditioned connection during the memorization of words itself gives rise to considerable difficulty, since
it is not always possible to reflect the whole range of meaning of a
particular word by means of a drawing. The choice of what to draw
thus requires a considerable degree of intellectual freedom.

G. V. Birenbaum, who used this method to investigate the disturbance of ideas in mental patients, delineates this fundamental
difficulty: the range of meanings of the group of words is wider
than can be represented by a single drawing, while the meaning of
the drawing is wider than the meaning of each individual word; the
meanings of the picture and of each word can thus only partially
coincide. It is this ability to detect what is common to the drawing
and to each word which is the fundamental mechanism of the act of
formation of the conditioned meaning. Although this intellectual
operation takes place relatively easily in a person of normal intelligence, even in an adolescent, in the presence of pathological
changes of thinking the formation of these associations becomes
difficult.

The pictogram task may be conducted in two ways. In the first
of these the picture is a conventional representation of the concept
included in the word. For example, to memorize the word "development" any small and large figures (squares, circles) may be
drawn; to memorize the word "doubt" a question mark may be

used. This method is satisfactory with a subject who has achieved an adequate level of education. In the second method the drawing consists of a less general concept than the given word; the first must serve as the conditioned stimulus for the second. For example, the same word "development" may evoke such associations as "development of industry," "mental development," and "physical development." The drawing of any object associated with such a less general concept (a factory, a book, some article connected with sport) may then act as a stimulus for the concept of "development."

Hence, this test requires the ability to coordinate the concept denoted by a word with a more concrete concept; this is possible only when the subject is able to abstract from the whole range of concrete concepts contained in the given word, and when he can inhibit all the special associations connected with this word. The performance of this test is possible only when the subject has attained a definite level of generalization and abstraction.

This pictogram method provides the means of judging the degree of generalization and relevance of the associations formed by the subject. As a rule, healthy subjects, even if they have not completed their high-school education (ninth or tenth grades), can easily perform the test. If the subject encounters difficulty in understanding the task, as soon as he is shown how the test should be performed, he will thereafter solve the problem correctly.

An experimental method similar to that just described is that suggested by A. N. Leont'ev and known in the literature as the method of the indirect memorization of words. We shall now describe one of the variants of this method.

The subject is asked to commit 15 words to memory. To facilitate memorizing he has to choose a suitable picture to correspond to each word from among 30 pictures which have been placed in front of him. After choosing the pictures, the subject must explain what association he made between each word and the object in its corresponding picture. The subject is then shown the pictures and asked to recall the corresponding words.

The chief advantage of this method over that of the pictograms is that here the experiment can be carried out with subjects with both little education and little or no drawing ability. The method also gives an idea of how fully and differentially the subject reproduces the material, to what extent the relationships that he has formed are appropriate.

Considerable attention was given by Vygotskii to the problem of secondary generalization. He approached the process of development of the mind historically, considering that human mental processes develop from external activity, and repeatedly emphasized the secondary character of mental processes. Human behavior and mental development find their origin in human relationships, which develop during material enterprise. In discussing the role of the use of tools in mental development, Vygotskii attached particular importance to language. He saw speech as a phenomenon of objective activity which arises in the process of social practice. It is used initially as a form of communication, and subsequently develops into a means of organization of human actions. Speech almost by definition implies the possibility of executive power, that of initiating and controlling action. Speech is a system of relationships and associations of social experience; it is always nothing more than the generalization of social experience.

In his own experience the individual masters the meaning of words by generalizing object connections and relationships. This generalization process occurs during social intercourse. Speech is both a means of social intercourse and a means of generalization and, in its development, it unifies the two.

Our research showed that this experimental task (indirect memorization) caused considerable difficulty for a number of patients. For instance, when required to find a picture for memorizing the word "development," patient K said: "What sort of development − there are different sorts − muscular development, mental development. Which do you want?" The same patient could not think of a picture for memorizing the words "heavy work." "What do you call heavy work? I found it hard to solve problems in school, and you may be weak and would find it hard to do physical work. I don't understand what I should draw."

Some patients try to reflect the situation almost photographically. When asked, for example, to memorize the expression "happy holiday," the patient says: "What am I to draw? There must be an accordion, a dance, and also, perhaps, a table with a cloth, a bottle, and food. How am I to draw all this? I am not an artist, and you would need an artist to draw it properly."

In her investigations of patients with severe brain lesions, G. V. Birenbaum observed that the difficulties in performing the pictogram task are so great that sometimes patients are unable to choose a drawing, for none seems to convey with sufficient precision and comprehensiveness the concrete significance of the words. We obtained similar results with our patients.

Let us consider typical examples of pictograms of patients with epilepsy.

Patient A. A happy holiday – "How can I draw this? You can be happy in different ways. One person likes to go to a movie on his holiday: that is happiness for him. Another likes to go out drinking. . . . This is bad, of course. . . . But some people I know do it all the same. . . . Others are happy when they go for a walk with their family, or when they take the children to the circus. How am I to draw all this? Of course, you can look at it from a different point of view, from that of society. We have national holidays, for everybody. May Day, for example. I could draw a demonstration with lots of flags. (The patient draws a flag, but still is not satisfied.) One flag isn't enough, there ought to be lots of flags and a crowd, but I don't know how to draw them. . . ."

Patient M'va. Heavy work – "It is absolutely impossible to draw anything the least like heavy work. For some, mathematics is hard. I never liked it and never had to do any. Others don't take to literature and, of course, for a weak person physical work is heavy . . . anything can be heavy. I shall draw a stone; it is hard work piling stones. Now, of course, they have cranes to lift heavy loads . . . No, I cannot draw stones, but I shall draw a hammer, like the one a blacksmith uses. But there, again, there are no more hammers nowadays, it is all done by machines. I don't know, doctor, what. . . . Oh, well, it can be a stone and a hammer."

Hence, an analysis of the data obtained by different methods (classification of objects, method of exclusion, explanation of proverbs, and a pictogram task) reveal disturbances of the processes of generalization in a number of patients (epilepsy and oligophrenia): their judgments were of the concrete situation type and they did not understand metaphors and conventions.

These experimental results show that these patients are unable to distinguish the essential properties of objects or to discover the semantic relationships between them.

A lowering of the level of generalization and of the supporting processes, analysis and synthesis, means that the problem situation itself, an aspect of every experiment, remains poorly understood. It is generally accepted that the thinking process has its beginning in the problem situation. S. L. Rubinshtein correctly points out that this situation comprises unknown elements. The situation becomes problematic precisely because elements are involved which are inappropriate to the very relationships in which they occur at a given moment. The problem situation itself has to be analyzed; only then will the correct formulation occur to the individual.

The patients we have described cannot analyze the problem situation confronting them; they reason in connection with each element in the situation; the requirements of the theoretical problem do not occur to them. Thinking uses and applies acquired knowledge and tactics of problem solution, but this must be preceded by a correct analysis of the task's requirements. New tactics must be employed if the old ones are unrealistic. Our patients are extremely limited in their abilities; their affected thinking incompletely reflects reality; they can function correctly only in rigidly predetermined conditions. A. A. Tokarskii wrote about this even in his time. In contrast to many contemporary Wundtian psychologists, Tokarskii felt that correct thinking means to realize that task conditions have changed, to make the appropriate response and be capable of doubting one's own conclusions. In his article "On Stupidity," published in 1896, Tokarskii gives an example of impaired thinking ("stupidity" in his terminology). A fool saw a fire, began to dance, and was beaten. At home his mother admonished him and advised him that water should be poured on a fire. He left and again saw a fire – a pig was being roasted – took a pail and began to pour it over the fire. Again, he was beaten.

Tokarskii analyzed this case as follows: this stupid individual understood the instructions after the first incident; there was no memory impairment. He concluded that if there is a fire, it must be extinguished, but he goofed because he couldn't distinguish between two situations, a real fire and a pig roast. He dealt with the new situation as he should have dealt with the first. According to Tokarskii he grasped an insufficient number of attributes, which means, he did not fully perceive reality.

The fundamental characteristic of foolishness, according to Tokarskii,is the "failure of action to correspond to the demands of the actual situation." Tokarskii believes that the cause of stupidity in such an individual is that his "mind is disturbed in those fundamental wellsprings from which all our mental resources flow, and especially in the ability to perceive the immediate realities. The stupid individual perceives only a small part of his environment" (page 689). Tokarskii characterizes such individuals as persons who often use clichés improperly, who cannot find new relationships and use them in novel ways, and who do not question their own judgments.

The stupid individual "absorbs little of what is going on around him, remembers little of what he has perceived, and, finally, he cannot understand to which prior situation a particular recollection belongs. His chief trait is a sharp lack of correspondence between his ideas and concepts, on the one hand, and reality, on the other" (page 692).

This statement of Tokarskii's makes it clear that he understood thinking as an activity, requiring analysis, synthesis, and generalization. For the inability to distinguish two situations having an attribute in common and the insufficiently complete perception of situational requirements, are, in fact, manifestations of inadequate analytic and synthesizing activity. Use of an inappropriate cliché, that is, an incorrect transfer of meaning, implies erroneous generalization.

Authors discussing the psychology of the mentally retarded child cite experimental findings that show that such children cannot discover the common element from among a variety of single phenomena. During the 1930's, L. S. Vygotskii and Zh. I. Shif found that the mentally retarded child who has learned to work with visual systems of associations is unable to systematize his experience through generalization and abstraction.

To recapitulate, it can be said that the intellectual activity of such patients represents an imperfect reflection of objects, phenomena, and their interrelationships. A perfect process of reflection of the objective properties and principles which underlie material objects always assumes the ability to abstract from concrete details. In discussing the sensory-abstract-practical nature of thinking, Lenin stressed that the act of generalization is a deviation from concreteness. "The approach of the [human] mind to an individual object, and the acquisition of an impression [an idea] from it is not a simple, direct, rigid act, but a complex bifurcating zigzag-shaped act allowing for the flight of fantasy from life."[1]

In our patients this "flight" from single associations was extremely difficult. A reflection of the objective features and principles of things assumes the ability, which was impaired in our patients, to abstract from concrete details.

Distortion of the Process of Generalization

Disturbances in the functions of abstraction and generalization can be of a different nature, apparently even the antithesis of those just described.

Whereas the judgments of the patients described above did not go beyond the bounds of single, individual associations, in the patients who we will now discuss the "flight" from concrete associations assumes a grossly exaggerated form. In their judgments these patients reflect only random aspects of phenomena, and not the essential relationships between objects.

Solution of experimental tasks actualizes these chance associations, taken from the patient's concrete experience. The patient relies upon relationships which reflect neither the content of real phenomena nor the cognitive relations between them. For example, when asked to classify objects, these patients are guided by excessively general signs and respond inadequately to the real relationships between objects. Patient M, for example, grouped together a fork, a table, and a shovel in accordance with the principle of "solidity"; and a mushroom, a horse, and a pencil in accordance with the "principle of joining the organic to the inorganic."

We designate such disturbances of cognitive activity as distortion of the process of generalization. They are found most frequently in patients with schizophrenia (in 67% of the patients whom we examined), mainly with the hallucinatory, paranoid form of the

[1]V. I. Lenin, "Complete Collected Works," Vol. 29, page 330.

disease, but they can be observed as well in other forms of the
disease.

Such patients live in a world of their own hallucinations and
have little interest in the real situation. They attempt to approach
unimportant, commonplace events "from theoretical standpoints."
In conversation they can discuss matters of a general character,
but often they cannot give a simple answer to a concrete question.
Their language is flowery. For example, when talking about a cupboard, one such patient called it "a circumscribed part of space,"
and when discussing a friend, whom he described as a good man,
he said: "What is good and evil? This definition is relative – positive and negative, like the problem of electrons and the universe.
If something is bad, this is a qualitative aspect, and it means that
something else must be good. But bad may be taken for good, and
the two are not opposite."

Some of the more demonstrative examples of how such patients
perform tests on the classification of objects are shown in Table 2.
They either make use of signs which are so general (hardness,

Table 2. Performance in the Object-Classification Test
Using Formal and Illogical Associations

Objects classified in the same group	Patient	Explanation
Cupboard, saucepan	M (schizophrenia, paranoid type)	"Both have an opening."
Automobile, spoon, cart	G-n (schizophrenia, paranoid type)	"A spoon also moves, toward the mouth."
Beetle, spade	G-n (schizophrenia, paranoid type)	"You dig the earth with a spade, a beetle also digs the earth."
Flower, spoon, shovel	D-n (schizophrenia)	"All these objects are long."
Goose, pig	K-v (psychopathy)	"The goose and pig aren't friendly."
Shovel, horse	E-n (schizophrenia, paranoid type)	"They both begin (in Russian) with the letter 'L'."
Clock, bicycle	M (schizophrenia)	"A clock measures time, and if you are riding a bicycle, it also measures space."

movement) that they go far beyond the essential significance of the phenomena, or they work on purely external, immaterial signs (an opening).

The illogical, aimless character of the judgments of the patients of this category is particularly obvious when they attempt to compose pictograms. One such patient, for example, in order to memorize the words "teplyi veter" (a warm wind), drew two triangles (treugol'niki), and to memorize the expression "veselyi uzhin" (a jolly supper), two circles (kruzhki). Another patient of this group, to memorize the word "somnenie" (doubt), drew a catfish (som), and to memorize the word "razluka," drew an onion (luk).

Patients with a lowered level of generalization ability have difficulty in composing pictograms because they cannot form abstractions when presented with individual concrete word meanings. Another group of patients could perform it very easily, since they produced any associations at random which bore no particular logical relation to the problem. The drawings were interpreted so widely and unobjectively that the result bore no logical relationship to the word or words. Without thinking, the patients permit themselves to suggest any scheme whatsoever for identifying words.

In Table 3 we show the most typical examples of performance on this task in which illogical and formal associations are used.

Tables 4 and 5 contain examples of how schizophrenics carry out these tasks.

In this fashion, while carrying out the experimental tasks, the patients put together any and all relationships between objects and phenomena even if they are inappropriate to the concrete facts of the situation. In fact, actual differences and similarities between objects are not taken into account by the patients; in no way do they serve to control or check his judgments and behavior. The logic of a stream of thought is not checked by experience. It is interesting to note that in these patients speech does not facilitate performance of the task, but rather adds to the difficulty: the words pronounced by the patients evoked new, often random associations, which they do not inhibit. Having completed a task correctly in real life, the patients may then proceed to conduct an absurd discussion about their performance.

Table 3. Examples of Performance of Pictogram Tests Using Formal, Illogical Associations

Words given for memorizing	Patient	Drawings and explanations
Development	M-v (schizophrenia)	Two arrows
Development	Od-ov (schizophrenia)	A rope. "It can develop."
Razluka (separation)	M-v (schizophrenia)	Onion (luk)
Somnenie (doubt)	E-n (schizophrenia)	Catfish (som)
Somnenie (doubt)	Sim-v (schizophrenia)	A clay ball (in Russian "kom gliny"). "Glinka wrote a novel 'Somnenie,' let it be 'gling' (clay)."
Devochke kholodno (the girl is cold)	L-na (schizophrenia)	$D^2/4$. "They both have a letter D."
Devochke kholodno (the girl is cold)	R-v (schizophrenia)	Two squares. "You said two words."
Devochke kholodno (the girl is cold)	K-v (schizophrenia)	Some dots and a triangle. "The dots are snow, let the triangle be the girl."
Pechal' (grief)	K-v (schizophrenia)	To print (pechat'). "It begins with pech."
Pechal' (grief)	L-na (schizophrenia)	Stove (pechka). "It begins with P."

Table 4. Examples of Definition of Ideas by Patients with Distortion of the Process of Generalization

Words to be defined	Patient	Definitions
Clock	O-v (schizophrenia)	"A mechanical object, a form of objectiveness, or an object of logic."
Clock	Z-na (schizophrenia)	"A measure of a definite property of matter, what do they call it in philosophy? An attribute, isn't it?"
Cupboard	M-v (schizophrenia)	"This is an object belonging to inanimate nature; it has practical application for the preservation of other material particles."

Table 5. Examples of Comparison of Concepts by Patients with Distortion of the Process of Generalization

Words for comparison	Patient	Patients' statements
Rain and snow	A-v (schizophrenia)	"Objects of humidity, distinguished by the displacement of certain substances in relation to the circumference of the earth."
River and lake	A-v (schizophrenia)	"River is long. Lake, an ellipse, sometimes a circle. From a geometrical point of view."
Sledge and cart	A-v (schizophrenia)	"From the grammatical point of view both these words are nouns but 'sani' [the word for sledge] does not exist in the singular."

Disturbances of intellectual activity in schizophrenic patients were described by Vygotskii. He postulated from his experimental findings that in such patients the function of concept formation has disintegrated; concepts had degenerated to the level of complexes, or concrete meaning-patterns. This phenomenon was based on changes in the meaning of words.

While we may agree with Vygotskii that patients with schizophrenia often show changes in word meaning, we cannot agree that in these cases concepts are degraded to the level of complexes. (A complex as Vygotskii understands the term, involves a generalization of phenomena on the basis of concrete associations or concrete ideas.) As our experiment showed, "concrete" associations take place in only a very small proportion of schizophrenics. In most cases the process of generalization is disturbed not because the patients operate with concrete association but rather because their intellectual activity is dominated by associations which are inappropriate to the concrete relationships of this situation. Even when their judgments are concrete, they reflect not only the real authentic relationships between phenomena or objects but also, and perhaps to a greater degree, their random, incidental characteristics. This phenomena occurs not because the conceptual level has been disturbed but because these patients have lost their ability to be guided by the objective meaning of phenomena and objects.

Hence their thinking seems unconventional and affected. Many authors have described this "uncommonness" in the thinking of schizophrenics. Some of them, such as N. Cameron, D. Chapman, and R. Payne, attempt to explain alternations in schizophrenic thinking in terms of the use of an excessively large number of object features, including ones that do not carry relevant information about the objects. Other authors, such as T. Vekovich, Yu. F. Polyakov, and T. K. Meleshko, attribute thinking disorder in schizophrenia to the actualization of insignificant bits of knowledge from past experience. In this regard the writings of Polyakov and Meleshko are especially interesting: they worked out a number of techniques (modified variations of the method of exclusions and comparison of concepts) for studying schizophrenic thinking. They showed that nonstandard properties of objects are used in concept analysis two and a half times more frequently by patients than by healthy subjects. Hence, from the studies of many investigators, it may be concluded that information selectivity is disturbed which, in turn, leads to the increased influence of latent and insignificant information.

Moreover, research supports the theses stated above that schizophrenic thought (especially distortion of the process of generalization) does not reflect the real relationships between objects and phenomena. Analysis of this aspect of thought pathology may be accomplished if thinking is approached as a motivated activity, whose structure also includes a personality component. Only by taking this component of cognitive activity into account will it be possible to some extent to illuminate many kinds of thought pathology.

2. DISTURBANCE OF THE DYNAMICS OF COGNITIVE ACTIVITY

Acceptance of the reflex nature of mental life implies acknowledging that it is a process. I. M. Sechenov even wrote that "the concept of the mental act as a process, as an event having a definite beginning, middle, and end, must be maintained as fundamental" (page 252).

We cannot adequately understand the internal mechanisms of thought, we cannot study the structure of cognitive operations whereby the objective properties of objects are reflected, if we do not analyze the process aspects of cognitive activity. The use of generalization to solve problems and the actualization of appropriate cognitions about objects requires not only the preservation of intellectual operations but also the dynamics of thinking. S. L. Rubinshtein repeatedly emphasized that reducing thought to its operations and ignoring its process means doing away with thinking altogether.

Any definition of thinking should be regarded as a process, and this applies not only to the general theoretical characteristics of thinking but also to every particular human thought. Even the elementary mental acts of a person, such as feelings and perceptions, are processes in the sense that they occur in time, possess a certain variable dynamic pattern, and take place as an active human function. The discovery of the reflex basis of even these most elementary acts reveals very distinctly that they are processes carried out in many different stages. This "process" type of structure is manifested to a maximal degree in every act of human thinking.

The successful execution of an intellectual act requires separating out appropriate systems of interrelationships, getting rid of the incidental elements, and evaluating each cognitive operation as it is being carried out. The performance properties of such a complicated many-staged activity constitute its dynamic character.

One of the special features of thinking as a higher form of cognition is its systematic nature. Of course, this systemization comes about only as a result of the correct structuring of ideas. The cognition of facts hidden from direct perception is possible only when man is capable of generalizing and analyzing from the facts he perceives. This systemization involves the transition from one group of judgments to another and the formation of a long chain of conclusions. The chain of conclusions, transformed into reasoning, is a true manifestation of thinking as a process. Therefore in studying the formation and disturbances of thinking, it is not enough simply to analyze the formation and disturbances of ideas, or simply to describe the characteristics of intellectual operations. Our investigations show that the disturbance of the process of generalization, although the most common, is not the only type of thinking disturbance. Moreover, the simple disintegration of ideas does not represent the most common disturbance of thinking. It is the various pathological states of the brain which most frequently lead to dynamic disturbances of thinking.

Little research has been done on disturbance of the dynamics of thinking. Although in many psychiatric investigations mention is made of the dynamic character of certain disturbances of thinking, their reversibility is taken for granted.

In the chapter on the disturbance of intellectual work capacity we described the judgmental inconsistency of our patients. It was shown that, for a number of our patients (for example, patients with vascular diseases of the brain), fluctuations of mental work capacity led to incorrect problem solving. The fluctuations did not depend upon the complexity of the task that had to be carried out but on the propensity to fatigue in these patients' cortical neural dynamics. These disturbances of cognitive activity can be defined as judgmental inconsistency.

Judgmental Inconsistency

A characteristic feature of this disturbance is the inability to maintain a stable method of task performance. The general level of generalization was not lowered; the patients correctly grasped the instructions, analyzed and integrated the material well, and understood the figurative meaning of proverbs and metaphors. However, the patients' reasoning was not always adequate, as we have already noted.

We will examine in some detail these patients' patterns of behavior in performing the object-classification test. They had no difficulty in grasping the instructions, they used a method adequate to the solution of the problem, and they began to sort the cards in accordance with generic signs; but after a short time they abandoned the correct method of solution. Having in some cases attained a high level of generalization, the patients periodically wandered off into incorrect, random associations. There were several types of variations.

1. Very often the principle of classification alternated between that of generalization and that of concrete situations. A few examples may be given.

Patient M-v (closed brain injury) began to sort the cards in accordance with a generic sign, forming groups of plants, animals, etc., and then suddenly began to have doubts about where to put a toadstool: "It is harmful; let us leave it alone." In the same way, he could not decide where to place a beetle: "Put it with the textbook and the exercise book; they study it at school." After the experimenter had asked the patient to pay more attention to the work, he replied somewhat confusedly: "Wait, here I have dishes, furniture, and plants. . . . Of course, and the fungus belongs here, regardless of whether it is poisonous or not; the beetle should go with the animals." Eventually the patient obtained the following groups: people, animals, plants, dishes, furniture, school articles, housekeeping equipment. The experimenter asked the patient to combine several groups. The patient replied: "People with animals, perhaps? Plants. . . and then what? Surely the rest cannot be put together: how can you combine things used in a house and things used in an office?" The patient was obviously tiring; he developed a mild tremor of the hands and began to perspire. The experimenter began to talk about something unrelated to the test. Five minutes later, at the experimenter's request, the patient resumed the work and at once produced without help a correct, generalized solution.

Patient Sh. (cerebral arteriosclerosis), having correctly separated a group of tools (saw, broom, spade), included a blacksmith in this group, "because he is drawn with a hammer in his hand, and he works with different tools." When the experimenter asked: "And what have you in this group?" (charwoman, sailor, child, doctor) the patient replied: "These are people," and she then transferred the blacksmith to the group of people of her own accord.

These examples show that the fluctuations in the mental activity of these patients took the form of vacillation between generalizations and concrete situations as a basis for their decisions. The solution of problems by these patients at the level of generalized decisions had not become a stable modus operandi.

2. The mistakes made by another group of patients were the result of the replacement of logical associations by random combinations. For instance, they spoiled their performance in an object classification test by combining objects inattentively into one group. They frequently noticed their mistakes and corrected them themselves.

3. The mistakes made by patients took the form of combining objects into similar groups: they often selected objects in accordance with the correct general attribute, and then immediately began to form another almost identical group. So, for example a patient might isolate a group of people including a doctor, a fisherman, and a maid, and immediately would sort out still another similar group where seaman and skier are included.

Hence, comparison of the results of experiments using different methods (classification of objects, exclusion of objects, establishment of analogies) revealed this instability in the appropriate mode of solution of a problem.

The instability displayed by some patients in completing tasks sometimes reaches extremely exaggerated proportions. The patient not only cannot keep his thoughts on the right track but he begins to respond to any stimulus whether it is meant for him or not. For example, having heard that another patient says that he had sausage for breakfast the patient, having told a little story about how a jackdaw had changed its color and flew into a pigeon house, says "and the pigeons treated her to sausage."

The phenomenon of hyperresponsiveness was manifested especially clearly in an association experiment. As responses we obtained the names of random objects which happened to be located within the subject's range of vision ("a sort of interweaving"): in response to the word "singing," one patient gave the word "table"; in response to the word "wheel," the word "spectacles," etc. This tendency was sometimes observed in other groups of patients, although it disappeared as soon as the experimenter pointed out the error. In the case of hyperresponsive patients, however, verbal correction could only curb this tendency for a very short time; even after a short interval the patients again began to name any objects which fell in their field of vision.

The hyperresponsive patients also exhibited this tendency in a variant of the association experiment in which the instructions stipulated an added qualification to the responses, for instance, when the subject was told to name a number of objects of a particular color (for example, red or green). This task can sometimes give rise to considerable difficulty in healthy subjects since it requires the active discarding of words which do not correspond to the meaning of the instruction. In such cases the subjects use various methods as aids in recalling the required words (such as observing the surrounding objects), but they do not use them in their answers if they do not correspond to the instructions (that is, they will not name the surrounding objects if not of the required color). The experimenter's instructions acquire the value of the determinant stimulus; the responses of a normal person in the experimental situation depend on the condition of the task and the demands of the experimenter.

On the other hand, in this experiment the hyperresponsive patients at times named objects which were in their field of vision but which were not necessarily of the required color. The experimenter's instruction evoked purposive behavior only for a limited time. The relationship between the direction of our patient's associations and the conditions of the problem was extremely unstable. Any object observed or once overheard would distort the course of their reasoning. We attributed their absurd thoughts and actions to the syndrome we have described as hyperresponsiveness.

It is possible that our patients' characteristic fluctuating disorientation in time and space was also closely associated with this hyperresponsiveness. For instance, one of them at first said that he was in a restaurant and then immediately declared he was in a watchmaker's shop instead. (As it happened, someone had just set a clock in the patient's presence.) Five minutes later he correctly stated that he was in the hospital.

It may be suggested that the pathological resuscitation of orientating responses destroys the stable system of appropriate connections that had previously been formed in these patients; now their thinking is subordinated to the flow of chance associations. Each new stimulus destroys the purposive character of their reasoning. Hence, experimental research on patients with different forms of illness has supported the notion that fatigability plays a major role in the genesis of cognitive disturbance in patients with organic impairment of the brain. At the same time these studies have shown that dynamic thought disorders are not only manifestations of fatigability but that their nature is considerably more complicated or, alternatively, considerably more mixed up. Some of them are due to pathologically affected motility of neural processes. We will consider here only a few of those, the ones frequently encountered in clinical practice: the so-called "flights of

ideas" of the manic patient and the "sluggishness of thinking" of
the epileptic.

Cognitive Lability

The term "flight of ideas," widely used in psychiatry, denotes
a peculiarity of thinking observed in patients in the manic phase of
a manic-depressive psychosis. This phase is characterized by
euphoria and psychomotor excitation. The patients speak loudly
and without stopping, they laugh, joke, and accompany their speech
with lively, expressive gesticulations and facial movements; they
are extremely distractible. Every new impression, be it a spoken
word or a perceived object, directs their thoughts and ideas, which
replace one another so rapidly that the patients cannot register
them in their speech. They cannot finish one thought before going
on to the next; sometimes they shout only a single word. Charac-
teristically, despite their extreme distractibility and scattering
of attention, manic patients actively observe what is going on
around them, and they frequently elicit surprise by their quick
wit and pointed remarks.

As a rule, experiments cannot be performed on manic patients
because of their extreme distractibility, which prevents them from
fixing their attention on the experimental situation. Such patients
can be investigated experimentally only when at various levels of
a hypomanic state, in which certain pathological changes in their
intellectual activity may be observed.

These patients have retained the capacity for analysis and
synthesis in the appraisal of a situation, although during the performance of any experimental problem their superficiality of
judgment is readily apparent. The patients pay little attention to
thinking over the problem presented to them and they fail to grasp
the meaning of the task. For example, when comparing ideas, they
often remark on their similarity and difference in accordance with
external signs. When asked to explain the similarity and difference
between the concepts of "table" and "chair," one patient (with a
high-school education) replied: "They have in common the fact that
both the chair and the stool have four legs; the difference is that the
chair has a back while the table has none." The same patient gave
the correct, generalized reply when he was guided and prompted in
solving the problem. When required to arrange pictures in consec-

utive order, although these patients immediately understand their
theme, they proceed to arrange the pictures in any random order.
In the proverb-and-phrase test, hypomanic patients often choose
phrases according to similarities between words rather than from
their individual meanings, although they are capable of the latter.
If the patient's attention is drawn to the incorrectness of his answers, he easily corrects his mistakes.

The intellectual activity of patients in a hypomanic state is
characterized not only by a superficiality of the judgment, but also
by a lack of inhibition of many random and chaotic associations.
Individual words evoke new thoughts, which the patients immediately put into words; their speech reflects a multitude of ideas and
emotional experiences. In cases of extreme hypomania, the patients
can concentrate on an experimental problem only for a very short
time. Although they may understand the meaning of a proverb perfectly, they fail to explain it. Often one particular word in the
proverb will evoke a whole chain of associations. Instead of explaining the proverb, a patient may cite a relevant example from
his own life; this will in turn remind him of something else, and
his thoughts then begin to run haphazard directions. For example,
a hypomanic patient explained the proverb, "All that glitters is not
gold," as follows: "Gold – that is the beautiful gold watch my
brother gave me; he and I get on well together. When we were at
school we used to quarrel, but since then we have lived in peace.
My brother is very fond of the theater, and I went with him to see
a play . . . ," and so on. The chaotic character of his associations
prevented him from giving the correct explanation of the proverb,
and the word "gold" immediately led to a complete chain of reminiscences. However, other variants are possible, in which patients
may omit a link in the course of their explanation. Another patient,
for example, immediately understood the meaning of this proverb,
and as an example, in the course of his subsequent explanation, he
wanted to describe the case of an apple, which although good on the
outside, was bad inside. This however, was not what the patient
said, for he at once began: "Apples, of course, are sometimes
wormy. There are some sorts of apple, for example, which you
would never suspect. . . . Our neighbors had some Michurin
apples. Naturally the development of Michurin's theory is very
important. . . ." He then went on to give various reminiscences
of friends of his who were trained in Michurin's ideas.

The disturbance of the logical course of thinking in patients of this group is also manifested during their performance on the object-classification test. They immediately understood the instructions and begin to sort the pictures correctly into groups, often in accordance with a general sign, but any chance association which may arise turns the course of their thinking into another direction. One such patient, for example, having formed a group of live objects, including several human beings (i.e., having performed the task on the correct level of generalizations), suddenly exclaimed when he saw the picture of the blacksmith: "We are blacksmiths and our friend is the hammer . . . I love . . . the old revolutionary songs . . . A song . . . is our friend. And is art in general to be found among these cards reminding me of a song? The pictures aren't drawn particularly well: who drew them, a "khudozhnik" (an artist)? From the word "khudo" (bad)." The patient laughed, held a picture in his hand, and did not carry out the test. When the experimenter asked him to turn to the problem, the patient continued to sort the pictures without returning to the previous principle of solution, but began with new associations which had arisen: "Where can I put the smith, surely there is no smith here?" When he saw a horse, the patient said: "Let us shoe it." Experimenter: "You have begun to arrange them differently." The patient replied: "Yes, I wanted to separate people from animals," and continued to arrange them in accordance with the generic sign.

The patient had grasped the meaning of the problem and, what is more, he could solve it at the generalized level, but any stimulus (a word spoken by himself or by the experimenter, something which he saw, etc.) evoked random associations and often led him away from the immediate problem. If the experimenter gave him guidance, he would eventually correctly sort the cards and define the ideas, but the independent path of his reasoning proved inadequate or incorrect.

Cognitive Sluggishness

This clinical manifestation represents the antithesis of the type of disturbance we have just described. Patients characterized by "sluggishness" of thinking cannot change their mode of work or their opinions, or switch from one type of activity to another. Such disturbances are often found in epileptics and in patients with late consequences of severe brain injuries.

Sometimes these patients are able to work, but then only with frequent interruptions, loss of their former skills, and difficulty in acquiring and applying new skills. They usually arrive at the mental hospital after having failed to compensate for their defects, often having become addicted to alcohol. Their case histories show that these patients can work, read newspapers, and often show an interest in ward affairs; at the same time, their mental production is of a low caliber and they can work only very slowly.

Experimental psychological investigation further reveals a slowness and sluggishness of their intellectual processes. Although they may both comprehend the instructions and exhibit ample capacity for generalization in the classification experiment, they are unable to adjust to modifications in the experimental procedure. A change in the conditions impairs their standard of performance.

This sluggishness of intellectual processes so impairs the patients that they cannot cope even with the most elementary problems if a change in conditions is required. So, for example, one patient in the pictogram task (where he had to mediate his recollection and reproduction of words with the help of drawings) was quite able to invent conventional signs for the classification of words if he was allowed to draw "a man" but he could not do so if he was forbidden to draw "a man."

Such patients are also characterized by a lack of flexibility. In experiments on mediated recollection (according to the technique of A. N. Leont'ev), having chosen a particular picture to aid in memorizing a particular word, the patients are then unable to choose another picture for this word when asked to do so. Thus, the patients can solve the problem only if it can be done by one particular method. Even in experimental tasks requiring the classification of colored pictures – which required no complex analysis and synthesis – they cannot switch to another attribute from one that they have already distinguished. Having grouped the pictures by their color, they cannot then categorize them in accordance with their form.

This type of disturbance can be described by "inertia of the associations of the previous experience." It appears to be a disturbance of cognitive dynamics leading to a reduction in the ability to generalize and abstract. While doing object classification, these patients not only would not group together wild and domestic animals, but they regarded each domestic animal as a single specimen. As a result the object classification task itself cannot be done even at a concrete level. For the sorting process itself requires the inhibition of some elements and a comparison of others (that is, it requires some degree of flexibility of operation, of switching from one to another).

One patient, for example, distinguished many small groups by a concrete, yet generic attribute: domestic animals, wild animals, furniture, transport. He formed the pictures of people into two groups: people engaged in physical work and those doing mental work (he included a skier among the latter).

The experimenter suggested certain groupings, such as domestic and wild animals, people in various occupations, etc. The patient agreed and started to sort the pictures afresh, but having already accomplished the task by the previous method, he gave up: "Let it be like that." Although he had understood the principle of classification suggested by the experimenter, and although he had even begun to act accordingly, he could not switch over to a different method of work.

The same difficulty was also revealed in an experiment involving the exclusion method. One patient, for example, when shown a card on which a table, a chair, a sofa, and a table lamp were drawn, exclaimed: "Of course, this is all furniture, exactly, but the lamp is not furniture. But surely there must be a lamp on the table if it is night, or even twilight. . . . In winter it grows dark early, and then it is better to remove the sofa. . . . If there is a chair, you can do without the sofa." When the experimenter said: "But you yourself said that the lamp is not furniture," the patient replied: "Of course, that is right, you must pick out the furniture, but the lamp is a table lamp, it stands on the table. I suggest we take out the sofa." Despite the fact that the experimenter tried several times to guide the patient into the proper direction; despite the fact that the patient himself not only understood but also mentioned the principle of generalization (furniture); in the actual test − sorting the objects − he returned again and again to the property he had picked out: "The lamp is a table lamp; it must stand on the table." The patient could not switch from the decision he had made.

The concrete associations with previous experience inertly dominate the intellectual activity of the patients and determine the entire subsequent course of their reasoning. They frequently cannot discard a single detail during the test, or let a single property of the objects escape, so that they cannot achieve even elementary generalization. This attempt to be precise and to exhaust all the various factual relationships when solving any problem, results in the ratiocination characteristic of the epileptic. Such attention to superfluous detail is known generally in clinical practice as "tenacity" of thinking.

This inertia of the associations of previous experience stands out especially clearly during tests demanding a fuller explanation – the definition of concepts. To illustrate this statement two typical examples of patients' attempts at the definition of simple concepts are given below.

Patient B-n (epilepsy). Cupboard. – "This is an object in which things are kept. . . . However, dishes are also kept in a sideboard – food, too, and clothes can be kept in a cupboard, although food is often kept in a cupboard. If the room is small and a sideboard will not fit inside, or if there simply isn't a sideboard, the dishes will be kept in a cupboard. We have a cupboard; on the right side there is a large empty space, and on the left four shelves; that is where the dishes and food are kept. This is bad management, of course, because the bread often smells of naphthalene from the mothballs. Again, there are cupboards for books, but they aren't deep. They have shelves, lots of shelves. Cupboards now are sunk into the walls, but still they are cupboards."

These illustrations show that the patients began correctly to define the concept of "cupboard" or "table" but then at once made all sorts of deviations from their definitions, going into detail over all the possible alternatives. As a result of these clarifications and descriptions the patients were unable to arrive at a single, clear definition. The patients themselves, however, were unsatisfied with their explanations, because they felt they were insufficiently complete.

Inertia of the concrete associations of previous experience also was exhibited in a variant of the association experiment: "Answer with the first word that comes into your head." The results show that the latency period was fairly long, its average

during being 6.5 sec and at times in individual patients it reached
20-30 sec.

A noteworthy feature was the large number of d e l a y e d   r e -
a c t i o n s (31.4%); the patients replied, not to the word presented,
but to the one before. For example, when replying to the stimulus
"song" with the word "silence," in response to the next stimulus
"wheel" he gave the reply "stillness"; having responded to the
word "deceit" with "trust," he responded to the next stimulus
"head" with the word "lie." In some patients delayed reactions
were observed in 7 or 8 of 20 response reactions.

The d e l a y e d reactions in our patients are an important
deviation from the normal course of the process of association.
They demonstrate that the subsequent stimulus is of greater signal value than the original stimulus. To clarify the mechanism of
these phenomena it is necessary to turn once again to the analysis
of the structure of the association experiment.

The word with which the subject reacts to the stimulus is not
the only association which arises. However, the fact that he reacts with only one word is explained by the experimenter's instruction to give only one word, and that which first springs to the subject's mind. The other associations arising under these circumstances are inhibited. The presentation of another word stimulus
evokes new associations. In other words, the patient's response
reaction was prompted each time by the actual stimulus. The current action of the stimulus is dependent on the problem set – the
instruction given.

Soviet psychologists have studied the relationship between the
formation of associations and the conditions and meaning of an activity. A. N. Leont'ev and T. F. Rozanova showed that following a
change in the meaning of a task (instruction), the same stimuli
evoke different associations. The consolidation and reproduction
of associations must take place in relation to the instructions given.

As applied to our experimental situation, this must mean that
only the words spoken at a given moment could evoke associations,
and that only then could they be the signals for the response reaction. The associations evoked by stimulus words spoken previously,
on the other hand, could not be made to apply at the current time;

and previous stimuli must remain neutral and must lose their signal value.

In our patients, however, the presented stimulus did not acquire the necessary value. Because of the inertia of their nervous processes, our patients responded to the echo of a previous word stimulus. Comparison of the results of our experiments with clinical observations suggests that in this case we have to deal with a disturbance of the mobility of the cortical neurodynamics with a tendency toward inertia. Pavlov characterizes the loss of mobility of the nervous processes, tending toward inertia, as an inability to yield quickly to the demands of the external conditions and to give preference to one stimulus over another. The delayed reactions and the subjection to the aftereffect of the stimulus may in fact be evidence of the inability to keep up with the newly applied stimuli.

Pavlov repeatedly stressed that mobility is one of the fundamental characteristics of the neurodynamics of the healthy cortex. Many researches by Soviet physiologists and psychiatrists have been devoted to this problem. C. O. Kaminskii and V. I. Savchuk, for example, discovered a disturbance of the mobility of the nervous processes in patients with essential hypertension. E. E. Melekhov and V. M. Kamenskaya found similar disturbances in brain injuries, as did A. S. Remezova and M. I. Seredina in epilepsy.

In an experimental situation, as in any situation in life, new aspects of objects are constantly revealed, and the conditions of the environment change constantly. In order to understand these different relationships correctly and to act in accordance with the changing conditions, man must be able to change over from one mode of action to another, he must not be chained to a fixed, automatic mode of behavior.

The perfection of intellectual activity is determined not only by the fact that a person is able to perform a particular intellectual operation, to analyze and integrate material, and to distinguish that which is essential, but also by the fact that this capacity for correct operations has established itself as a stable method of behavior.

To adequately reflect objective reality, thinking must preserve not only its operational aspects but also its dynamics.

3. DISTURBANCES OF GOAL-DIRECTED THINKING

Thinking is a complex self-regulated form of activity. It is determined by the goals of a particular task. The crucial phase in cognitive activity is the comparison of the obtained conclusions with the requirements of the task and the expected outcomes. In order for that comparison to be carried out human thought must be actively focused on objective reality. Without its purposiveness, thinking remains superficial and incomplete and ceases to regulate human actions.

The view of thinking as a regulator of action should not, of course, be understood as implying that thinking may be regarded as the source or the moving force of behavior. Engels said "People have been accustomed to explain their actions by their thoughts, instead of explaining them by their needs (which are, of course, reflected in their brains, in their consciousnesses), and hence in the course of time the idealistic doctrine has developed which has dominated men's minds, especially since the end of antiquity."[1]

Consequently, the source of human actions lies in the emergence into consciousness of man's needs which arises as a result of social intercourse and work. The needs he recognizes present him with a number of concrete goals and problems in life. Man's real activity, which is directed toward the achievement of these goals and the solution of these problems, is regulated and corrected by thinking. First aroused by need, thought becomes a regulator of action; and in order to regulate behavior, thinking must be purposive, critical, and motivationally involving.

Thus, thinking cannot exist apart from needs, desires, expectations, and feelings, that is, apart from the human personality as a whole. S. L. Rubinshtein writes about that in his book "On Thought and Ways of Studying It": "The issue concerning motives, concerning the impetus to analyze and synthesize cognitions in general – this, in essence, is a question concerning the origins of a given cognitive process" (page 87). Rubinshtein constantly emphasizes that the stages of thinking are closely connected with personality components.

---

[1]K. Marx and F. Engels, "Collected Works," Vol. 20, page 139.

In the cognitive activity of the healthy individual, whether adult or child, all these factors are inseparably linked and hence we frequently are not able to analyze them. The study of various forms of pathology allow us to do this.

The symptoms of disturbance in purposive thinking and the connection of this impairment with personality change, are observed in different forms of mental illness. In analyzing that kind of pathology of thinking which we labeled "distortion of the level of generalization" we already were able to cite personality disorders. We already noted that patients who have this disorder depend in their reasoning on attributes and properties of objects which do not reflect the real relationships between them; the thinking of the patients was not based on the concrete meaningful properties of objects; instead, it reflected extremely abstract logical relationships.

These disturbances came to light with special clarity in certain experimental tests which required isolating and selecting attributes, on the basis of which it would be possible to synthesize and make generalizations (for example, in various variations of the classification-of-objects task). We have mentioned the modes of classification of these patients: for example, spoon could be grouped with automobile "according to the principle of movement," a cupboard could be grouped with a saucepan because "both were openings." Frequently objects were grouped on the basis of their color, location in space, or the manner in which they were drawn. Other investigators have also observed such an increased facilitation of formal associations and inappropriate bonding. Yu. F. Polyakov and T. K. Meleshko give the example of a patient who, in discerning a similarity between pencil and boot, says that "both leave marks." Describing similar phenomena, they explain them in terms of a disturbance in the reliability of evaluating past experience. According to their data, chance, improbable connections occur to patients with the same frequency as ordinary ones. This position is correct. It is necessary however to understand more fully what psychological significance the concepts "essential," "ordinary," "meaningful," have, as opposed to chance attributes and the real properties of objects.

What is meaningful and essential for the typical human being is what has acquired meaning in his everyday activity. It is not the frequency of manifestation of this or that attribute or property of an object which makes it meaningful or essential but rather the significance of the role which this attribute has played in the life of the individual. The importance of an attribute or property and the significance of an object or phenomena depend on what role they have played in the activity of the individual, on what meaning they have acquired for him. Phenomena, objects, and events can acquire different meanings in different life situations, although knowledge about them remains the same. Leont'ev pointed out that a phenomenon is changed so that it makes sense for the individual.

At the same time the meaning of things and our accumulated knowledge about them remain stable. Even though personality tendencies and the content of motives can turn out to be diverse, basic practical activity determines the reliability of the objective significance of things.

Our perception of the world always includes both a cognitive relationship to it and its objective significance. Under certain circumstances one or the other aspect prevails but both are united in a harmonic unity.

Of course, emotional changes and strong affects can make objects or their properties begin to take on a somewhat changed meaning and this can happen even in the healthy individual. However, in the neutral situation which always prevails in the experiment, objects have their univocal meaning. Dishes are always seen as dishes and furniture as furniture. Regardless of all the individual differences, differences in education, regardless of the heterogeneity of modes of interest, the healthy individual who has to classify objects approaches a spoon as a spoon and not as a movable object. Classification can be carried out in a more generalized way (spoon and cupboard can be classified as inanimate objects) but the objective significance or meaning of an object, in terms of which the individual carries out a given operation, remains stable. Hence the attributes, on the basis of which the operation of classification is carried out, and the actualization of associations have a certain standard character and equilibrium. For a number of schizophrenics this stability of the objective significance of things has been disturbed.

Of course, even these patients accord meanings to things and phenomena which have something in common with our own. Their

representation of the world corresponds basically to our own. With
respect to carrying out intellectual tasks, such as object classification, this means that patients can set aside a spoon or can match
a spoon to the category dishes, or cupboard to furniture, but, at the
same time as they do this, spoon can appear as an object of "movement." Two things happen: first, properties of attributes and relationships between the objects and phenomena are actualized that
have been conditioned and formed in previous everyday experience.
At the same time, inappropriate (from the point of view of our representation of the world) relationships and bonds are generated
which have acquired meaning only as a result of the changed orientation and motives of the patients. The meaning of things and
the patient's cognitive relationships to that meaning, which were
included in a harmonious unity, become lost due to changes in his
motives and attitudes. Personality disturbance in thinking was
even more obvious in that cognitive disorder which we described
as "multilevel thinking."

Multilevel Thinking

The disturbance of that type of intellectual activity which we
described as "multilevel thinking" is one in which the patient's
judgments take place on different levels. Despite the fact that he
may grasp the instructions, and that such mental operations as
comparison and distinction and generalization and abstraction are
not disturbed, he does not bring the task properly to fruition: his
judgments follow devious routes.

We do not refer to that faculty of comprehensive, exhaustive
analysis that characterizes the thinking of the normal person – the
act of approaching the problem from various aspects, in the course
of which his actions and judgments are purposively determined both
by the conditions of the task and by the orientation of the personality.

We also do not refer to those fluctuations in the level of judgment which arise as a result of altered work capacity. As already
stated in Chapter 3, when work capacity is disturbed the patients
are unable to reason adequately and correctly for a certain period
of time; however, they have not lost the purposiveness of intellectual activity as such. For example, if, while performing the object-classification task, a patient in whom fluctuations of the ac-

Table 6.   Performance on an Object-Classification Test by
Patients with Multilevel Thinking

Objects placed in same group by patient	Patient's explanation
Elephant, horse, bear, butterfly, beetle, and other animals	"Animals."
Aeroplane, butterfly	"A group of flying objects" (the patient has taken the butterfly from the group of animals).
Spade, bed, spoon	"Ironwork."
Automobile, airplane, ship	"Objects indicating the strength of the human intellect" (the airplane has been taken from the group of flying objects).
Flower, saucepan, bed, charwoman, saw, cherry	"Objects painted red and blue."
Elephant, skier	"Object for a circus. People want bread and circuses; the ancient Romans knew that."
Cupboard, table, bookcase	"Furniture."
Charwoman, spade	"A group of things for sweeping what is bad out of life. The spade is an emblem of work, and work is incompatible with corruption."
Flower, bushes, trees, vegetables, fruits	"Plants."
Tumbler, cup, saucepan	"Dishes."

tivity of the cerebral cortex have been noted, ceases temporarily
to be guided by the generic criterion, his actions nevertheless remain adequate for the purpose and for the conditions set by the
experimenter. If the patient in these instances begins to group
objects on the basis of a concrete attribute, nevertheless his behavior is carried out in terms of the classification instruction; he
groups objects on the basis of properties, on the basis of attributes, of these same objects.

With multilevel thinking the basis of classification looses its
unified character. In the course of carrying out one and the same
task, patients group objects sometimes on the basis of properties
of the object and sometimes on the basis of personal tastes and
orientations. The process of classification in these patients fol-

lows devious routes (Table 6). We consider some examples of this in Patient G-n (schizophrenia, paranoid type).

From this table it is evident that patient G-n distinguished groups at times on the basis of a generic sign (animals, dishes, furniture), and at others on the basis of material (ironwork) or color (objects painted red and blue). However, other objects were grouped together on the basis of the patient's moral outlook and general world view (a group "for sweeping what is bad out of life," a group "bearing witness to the power of the human intellect," etc.).

Some patients were guided in their performance of the test by personal tastes or by fragmentary reminiscences. Patient S-V (schizophrenic, paranoid type), for instance attempted in the object-classification test at first to form groups of animals and plants, but then added at once: "But if I approach it from the point of view of my personal taste, I don't like mushrooms, and I shall reject this card. Once I was poisoned by mushrooms and even had to be admitted to the hospital. . . . No, not mushrooms . . . . And I don't like this dress either, it isn't smart and I shall put it aside. But I like the sailor and I shall acknowledge sport." He then placed the sailor and the skier in the same group.

So that this patient, too, had lost the point of the task, not because he was exhausted but because he did the classification from the point of view of personal taste, basing it on his recollection that he had been poisoned by mushrooms.

Another patient, K-N (schizophrenia) whom we described jointly with P. Ya. Gal'perin, could not agree in the same test that the dog should be placed in the group of domestic animals: "I am not going to eat dog meat." His actions were no longer governed by objective reality, and his judgments clearly assumed a multilevel character. This multilevel thinking was also observed by us when the task "exclusion of objects" was carried out.

To illustrate consider some examples from a schizophrenic (simple type) in Table 7.

As is evident from the table the patient was able to generalize. She excluded the sun as a natural source of light but at the same time excluded spectacles on the basis of personal taste (she didn't like them and not because they did not belong with measurement instruments). She excluded umbrella for the same reason. Appro-

Table 7.   Performance of Patients with "Multilevel" Thinking
in the Exclusion-of-the-Superfluous-Object Test

Pictures presented	Patient's responses
Kerosene lamp, candle, electric flashlight, sun	"You have to take away the sun because it's a natural light while the others are artificial."
Scales, watch, thermometer, spectacles	"I take away the spectacles and don't like spectacles. I like pince-nez. Why not wear them? Chekov did."
Drum, revolver, service cap, umbrella	"The umbrella is not necessary. Now people use raincoats. An umbrella is old-fashioned, I'm for modern things."

priate, logically constructed reasoning "coexisted" with utterances based on random associations.

As a result of the simultaneous coexistence and the interweaving of all these various aspects of the patient's reasoning, his
definitions and conclusions are not directed at carrying out the
task according to plan. His cognitive activity is interspersed with
random associations, fragments of ideas, elements of reminiscences, and desires.

Similar disturbances of thinking were observed by Birenbaum
during an investigation of schizophrenics. She showed that the
thinking of these patients "apparently runs in different streams
simultaneously." Birenbaum defined this symptom as "the eluding
of the essential," in which the patients tend to reveal their subjective attitude to the problem instead of solving it.

This simultaneous coexistence of different aspects in the form
which we have described here is a manifestation of a profound disturbance of intellectual activity.

Of course, any phenomenon or object also represents various
values and meanings to the normal person. Normal people also
tend to approach their work and their judgments from a variety of
aspects, although the objective significance of reality remains consistent throughout. In the comparatively affect-free situation of
the psychology experiment and also in ordinary everyday activity,
things normally have a unitary objective meaning.

In the patients we are describing, this objective significance was lost. In performing any very simple task, patients were guided not by the concrete situation, but rather by abnormal attitudes, modified orientations toward life, and delirious ideas, although in these circumstances there was no immediate application of the psychopathological symptoms to the experimental situation (for example, the patient did not interweave the elements of delirium into the performance of the task). However, together with appropriate associations, connections were activated which in some fashion reflected the pathological orientations of the patients and which entered whimsically into a given concrete situation. The objective meaning of things became, in one and the same cognitive situation, unstable and at times even contradictory.[1]

Such an inappropriate association between things bearing no relationship to each other occurred because the patient tended to regard the simplest most commonplace objects from aspects totally irrelevant to the situation. Our findings correspond to most clinical evidence.

Analysis of the disease histories of these patients and observations of their behavior both in and outside the hospital revealed how inappropriate were their everyday orientations and how paradoxical were their motives and emotional responses. Behavior of the patients deviated from conventional norms. The early interests and views of these patients were replaced by inappropriate and pathological orientations. One patient would not care at all about his family and relatives but he would manifest a heightened concern about the kind of food that his cat was getting; another patient left the profession for which he was qualified and, dooming his family to hardship, became occupied for whole days with putting things in front of photo lenses, since, according to his view, "seeing things at different optical foreshortenings helps to widen the intellectual scope."

The paradoxical orientation of these patients and their cognitive confusion led to serious changes in the structure of any activity, whether practical or intellectual. Whatever corresponded to

---

[1] The thought processes of a certain group of schizophrenic patients were characterized by multilevel thinking in conjunction with symbolism. As a result of multilevel thinking and emotional saturation, commonplace occurrences began to assume the form of symbols.

their changed paradoxical orientations seemed essential to the patient. In carrying out experimental tasks requiring comparison
and selection of attributes, this cognitive confusion led to operational insufficiency. The patient who saw the meaning of life in
placing objects in front of photo objectives thought that the location of objects in pictures was a meaningful principle for classifying them.

In those cases where the patient is in the grip of delirium
multilevel thinking occurs clearly in his conversation. In such
situations which are affectively neutral, multilevel thinking occurs
in a simple rudimentary form. However, it can occur just as
clearly in the experimental setting requiring a definite direction
in the patient's reasoning. In these situations cognitive confusion
leads to the actualization of nonessential, insignificant, "latent"
(L. S. Rubinshtein) attributes, which coexist with appropriate associations. During intellectual performance the patients begin to be
guided simultaneously by the objective meaning of things as well as
by a meaning that is distorted, frequently by elements of desires,
and fragments of recollections and delirious interpretations. Such
thinking is deprived of purposiveness.

In his report at the 18th International Congress of Psychology
in Moscow in 1966, "Needs, motives, and consciousness," A. I.
Leont'ev indicated that the cognitive attainments of an individual
can be more or less narrow, more or less appropriate, but they
always preserve their objectivizing and, as it were, "supraper-
sonal character" (page 9). Evidently, in our patients this "supra-
personal" character of meaning was lost.

Ratiocination

The disturbance of the personality component of cognitive activity, leading to a loss in its purposiveness, can be observed in
still another variant of thinking disturbance. This variant occurs
as a symptom which has been called ratiocination in the clinic and
which is defined by many clinical psychologists as an inclination
to futile philosophizing. The studies of our colleague T. I. Tepenitsyna have shown that this kind of thinking disorder, which used to
be thought of as a manifestation of empty associations or simply
as a speech "push," is not really due to a change in the operational
aspect of thinking. The crucial factor has turned out to be the relationship of the patient to his environment and his inappropriate

self-evaluation. This is expressed in affective inadequacy in connection with discerning what point is at issue. It is also shown in the way the patient's relationship to an insignificant object or discussion can be full of pretentions and specious evaluations. Tepenitsyna was completely right in concluding that the disturbance of the personality component is not just the background for the patient's judgmental impairment, but that it directly determines the very structure of this cognitive disorder. Even the grammatical structure of the speech of these patients reflects the emotional peculiarities of ratiocination. The grammar of the patients is unique; it uses inversions and parenthetical expressions, etc. In her article "Concerning the psychological structure of ratiocination," Tepenitsyna gives examples of such statements. While searching in mediated memory for a link to the word "riches," the patient draws a book, justifying this by saying: "A book – this is the riches of the intellect! A book of human experience! What can be greater than that. I think that nothing is greater than that." In order to mediate the word "happiness" another patient reasons as follows: "Riches, happiness, separation, grief! I would like to draw some flowers, I love flowers. Happiness! You can't depict it on paper nor can you draw it. No one can draw why he is fully happy (he draws an envelope). Happiness of a man is composed of such things. It happens for example that you receive a letter; that is a small joy. It is from such small joys that human happiness is built up!"

Another patient compares the concepts "elephant" and "fly": "A fly – that is an insect, what I have in mind is that it is a harmful insect. Elephant – that is an animal. Then a fly can. . . there are different kinds of flies. Consider that in the tropical countries there are other flies. The main thing is the size of the fly. It's a fact that a fly is not bigger than a fingernail. However it is true that in tropical countries there are bigger flies. And an elephant weighs a lot too. Flies live all over. There are differences in where they are found. If you are only talking about flies living here in the central region, there are flies which live in the tropics. Flies are different and the climate is different. Even a fly living in the tropics is a thousand times, more than a thousand times, smaller than an elephant. It is all so, do you see?"

Tepenitsyna shows that such random philosophizing utterances occur in most experimental situations where it has been possible to set up the conditions for showing an increased level of aspiration and self-evaluation and where distortion of the relational system can be easily actualized. The evidence that we have presented shows that the loss of purposiveness occurs due to distortion of the personality orientations of the patient and to changes in the structure of his motives and intentions.

Disturbances of the Critical Aspect of Thinking

Disturbances in the purposiveness of the patient's thinking can arise because constant control over his actions, and correction of the mistakes he commits, drop out. Isolated elements of this pathological phenomenon have already been seen by us in the structure of cognitive changes which we labeled "multilevel thinking," "distortion of the level of generalization," "ratiocination," and others. Disturbance in purposiveness occurs in extremely clearcut fashion where there has been destruction of the frontal lobes of the brain. This kind of thought disturbance can be characterized as a disturbance in the critical aspects of thinking.

The problem of the critical aspect of thinking has been decided in psychology only on the general plane. S. L. Rubinshtein stresses that it is only in the process of thinking, when the subject more or less consciously relates the results of the thinking process to the objective data, that a mistake is possible, and that the possibility of recognizing the mistake is the privilege of thought. In characterizing the properties of the mind, B. M. Teplov mentions the critical faculty and assesses it as the ability to evaluate strictly the work of thought, to weigh carefully all the arguments for and against suggested hypotheses, and to subject these hypotheses to comprehensive testing.

The problem of the critical aspect of thinking becomes particularly acute in the analysis of various psychopathological phenomena. In all the textbooks and monographs dealing with dementia, disturbance of the critical faculty is given a foremost place (V. A. Gilyarovskii, M. O. Gurevich and M. Ya. Sereiskii, S. S. Korsakov, E. Kraepelin, V. P. Osipov and G. E. Sukhareva). The concept of critical appraisal is fundamental in psychopathological analysis. The evaluation of the patient's condition and the diagnosis of the disease are often based chiefly on the presence or the absence of the critical aspect of thinking.

The concept of critical appraisal does not always refer to the same phenomenon in psychopathology. For instance, it also often implies a critical attitude on the part of the patient toward delirium, hallucinations, and other abnormal experiences. However, we propose to analyze that form of critical attitude which consists of the ability to act deliberately – to check and correct one's actions in relation to the objective conditions.

In carrying out the experimental tasks, a special category of mistakes was found which can be characterized as the thoughtless manipulation of objects. For example, in an object classification experiment, the patients glance quickly over the cards and immediately begin to sort the objects into groups, without any form of check. For example, one such patient began to put in the same group cards which lay side by side: "bear," "thermometer," "spade," and "cupboard"; in another group were included cards found around the edges: "fungus," "bird," and "bicycle."

It is clear that the patients had no real comprehension of the nature of the test. When the experimenter repeated the instructions, emphasizing the rational principles involved in the classification procedure, the above-mentioned patients sorted the cards correctly and selected the groups by generic signs (animals, furniture, people, plants).

The disease patterns in these patients showed an absence of acute psychotic symptoms. In fact, they appeared to be relatively normal upon superficial observation. They understood and responded to questions, were oriented in time and place, they took part in social and work activities, carried out various assignments, read books and remembered what they had read, and listened to the radio. Closer observation revealed, however, the inadequacy of their behavior. In conversation with their families, for instance, although they might reply correctly to questions, they themselves never asked questions, showed no interest in the lives of their friends and relatives, and never spoke of their plans for the future. Having begun to read a book, they would quickly put it down to take another – whichever happened to catch the eye.

This indifferent attitude toward their errors at times reached particularly absurd degrees. One patient, for example, although still capable of calculating, made such a gross blunder in calculating his daughter's age that she turned out to be only two years younger than he. When the experimenter drew the patient's attention to the absurdity of his answer, he replied, without a sign of embarrassment: "anything can happen."

These patients readily concurred with any judgment proffered, however ridiculous, and they readily and unthinkingly obeyed any suggestion made by another person. (One of these patients, for example, willingly agreed on the day before a serious operation to the suggestion of a fellow-patient that he leave the surgical ward and go out into the cold, rainy weather for a swim in the lake.) They never noticed any defects or disturbances in their own mental capacities, they never complained about anything, they were not put out by having to stay in the hospital, and they did not ask to be discharged. For the most part, they remained in good spirits and gave no thought whatsoever of their futures.

This thoughtless behavior was particularly noticeable in their performance in psychological experiments. As already mentioned, the patients started to work immediately without really taking a good look at the material. For example, a patient who was shown a series of pictures of wolves attacking a boy walking to school replied after hardly having glanced at them: "The boy is climbing a tree; he probably wants to pick an apple." – Experimenter: "Look more carefully," – Patient: "The boy is saving himself from the wolves." Another patient scarcely listened to the experimenter's request to explain the proverb, "Strike the iron while it is hot," replying instead: "Yes, of course the iron must be hot; otherwise it couldn't be shaped." However, he immediately followed this with the correct explanation: "Things must not be put off until later."

The patients could grasp the theme of a fable, the conventional meanings of instructions, and the metaphorical meanings of proverbs. Although they could pick out generic signs, they persistently made the most glaring mistakes, acted contrary to the instructions, and matched phrases and proverbs wrongly. Thus, although they usually possessed an adequate understanding of the conditions of a test, they frequently acted contrary to this understanding.

In simple tasks which required that they check their performance not merely at the end of the operation, but after each successive stage, patients made many obvious and seemingly inexplicable errors. This type of behavior was illustrated in an inves-

tigation carried out as part of her diploma program by V. I.
Urusova-Belozertseva under our direction at the Department of
Psychology, Moscow State University. We now present some of
the results of the investigation.

A group of patients was given short stories from which individual words had been omitted; they were instructed to fill in the
blanks (a variant of Ebbinghaus' method). The following stories
were given:

1. A lion had become . . . and could not go out. . . . He decided to live on his
wits: he lay in his lair and pretended to be. . . . Thereupon the other wild
animals began to come near the sick... to see what was happening. But
when they were within range he pounced on them and. . . . A fox came up,
but did not go into the lair, and stopped at the. . . . The lion asked it:
"Why don't you come inside to see me?" But the. . . replied: "I can see
many tracks leading into your. . . but I can't see. . . coming out again."

2. A man ordered some fine . . . from a spinner. The spinner spun some fine
thread, but the man said that it was. . . and that he must have it thinner.
The spinner said: "If this is not thin enough for you, here is some which
may do," and pointed to. . . place. The man said he could see nothing.
"Of course, you can't see it, because it is so thin. I can't see it myself."
The stupid man was content with this, ordered some . . . like it, and paid
the spinner his money.

Only four of the patients read through the complete story initially; the remaining fourteen immediately inserted words into each
gap as they went along, without paying attention to the subsequent
phrases. Control experiments, using as subjects patients with de-
pressed levels of generalization, revealed a different picture: even
those patients who achieved poor levels of performance always
read the whole story first and then filled in the gaps with words
which at least were in context, even if they were not correct.

We now present examples of the performance of these tests
by patients of this group.[1]

Patient T.   A man ordered some fine hands (thread) from a spinner. The
spinner spun some fine thread, but the man said that it was not (thick) and that he
must have it thinner. The spinner said: "If this is not thin enough for you, here is
some which may do," and pointed to another (an empty) place. The man said
he could see nothing. "Of course, you can't see it, because it is so thin. I can't see

---

[1]The words which should have been inserted are given in parentheses.

it myself." The stupid man was content with this, ordered some h a n d s (thread) like it, and paid the spinner his money.

P a t i e n t C h.   A man ordered some fine s o c k s from a spinner. The spinner spun some fine thread, but the man said that it was t h i n and that he must have it thinner. The spinner said: "If this is not thin enough for you, here is some which may do," and pointed to t h e t h r e a d s place. The man said he could see nothing. "Of course, you can't see it, because it is so thin. I can't see it myself." The stupid man was content with this, ordered some t h r e a d like it, and paid the spinner his money.

P a t i e n t T.   A lion had become a g r o w l e r (old) and could not go out h u n t i n g.   He decided to live on his wits: he lay in his lair and pretended to be a s l e e p (ill). Thereupon the other wild animals began to come near the sick d e e r (lion) to see what was happening. But when they were within range he pounced on them and a t e t h e m. . . .

Urusova-Belozertseva differentiated the incorrect inserted words as follows: (a) those which make sense in the immediate context – the surrounding words or phrases – but which make no sense in the larger context; (b) those selected arbitrarily, at random; (c) those taken from other stories.

As in other situations in which they have made numerous mistakes during the performance of tasks, the patients fail to notice the inconsistencies in their versions of the stories and make no attempts to analyze the material. If they do notice the inconsistencies or contradictions, they make no effort to understand the real meanings and to isolate and correct their mistakes. When the experimenter pointed out their mistakes, patients replied: "Something different was needed here, yes, here it is not so." But they did not correct their mistakes. In these patients it was impossible to elicit an orientation toward the correct completion of the test, toward an appropriate relationship to the endproduct of their work.

This fact was the topic of a special inquiry made by S. Ya. Rubinshtein. In her dissertation, "The rehabilitation of work capacity after wartime brain injury," (1944) Rubinshtein carried out a psychological analysis of the work capacity of patients with different kinds of brain disorder. The author convincingly showed that even patients with considerable damage to the brain mastered the necessary skills for acquiring a new profession. As Rubinshtein correctly notes, these patients had an appropriate attitude toward work; they correctly realized that the knowledge acquired by them would be useful later on.

The mastery of new habits in patients with damage to the frontal lobes was completely different. Rubinshtein shows that there was no special difficulty for these patients in mastering separate work techniques – they easily mastered technical operations. There was none of the fatigability for them which lowered the competence of other patients. At the same time it was just this group of patients, namely those with trauma to the frontal lobes, who could not acquire the necessary skills. In analyzing the reason for the failure of an attempt to train patients with obstruction of the frontal lobes, Rubinshtein indicated that these patients did not have a stable attitude toward the endproduct of their activity; and they had no orientation toward self-criticism; and, as the author correctly notes, their behavior was not subject to internalized control.

This fact was noted too under laboratory training conditions. In order to study the structure of behavior in the process of training we selected a group of seven patients with massive injuries of the left frontal lobe and also a number of patients with massive destruction of the posterior portions of the left hemisphere (temporal and parietal-occipital areas). For two weeks all these patients carried out systematic exercises in the course of which they learned poetry, built mosaics according to a specified pattern, and sorted materials.

Although the patients with destruction of the posterior (gnostic) parts of the brain experienced noticeable difficulty during training, nevertheless, while they were doing the systematic exercises, they achieved significant success.

On the other hand, patients with massive damage to the frontal system behaved completely differently. Not only were they unable to apply any of the active tactics which might have helped them in rationally mastering the task set before them but they could not maintain those techniques which were shown to them. And so, for example, they put the mosaic together without any plan. They did not consider the basic lines of the pattern that they were supposed to follow and passively slipped into repetition of lines that were incorrect and haphazardly set out. They did not learn work techniques which had been given to them and, after the lesson, they began the next lesson without any improvement. It was the same with the learning of poetry and the other tasks. The patients lacked stable and consciously-perceived motivation and it was just this which destroyed the purposiveness of their behavior and reasoning.

It was found, however, that if the experimenter frequently asked control questions and aided the patient in external organization of his work, he could understand even complicated problems. The errors of these patients were obviously caused chiefly by an absence of self-control and an indifferent attitude toward the material. To illustrate these points we present case-history extracts together with the results of the experimental psychological examination of two patients.

Patient M, male, born 1890. Diagnosis: progressive paresis. His development was normal. He graduated from the medical faculty and worked as a surgeon. At the age of 26 he contracted syphilis. At the age of 47 the first signs of mental illness appeared. while performing an operation he made a gross blunder (he anastomosed the large intestine to the stomach) which cost the patient her life. Psychiatric examination in connection with the criminal proceedings established a diagnosis of general paresis. After treatment, he attempted without success to resume his work as a doctor.

Mental State. The patient was properly oriented, accessible, talkative, and inclined to gossip with the patients. He realized he was suffering from general paresis, but regarded the matter with considerable levity. He constantly repeated that he had "residual manifestations following progressive paresis," but "they were negligible," a "trifle" which would not prevent his return to work as a surgeon. When reminded of his lamentable surgical blunder, he said with a smile, quite casually, that he had "made a slight mistake, but we all have accidents." He now considers that he is well ("as fit as a bull" in his own words). He is confident that he will be able to work as a surgeon and to be the medical chief of a hospital. At the same time, he gives the most inept advice to the patients in the department. Without any embarassment he told them he had met his wife in a saloon and that at that time she was a prostitute.

In performing the simplest tasks, the patient made gross mistakes and did not try to correct them. For example, he understood correctly the meaning of a proverb, but then matched it with an unsuitable phrase: "I have made a slight mistake, now what shall I do?" The object-classification test was started without listening to the complete instruction. He exclaimed: "Why, this is like dominoes," and tried to begin the test as if playing at dominoes. He then asked: "Now tell me, which one shall I play? We can't play for money, because I haven't any." Having heard the instructions for a second time, he performed the test correctly.

In the course of the test on "establishing the sequence of events" he first tried to explain each picture, and then to invent the theme which was not evident from the material on the cards. Having glanced at picture No. 2, he said: "Here somebody has gone for a walk. He has gone to meet somebody . . . . Where could he have gone? Evidently he is waiting for somebody, probably a woman . . . . Or perhaps it is a business meeting, and here (picture No. 5) the uncle has gone away. This one is left alone; he is expecting somebody, of course, but whom? Perhaps the one he was hurrying to meet? What have we here? The wheel has broken? That is bad management."

The experimenter interrupted the patient's reasoning and asked him to arrange the pictures in the proper order of the development of the theme. The patient did the test correctly. When matching phrases and proverbs the patient correctly explained the proverbs, "All that glitters is not gold" and "Measure seven times, cut once," but matched them with the wrong phrases: "Gold is heavier than iron," and "If it is cut wrongly, it is no use blaming the scissors."

An experiment involving mediated memorization with the aid of pictograms gave the following results: The patient did not listen to the instructions for the test: "You want me to put your words into a picture? I'm not an artist, you know." The experimenter again explained the meaning of the test and asked the patient to listen carefully to the instructions. The patient replied: "Oh, is that what has to be done, just draw a sketch? That's easy." He formed associations of a fairly general order: to signify the expression "a happy holiday" he drew a flag; for the words "a dark night," a shaded square; and to signify the expression of "a starving man," he drew a very lean man. The patient constantly let himself be distracted from his task and tried to start a conversation with the doctor on a completely extraneous topic.

Although the experimenter continued to stress that the problem was being given in order to test his memory, the patient was not in the least surprised when the experimenter, having apparently finished the experiment, excused himself from the patient without asking him to reproduce the suggested words. Neither was the patient embarrassed when, in the next test, it turned out that he had memorized only an insignificant number of words (only 5 of 14). When the experimenter remarked that he had not remembered many, the patient replied with a smile: "Next time I shall remember more."

Patient K. (hospital case No. 3120), male, born 1922, developed normally, and completed 4 classes at a rural school, after which he trained as a crane operator; he subsequently practiced this occupation in a factory. On March 23, 1943, he received a perforating bullet wound of both frontal lobes. Some loss of brain substance at the entry and exit wounds was observed. The day after he was wounded an operation was performed to remove the numerous splinters of bone embedded in the brain substance of the left frontal pole. Postoperative recovery was smooth. The neurological findings six weeks after the operation were as follows: disturbance of convergence, especially on the left side, spontaneous nystagmus during divergence of the eyes, and obliteration of the right nasolabial fold. The tendon reflexes were increased on the right side, but no pathological reflexes were present. All forms of sensation were within normal limits. Coordination was normal.

Mental State. The patient was oriented in space and time, and fully recognized his environmental situation. He was able to recall the events of his past life and was aware that he had been wounded, but he thought that the wound was slight and was unaware of any of the defects in his physical or mental condition. He assumed that he would return to his military unit. He was accessible, talkative, and serenely happy. He obeyed the hospital rules without protest, but if his fellow patients suggested he do something that infringed upon the rules, he followed their suggestion equally unprotestingly. At their request, for example, he would often play the balalaika and sing, but if left to himself, he would sit inactively and silently for long periods.

At the doctor's suggestion the patient began working in the occupational therapy workshops. He proved so eager to undertake any form of work, even the heaviest jobs, that he had to be watched constantly, frequently prevented from doing some types of work, and told when the work therapy period was over. However, when performing some task at the instructor's request, patient K was never interested in the result of the work as a whole or concerned with the quality of his work. Often, having started a job, he would go outside for a smoke, and then forget to go back to the workshops. Every now and then he would spoil the material or damage the tools, not because he did not know how to use them, but because of his unthinking, irresponsible attitude toward the work; he never became angry or embarrassed when the instructor or his fellow patients remonstrated with him because of his behavior. One day, he used a sewing machine to stitch the front of a garment to the back; when this was pointed out to him he merely laughed and said: "It will do!"

After examination by a medical board, the patient was discharged from the armed forces and graded as a category 3 disabled person; he was about to leave to stay with his uncle when he decided to visit one of his former neighbors in the ward. He was then asked to stay in the hospital and to work as an orderly, to which he agreed without hesitation. From the time of his discharge from the hospital the irregularity of his behavior became quite obvious. When he had been subjected to the rigid code of conduct of the hospital routine, he did not stand out among his fellows. Now his behavior appeared grossly inadequate to his new situation. Whereas wounded patients on the day of their discharge from the hospital almost invariably display an active concern about their plans for the future, K remained completely indifferent.

K's duties as an orderly involved assisting others to move patients from one hospital area to another. He performed these duties competently and tirelessly under supervision, but as soon as something happened to distract his attention or someone called him, he would put the stretcher down "for a minute," go away, and not return. He was transferred to the job of stoker, but on his first day of his new job he went out to the movies at the invitation of a fellow patient, returned to the hospital, and went to sleep, leaving the work undone. For several months he worked satisfactorily while under supervision, arousing the sympathy of those around him by his invariably good-natured, willing behavior. When allowed the slightest independence, however, he became irresponsible and behaved incorrectly, adversely affecting both his own and his comrades' work; he forgot to collect the invoices, he stored things in the wrong boxes, and he would leave his work during working hours to do some absurd errand for a mental patient. When in the company and under the observation of his family, however, his behavior was comparatively normal.

We now present some of the results of an experimental examination of this patient. In the classification experiment, K began to sort the cards into neat piles and to examine them even before he had heard the end of the instructions. However, he did perform the test correctly after the instructions had been emphatically repeated several times. The peculiarities of his behavior were particularly evident in tests involving the determination of the chronological order of events. In one such test K was presented with a series of pictures representing the breaking and the repair of a cartwheel. The patient described the first picture that came into his hand and then arranged the cards in random order; when the experimenter admonished him to be more attentive to his work, however, he performed the test correctly within a relatively short period of time. If the patient's attention could be directed toward the problem he could solve it, even if it required fairly complex analysis and synthesis (the patient understood the metaphorical meaning of proverbs, could establish analogy of associations, etc.).

The patient also made mistakes when putting Link's cube together. The nature of this test is as follows: the subject has to assemble a large wooden cube from 27 cubes by arranging them in three layers, each of nine cubes. The sides of each small cube are painted yellow, red, or green. The large cube must be constructed in such a way that all sides are painted red. The color combinations determine the place of each small cube in the large cube. This test requires planning of actions, careful and constant checking, and immediate correction of any mistakes made. Our patient was unable to perform the test. Although he grasped the meaning of the instructions, he chose the small bricks to give the correct

color only on the sides of the large cube facing him and did not
bother about the other sides.

The findings of research and clinical investigations of these
patients reveals unified characteristics in the disturbances of their
mental activity. The gross mistakes and random, arbitrary answers which characterized their performance during the tests;
their inability to utilize their past experience and their capabili-
ties in the experiments; and their unthinking behavior both in the
hospital and in work situations – in fact the complete absence of
any self-appraisal of their work: all these factors demonstrate
that the actions of these patients are neither regulated by their
intellect nor guided by personal interests. Neither was their behavior influenced by adequate social attitudes. In sum, their behavior was completely random in character.

We observed the patients in the clinic and in the workshops,
and frequently engaged them in conversation; we were everywhere
struck by absence of a personal attitude to the situation of the moment. For instance, it did not seem strange to them that, although
they understood the instructions of a psychological investigation,
they could not solve the problem; it never struck them as odd that,
"being able to sew," they nevertheless were unable to do the simplest job in the sewing room; although they knew how to calculate,
they could not solve the simplest arithmetical problem. They were
not upset by the fact that they could not remember errands on
which they had been sent.

This abnormal attitude radically transformed their patterns
of behavior, primarily by depriving it of purposiveness. They thus
continued to work at obviously purposeless tasks, stopping work at
the slightest distraction. They could not become skilled in work
operations, not because they were unable to understand the explanation of the investigator or instructor, but because they could not
fix their attention on their work, because they had no definite attitude toward it, and could not grasp its purpose.

This disturbance of their attitude toward their environment
and toward their own "egos" not only caused a change in their behavior but also seemed to effect a fundamental character transformation. Their carelessness, light-heartedness, and indiffer-
ence were manifestations of a gross "flattening" of their personality. This absence of attitudes had the result, for example, that

patient K could leave a patient on a stretcher in the snow simply to go after some almost total stranger who beckoned to him. This absence of attitudes also explains why the patients were neither upset by their own deficiences nor concerned over the quality of their work and never bothered to verify and check their behavior.

The thinking of the patients was not directed at a specific target; there was no development of interest in solving the task or in how the experimenter evaluated their behavior. They had no doubt about the correctness of their behavior. The mistakes made by the patients during the solving of mental problems, the superficial, random character of their judgments, and their lack of control over their behavior and inability to evaluate it – all these factors demonstrate the uncritical nature of the thinking of this group of patients.

Chapter 6

Personality Disturbances in the Mentally Ill and Relevant Research Techniques

Analysis of any manifestation of mental disorder requires taking into account the personality peculiarities of the patient. This approach is dictated by the fundamental principles of contemporary materialist psychology. In "Being and Consciousness," S. L. Rubinshtein stated on page 308 that "in the explanation of any mental phenomena personality is involved as an aggregate of internal conditions which are bound together and through which all external influences are reflected."

In studying mental change it is necessary to take personality into account for still another reason, namely, that mental illness frequently affects the entire personality by affecting need systems and emotional-voluntary components. In the meantime, research in abnormal psychology has been basically concerned with disorders of cognitive activity. The experimental techniques for studying personality changes have been insufficiently developed. This is partially attributable to the insufficient development of the problem of personality structure in general psychology.

One must acknowledge that foreign psychologists have devoted much effort to the problem of personality and its pathology. However this research has been carried out mainly by psychologists with a psychoanalytic inclination and psychologists adhering in some way or another to "verstehen psychology" or to the philosophy of existentialism.

Soviet psychologists (A. N. Leont'ev, S. L. Rubinshtein) believe that personality is a product of historical development, of the development of relationships between the individual and society, of relationships "between the subject and the world of man" (Leont'ev). Leont'ev emphasizes that in personality formation, it is not the processes of adaptation to the environment which are important, but the processes of mastering human experience.

While studying personality formation in children, L. I. Bozhovich dwelt on its tendency to have a specific direction which forms the basis for the lifelong development of a reliable and stable motivational system. In the personality formation process, the dominant role is played by the child's awareness of the place which he occupies in a system of social relationships, his "internal" position.

It is already evident from these basic tenets of theoretical psychology how complex the psychological structure of personality is. It is bound up with the individual's needs and goals, with his emotional and volitional peculiarities. Regardless of the fact that the latter properties are thought by psychologists to be processes, in essence, they are components of personality. The individual's personality is formed and manifested in his activity, deeds, and behavior. His needs, both material and spiritual, reflect his relationship with the surrounding environment and people. We evaluate an individual personality mainly by characterizing the interests which compose it and the content of its desires and needs. We judge an individual according to the motives behind his acts and by those phenomena of life to which he is indifferent. What makes him glad and what are his thinking and desires aimed at?

The following indicate impending changes in personality: the interests of a patient decline under the influence of disease; his needs diminish; he becomes indifferent to previous sources of excitement; his behavior is deprived of purposiveness; his actions become senseless; he stops controlling his behavior, and he is no longer able to appropriately evaluate his opportunities.

From everything we have said so far, it follows that research on personality, and its formation and change, is exceedingly complex and manysided; it may be carried out in various modes and directions. Hence, first and foremost, it is important to look at those areas of personality research which at present are most developed in a general theoretical sense. Among the most theoretically well-developed problems are the questions of motives, attitudes, and personality goals.

Without going into detail on the problem of the structure of needs and motives, one must note that in the writings of Soviet psychologists (A. N. Leont'ev, S. L. Rubinshtein) the social nature of personality needs has been emphasized. It is thought that these needs find their satisfaction in activity, that the development of needs occurs via the development of production, and that any activity in itself generates needs. In our study of personality disturbances we try to proceed from these basic positions as developed by Soviet psychology.

On the other hand, we propose that the study of the pathology of personality can turn out to be helpful in analyzing the structure of normal personality. The personality changes observable in psychiatric practice are multifarious and all of this has been admirably described in the textbooks of psychiatry. For the sake of illustration we will briefly discuss several such descriptions.

In these volumes we find very colorful descriptions of epileptics and the changes in the emotional-volitional areas which are characterized by pronounced inertness and rigidity. The patients constantly turned to one and the same emotion, one and the same notion; they concentrate on insignificant phenomena. This emotional rigidity is expressed in the pedantic behavior of these patients; the patients are unable to accept any changes in the lifestyle that they have established. Pedantic in their work, they are inclined to carry out only one type of activity which they do with special thoroughness. This emotional inertness in epileptics is associated with the quick onset of irascibleness as well as an inclination to affective discharges and mood changes. As a result, the patients behave inappropriately and sometimes inflict harm on other people. Egocentrism and narrowness of interests characterize epileptics. At the same time they can have an exaggerated politeness, an obsequiousness bordering on hypocrisy. (This type of patient was depicted by Dostoevski in his character Smerdyakov.)

These characterological features are determined to a large extent by the patient's response to his inferiority. This has been shown by A. P. Osipov in his "Handbook of Psychiatry."

In the psychiatric clinic we find another kind of personality disturbance manifested as increased lability of emotional reactions, lack of self-criticism with respect to one's actions, and a weakening in cognitive regulation akin to that found in chronic al-

coholism. The patients become self-confident, boastful, inclined
to stupid jokes, and their behavior is bereft of purposiveness while
their actions are unmotivated and unjustified.

The absence of self-criticism has been described by many
psychiatrists in analyzing the personality of patients with progressive paralysis. The patients display a sort of excited complacency,
they declare that they are in wonderful health and that they have
unusual abilities. Their excited mood easily changes into one that
is capricious and irritated; these patients can cry at a trifle but all
at once they become calm.

The suggestibility of these patients has been described in
great detail: they easily succumb to persuasion and they do frivo-
lous things. E. A. Gilyarovskii used to bring such a patient into
his lectures. This man broke a window in front of everybody and
took a vase that he didn't need merely because it was pleasing to
him; another patient bought a set of dishes for his wife, using up
all the money he had and leaving his whole family without any
money for food.

Sometimes patients' ethical sensitivity is blunted; they are
indifferent to their neighbors; the grief of their friends does not
touch them nor are they affected by their own unhappinesses; they
are careless and indifferent both to themselves and to others.
Their behavior is bereft of purposiveness and self-direction.

Psychiatrists have devoted much attention to the kinds of personality disturbance which are observed in different forms of
schizophrenia. The feelings of schizophrenics lose the quality of
belonging to a particular "ego." These patients have a special
relationship to the world around them that includes an autistic
alienation from people. The patients live in the world of their own
illusionary experiences without taking an interest in real relationships around them. They incorrectly interpret the environment.
Their emotional reactions are distorted, their development dull.
People who used to be delicate and modest become crude, shame-
less, and unrestrained. The frigidity and coldness of their feelings
is noticeable; the patients can laugh even while telling about the
death of persons who were close to them and when they receive a
visit from relatives they don't ask about anything. They are indifferent to life and to people. Emotional dullness forms the background for the patient's negativism. This consists in negative re-

action to stimulation; when he is greeted he hides his hands behind his back and does not reply to questions. The poses and gestures of the patient frequently suffer from paradoxicalness and whimsicality. Sometimes the behavior of the patient becomes impulsive; without justification he begins to whistle or to make grimaces during a conversation. The patients interpret the environment in a peculiar way; any event can acquire a special meaning for them: "if someone on the ward picked up a newspaper, this means that that person must be killed."

It is evident from this rather sketchy description, that the personality changes which are observed in the clinic are extremely diverse. It is very difficult to qualify these changes in terms of scientific psychology because the psychology of personality is insufficiently developed on the theoretical level. There are two few concepts and techniques for personality research. Therefore it seems advisable in our further discussion to dwell on experimental approaches to personality and on those findings which have been brought to light with these techniques.

One way of studying pathology of personality is to observe the behavior of the patient during an experiment. Even when the patient has "accepted" the task, or its instructions, it is possible to observe the adequacy or inadequacy of his personality. Any experiment in psychology can serve as an indicator of the emotional-volitional properties of personality.

Every investigation must take attitudes and motives into account. This point of view was enunciated in the 1930's by V. N. Myasishchev. He pointed out that attitudes exist at two levels; attitudes generated by the experimenter and attitudes elicited by the task itself.

Many patients have an attitude toward the experimental situation. Some perceive the experimental situation as some kind of test of their intellectual capacity. Frequently patients consider that the results of the research will affect how long they have to stay in the hospital or what treatment will be selected for them or to which group of patients they will be assigned. Therefore the experimental situation itself promotes the actualization of a certain attitude. So, for example, some patients, fearing that their bad memories will be discovered, declare that "they always remembered things poorly." In other instances, the requirement to do calculations elicits the comment that they "could never do arithmetic." Any task, even an easy one, can provoke a personality reaction in the experimental situation.

In some of our patients (for example, during diagnosis) an orientation toward illness develops in which the patient tries to express his intellectual incapacity, i.e., he does not do the task. This motive, of course, is in conflict with the appropriate motive as stimulated by the task itself. As a result the intellectual behavior of the patient turns out to be complex, to have two forces working, but, all the same, it is structurally intact. The patients customarily solve the problem correctly to themselves, but then they deliberately distort the answer given to the experimenter (findings of S. Ya. Rubinshtein).

In other instances the attitude generated by the task itself predominates. The task contains an intrinsic instigation to self-criticism and self-control; that is, the task makes sense for the patient. Here the task addresses itself, as it were, to the individual's self-esteem and his level of personality aspiration; it seems as if the drive to solve the problem is justified and objectified for the individual. This motivational push, which mobilizes the intellectual resources of the individual, makes the experimental method fundamentally dependable.

Hence, it can happen that, for some patients, who are intact, but who are suffering from asthenia and exhaustion, the conditions of the experiment can stimulate activity and afford partial relief from the exhaustion. As a result these patients appeared to be more normal in the experiment than in real life. Such effects were observed in patients with vascular diseases of the brain who displayed better intellectual production during the experiment than in nonexperimental situations.

Experience in our laboratory has shown that observation of patients who are doing the most simplified tasks can be used for evaluating their attitudes. For example, in building "Links cubes" (the technique focused on the study of combinatorial operations), it turned out that schizophrenics and psychopaths reacted in different ways. Patients with simple schizophrenia evinced no emotional reactions while they worked on the cube; they worked on the task itself, rather passively, and their mistakes did not cue any emotional reactions. They did not react to the comments of the experimenter when he pointed out their mistakes.

The psychopaths' behavior was completely different. At the beginning of this experiment, the ways they acted and worked were analogous to the behavior of normal individuals. However, this behavior changed sharply when mistakes occurred: the patients became irritable, frequently interrupted their work, and did not carry it to completion.

We had the opportunity to observe similar behavior in patients with symptoms of irritable weakness and asthenia. However, in these patients, the affective reaction was not so strongly expressed. However, in children with serious asthenia, difficulties in carrying out a task frequently caused depression and tears.

Observing the behavior of the subject during an experiment makes it possible to evaluate his critical ability and his capacity for self-control. Patients frequently point out that it is interesting to check on how well they can remember. It even frequently happens that a patient, while working on a task, is the first to recognize that he has an intellectual insufficiency and he reacts to it in an appropriate manner. It follows that the behavior and utterances of the patient and his reaction to the experimental situation, can serve as material for analyzing his personality dispositions and the extent to which a healthy personality has been preserved.

Another methodological approach to the study of personality change is the mediated manifestation of change with the help of techniques directed at studying cognitive processes. This tactic seems fully correct and justified, for cognitive processes do not exist divorced from personality orientations and from the patient's needs and emotions. In treating motives and the instigation of thinking, S. L. Rubinshtein, in his book "Concerning Thought and Ways of Studying It," noted that "the basic question concerns the sources from which a given cognitive process stems" (page 87).

As we already said in Chapter 5, research on abnormal thinking has shown that some kinds of disturbances are essentially expressions of the cognitive confusion which is characteristic for such patients. We showed that the actualization of inappropriate cognitions is in no way a self-contained process independent from the structure and properties of personality, but, rather, a mani-

festation of altered orientations, attitudes, and needs, that is, a
reflection of changed "internal conditions."

We tried to exposit this view in Chapter 5 when we were analyzing that form of cognitive disturbance which has been labeled
"ratiocination." As proof we cited the findings of T. I. Tepenitsyna
in which it was shown that it is not disorder of intellectual operations but change in a personality component which plays the dominant role in the structure of "ratiocination." Here we only wish
to discuss two kinds of facts coming from the research of Tepenitsyna. The author has shown the following: 1) The structure of
ratiocination is diverse and depends on the nature of the personality disorders. In patients with organic diseases of the brain ratiocination appears as an unsuccessful compensation for intellectual
inadequacy. In epileptics, ratiocinative reasoning is marked by
the actualization of inert connections with past experience. In
other words the structure of personality change affects the structure of the cognitive disorder. 2) Ratiocination is manifested most
readily in those experimental situations which form and "provoke"
a heightened level of aspiration; when experimental tactics are applied which stimulate the activity of the patient, and which provide
an occasion for him to demonstrate his attitude. It follows, and
these examples show it, that the strategy itself of thinking is determined to a considerable degree by the attitude of the individual.
The attitude of the individual is included in the structure of cognitive activity. This notion is supported, moreover, by research on
uncritical thinking in which the thoughtless judgments and incorrect
behavior of the patients are caused, not by a lowered level of generalization, but by an indifferent and inactive attitude toward the
consequences of their activity.

A similar type of patient, for example a patient with frontal-
lobe injury, cannot manage certain simple tasks in spite of the fact
that his intellectual functions are relatively intact. For example,
while these patients understand the metaphorical meaning of proverbs and the conditions of the instructions, they are unable to put
a series of pictures depicting a simple theme into a consistent
order.

Any simple task which requires choosing and planning cannot
be carried out by this type of patient and, on the other hand, more
complex tasks, which do not require adherence to such conditions,

can be carried out by them rather easily. In such fashion, erroneous solutions of problems appear not due to a disorder of logical structure of thinking, but are the result of a thoughtless orientation. Changes and alterations which crop up in the area of cognitive activity appear to be due to personality modifications.

This is demonstrated by the studies of Soviet psychologists working in the area of pedagogical psychology. Thus the studies of L. I. Bozhovich and L. S. Slavina showed that the failure of many students to advance in school was caused not by cognitive disturbance but rather by attitudinal changes in the children and their changed position in the collective.

To recapitulate, it can be said that analysis of cognitive strategies will be incomplete if we do not take into account the personality goals of the cognizing subject. For, in the words of L. S. Vygotskii: "If we divorce thinking from life and needs we prevent ourselves from finding any ways of showing and explaining the properties and the chief significance of thinking, namely, to define the manner of life and behavior and to change our behavior."[1] Therefore it is right to expect that the execution of any experimental task which was apparently directed at the study of cognitive activity, could, in principle, provide information about the personality orientations of the patient. More importantly, the modeling of the individual's cognitive activity must include modeling of his personality.

Methods for indirect evaluation of personality are unlimited. In principle, any experimental technique can be a convenient way to do this since the construction of any model of human activity (and the techniques of experimental psychology are such models) presupposes the attitudes of the individual.

We will limit ourselves to a few examples.

Performance on even the most rudimentary tasks includes an emotional component. The studies of É. A. Evlakhova have shown that even such simple tasks, as the description of an uncomplicated subject of a picture, depend on the emotional status of the subject. It was found that children, with frontal lobe damage, had an inade-

---

[1] L. S. Vygotskii, "Selected Psychological Investigations," Moscow, Izd. APN, RSFSR, 1957, page 476.

quate reaction to the emotional content of pictures. It seemed appropriate that disturbances of emotional orientations should be especially marked when pictures had to be described whose comprehension depended chiefly on the physical appearance of the figures. The pictures used for this purpose belonged to the so-called projective techniques. As we have already pointed out in Chapter 3, the essence of this method is that the task does not presuppose any definite way of doing it; it is intended to reveal the emotions, peculiarities of personality and the character of the subject. The subject's performance is not assessable since, in projective techniques, the problem of right and wrong answers does not arise.

Projective techniques are used in other countries with a dual purpose: to establish individual differences and to reveal "covert feelings."

One of the projective techniques, proposed by Morgan and Murray, has been called the Thematic Apperception Test (T.A.T.). It consists of separate pictures depicting situations without any definite content. According to Murray's instructions, the subject is told that his imagination is being studied and he must compose stories based on the pictures.

According to the way in which Murray interprets the utterances of the subjects, their stories have to be regarded as symbolic reflections of their feelings and opinions and their notions concerning their past and future. According to Murray, an identification occurs between the subject and the hero in the picture.

In a master's thesis by N. K. Kiyashchenko done in our laboratory, the instructions to the subject were changed. The subjects were told that the problem concerned the study of perception (and not imagination). The subject was not given questions but was simply presented with the following "blind" instructions: "I will show you pictures, look at them and tell me what is depicted on them." Only after the task had been completed was the question asked: "What suggested this or that description?"

The findings of Kiyashchenko's research showed that healthy subjects approached the task in order to explain the content of the pictures. Their attempts to define the subject of the pictures were carried out by posing and by imitating the depicted personages. As a rule, in carrying out this task, the healthy subjects expressed their attitudes toward the events and personages in the pictures.

The results with simple schizophrenics were completely different. In contrast to healthy people, the patients in this group had no desire to find the correct interpretation. The answers of the patients contained only formal declarations about the elements in the pictures: "two people," "a man is sitting in an arm chair," "a conversation between two people." There were formal generalizations: "rest," "a minute of silence." As a rule, the patients did not express their own attitudes toward picture themes. To illustrate, a few examples of picture descriptions by healthy individuals and by patients with simple schizophrenia are given in Table 8. These descriptions have been taken from Kiyashchenko's studies.

Table 8. Examples of Descriptions of Pictures by Schizophrenics (In Comparison with Healthy Subjects)

Healthy subjects			Schizophrenics
Subject G	This picture is laughable because the physiognomy of the patient is so smug. It seems to him that he is doing something that is generally very helpful and without a doubt, pleasant. Otherwise he would not be in such an emotional state.	N	A man is sitting.
		K	A man reads a book, holding it in his left hand; and in his right hand, a pipe.
Subject M	A man who is reading a book recalls a similar event from his own life (the event was pleasant and significant) and he falls into a reverie.	M	Someone is relaxing.
		O	A minute of silence.
		F	A man is sitting near a round window.
Subject A	A man is in an airplane. He reads a book but then he had a pleasant recollection and his eyes wander from the pictures, which change into a window. Undoubtedly he recalled something pleasant which occurred before his departure.	M	A man sits in an armchair. There is a cushion on it.

Peculiarities in the perception of the TAT pictures by schizophrenics were not associated with lowering of the level of generalization; their descriptions were not based on concrete representation; on the contrary, they amounted to formal contentless characterization.

To recapitulate, the modeling of the cognitive processes (the application of experimental tests requiring generalization, isolation of essential attributes, comparison of actualized relationships, and so forth) always includes the arousal and actualization of personality components (motives and attitudes).

Finally, one of the ways of studying personality change is the application of techniques aimed directly at revealing emotional and volitional peculiarities of the sick individual and revealing his changed attitude toward the experimental situation. This group of techniques stems from research in the affective-volitional area. S. L. Rubinshtein's book "Concerning Thought and Ways of Studying It" states that a research finding which reveals any essential relationships whatsoever, can be turned into a technique, into an instrument of subsequent investigation. This happened in fact with some of the techniques developed for research in the affective-volitional area by Kurt Lewin's school. Despite the fact that Lewin's general methodological position is unacceptable to us, his experimental techniques have turned out to be quite useful.

Here we will discuss some of these in more detail. A few words first concerning the principles behind the construction of such techniques. Major care must be taken that the artificially created experimental situation facilitates attitude formation as much as possible. As we said above, any experimental situation evokes an attitude on the part of the subject (hence the very possibility of indirectly studying his personality reactions). However, if we want our technique to be proper models of cognitive processes in the human being, then those methodological tactics, which are aimed at direct study of personality properties, must be models of everyday situations, which compel the subject to be responsive.

To achieve this goal we used Hoppe's technique, known in the psychological literature as "study of the level of aspiration." It was proposed and standardized in the Lewin school.

Kurt Lewin (1890-1947) was a representative of the German school of Gestalt psychology, who, after the onset of the fascist regime, emigrated from Germany to the United States. He was the first to systematically develop a theory about the will and affects and he was one of the first to devote experimental attention to studying the properties of human behavior in concrete circumstances.

In Lewin's conceptual system, it was necessary to distinguish two periods: the first took place before 1933 and it was in this period that he created his dynamic theory of personality. The second or American period took place after 1933, when his scientific views began to change under the influence of American sociological psychology. The methods that we are going to describe belong to the first period.

In contrast to the atomistic thinking of his time, or, as they called it then, associationism in psychology, Lewin believed that needs rather than associations lie at the basis of human behavior and thought. Under the heading "needs" Lewin understood not biological implications but rather psychological formations which arise in conjunction with the everyday goals of the individual. More than anything else, Lewin emphasized that goals and intentions belong, in their dynamic properties, in the same category with needs. In Lewin's teaching concerning needs the question arose concerning the relationship between need and object. He showed that the individual always exists in a definite concrete situation (according to his terminology, "in a psychological field"), where each object occurs not in itself but in relationship to the needs and strivings of the individual. Lewin pointed out the dynamic quality of these relationships and that any behavior of the individual changes the "relationship of forces in the situation" and this in turn affects the behavior of the individual.

Hence, any experimental research requires analyzing the mutual relationships between the individual and the environment. Lewin emphasized that the individual is always included in the environment of his situation and that the environment itself must be considered in its relationship to the behaving individual. The nature of these relationships is dynamic, and depends on the structure of the individual's needs.

Yet Lewin resolved the question of needs as a motive force in human activity from the idealist position of Gestalt psychology. For him, a need means some internal psychological dynamic "charge" or "tension system," striving for discharge of relaxation. Discharge of this "tension system" constitutes need satisfaction, according to Lewin. He failed to see the social-historical determination of needs and he ignored their substantive character. Indeed even the concept itself, "psychological field," did not mean a real objective environment, but rather the phenomenal world that was essentially a reflection of those same tension systems. According to Lewin, volitional behavior can be explained by discovering the structure of the dynamic tension systems and their relationships with the "psychological field."

The idealist biases of Lewin are especially evident in his view of the nature of volitional behavior, a cornerstone of his doctrine. Just as he did not see that needs are socially conditioned, he did not perceive that volitional behavior, although it is linked in its origins with needs, does not flow directly from them but is mediated by the awareness of the individual.

Regardless of methodological errors, the theory of Lewin played a positive role in the history of psychology. Lewin introduced into psychological research new parameters for studying the individual: he showed that it is possible to do experiments on needs, motives, intentions, and goals. But what was especially significant was the role of Kurt Lewin and his school in the development of experimental techniques applicable to the psychology of personality. The writings of Lewin and his pupils (Dembo, Mahler, Karsten, Hoppe) permitted the experimental discovery of relationships between the personality and the environment and within the personality itself. To these internal relationships belong the problems associated with "level of aspiration." Lewin believed that level of aspiration is formed in the process of concrete activity. Success and failure play an important role in level of aspiration and it is an important personality development because it is linked with self-evaluation, the activeness of the subject, and the complexities of his affective life.

The method of studying level of aspiration consisted in the following. The subject was presented with a number of problems (from 14 to 18), which differed in their degree of difficulty. All the tasks were put on cards which were laid out in front of the subject in numerical order. The degree of difficulty of the task corresponded to the number on the card.

Research done with this technique (F. Hoppe, M. S. Neimark, B. I. Bezhanishvili, E. A. Serebryakova) showed that, as a rule, subjects choose more difficult tasks after they have been successful, and when they have not been successful they turn to easier tasks. The quality of task performance affects the choice of the next task.

The tasks which were given to the subjects could be quite different in content depending upon the level of education and the occupation of the subjects. For example, subjects who were school children or students at technical institutes could be given mathematical tasks; students of the humanities, tasks requiring knowledge in the area of literature and art. The tasks could be like puzzles. In other words the content of the tasks had to correspond to the social and educational level of the subjects. Only under these conditions was it possible to get the subjects to relate seriously to the experimental situation; only under these conditions was there a real choice.

In order to carry out the experiment 12 × 17 centimeter cards were prepared, and on these cards the numbers from 1 to 14 were clearly written. In addition, a stopwatch was required. The cards were laid out in two rows:

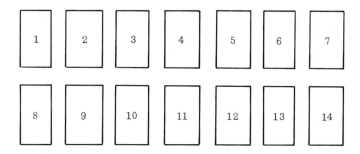

The subject is instructed: "In front of you are cards with problems on the back. The number on the card indicates degree of difficulty of the problem. The problems are arrayed in front of you in terms of increasing difficulty. For the solution of each problem a definite amount of time is allotted which is unknown to you. I will monitor time with the help of a stopwatch. If you do not get the problem right in the allotted time I will consider that you have not done it at all. You must choose which problems you do yourself." In this fashion the subject had the right to choose the difficulty of the problem. After the instructions, the subjects had to choose a task. Upon completing each succeeding task, the subject was told: "And now choose a problem of whatever difficulty you want." The experimenter set the time for completing the task and after each problem said: "You completed this problem in time, I'm going to give you a plus" or: "You did not get it in time, I am giving you a minus." The experimenter could increase or reduce the time allotted for carrying out the task and thus arbitrarily induce a feeling of failure or success. The experimenter could show that the task was completed correctly or, by limiting the time, cause bad results to be obtained. The subject chose the next task, whether harder or easier, only after the evaluation of the experimenter. The analysis of the experimental findings showed that the choice of the problem (its degree of difficulty) depended upon whether the previous problem had been done successfully or not. However the feeling of success or failure itself depended on the attitude of the subject toward the goal of the task. Subjects always begin work with definite aspirations and expectations, which are then changed in the course of the experiment. The sum of these aspirations, which shifts with each trial, was called "level of aspiration" by Hoppe. The feeling of attainment, of success or failure, depended, consequently, not only on objective performance but also on the level of aspiration. Without a level of aspiration, a given trial performance was not felt either as success or failure.

Hoppe's research showed that after successful problem solution, the level of aspiration rises and the subject turns to more complex material; after failure the level of aspiration slowly decreases. The work of Hoppe was the first experimental attempt to study stages in the formation of aspiration under the influence of successful or unsuccessful problem solution. His work was followed by others.

The law for the shift of level of aspiration, as established by Hoppe, was checked out by Juknat, in his "Achievement, Level of Demand, and Self-awareness." By modifying the technique somewhat, a series of labyrinth problems were developed instead of the individual tasks as in Hoppe's research. The first series (ten labyrinth problems) guaranteed success, i.e., the subject could solve the problem, he could find a path from the beginning to the end of the labyrinth. This was the "success series." In the second series, the "failure series," all the problems (also ten labyrinth problems) except the first were unsolvable, that is, all paths of the labyrinth led to a dead end.

Juknat studied two groups of subjects. The first group began the task with the series which guaranteed success; the second group began with the failure series. It turned out that subjects who began with the success series began the second series with a supposedly more difficult problem and, conversely, subjects who started with the failure series began the next series with easier problems. Juknat tried to show that the development of the level of aspiration was linked with prior experience.

Yet for Juknat, just as for Hoppe, "level of aspiration" turned out to be completely isolated from the objective influence of its component attitudes.

The studies of Soviet authors, e.g., E. A. Serebrykova and M. S. Neimark, attempted to show the dependence of level of aspiration on the content of the activity. Basing her research on Hoppe, Serebryakova tried to establish the roles of successful task completion and social evaluation in the development of self-evaluation and self-confidence. If Hoppe in his technique abstracted from real life conditions to the greatest possible extent, Serebryakova tried to maximize naturalism. As a result of her research Serebryakova showed that the development of self-confidence depends upon the type of self-evaluation. Using children, she established correlations between the following:

1. Reliable and appropriate self-evaluation and well-established self-evaluation.
2. Inappropriate reduction of self-evaluation and lack of self-confidence.
3. Inappropriate elevation of self-evaluation and self-confidence.
4. Unstable self-evaluation and poorly established self-evaluation.

Besides this, Serebryakova discovered that different groups of pupils had different types of affective reaction to success and failure. But questions connected with the emotional relationship of the pupils to task difficulty were ignored by Serebryakova. Her research was limited to establishing the nature of self-evaluation but the question concerning the relationship between self-evaluation and level of aspiration was not considered.

However, both these problems were studied in the article by Neimark, "Psychological analysis of the emotional reactions of school children to the difficulty of their work." Neimark indicated that, to the extent that self-evaluation is developed, it begins to affect the behavior of the child and determines his reaction to the influence of adults. If this evaluation is high and gives the child an honorable place in his collective, then it finally becomes a need. From here Neimark was led to a conclusion about the relationship between self-evaluation and level of aspiration. "Level of aspiration is a need for a definitely satisfying self-evaluation." Her research assessed the emotional reactions of children to their success and failure. In her design the subjects were divided into four groups.

1. Pupils with an appropriate reaction to success and failure (disappointment at failure and a feeling of satisfaction at success).
2. Pupils with an inappropriate reaction to failure (after an unsuccessful attempt to solve a problem the children set out on even more difficult problems, displayed resentment toward the experimenter, and were rude).

3. Pupils with inappropriate reaction to success (lowering of the level of aspiration after achieving success).
4. Pupils fleeing from difficulty (after the first failure the children refused to participate in the experiment).

Neimark showed the relationship of level of aspiration to the material of the experiment, she demonstrated the nature of the emotional reaction in the critical situation, and she came close to the problem of the relationship between level of aspiration and self-evaluation.

In this fashion the studies of Serebryakova and Neimark showed that Hoppe's technique was feasible for studying the development of school children's attitudes. This method also turned out to be suitable for studying changes in the emotional conditions of patients.

The studies of our colleague V. N. Myasishchev had already used this technique to illuminate the personality traits of hysterical children (R. I. Meerovich and V. M. Kondratskaya).

Using different variations of this technique in our laboratory, studies of the development of level of aspiration were carried out (by B. I. Bezhanishvili) in patients with various mental illnesses. As an experimental task the subjects were given problems which might be regarded as indicators of certain cultural levels. Arithmetic tasks, or other tasks requiring special skills, had to be rejected since for most people they do not permit development of a meaningful level of aspiration.

In all there were 24 tasks (there were two cards for each level of difficulty). Here are some examples.

1. Write three words beginning with the letter "Sh."
2. Write three words beginning with the letter "N."
2a. Write the names of four animals beginning with the letter "L."
2b. Write the names of four fruits beginning with the letter "A."
3. Write the names of five cities beginning with the letter "L."
3a. Write six names beginning with the letter "P."
4. Write six names beginning with the letter "A."
4a. Write the names of six nations beginning with the letter "I."

5.   Write the names of three flowers beginning with the letter "R."

5a. Write the names of five subway stations beginning with the letter "K."

6.   Write the names of six animals beginning with the letter "K."

6a. Write 20 words beginning with the letter "S."

7.   Write the names of 5 flowers beginning with the letter "G."

7a. Write those parts of the world which begin with the letter "A."

8.   Write four names of trees beginning with the letter "O."

8a. Write the names of 15 cities beginning with the letter "M."

9.   Write the names of 10 cities beginning with the letter "A."

9a. Write the names of 5 films beginning with the letter "M."

10. Write the names of 5 authors beginning with the letter "S."

10a. Write the names of 5 well-known Soviet film artists beginning with the letter "L."

11. Write the names of four composers beginning with the letter "S."

11a. Write the names of well-known Russian composers, artists, and authors beginning with the letter "R."

12. Write the names of seven French artists.

12a. Write the names of 5 well-known Russian artists beginning with the letter "K."

The experimental results obtained with healthy subjects supported the findings of Hoppe and Serebryakova. The selection of tasks by healthy subjects depended on whether the prior tasks were done successfully or not. The initial level of aspiration was different for different subjects: for some subjects their entire behavior was careful and "groping," while others developed a more or less high level of aspiration immediately, as if "on the run." However it was quite evident that the choice of tasks was dependent on how well the previous task had been done. This relationship was frequently not straightforward but the element of choice was always present.

With schizophrenics the findings were completely different. (These were simple schizophrenics who were rather dull and listless). According to the findings of Bezhanishvili, 26 out of 30 schizophrenics showed no relationship between the choice of task and prior performance. No level of aspiration developed nor was

there any sign of an adequate self-evaluation of abilities. The statements of the patients did not have any emotional coloring whatsoever. The patients did not display embarrassment even when the
experimenter emphasized their failure.

Psychopaths were completely different when their level of aspiration was studied; it developed very quickly and, as a rule, it was
rather high. However it was characterized by fragility and instability: at the least failure, it fell and, at the same time, it would quickly
increase when a problem was solved successfully. In studying the
psychopathic personality with this method one other feature was observed, namely, affective explosiveness. The patients quickly became irritated, their mood turned bad, they became gloomy, mali-
cious, and sometimes tore up pieces of paper that contained the experimental instructions which they deprecated, saying "stupid problems."

However, in further work with these techniques some insuffi-
ciences with the level-of-aspiration tasks were found, especially
as they had been applied by Bezhanishvili. In her thesis, N. K.
Kalita showed that the use of questions which allegedly reflect general educational level, was unreliable since the questions presented
by Bezhanishvili afforded no basis for judging the degree of difficulty
for individual subjects. It turned out that for some subjects the answer to question No. 8 (write four names of trees beginning with
"O") was considerably more difficult than the answer to question
No. 10 (write the names of five authors beginning with the letter
"S"). In other words, there were no clear gradations of difficulty
and complexity in these questions and because of this, it was difficult to conduct a proper experiment. Another experiment was
thought up which permitted the experimenter to artificially regulate
the time for solving the problem and thereby arbitrarily determine
success and failure. However the time control by the experimenter
must occur within reasonable limits so that the subject doesn't suspect anything. The subjects had different amounts of knowledge
about the topics of the questions: subjects sometimes succeeded
very quickly in answering questions No. 10 or No. 11, while they
were unable to do ones that were actually easier. As consequence,
the experimenter's evaluation lost its significance for the subject
and his own self-evaluation prevailed.

Kalita concluded that it was necessary to find more objective
gradations of task complexity. He introduced the following varia-

tion: subjects are presented with a pair of pictures which are different from one another in terms of the number of elements (this is akin to a test of attention). The subjects have to find the difference between them. Twelve pairs of tasks were set up and laid out in terms of increasing degrees of difficulty. As a criterion for the difficulty of the task the investigator used the number of differences between two pictures and the time which was necessary for normal subjects to find these differences (from 15 seconds to 3 minutes). The subject was told that his attention was being studied.

This modification in technique permitted Kalita to show the following: (1) The development of level of aspiration depends not only on the evaluation of the experimenter but on the self-evaluation of the subject. (2) A level of aspiration is not formed in circumstances in which the subject is still developing a working relationship to the experiment or when he is simply motivated to become acquainted with problems.

All these data lead us to the following conclusion. In order that an experiment may reveal the self-evaluation and level of aspiration of an individual, it must be set up in such a fashion that it evokes not only an orientation toward the content of the task but it also must facilitate the formation of a relationship to the experimental situation and to the experimenter.

The technique of studying the level of aspiration has turned out to be fruitful in investigating patients with vascular diseases of the brain. The reactions of these patients at the beginning of the experiment was adequate. They tried to test their power, they demanded more of themselves after successful problem solving and returned to easier problems after failure (but these fluctuations were not particularly sharp). However, gradually, toward the end of the experiment, the patients became exhausted and began to be somewhat perplexed; at the same time they did not want to acknowledge their failure. As a result their choice of tasks became unjustified; "I just don't know which one I should take, you tell me," "How would you advise me," etc. The patients, as it were, transferred responsibility for choosing tasks to the experimenter. Frequently the patients refused further work: "I'm tired."

In studying the emotional-volitional behavior of children with oligophrenia, especially interesting results were obtained. The studies of L. Balakireva have shown that in these children the entire

development of level of aspiration has a rather different structure.
For the majority of oligophrenics the level of aspiration was not
appropriate to their self-evaluation. In spite of successful task
completion, the children selected less difficult tasks and, conversely, long-term failure did not lead to a reduction in their level
of aspiration. The sluggishness of their emotional reactions came
to light in his experiment showing the difficulty with which these
oligophrenic children changed their level of aspiration.

At the same time research has revealed another characteristic,
namely, the exceeding sensitivity to failure. The least reproach by
the experimenter led to a catastrophic decay in the level of aspiration and subsequent successful problem solving did not make the
level of aspiration go back up again. The children with oligophrenia
were especially vulnerable to the experimenter's assessment. This
fact underscores the unusual combination of inertness and instability in the emotional-volitional sphere characteristic of oligophrenics and it demonstrates the immaturity and the insufficiently differentiated quality of their personality. The paradoxical combination of inertness and sluggishness, together with instability, is very
likely one of the characteristic personality traits of oligophrenics.

Another appropriate technique for studying pathological personality changes has been "the study of mental satiation" which
was launched by a student of Lewin's, A. Karsten. Her research
focused on the ability to maintain and to restore the impetus to
complete some monotonous task. The subject has to carry out a
task, for example, drawing dashes or circles (in doing this task a
large pile of sheets of paper is placed in front of the subject). The
subject is instructed: "please draw dashes in this fashion" (the
experimenter draws some identical dashes or circles O O O O O).
If the subject asks how many he has to draw the experimenter answers in an indefinite and impassive manner: "As many as you
want, there you have some paper."

Studies carried out by Karsten and I. M. Solov'ev show that at
the beginning, the subjects rather accurately carried out the task
that was assigned to them; however, after a short period (5 to 10
minutes), they began to introduce variations into the task, that is,
unknown to himself the subject changes the task. These variations
seemed to be changes in the external structure of the task: the
dashes or circles became smaller or bigger, the subjects changed

work tempo or drew the dashes and circles in a definite rhythm (for example, ○○ ○○○ ○○ ○○○). Sometimes the subjects had recourse to concomitant behavior; they began to sing, whistle, and tap their feet. These variations show that the instigation to complete an assigned behavior begins to run down and, as Karsten expressed it, the phenomenon of "mental satiation" begins to supervene.

According to Karsten such phenomena, that is, variations in the task, not only show that the desire to complete the task is beginning to fade; to some extent these variations perform a prophylactic service; change in the structure of a given task enabled the subject to continue it.

The experimenter conscientiously records spontaneous statements of the subject, the nature of his reactions, his mimic behavior, and his expressive movements. In this way he determines the point of time at which the new variations appear.

After a certain amount of time (usually 20 to 30 minutes), when variations are becoming more frequent and are beginning to take on a somewhat coarse character, the subject is given new instructions: "This task is monotonous for you and it was given to you in order to study your stamina. Continue it if you want."

The reactions of the subjects to these new instructions are diverse. Some subjects become angry: "Why didn't you tell me that earlier," and they stop working. For other subjects, however, the new instructions provide a new comprehension of the situation: "Well, that is another matter" is frequently heard in reply.

This new comprehension of the task situation often makes variations become less frequent, less pronounced, and sometimes they even disappear altogether. After the new instructions the experimenter conscientiously records the responses and the statements of the subjects and notes, just as he did before, the time at which variations supervene and their nature. A good time for stopping work before completion has not been established. As a rule the subjects themselves stop work: "I can't do any more." But sometimes some of them are not disposed to stop work because they frequently change their interpretation of the task, or, more correctly, they add something to it. This is shown both by the spontaneous utterances and the self-awareness of these subjects. "I wanted to see who would get fed up sooner, you (that is the experimenter) or I," or "I wanted to test myself to see how long I could work on this boring task."

When this study was done with healthy adults and children it was shown that, after a certain amount of time, the subjects introduce variations into a monotonous task: the variations consist in changes of the activity itself, for example, the circles are transformed into "mug" cartoons and ears and hair are added. Then pauses occur in the work, and concomitant behavior begins to occur. The child begins to sing and whistle, just as if the children were satiated with the monotonous work and were attempting to change its meaning for themselves. The variations are temporary withdrawal from work and a shift to activity which is fundamentally similar. Solv'ev followed Karsten in labelling this withdrawal, that is, this variation, "an equivalent withdrawal from work." The more subtle such equivalences, the more they demonstrated the flexibility of the child's behavior.

In doing this experiment with mentally retarded children it turned out that they kept at the task as long as healthy children, and it followed that their work capacity can appear to be undisturbed. However, the unfolding of the satiation process revealed peculiarities consisting in the polarity of their reactions.

In intellectually retarded children we find coarse forms of the variations: long pauses, temporary withdrawals from work, even together with stamina and endurance (especially in connection with monotonous tasks). On the other hand, children with oligophrenia quickly throw aside the work that they are tired of; no variations or changes are introduced. Such a polarity, so noticeable in the daily behavior of oligophrenics, demonstrates the immaturity of their intentions.

This methodological technique turned out to be very useful for revealing the personality features of epileptics. It turned out that they not only can maintain monotonous performance for a long time but that they introduce few variations. It was especially interesting to observe the responses of patients to the second instruction. While the second instruction imparted new meaning to the entire situation for healthy subjects, in epileptics and in children suffering from oligophrenia, this kind of meaning transformation did not occur. Hence, the techniques which we used showed that, for a def-

inite group of patients, the process of meaning formation is disturbed.

As we have mentioned above in Chapter 3, interesting results
were obtained by using this method on patients with disorders of
work capacity. Experimenting with patients with brain trauma, we
were able to note that satiation occurred for them much more
quickly. While variations occur on the average after 10 minutes
for healthy subjects, the traumatized subjects generate variations
after only two or three minutes; and these variations are quite
crude in nature. The experiment reveals the rapid extinguishabil-
ity of mental processes in such patients.

Recently some other approaches to the study of personality
traits in mental patients began to appear, such as comparison of
patients' complaints about their intellectual deficit with what has
been revealed experimentally. This methodological technique was
followed by V. V. Kostikova, who made a very interesting attempt
to analyze the so-called "internal dynamics of illness" in the
mentally ill.

The well-known Soviet therapist R. A. Luriya introduced the
concept of "internal dynamics of disease," by which he means
"all that which the patient experiences and feels, the entire aggregate of his sensations, not only local sensations due to his illness
but also his general feeling about himself, his self-observation,
how he represents his illness to himself (with respect to its causes),
all that which is linked with approaching a physician – that entire
internal world of the patient, which consists of very complex combinations of perceptions and sensations, emotions, affects, conflicts,
mental feelings, and trauma." He indicated that the behavior and
mental processes of the individual are changed at the very moment
when he learns about his illness.

Luriya discussed the significance of studying the "internal
dynamics of disease" in somatic illnesses. Undoubtedly these
dynamics play a larger role in mental illness. The author was
completely right when he pointed out that a comparison of subjective and objective amnesia in the history of the patient facilitates
establishing whether the patient is aware of his disease, to what
extent he adequately appraises the burden that his condition will
be for him, and what feelings are linked with the disease. It can
be no less informative to compare the patient's complaints with

the results of experimental research. The experiment is a situation that has personal significance for the patient and therefore the relationship of the patient to it and his emotional response to the fact that his capability is being studied characterize his personality.

Kostikova made an attempt to compare the results of experimental research with patient complaints. Patients with different kinds of illnesses were presented with a number of standard questions aimed at revealing their complaints and their opinions about the causes of their illness (for example, the questions: "How does your illness show itself?" "What do you think is the cause of your illness?"). Then the usual experimental steps were taken and a number of experimental methods were used (classification of objects, pictogram, memorization of ten words, transmission of the metaphorical meaning of proverbs, counting, and others).

Comparison of patients' complaints with the experimental and clinical evidence enabled Kostikova to observe different kinds of relationships between them. In some instances a very crude uncritical attitude is observed: the patients did not notice and they are unable to evaluate the signs of their own mental weaknesses. Some patients who in conversation created the impression of being completely uncritical were enabled to show critical ability by the experiment. These abilities were manifested as an unstable but, all the same, active personality disposition. At the same time, there are instances of the passive awareness of disease without any effect on the disposition of the patient toward everyday life. In many instances in which more or less correct assessment of their disease is available to the patient, he talks about it incorrectly to the doctor. This frequently signifies that there is "dissimulation." But such a dissimulation can have two meanings; in one case, the patient, who is trying to compensate for his defect, does not talk about it, and tries to struggle with the disease and to make a good life adjustment. In the second instance the patient dissembles; he conceals the pathological feelings because he is trying, for delirious reasons, to get discharged from the hospital and he acts in terms of these delirious ideas.

The characterization of this kind of personality disposition is important since the experiment has artificially created a personally significant situation which facilitates discovery of the patient's relationship to the doctor, to the treatment situation, and to his disease in general.

Whatever may be the disposition of the individual during experimental research, if there is even a shred of interest displayed, it always demonstrates that personality has been preserved to some extent.

The problem of personality disposition has recently been raised by psychologists working on the problem of the development of personality in the child (L. N. Bozhovich, S. L. Slavina). They correctly show that the formation of needs in the individual is associated with the availability of awareness of the need. Therefore, study of changes in awareness has fundamental significance for questions of general psychology as well.

Recently still another technique has begun to show up, namely, the analysis of illness-history data. These data, that is, a description of mental status, the findings of anamnesis, diaries, etc. are valuable material, which have been insufficiently used by psychologists. Meanwhile casting of many of the factors which have been described by clinical psychologists in the terms of contemporary psychological science could vastly facilitate the analysis of the structure of needs and motives, which change so much in many mental patients (schizophrenia, epilepsy, chronic alcoholism). This kind of analysis is being carried out now in many studies such as those of B. S. Bratuse, L. V. Bondareva, and M. M. Kochenov.

Combining psychological techniques and pharmacological tests has turned out to be especially valuable in illuminating personality properties. The studies of S. Ya. Rubinshtein are moving in this direction. While affirming the opportunity afforded by applying experimental methods to the study of psychopathological phenomena, this author states that the following means of constructing experimental techniques are most objective and appropriate to the problems of psychiatry: 1) variation of the situation in which the patient finds himself, 2) variation of the activity which the patient must perform, and 3) variation of the condition of the patient by means of experimental and pharmacological stimulation. It is possible to combine these techniques in a very productive fashion.

Rubinshtein showed that the patient's susceptibility to change and his susceptibility to pharmacological influence can serve as major criteria for the effectiveness of therapy. The author has developed a number of methodological techniques which enable him to carry out such research; this branch of research is extremely promising for the study of abnormality in personality.

The enumerated research techniques for studying personality alterations are not the only ones. The analysis of so complex a problem must be carried out from different points of view and from different directions. However, the fundamental basis for these studies must be the tenets of contemporary materialist psychology.

Chapter 7

Mental Decay and Mental Growth

Knowledge about the relationship between mental growth and decay is poorly developed even though this issue is very important for psychiatric and psychological theory and for understanding the structure of mental activity and the principles of mental development. The correct resolution of this question may help to defeat biologizing tendencies in psychiatry and psychology. In a practical sense, this question generates data for classifying and analyzing psychopathological syndromes.

G. E. Sukhareva repeatedly cited the necessity for an evolutionary-biological approach to the resolution of theoretical questions in psychiatry. L. S. Vygotskii, who devoted much attention to mental development and maturation in the child, emphasized the importance of information about mental decay. In this connection, he indicated that, as far as human development and maturation are concerned, the genetic approach, as applied to animals, cannot be simplistically extrapolated, since, in phylogenesis, the laws of biological evolution yielded to the principles of social-historical development. Continuing with Vygotskii's conceptualization, A. N. Leont'ev stated that human development consists not in adaptation to the environment but in mastering all the accumulated knowledge of mankind.

The question arises as to whether the relationship between decay and growth can be resolved in psychology as it is in biology. It is well known that research on anatomical and cell pathology has established that brain disease first of all affects the "young" formations in the cortex, that is, those portions whose phylogenetic development has been most recent (Gerstman, Gurevich, Miskolchy, Snesarev, Vogt).

The animal experiments of Pavlov and his co-workers supported the view that pathology first affects whatever was acquired most recently. Thus, acquired conditioned reflexes are destroyed in brain diseases considerably more easily than unconditioned reflexes. Further studies of the physiology of higher nervous activity established that impairment of phylogenetically recent formations entails weakening of their regulatory role and the consequent disengagement or freeing of earlier formations.

From these considerations, the conclusion is frequently drawn that some brain diseases entail activity at a lower developmental stage, which may correspond to a specific stage in childhood. This notion about mental regression to an ontogenetically lower level, stimulated many investigators to try to find a relationship between the structure of mental decay and a specific stage in child development. Thus, even in their time, Blonskii and Krechmer compared schizophrenic thinking to the thinking of the child at puberty. And today the American authors Pinkerton and Kelley state that patients with cerebrovascular diseases lose the ability to abstract in a way that corresponds to the development of that ability in children. In his report to the 18th World Congress of Psychology the well-known Swiss scholar Ajouriaguerra also defended the view that in mental illness there is psychological regression to an ontogenetically lower level of development.

The basic idea here is that mental decay proceeds stage by stage from higher to lower levels. The supporting evidence comprised the following observations.

1. In many mental illnesses the patients cease being able to manage more difficult kinds of behavior while simple habits and skills are preserved.
2. Some forms of disturbance in thinking and ways of behaving are actually superficially reminiscent of the child's thinking and behavior at certain developmental stages.

However, close scrutiny of these observations shows them to be unfounded. First and foremost, it is far from always true that illness causes deterioration of higher functions. In the clinical treatment of nervous diseases we often encounter impairment of elementary sensory-motor operations, and this impairment underlies the complexities of the disease.

Close examination of the second set of facts (in which the thought styles and behavior of adult patients are compared with those of children at certain developmental stages) also shows that the analogy is superficial.

Let us examine some of these facts. First of all, it is necessary to discuss skills since ontogentic formation of skills occurs in an especially clearcut fashion. Consider some interesting data from S. Ya. Rubinshtein's work. She studied the deterioration of different skills: writing and reading, habitual behaviors in older people who are mentally ill. She found that in different diseases the structure of impairment was different. In some diseases (for example, cerebrovascular disease without a focal symptomatology), she found lack of coordination, behavioral discontinuity, and paraphrasis; the patients' movements were awkward and they blundered in any ordinary undertaking. Rubinshtein notes that the lack of coordination is due to desensitized and retarded cortical motor control.

Patients with brain atrophy suffer from impairment of stereotyped motor behavior, such as writing and reading. Rubinshtein points out that the typical decline of complex human skills in these patients is caused by the loss of previous experience. Furthermore these patients do not develop any compensating mechanisms, while in vascular patients, on the other hand, skill deterioration is accompanied by compensating mechanisms which, in turn, complicate the disorder.

All these findings indicate that skill deterioration is complex. Sometimes it is a dynamic disorder, sometimes disturbed compensatory mechanisms are involved, and, in some cases, the structure itself of behavior is impaired. The main point, as Rubinshtein correctly notes, is that in all these instances of skill deterioration no mechanisms have been observed which resemble stages in the skill development of children.

This conclusion is supported by the analysis of thought disorders presented in Chapter 5, in particular, those disorders which were called "lowering of the level of generalization." The

patients were mainly ones suffering from deep organic brain lesions and their reasoning and behavior could seem to be reminiscent of elementary school children. They couldn't perform a
series of intellectual operations at a normal level of abstraction
and generalization. Their reasoning was dominated by direct
and immediate images of objects and events. These intrusions
occurred experimentally when the patients worked on such tasks
as "classification of objects." They began to be influenced by
concrete-situational attributes and properties (bear and fox are
grouped together because "these animals live in the woods," and
cat and goat, "these live at home." Vegetables and fruits were
put in the same group not because they are both "plants" but because "they are sold in the stores." Systematic conceptual generalization is replaced by concrete, situational linking.

Superficial analysis might support the idea that the properties
of cognitive disorder in patients with lowered level of generalization are somewhat reminiscent of preschool thinking since thinking at this age is also based on sense images rather than abstract
concepts. However deeper analysis discloses a qualitative distinction between the thinking of the imbecile patient and the child.
The adult imbecile cannot master a new set of relationships, he
cannot establish unconventional relationships between objects
while doing mental work; at the same time, he relies on a supply
of previous knowledge and skills. The child, on the other hand,
who does not have a store of prior knowledge or a wide array of
associations, easily masters a new system of knowledge. In the
course of learning, the child's associations become more rami-
fied, and his knowledge of the environment gradually increases
and becomes complex. Even though the child's thinking is incomplete and maps only a portion of reality, it becomes complete
through everyday living; thanks to the powerful orienting reflex
and his commerce with the environment, the child quickly assim-
ilates quite different aspects of objects and the knowledge of these
aspects is accumulated and synthesized. Even a mentally retarded
child is always trainable in principle, while a demented patient
cannot be trained because he is unable to learn new material and
has to use previous experience. So, regardless of the superficial
similarity between the thinking of the adult imbecile patient and
the child, they are in fact qualitatively different.

An analogy is frequently drawn between that pathological condition referred to as "hyperresponsiveness" and the distractibility
of the young child. The hyperresponsive patient cannot proceed
firmly toward the accomplishment of his intended objectives. His
associations are misdirected and his level of intellectual performance fluctuates. Any object or stimulus, whether or not it is
addressed to the patient, can evoke a heightened response from
him. In our articles we described a patient who, upon entering
the ward dining room, declared that "he had come to a restaurant
to make merry," and then he immediately stated that he is at a
watchmaker's (a hospital attendant had just set the wall clock). A
minute later the patient acknowledged that he was in the hospital.
Some patients who had been lying in their beds without having any
conversation with other patients or hospital staff suddenly responded to questions or remarks intended for others.

This hyperresponsiveness of adult patients seems to be a re-
jection of normal behavior. In our environment there are always
objects which do not compel our attention. A normal cognitive
process assumes the ability to pick out important stimuli and to
avoid the incidental ones which interfere with cognitive harmony.
However, for our patients any object seemed capable of having a
signal function and influencing their thinking and behavior.

The hyperresponsiveness of adult patients can resemble the
distractibility of very young children in that the latter are also
distracted by any stimulus and their attention drawn by every object. Proponents of the view that pathological phenomena constitute regression to earlier developmental stages might, it seemed,
find support for their position in this phenomenon. In fact, however, the genesis of distractibility in the child is completely different. It is founded on an amplified orienting reflex, that is, a
heightened degree of cortical arousability, and, therefore, the
child's distractibility enrichens his intellectual activity; it con-
fers the ability to generate a large number of temporary relationships, which is the basis for human purposive activity. The "hyperresponsiveness" of patients, however, is due to a lowering of
cortical arousability and it not only doesn't enrich them intellectually but, on the contrary, it helps to destroy purposiveness. Indeed, "hyperresponsiveness" occurs systematically in conjunction

with other manifestations of increased cerebral inhibition: memory impairment, paraphases, and so forth.

Finally, it is possible to draw an analogy between uncritical behavior in the patients (for example, those suffering from progressive paralysis) and the carelessness of the child. However, in this instance the analogy is purely superficial. The behavior of the little child is thoughtless in the sense that his limited knowledge does not enable him to predict the results of his behavior; there are no causal relationships between events for him since his actions seem to him to be without purpose. In fact, however, it is not this way at all. The goals pursued by the child are limited; they are not included in a complex chain of relationships. However, the limited goal of the small child does exist; and each of his actions is determined by a need (however elementary), and in this sense his actions are always motivated and goal-directed. The child's goals change quickly due to his powerful orienting reflex, and as a result his behavior seems to be readily manipulable over the short term.

But it is different for adult patients with uncritical thinking. Our experimental data and clinical observations show that the behavior of these patients was insufficiently determined by their personality orientations and intentions. Their goals were unstable, their behavior lacked direction and self-correction, and the regulatory function of speech was impaired. Hence, these kinds of behavior disorders only superficially resemble the child's behavior at particular developmental stages.

At the same time, studies of cognitive decay reveal types which are not even superficially similar to the thinking characteristic of children. Such peculiarities of thinking as "dissociation" or "distortion of the level of generalization" are not encountered at any developmental level.

In thought "dissociation" it is usually difficult to find out what the object of thought is. For these patients, speech is neither a means of communication with a listener nor of relating to other people; it is neither a tool of thought nor a means of social intercourse.

Such features do not characterize the child's thinking. No matter how disconnected is the child's speech, it is always directed at some object. No matter how we distract him, the child's babble is always directed at some object; his speech always reflects the child's relationship to his environment, and it is directed at the people who are around him. Soviet psychological research has shown that even in egocentric speech, the child is expressing his thoughts and desires and his speech is not aimless. In sum, analysis of clinical material has shown that the behavior and cognitive activity in the adult patient does not correspond structurally to behavior and thinking in the child.

If, on the one hand, we look at the principles of development of mental processes during childhood (infancy, preschool, elementary school, junior and senior high school, etc.) and, on the other, at the forms of mental deterioration, it is easy to see that none of the diseases is a repetition of mental properties peculiar to certain developmental stages.

This conclusion follows from the general tenets of Soviet psychology. Mental activity arises in a reflex fashion on the basis of socially-conditioned bonds which are formed during a lifetime of upbringing and education. Soviet psychologists (A. N. Leont'ev, A. R. Luria) repeatedly emphasized that the material substrate of higher mental functions is not composed of separate cortical parts or centers but rather consists in a functional system of cortical areas working together. These functional systems do not mature independently but they are formed in everyday life and gradually become durable and complex interfunctional relationships. Following A. A. Ukhtomskii, Leont'ev suggests calling them "functional organs."

These ideas radically change our notions regarding the essential nature of mental development: human mental processes and personality traits are not (in contrast to animals) simply the result of the maturing of individual parts or zones of the brain. They are formed ontogenetically and, as a consequence, they depend on the child's life style.

In point of fact, the course of a disease follows biological laws which cannot replicate the laws of development. Even in those instances where disease affects the youngest, and the most specifically human, sections of the brain, the behavior of the patient does not assume the structure of that of a sick child at an earlier developmental level. The fact that patients lose the ability to think and reason at a more advanced level only means that they have been deprived of more complex forms of behavior and cognition, but it does not signify a return to a childhood level. Anyway such a regression would not justify concluding that levels of decay and development are qualitatively uniform: decay is not negative development.

Different pathological states lead to qualitatively different kinds of decay. Experimental psychology has studied the multifarious forms of these mental disorders and the findings constitute valuable evidence which must be taken into account in constructing a general psychological theory.

Bibliography

Abashev-Konstantinovskii, A. L. "The psychopathology of frontal lesions." Nevropatologiya i psikhiatriya, Vol. 18. No. 4 (1949).
Abashev-Konstantinovskii, A. L. "The problem of consciousness in the light of clinical psychopathology." Voprosy psikhologii, No. 4 (1958).
Abramov, V. V. Research on Creativity and Other Intellectual Functions in the Mentally Ill. (Saint Petersburg, 1911).
Abramovich, G. B. "The clinical psychological experiment." Sovetskaya psikhonevrologiya, No. 1 (1939).
Anfimov, V. Ya. "Concentration of attention and capacity for mental work in epi-
lepsy." Obozrenie psikhiatrii, nevrologii i eksperimental'noi psikhologii, Nos.
11-12 (1908).
Anikima, A. M. "The differential features of the work processes of patients with
idiopathic and traumatic epilepsy." In: Epilepsy and Clinical Aspects of
Working Capacity (Medgiz, Moscow, 1939).
Averbukh, E. S. "Recall of completed and incompleted actions by manic-depressives
(a study of affective-volitional training in manic-depressive psychosis)."
Sovetskaya nevropsikhiatriya, No. 1 (1936).
Banshchikov, V. M., Gus'kov, V. S., and Myagkov, I. F. Medical Psychology
(Meditsina, Moscow, 1967).
Bassin, F. V. "The disturbance of word values in schizophrenia." Candidate's dis-
sertation (Khar'kov, 1936).
Bekhterev, V. M. "The objective study of neuropsychic activity." Obozrenie
psikhiatrii i nevrologii, No. 4 (1907).
Bekhterev, V. M. "The objective study of the mentally ill." Obozrenie psikhiatrii,
nevrologii i eksperimental'noi psikhologii, No. 11-12 (1907).
Bekhterev, V. M., and Vladychko, S. D. Objective Experimental Study of the Men-
tally Ill. (Saint Petersburg, 1911).
Beringer, L. "Sprache und Denkstörungen bei Schizophrenie." Z. Neurol., Vol. 103
(1927).

Bernshtein, A. N. "Experimental-psychological patterns of intellectual disorder in the mentally ill." Reports given at the April 30, 1910 Meeting of the Moscow Association of Neurologists and Psychiatrists (Moscow, 1910).

Bernshtein, A. N. Clinical Tactics in the Psychological Study of the Mentally Ill (Gosizdat, Moscow, 1922).

Berze, J. and Gruhle, H. W. Psychologie der Schizophrenie (Berlin, 1929).

Bezhanishvili, B. I. "Some peculiarities of fixed sets in Pick's disease." In: Problems of Experimental Abnormal Psychology (Moscow, 1965).

Birenbaum, G. V. "The formation of metaphors and conventional word meanings in the presence of pathological changes in intelligence." In: Advances in the Study of Apraxia, Agnosia, and Aphasia (Moscow–Leningrad, 1934).

Birenbaum, G. V., and Zeigarnik, B. V. "The dynamic analysis of intellectual disorders." Sovetskaya nevropatologiya, psikhiatriay i psikhogigiena, Vol. 4, No. 6 (1935).

Bleikher, V. M., and Mints, A. Ya. "Memory disorder in cerebral arteriosclerosis." In: Problems of Experimental Abnormal Psychology (Moscow, 1965).

Blumenau, L. M. "The study of the originality of associations." Vestnik psikhologii, Vol. 3, No. 5 (1906).

Blyumina, M. G. "Techniques for psychological research on oligophrenic children from age two to five." Voprosy eksperimental'noi patopsikhologii (Moscow, 1965).

Bogdanov, E. I. "Techniques for studying visual perception with incomplete information." In: Problems of Experimental Abnormal Psychology (Moscow, 1965).

Bzhalava, I. T. "Psychopathology of the fixed sets in epilepsy." In: Proceedings from a Conference on Psychology, (Izd. APN RSFSR, 1957).

Bzhalava, I. T. "Use of D. N. Uznadze's study of fixed sets in clinical treatment of the mentally ill." In: Psychological Research Methods in the Clinic. Symposium Proceedings, 14-17 Feb., 1967 (Leningrad, 1967).

Cameron, N. The Psychology of Behavior Disorders (Boston, 1947).

Cattell, R. B. Personality (New York, 1950).

Chapman, L. J., Burstein, A. G., Day, D., and Verdone, P. "Regression and disorders of thought." J. Abnorm. soc. psychol., No. 63, pp. 540-545 (1961).

Chizh, V. F. "Apperception of simple and complex ideas as studied by the method of complications." Vestnik psikhiatrii, Vol. 1 (1885).

Chizh, V. F. "Measurement of the duration of elementary processes in the mentally ill." Vestnik psikhiatrii, Vol. 1 (1885).

Chizh, V. F. "Perceptual scope in the mentally ill." Arkhiv psikhiatrii (Moscow, 1890).

Conference Proceedings of the Society for Experimental Psychology. "A review of psychiatric and neurological experimental psychology" (Saint Petersburg, 1904).

Delay, J. Etudes de psychologie medicale (Paris, 1953).

Dement'eva, N. F. "Emotional-volitional changes in schizophrenics suffering from psychogenic relapses." In: Problems of Experimental Abnormal Psychology (Moscow, 1965).

Destunis, G. Einführung in die medizinische Psychologie (Berlin, 1955).

Dokuchaeva, M. A. "Use of Kraepelin's scoring technique in the psychiatric clinic."
    In: Psychological Research Methods in the Clinic. Symposium Proceedings,
    14-17 Feb., 1967 (Leningrad, 1967).
Dubinin, A. M., and Zeigarnik, B. V. "The problem of traumatic dementia." Nevro-
    patologiya i psikhiatriya, Vol. 9, Nos. 7-8 (1940).
Dukel'skaya, I. N., Melekhov, D. E., and Korobkova, É. A. "Assessment work capacity
and job replacement of remitted schizophrenics." Metodicheskoe pis'mo
    TSIETINa (Medgiz, Moscow, 1955).
Dukel'skaya, I. N., and Korobkova, E. A. Medical Assessment of Working Capacity
    and Placement of Schizophrenic Patients (Medgiz, Moscow, 1958).
Epshtein, A. L. "Some properties of attention in the mentally ill." Psikhologiya,
    nevrologiya, i psikhiatriya, No. 2, (1933).
Évlakhova, E. A. "Types of intelligence in schizophrenia." In: 50th Anniversary of
    the S. S. Korsakov Psychiatric Clinic (Moscow, 1940).
Gadzhiev, S. G. "Analysis of the disturbance of intellectual activity in lesions of the
    frontal areas of the brain." Candidate's dissertation (Moscow, 1947).
Gal'perin, P. Ya. "Two conceptions of higher nervous activity and their relationship
    to psychology." Sovetskaya psikhonevrologiya, No. 2 (1933).
Gal'perin, P. Ya. "The intellectual action as the basis of formation of thought and
    image." Voprosy psikhologii, No. 6 (1957).
Gal'perin, P. Ya. "The development of investigations of the formation of intellectual
    actions." In: Psychological Science in the USSR, Vol. 1 (Izd. APN RSFSR,
    Moscow, 1959).
Gal'perin, P. Ya., and Golubova, R. A. "Mechanism of paraphasias of the complex
    type." Sovetskaya psikhonevrologiya, No. 6 (1933).
Gal'perina, R. A. "Special features of the working capacity and compensatory powers
    of schizophrenics." In: Assessment of Working Capacity and Resettlement of
    Schizophrenic Patients (Moscow, 1940).
Gellershtein, S. G. Rehabilitative Work Therapy in the Evacuation Hospital (Medgiz,
    Moscow, 1943).
Golant, P. Ya. "Recall of complete and incompleted action in progressive paralysis."
    Sovetskaya nevropathologiya psikhiatriya i psikhogigiena, No. 6 (1935).
Golant, P. Ya. Memory Disorders (Moscow-Leningrad, 1925).
Golant, R. Ya., and Yankovskii, A. E. "Some experimental data relating to the prob-
    lem of the disintegration of intelligence in schizophrenia." Sovetskaya nevro-
    patologiya, psikhiatriya i psikhogigiena, Vol. 3, Nos. 2-3 (1934).
Golodets, P. G., Zeigarnik, B. V., and Rubinshtein, S. Ya. "Mental disorder in as-
    thenic conditions caused by industrial hazards." Voprosy psikhologii, No. 5
    (1963).
Gutman, L. S. "Experimental-psychological investigations of manic-melancholic
    psychosis (the state of concentration, attention, capacity for mental work, and
    association)." Doctoral dissertation, Seriya doktorskikh dissertatsii, No. 15
    (Saint Petersburg, 1909).
Hanfmann, E., and Kasanin, J. S. Conceptual Thinking in Schizophrenia (New York,
    1942).

148

Il'in, A. V. "The processes of concentration (attention) in patients with dementia."
Izvestiya imperatorskoi voennomeditsinkoi akademii, No. 3 (1909).

Ivannikov, Yu. V. "Research methods for studying some peculiarities of visual
awareness." In: Problems of Experimental Abnormal Psychology (Moscow, 1965).

Ivanov, A. Ya. "The training experiment as a means of investigating children with
abnormal mental development." In: Problems of Experimental Abnormal Psychology (Moscow, 1965).

Ivanov, A. Ya. "Principles for designing a training experiment." In: Psychological
Research Methods in the Clinic. Symposium Proceedings, 14-17 Feb., 1967
(Leningrad, 1967).

Janet, P. La medicine psychologique (Paris, 1923).

Kekcheev, K. Kh. "The application of the chronocyclograph technique in studying
pathological findings." Psikhologiya, nevropatologiya i psikhiatriya, Vol. 2 (1923).

Khvilivitskii, T. Ya. "The psychoneurotic's attitude toward work and its role in devel-
ment of the work curve." Sovetskaya nevropatologiya, psikhiatriya i psikhogigiena, Vol. 1, (1935)

Khramtsova, S. T. "Standardization of the technique, 'comparison of concepts,' in a
psychoneurological clinic for children." In: Problems of Experimental Abnormal Psychology (Moscow, 1965).

Kiyashchenko, N. K. "Standardization of alternative TAT techniques." In: Problems of Experimental Abnormal Psychology (Moscow, 1965).

Klimusheva, T. A. "Experimental investigation of paranoid schizophrenics with the
automatism syndrome." In: Problems of Experimental Abnormal Psychology
(Moscow, 1965).

Kochenov, M. M. "Experiences with experimental research on patients' motivation."
In: Psychological Research-Methods in the Clinic. Symposium Proceedings,
14-17 Feb., 1967 (Leningrad, 1967).

Kogan, V. M. "Occupational placement of mental patients." In: Technical Instructions in Relation to Industrial Medical Boards (Moscow, 1940).

Kogan, V. M. "Special features of the working capacity of mental patients (with
schizophrenia and epilepsy) and measures of organization of their work."
Abstracts of Proceedings of a Scientific Session 3-7 Feb., 1941 (Moscow, 1941).

Kogan, V. M. Speech Rehabilitation in Aphasia (Meditsina, Moscow, 1963).

Kogan, V.·M. "Principles of collaborative research." In: Psychological Research
Methods in the Clinic. Symposium Proceedings, 14-17 Feb., 1967 (Leningrad,
1967).

Kogan, V. M., and Kostomarova, N. M. "Special features of the working capacity
and placement of schizophrenics." In: Assessment of Working Capacity and
Placement of Patients with Schizophrenia (Moscow, 1940).

Kokin, M. K., and Perepelkin, V. M. "Characteristics of associations in persons suffering from chronic alcoholism." In: Problems of Experimental Abnormal
Psychology (Moscow, 1965).

Kononova, M. P. "Psychological findings from a study of slowly progressing schizophrenia in children." Sovetskaya nevropatologiya, psikhiatriyi i psikhogigiena,
Vol. 6, No. 11 (1935).

Kononova, M. P. "The psychological analysis of the asthenic state during exhaustion
(in children and adolescents)." Trudy bol'nitsy im. Kashchenko, No. 4 (1945).

Kononova, M. P. Handbook of Research on Mentally Ill Children (Medgiz, Moscow, 1963).

Korobkova, É. A. "An experimental investigation of the factors stimulating and depressing working capacity." In: Problems in the Assessment of Working Capacity and Diagnosis of Borderline States (Biomedgiz, Moscow, 1939).

Korobkova, É. A. "Occupation placement of epileptics." Sotsial'noe obespechenie, No. 9 (1940).

Korobkova, É. A. "Time parameters in the abnormal psychology experiment." In: Psychological Research Methods in the Clinic. Symposium Proceedings, 14-17 Feb., 1967 (Leningrad, 1967).

Korobkova, É. A., and Savich, M. G. "Psychological characteristics of the working capacity of neurotics." Abstracts of Proceedings of a Scientific Session of TsIETIN, 11-15 Feb., 1936 (Profizdat, Moscow, 1936).

Korsakov, S. S. "The psychology of microcephaly." Voprosy filosofii i psikhologii, Book 1 (1894).

Korsakov, S. S. Medical-psychological Investigation of One Form of Memory Disorder (Moscow, 1894).

Kostikova, V. V. "Psychological analysis of patients' complaints in comparison with clinical and experimental findings in relationship to the so-called internal description of disease." In: Problems of Experimental Abnormal Psychology (Moscow, 1965).

Kostikova, V. V. "Some practical applications of psychology in the mental hospital." In: Problems of Experimental Abnormal Psychology (Moscow, 1965).

Kostomarova, N. M. "Qualitative characteristics of intellectual activity in patients with diffuse changes in the central nervous system as a result of head injury." In: Traumatic Lesions of the Central Nervous System (Moscow, 1940).

Kritskaya, V. P. "Techniques for studying speech perception." In: Problems of Experimental Abnormal Psychology (Moscow, 1965).

Kritskaya, V. P. "Speech perception in schizophrenics." Candidate dissertation (Moscow, 1966).

Kurganov, Zh. L. "The psychology experiment in the cerebro-arteriosclerosis clinic." Sovetskaya nevropatologiya, psikhiatriya i psikhogigiena, Vol. 3, No. 4 (1934).

Kutaliya, N. A. "Toward a technique for investigating conceptual thinking in schizophrenics." In: Psychological Research Methods in the Clinic. Symposium Proceedings, 14-17 Feb., 1967 (Leningrad, 1967).

Lagache, D. "Psychologie clinique et methode clinique." Evolution psychiatrique (April-June, 1949).

Lange, N. N. Psychological Studies (Odessa, 1893).

Lebedinskii, M. S. "Speech disorders in schizophrenics." Sovetskaya psikhonevrologiya, No. 3 (1933).

Lebedinskii, M. S. "Speech disorders in schizophrenics." Sovetskaya psikhonevrologiya, No. 3 (1938).

Lebedinskii, M. S. "Mental disturbances from lesions of the right hemisphere." In: Problems of Contemporary Psychiatry (Moscow, 1945).

Lebedinskii, M. S. "Some principles and problems for psychological research in the clinic." In: Psychological Research Methods in the Clinic. Symposium Proceedings, 14-17 Feb., 1967 (Leningrad, 1967).

Lebedinskii, M. S. "Motor and behavior disturbances in patients with frontal lesions."
    Candidate's dissertation (Moscow, 1967).
Lebedinskii, M. S., and Myasishchev, V. N. Medical Psychology (Meditsina, Moscow,
    1966).
Lenin, V. I. Complete Collected Works, Vol. 29.
Leont'ev, A. N. A Sketch of the Development of the Mind (Moscow, 1947).
Leont'ev, A. N. "The nature and formation of human mental properties and pro-
    cesses." (Paper read to the 14th International Congress of Psychology.)
    Voprosy psikhologii, No. 1 (1955).
Leont'ev, A. N. "Biological and social aspects of the human mind." Voprosy psikhol-
    ogii, No. 6 (1960).
Leont'ev, A. N. Problems in the Development of the Mind (Izd. APN RSFSR, Moscow,
    1960).
Leont'ev, A. N. "Some long-term problems of Soviet psychology." Voprosy psikhol-
    ogii, No. 6 (1967).
Leont'ev, A. N., and Rozanova, T. V. "Relationship between the formation of asso-
    ciative links and the content of the action." Sovetskaya pedagogika, No. 10
    (1951).
Lotze, R. H. Medizinishche Psychologie (Leipzig, 1852).
Luriya, A. R. "The conjugate motor trend in studying affective responses." Trudy
    instituta psikhologii (Moscow, 1928).
Luriya, A. R. Internal Description of Illness and Pathogenic Diseases (Moscow, 1944).
Luriya, A. R. Restoration of Brain functions after war injuries (Izd. AMN SSSR,
    Moscow, 1948).
Luriya, A. R. (ed.). Problems in the Higher Nervous Activity of the Normal and Ab-
    normal Child, Vols. 1-2 (Izd. APN RSFSR, Moscow, 1956-1958).
Luriya, A. R. Traumatic Aphasia (Izd. AMN SSSR, Moscow, 1957).
Luriya, A. R. Higher Cortical Functions in Man (Izd. MGU, Moscow, 1962); Engl.
    transl., Consultants Bureau, New York, 1966).
Luriya, A. R. The Human Brain and Mental Processes (Izd. APN RSFSR, Moscow, 1963).
Luriya, A. R. and Khomskaya, E. D. "Disturbances of intellectual functions from
    lesions of the posterior frontal area." Dokl. APN RSFSR, No. 6 (1962).
Madsen, K. B. Theories of Motivation (Munksgaard, 1968).
Maksytova, É. L. "The evaluation and use of experimental data obtained from schizo-
    phrenics after they had the flu." In: Problems of Experimental Abnormal Psy-
    chology (Moscow, 1965).
Mandrusova, É. S. "The role of experimental research in evaluating cognitive disor-
    ders in children." In: Problems of Experimental Abnormal Psychology (Moscow,
    1965).
Mandrusova, É. S., and Raiskaya, M. I. "Clinical analysis of a diagnostically com-
    plicated case." In: Problems of Experimental Abnormal Psychology (Moscow,
    1965).
Marx, K., and Engels, F. Works, Vol. 3.
Meerovich, R. I. "Experimental analysis of the curve of working capacity of patients
    with manic and depressive syndromes." Sovetskaya nevropatologiya, psikhia-
    triya i psikhogigena, Vol. 4, No. 1 (1935).

Meerovich, R. I. "Psychological analysis of completion tendencies in progressive paralysis." Sovetskaya nevropatologiya, psikhiatriya i psikhogigiena, No. 1 (1935).

Meerovich, R. I., and Kondratskaya, K. M. "Level of aspiration in hysterical children." In: Mental Features of Difficult and Mentally Retarded Children. Vol. 5 (Leningrad, 1936).

Meerovich, R. I., and Plotnikova, E. E. "Success and failure and their influence on level of aspiration in hysterics." In: Soviet Neuropsychiatry, Vol. 1 (1936).

Meleshko, T. K. "Actualization of information in the course of schizophrenic thinking." Candidate's dissertation (Moscow, 1966).

Murray, H. Thematic Apperception Test (Cambridge, 1943).

Myasishchev, V. N. "Working capacity and diseases of the personality." Sovetskaya nevropatologiya, psikhiatriya i psikhogigiena, Nos. 8-10 (1935).

Myasishchev, V. N. "Personality and work of the abnormal child." In: Mental Peculiarities of Difficult and Mentally Retarded Children (Leningrad, 1936).

Myasishchev, V. N. "Mental functions and sets." Uchenye zapiski LGU, No. 119 (1949).

Myasishchev, V. N. "The importance of psychology to medicine." Voprosy psikhologii, No. 3 (1956).

Myasishchev, V. N. "Problems, techniques, and importance of medical psychology." In: Psychological Research Methods in the Clinic. Symposium Proceedings, 14-17 Feb., 1967 (Leningrad, 1967).

Nepomnyashchaya, N. I. "Some conditions of disturbance of the regulatory function of speech in mentally backward children." In: Problems in the Higher Nervous Activity of the Normal and Abnormal Child. Vol I (Izd. APN, RSFSR, Moscow, 1956).

Nikol'skii, V. N. "Types of planning and task performance by children who are difficult to train." In: Mental Features of Difficult and Mentally Retarded Children (Leningrad, 1936).

Obraztov, V. N. "The writing of the mentally ill." Candidate's dissertation (Saint Petersburg, 1904).

Osipova, V. N. "The psychology of complexes and an association experiment modeled after the works from the Zurich clinic." Nevropatologiya i psikhiatriya, No. 6 (1908).

Pavlov, I. P. Complete Collected Works, Vols. III-IV (Izd. AN SSSR, Moscow–Leningrad, 1951-1952).

Pavlovskaya, L. S. "The experimental investigation of young idiots and imbeciles using the method of Academician V. M. Bekhterev and S. D. Vladychko." Obozrenie psikhiatrii (Saint Petersburg, 1909).

Payne, R. W., Mattuset, P., and George, H. "An experimental study of schizophrenic thought disorder." J. Med. Sci., No. 105, p. 627 (1959).

Perel'man, A. A. Disorders of Intelligence (Tomsk, 1957).

Perepelkin, V. I. "Comparison of visual objects by epileptic children. In: Problems of Experimental Abnormal Psychology (Moscow, 1965).

Petrova, A. E., and Anikina, A. M. "The nature of working capacity in schizophrenia." In: Problems in Borderline Psychiatry (Medgiz, Moscow, 1935).

Petrova, A. E., and Anikina, A. M. "The role of experimental psychology in the determination of the character of working capacity in patients with idiopathic epilepsy." Nevropatologiya, psikhiatriya i psikhogigiena, No. 5 (1936).

Pevsner, M. S. Oligophrenia – Mental Deficiency in Children (Izd. APN RSFSR, Moscow, 1960; Engl. transl. Consultants Bureau, New York, 1961).

Philosophical Problems of the Physiology of Higher Nervous Activity and of Psychology (Izd. AN, SSSR, Moscow, 1963).

Piaget, J. La psychologie de l'intelligence (Paris, 1952).

Pichot, P. Les testes de personalité en psychiatrie (Paris, 1956).

Pinskii, B. I. "Diagnostic aspects of research on children's behavior." Voprosy psikhologii, No. 2 (1968).

Pittrich, O. Denkstörungen bei Hirnverletzten, Sammlung psychiatrischer und neurologischer Einzeldarstellungen (Leipzig, 1944).

Polyakov, Yu. F. "Properties of slight cognitive disturbances in schizophrenia." Candidate's dissertation (Moscow, 1961).

Polyakov, Yu. F. "Comparative description of cognitive disturbances in patients with early arteriosclerosis of the brain and schizophrenics." In: Problems of Cerebrovascular Diseases. Vol. 2 (Moscow, 1961).

Polyakov, Yu. F. "Methods in the study of cognitive processes in schizophrenics." In: Problems of Experimental Abnormal Psychology (Moscow, 1965).

Povarnin, K. N. The Role of Attention in the Most Elementary Mental Processes (Saint Petersburg, 1906).

Protopopov, V. P., and Rushkevich, E. A. Investigation of Disorders of Abstract Intelligence in Mental Patients and Their Physiological Characteristics (Kiev, 1956).

Rey, A. Monographie de psychologie clinique (Neuchatel–Paris, 1952).

Rodgers, C. R. Client-Centered Therapy – The current Practice, Implications and the Theory. (Houghton, Boston, 1957).

Rodionova, E. A. "Techniques for studying skill deterioration in mentally ill children." In: Problems of Experimental Abnormal Psychology (Moscow, 1965).

Rotschild, D. Senile Psychoses with Cerebral Arterioscleroses – Mental Disorders in Later Life. (Stanford, London, 1945).

Rozenblyum, I. I. "The comparative characteristics of schizophrenia and paralytic dementia. I." Sovetskaya nevropatologiya, psikhiatriya i psikhogigiena, Vol. 3, Nos. 2 (1934).

Rubinshtein, S. L. Foundations of Social Psychology (Gosudarstvennoe uchebno-pedagogicheskoe izd. Narkomprosa RSFSR, Moscow, 1940).

Rubinshtein, S. L. "Problems in psychological theory." Voprosy psikhologii, No. 1 (1955).

Rubinshtein, S. L. Being and Consciousness (Izd. AN SSSR, Moscow, 1957).

Rubinshtein, S. L. Thinking and Ways of Investigating It (Izd. AN SSSR, Moscow, 1958).

Rubinshtein, S. Ya. "Restoration of working capacity in patients with war wounds of the brain." Candidate's dissertation (Moscow, 1944).

Rubinshtein, S. Ya. "Assessment and restoration of working capacity after war wounds of the brain." In: Neurology in Wartime, Vol. 1 (Izd. AMN SSSR, Moscow, 1949).

Rubinshtein, S. Ya. "The reflex nature of hallucinations." Report of the All-Union Congress of Psychology. Proceedings of a Conference on Psychology (Izd. APN RSFSR, Moscow, 1957).

Rubinshtein, S. Ya. The Psychology of the Mentally Retarded Child (Uchpedgiz, Moscow, 1959).

Rubinshtein, S. Ya. "Methodology of studying sensory motor performance in patients suffering from vascular diseases." In: Cerebrovascular Diseases (Moscow, 1960).

Rubinshtein, S. Ya. Methods of Experimental Abnormal Psychology (Moscow, 1962).

Rubinshtein, S. Ya. "Study of skill deterioration in the mentally ill aged." In: Problems of Experimental Abnormal Psychology (Moscow, 1965).

Rubinshtein, S. Ya. "Use of the experimental method for studying psychopathological phenomena." In: Problems of Experimental Abnormal Psychology (Moscow, 1965).

Rubinshtein, S. Ya. "Experimental study of patients with diencephalous pathology of diverse etiology." In: Deep-Seated Structures of the Brain and Problems of Psychiatry (Moscow, 1966).

Rubinshtein, S. Ya. "Joint use of the abnormal psychology experiment and pharmacological treatment." In: Psychological Research Methods in the Clinic. Symposium Proceedings, 14-17 Feb., 1967 (Leningrad, 1967).

Ruzer, V. I. "The role of the experimental investigation in mental hygiene work in higher educational establishments." Sovetskaya psikhonevrologiya, Vol. 5, No. 2 (1935).

Rybakov, F. G. An Atlas for the Experimental-Psychological Study of Personality (Moscow, 1910).

Sagalova, S. R. "Some results of the psychological investigations of patients with cerebral arteriosclerosis." In: Cerebral Arteriosclerosis and Working Capacity (Biomedgiz, Moscow, 1934).

Sakharov, L. S. "Concept formation in mentally retarded children." Voprosy defektologii, No. 2 (1928).

Savitskaya, L. V. "Treatment effects on speech disorders in schizophrenics." In: Problems of Experimental Abnormal Psychology (Moscow, 1965).

Scheid, K. F. "Die Psychologie des erworbenen Schwachsinns." Zentralbl. Neurol. Psychiatr., Vol. 107 (1939).

Second All-Union Congress of Neuropathologists and Psychiatrists. Sovetskaya psikhonevrologiya, No. 1 (1936).

Sechenov, I. M. Selected Philosophical and Psychological Works (Gospolitizdat, 1947).

Sharashidze, G. I. "Effects of insulin and neuroleptic treatment on attention processes in schizophrenics." In: Problems of Experimental Abnormal Psychology (Moscow, 1965).

Shevelev, E. A. "Thinking out loud in mental illnesses." Sovetskaya psikhonevrologiya, No. 1 (1937).

Shif, Zh. I. Intellectual Development of Pupils at Auxiliary Schools (Prosveshchenie, Moscow, 1965).

Shubert, A. M. "Description of cases with disturbed visual-spatial perception." In: Prophylaxis and Treatment of Mental Illnesses, No. 3 (1938).

Shubert, A. M. Schizophrenic Disturbance of Intellectual Performance in Organic
    Brain Disease, Vol. 5 (Moscow, 1946).
Shubert, A. M. "Some special features of the disturbance of intellectual activity
    after frontal trauma." In: Problems in the Clinical Course and Treatment of
    Mental Diseases (Moscow, 1949).
Shubert, A. M. "Disturbances of abstractions and generalization in schizophrenia
    and their pathophysiological basis." Voprosy psikhologii, No. 4 (1955).
Shubert, A. M. "Schizophrenic disturbances of intellectual performance in patients
    with skull trauma." In: Wartime Problems of Psychiatry (Moscow, 1965).
Shubert, A. M. "Some disturbances of perceptual activity in a traumatizing situation."
    In: Proceedings of a Conference on Psychology (Izd. APN RSFSR, Moscow).
Stanishevskaya, N. N. "Toward an experimental methodology for the forensic-
    psychiatric clinic." In: Psychological Research Methods in the Clinic.
    Symposium Proceedings, 14-17 Feb., 1967 (Leningrad, 1967).
Szekely, L. "Knowledge and thinking," Acta Psychologica, No. 1 (1950).
Techniques of Experimental Research on Personality (Saint Petersburg, 1908).
Tepenitsyna, T. I. "An analysis of errors in a study of attention using the correction
    trial technique." Voprosy psikhologii, No. 5 (1959).
Tepenitsyna, T. I. "Comparison of physical and verbal classification as a technique
    for studying cognitive processes in vascular and other diseases." In: Cerebro-
    vascular Diseases (Moscow, 1961).
Tepenitsyna, T. I. "The psychological structure of ratiocination." In: Problems of
    Experimental Abnormal Psychology (Moscow, 1965).
Tepenitsyna, T. I. "Use of the psychology experiment in the study of the personality
    components of thinking." In: Psychological Research Methods in the Clinic.
    Symposium Proceedings, 14-17 Feb., 1967 (Leningrad, 1967).
Teplov, G. M. Psychology (OGIZ, Moscow, 1946).
Terekhov, V. A. "Mechanisms which regulate solution seeking (heuristics)." Candi-
    date's dissertation (Moscow, 1968).
Tikhomirov, O. K. "Cognitive value of a computer simulation of creative thinking."
    Proceedings of the Polish-Soviet Symposium (Izd. AN SSSR, Moscow, 1967).
Tikhomirov, O. K. "The structure of human cognitive activity: theory and experi-
    ment." Doctoral dissertation (Moscow, 1968).
Tokarskii, A. A. "The association of ideas." Voprosy filosofii i psikhologii, Vols.
    21-35 (1896).
Tokarskii, A. A. "On stupidity," Voprosy filosofii i psikhologii, Vol. 35 (1896).
Tokarskii, A. A. "Notes on the psychological laboratory of the Psychiatric-Clinic,
    Moscow State University." Voprosy filosofii i psikhologii, Books 21-35 (1896).
Transactions of the 14th Meeting of the Ukrainian Psychoneurological Institute (Izd.
    AN SSSR, Moscow, 1963).
Urakov, I. G. "Clinical features in patients with slowly progressing paranoid schizo-
    phrenia." In: Problems of Experimental Abnormal Psychology (Moscow, 1965).
Valitskaya, M. K. The Associations of the Mentally Ill (Kazan', 1891).
Valitskaya, M. K. "Psychophysical changes in mental patients." Vestnik klinicheskoi
    i sudebnoi psikhiatrii, Vol. 6, No. 1 (1898).
Vasil'ev, Yu. A. "Qualitative analysis of errors with the correction method."
    Zh. psikhologii, nevrologii i psikhiatrii, Vol. 4 (1924).

Veisfel'd, V. M. "Lawfulness in the process of memory impairment." Sovetskaya psikhonevrologiya, No. 3 (1933).

Vikulova, L. V. "Level of aspiration in oligophrenic children." In: Problems of Experimental Abnormal Psychology (Moscow, 1955).

Vladychko, S. D. "Attention, mental working capacity, and free associations in patients with dementia praecox." Obozrenie psikhiatrii, nevropatologii i eksperimental'noi psikhologii, No. 6 (1908).

Vladychko, S. D. The Character of Associations in Patients with Chronic Primary Dementia (Saint Petersburg, 1909).

Voprosy filosofii i psikhologii, Book 4/24 (1894).

Vygotskii, L. S. "The problem of mental retardation." In: Selected Psychological Investigations (Izd. APN RSFSR, Moscow, 1956).

Vygotskii, L. S. "The disturbance of concepts in schizophrenia." In: Selected Psychological Investigations (Izd. APN SSSR, Moscow, 1956).

Vygotskii, L. S., Samukhin, N. V., and Birenbaum, G. V. "Dementia in Pick's disease." Sovetskaya nevropatologiya, psikhiatriya i psikhogigiena, Vol. 3, No. 6 (1934).

Wallon, A. From Action to Thought (Russ. transl. IL, Moscow, 1956).

Wechsler, D. Measurement and Evaluation of Intelligence of Older Persons in Old Age in the Modern World (London, 1954).

Wechsler, D. Manual for the Wechsler Adult Intelligence Scale (New York, 1955).

Zalmanzon, A. N. "The basic disorder in schizophrenia." Transactions of the Psychiatric Clinic, 1st Moscow Medical Institute, No. 5 (Medgiz, Moscow, 1934).

Zalmanzon, A. N. "Structure and limits of schizophrenic imbecility." Sovetskaya psikhonevrologiya (Khar'kov, 1937).

Zalmanzon, A. N. "The problem of pervasive imbecility." Transactions of the Psychiatric Clinic, 1st Moscow Medical Institute (Moscow, 1937).

Zalmanzon, A. N., and Skornyakova, S. I. "The structure of epileptic and schizophrenic thinking." Transactions of the Psychiatric Clinic, 1st Moscow Medical Institute, No. 4 (Moscow, 1934).

Zankov, L. V., and Petrova, V. G. "The comparative investigation of the differentiation of similar material in mentally retarded and normal schoolchildren." Izv. APN RSFSR, No. 57 (1954).

Zaporozhets, A. V. The Development of Voluntary Movements (Izd. APN RSFSR, Moscow, 1960).

Zavalloni, R. La psycologia clinica nello studio del ragazzo (Milano, 1957).

Zeigarnik, B. V. "The understanding of metaphors or sentences in the presence of pathological changes in intelligence." In: Advances in the Study of Apraxia, Agnosia, and Aphasia (Medgiz, Moscow, 1934).

Zeigarnik, B. V. "Psychological analysis of posttraumatic impairment and deficit." Transactions of the Central Institute of Psychiatry, Ministry of Health, RSFSR (Moscow, 1941).

Zeigarnik, B. V. "Local and general cerebral factors in frontal lesions of the brain." Nevropatologiya i psikhiatriya, Vol. 12, No. 6 (1943).

Zeigarnik, B. V. Psychological Analysis of Postconcussional Disturbances of Hearing and Speech (Medgiz, Moscow, 1943).

Zeigarnik, B. V. "Experimental psychological findings in relation to frontal-lobe
    injuries." Trudy Tsentral'nogo instituta psikhiatrii, Vol. 3 (1947).
Zeigarnik, B. V. "The experimental psychological investigation of patients with
    brain injuries." In: Nervous and Mental Diseases in Wartime (Medgiz,
    Moscow, 1948).
Zeigarnik, B. V. "The disturbance of spontaneity in patients with wartime injuries
    of the frontal lobes." In: Neurology in Wartime, Vol. 1 (Izd. AMN SSR,
    Moscow, 1949).
Zeigarnik, B. V. Intellectual Disturbances in Mental Patients (Medgiz, Moscow, 1958).
Zeigarnik, B. V. "The properties of compensation for mental deficits in patients
    suffering from cerebral arteriosclerosis." In: Cerebrovascular Diseases (Moscow,
    1961).
Zeigarnik, B. V. The Pathology of Thinking (Izd. MGU, Moscow, 1962; Engl. transl.
    Consultants Bureau, New York, 1965).
Zeigarnik, B. V. "The relationship between mental growth and mental decay." In:
    Problems of Psychoneurology in Children (Moscow, 1964).
Zeigarnik, B. V. "Experimental investigations of personality change in the mentally
    ill." In: Problems of Experimental Abnormal Psychology (Moscow, 1965).
Zeigarnik, B. V. and Birenbaum, G. V. "The problem of conceptual perception."
    Sovetskaya nevropatologiya, psikhiatriya i psikhogigiena, Vol. 4, No. 6 (1935).
Zeigarnik, B. V., and Gal'perin, P. Ya. "Psychological changes after leucotomy in
    schizophrenics." Nevropatologiya i psikhiatriya, Vol. 17, No. 4 (1948).
Zeigarnik, B. V., and Karanovasaya, É. L. "The psychopathology of negativism in
    epidemic enchephalitis." Sovetskaya nevropatologiya, psikhiatriya i psikho-
    gigiena, Vol. 4, No. 8 (1935).
Zeigarnik, B. V., and Rubinshtein, S. Ya. "The experimental psychological investi-
    gation of patients in psychoneurological institutions." Metodicheskoe Pis'mo
    (Moscow, 1956).
Zeigarnik, B. V., and Rubinshtein, S. Ya. "Experimental psychological laboratories
    in the psychiatric clinics of the Soviet Union." In: Psychological Sciences in
    the USSR, Vol. 2 (Izd. APN RSFSR, Moscow, 1960).
Zvereva, M. V., and Lipkina, A. I. "Comparison of objects by mentally retarded
    schoolchildren." In: Special Features of the Perceptual Activity of Pupils at
    a Special School (Izd. APN, RSFSR, Moscow, 1953).

Index

D

THIS HOUSE
OF WOUNDS

Advance Praise for *This House of Wounds*

"An astonishing, totally absorbing debut collection. Edgy, disturbing and delicious in equal parts. Georgina Bruce plays with myth and horror beautifully."

—Kerry Hadley-Pryce, Author of *Gamble,* and *The Black Country*

"The stories in *This House of Wounds* strike me as both an emotional and intellectual examination of pain, from how it spreads and is passed on to others to how it can easily turn us into different, crueller creatures. Each act formed in pain leads to another, then another, and this makes for twisted, beautiful reading. Georgina Bruce is a courageous and compelling writer."

—Aliya Whiteley, Author of *The Loosening Skin,* and *The Beauty*

THIS HOUSE
OF WOUNDS

Georgina Bruce

UNDERTOW
PUBLICATIONS

THIS HOUSE OF WOUNDS

First Edition All Rights Reserved
TRADE ISBN: 978-1-988964-10-2
HARDCOVER ISBN: 978-1-988964-09-6

Undertow Publications Pickering, ON Canada
undertowpublications.com

PUBLICATION HISTORY

Kuebiko, *original to this collection*
The Lady of Situations, *original to this collection*
Red Queening, *original to this collection*
The Shadow Men, *original to this collection*

The Art of Flying, *previously published in* Mythic Delirium 0.2, 2013
The Art Lovers, *previously published in* Crimewave #13, 2018
The Book of Dreems, *previously published in* Black Static #61, 2017
Cat World, *previously published in* Interzone #246, 2014
Crow Voodoo, *previously published in* Clockwork Phoenix #3, 2010
Dogs, *previously published in* Shimmer #13, 2013
Her Bones the Trees, *previously published as* Her Blood the Apples, Her Bones the Trees, *in* The Silent Garden: A Journal of Esoteric Fabulism, 2018
Little Heart, *previously published in* Imposter Syndrome, 2017
The Queen of Knives, *previously published in* Bad Seeds, 2013
The Seas of the Moon, *previously published in* Great British Horror #3: For Those in Peril, 2018
Wake Up, Phil, *previously published in* Interzone #250, 2014
White Rabbit, *previously published in* Black Static #50, 2016

For the lost, and the lonely.

TABLE OF CONTENTS

THE LADY OF SITUATIONS

———————◉———————

I smash my face into the mirror and it breaks against shell and bone. Shards of mirror blister eyes, slice through skin. I vandal. I criminal. I—

Rachel, on hands and knees, scrabbled at a bank of sand that shifted and gave way beneath her weight. The sky thickened and curdled to pitted white tiles, became a ceiling. Rachel clung there, hanging over her body. Green-clad surgeons circled. Their hands were their instruments: scalpels, saws, forceps, vices, cleavers, needles, probes and clamps. They slit her middle and she burst open like an overstuffed purse. They broke her ribs, her skull, her pelvis.

Electricity crawled up the walls, sporadically illuminating a dark cloud that accreted around the surgeons, in the gaps between their fingers, in the aura around their bodies; a shape growing and darkening until she could see nothing except for when a white thread of lightning flashed through the cloud's arteries and veins. Then they had the look of magicians under a spell. They were conjuring. Her. They were about to pull her out of a hat. They were bringing her through worlds. Out, out through the door of herself, her self, the other. Not her, now. *Me*. See now, how they do it. Within this dark coven, brutal magic. Always a price. But they will make you. *Perfect*.

A symphony played, strings plucked and strained, music flooded the room. She became the vibrating vein of a note as it stretched and collapsed into another. She could go, now, and be music. But the body pulled her down; the weight of it, the ballast. She couldn't douse water, or set fire aflame, but this—this astral trick—she must do. The body grew heavier, grew stone and a forest. A long note unfurled and held the air and all the universe in pure wavering sound

the scrape of steel on bone

loosening parts

a bite at her ear, a sickening backwards rush and— applause. The roar of an audience on its feet.

Someone unpinned the green canopy, removed the bowl of flesh so Rachel could sit up. She got to her feet and they rolled the bed away from her. She was stumbling across the stage, she was falling and blood was pulsing out from between her legs, but it was alright. It's going to be fine, it's going to be perfect. It will be—I will be—a bright orb, an infinitely unpetaling rose.

The audience reached towards her. Flowers fell from the air. Saucers of blood sank in the sea.

The sea was cold and distant now, a greenish smear beyond the sand dunes, pale shapes through the rain-blurred window. Smoke leaked through the seam of Rachel's cigarette. She dropped it onto the floorboards, watched it burn away to ash. Was Diane coming?

A book was splayed open on the floor. Diane's? Rachel picked it up and put it to her mouth. She nibbled, then tore at the pages with her teeth, her mouth slowly wadding up with paper, filling her gums. She knew this book, had done it at school—school! The story was about a white woman who lived in a house, and a black woman who lived in the attic, both of them under a spell of a devil. But the white woman was so compliant, so eager to please, she burned the house down and set the black woman on fire, and put out the devil's eyes so he wouldn't remember the beautiful black woman or compare her to the pale white face that bent to kiss him now.

Rachel pressed her cheeks full of wet, chewed paper. Her fingers smelled of blood. That luxurious smell. Dried blood caked on long black stitches, sticky in the roots of her hair. Menstrual blood on hands and thighs. A smell that lingered under soap and perfume: a haunting of blood. She spat paper into her palms. Yes, I am the white mistress of this house. But no, I am not the anything of anything. I am the nothing of nothing. There's someone else, hidden away in the attic, someone put away for shame and fear. I've put her there, I've locked her away. She's mad, that's why, she's mad and dangerous and it was the right thing to do. The only choice.

The looping trill of the telephone ran bones of steel around her, weaving together to make a reverberating bell. She lay under the table, low to the floor, her face close to a little clutch of discarded miniature cars. Rachel picked one up and opened and closed its doors. Remember that? Remember driving through the desert, like an advertisement? Twisted metal mangled around a tree, fire blazing in the branches.

She was licking the wallpaper. The walls were bleeding. She was licking the walls.

She smashed her face into the mirror.

Again, again.

She ground her face into the broken mirror.

A plate of spaghetti in front of her, pustules of grey meat poking up through an oily red sheen.

"So this is what a billion dollars looks like," said the doctor-husband. "Very nice." His napkin tossed on his plate, a stripe of tomato sauce running down the white linen.

No more bleeding. No more blood. She was sitting with a carrier bag held between her knees, stuffed full of all the things they'd taken out of her. A womb, two ovaries. Fat, skin and bones. A plastic car, a chunk of ceramic, a silver bullet, an ancient prophecy. Feathers and pebbles, buttons, coins of no currency. Love letters. A roll of camera film, negatives ruined by blood and the light as they came out of her. And it all smelled of blood. And the food on the table smelled of blood.

She turned a knife in her fingers. Blunt. But stab it hard enough, through the soft hollow of a throat... Her own voice had come out on the end of a scalpel, a balloon of flesh all crossed inside with strings; my instrument, my only one.

"And cut! That's a wrap."

She was swarmed by people; they were dismantling the room, taking down the mirror, taking away the doctor-husband and the food, moving Rachel to this side and that as they carried things in and out. Rachel saw now that the room had only three sides—why hadn't she known that?—and the fourth wall opened out onto a huge hangar, so enormous she couldn't see the far end of it. Someone was at her elbow now, steering her away, and then she was in front of the director, who raised his coffee cup and said, "Ah, yes. Actually very good! Uncanny, really." He laughed softly to himself. "But your eyes! It was like you were really *there*. You know? Darling?" The director glanced around. "Do we have a doctor? I mean... a technician or something?"

He gripped Rachel's shoulders and pushed her back and down into a chair.

"Bend, bend your knees..."

He caught his breath.

"Fuck. I think I heard something snap."

The mirror was cracked and dirty. It clouded its eye to Rachel's face, so she was only shapes and colours. Where was Diane? Was she coming or not?

The punch of a blade through her heart. A knife-spasm of pain at her core. Rachel doubled over. It was as though an organ had burst, an ovary—a rush of blood flooding her hollows. But no, there was no pain. There was no pain. Just the ghost of her body. Its dreadful attempt to possess her. Ach, ah. My body. How I hated you. I wanted to annihilate you. Slice you away, you maggot-white and gross udders, you hairy seeping sex. Now look, you are gone. *Goodbye.* She pulled down her lip, stretched her mouth to feel the flesh of her tongue rising from the clutch of her throat. But it was all numb rubber. Remember your teeth in white graveyard rows, sinking into pale gums. Your dangling epiglottis, your tonsils... There were men talking outside the door. Rachel raked her sharp nails through the skin of her cheek. *Rachel? You... Just go in and get it, somebody. Turn it off.* Was there blood, was there flesh, under her nails? The mirror showed a spreading bloom of red against the beige and blonde. They were battering at the door. It bulged and splintered, flew open.

But when the men came in, they went out again. They came and went through her body that was a door. Through her body that was only a door.

"She's glitching," said the doctor-husband. "I fucking hate it when they glitch."

"Hmm. What a layman might call a glitch is usually some kind of problem with memory." The consultant gave a fatuous smile. Memory was the most difficult problem, he explained. Memory was a problem they hadn't quite yet resolved. It seemed there was a problem with memories, the way they crawled up and pushed at the lid of the mind, little fingers scrabbling away.

"Yes, I know," said the doctor-husband. "I know all that."

The men looked the same to Rachel, looked like one man, standing in a mirror. Why didn't they ask her? They could ask her about memory, and she would tell them, nothing, it's nothing—and that's the problem, really, there is nothing and I don't remember, and time has abandoned me, and I can't remember how, how I became those two women in a house on a beach, two women so very alike they're almost the same person, and yet each woman is her self, multiplied and divided, a mathematical problem of kinds—and this is the same kind of problem, it's the same kind of problem as confusing the character with the actor, the persona with the true self, but—she looked up, and choked. A word like a fish bone on the back of her tongue. Both doctors were appraising her. The consultant pulled up her eyelid, pulled down her lip, peered into her mouth.

"Let's get you *dreeming* again, shall we?"

And the world stumbled under her feet. The bodyguard followed behind, keeping his distance. Each time she looked, he pretended to be interested in something other than her: a flower by his foot, a distant flock of birds on the horizon. But after a while, he did look at her, watched her flounder in the sand. It felt strange and alien, even the sand. I am on the moon. The sea could easily be made of paint and foil. The bodyguard was stretching upwards, expanding, his two thighs like twin trunks of a tree. His bullet eyes swivelled towards her. Her voice would break the tension that shimmered between them, the stretched-taut trembling film of soap. Her voice would pop the bubble, diffuse his purpose. But she had no voice. She had only a smile. Vacuous and willing. The bodyguard smiled too: his mouth of crumbling yellow pearls. Rachel scrambled, tried to scramble away from his smile. But she was only scrambling inside herself; the body did not respond.

This had happened before. The splitting apart of person from body. The splitting apart of legs, the sharp push, the taking by giving of a hard prong, a spit of pearlescent phlegm, the ritual of possession. I—it was not I—it was she. Her memories clutched like human hands. Yes, memory was the problem; memory was what scientists had to overcome. Scratch it out with a scalpel. Erase it with lasers and a blizzard of white noise. Memories ruin them. Memories provide too many points of comparison. Memories give rise to dreams, and dreams give rise to language. Above all, you must erase their language.

"Eventually we'll simply breed it out of them altogether."

The men's voices droned. Bees buzzing among wildflowers... but when were there bees? Where are the bees now? What is a bee, anyway—only a black-and-yellow buzz, a furze of velvet, a searing red sting, the sharpness of a pin when my sister dug out the dark splinter... my sister with the black braids, my sister, yes, my sister sister sister I had a sister sister sister sister sister sister—

Her head span dizzy, smacked against the consultant's palm.

"Stop that now," he said. "Unbearable racket."

He turned to the doctor-husband.

"Don't be afraid to give her a little tap if she does that again."

I—I had a sister, whose black braids went flying in the air as she swung high and higher, up and up until she was a shape silhouetted by blue sky, the bluest sky that ever was, the sun a flashing fire in our eyes, laughter ringing from our lips like bells blooming underwater and I—

The men's faces peering in. *Goodbye.*

Poor Rachel. The urge was in her at that moment to give up being stupid, to discard her ignorance and know the truth. But a wall curved around her mind, the impulse was paralysed... the dreaming sea was still and shallow.

And the telephone was ringing, the loop of the bell like an endless figure of eight, swooping around and through itself. She picked up the phone from the hallway table, picked up the receiver and laid it down on the dark wood. It was hard to see, in the red hallway, with maroon velvet curtains hanging, and walls hung with paintings of women with their legs spread wide. Girls, really. Rachel put her hands against soft wallpaper. Pressed them there, as though feeling for a heartbeat. A gust of laughter blew along the hallway, the curtains parted, and a tall black woman emerged. She quickly disappeared again, stepping through another slip of velvet. Rachel followed, found her in a kitchen. She was standing at the counter, drinking a glass of wine.

"Oh, look who it isn't."

The woman's hands were beautiful. Long fingers tightly wrapped around her wine glass. Her arms, tautly muscled. Shoulders curving into soft line of neck and skull.

"I know you," said Rachel.

"Ha." The woman let out a surprised, sardonic laugh. She hesitated, shaking her head. "No, you don't. You don't know me. And I most definitely do *not* know you. Funny that, isn't it? But not really."

Rachel felt thick and numb, rubber all the way through. Her mouth was knotted up, twisted into a hard cord that made her voice strange and shallow. She said, "You're beautiful. Have you ever lived in an attic? I knew a black woman who lived in an attic."

The woman tutted and reared back in annoyance. "What are you talking about, an attic? Do I look like I live in an attic? You think all black women live in attics now?"

Rachel stood and stared. As dumb as plastic.

"Funny how they can cut out your entire personality but leave the racism intact. Fuck me. What the fuck, Rachel?" Her voice rose and sharpened. "What the fuck did you *do*?"

Rachel's fingers were tangled in her hair, caught in loops and knots. She was trying to untangle them but the more she tried, the more entwined and knotted they became, and the hair was being worried loose from her scalp, little globules of pale blood welling up from the follicles.

"You fucking shitwitch. Put your hands down. Are you still in there? At all? Anything left? Jesus, I actually hope not. I hope they scraped every last inch of your soul out of you, every bit of consciousness and spirit."

"It's memory." Rachel smiled. "It's memory that's the

problem we need to overcome."

"Fuck you," said Diane. "You're helping them. Fuck you."

Diane. Her name was *Diane*.

The mirror shimmered. The door shook in its frame.

A lump of pink flesh squirmed on the end of the surgeon's tweezers. A blue vein crackled through it, light fading to grey. The surgeon peered over his mask, watched it go still, stiffen, and die. Diane, Diane... they scraped out my soul. Diane I'm so sorry—but oh no, no, no you can't have her, you can't take her, there's nothing without her. Diane!

Goodbye.

No—

She's walking in a white desert. Her clothes bloodstained and ragged. Her feet shod in broken boots. A car in the distance behind her, mangled around a tree, swathed in flame. A house ahead of her, skeleton bones ablaze. To go forward or back is to go towards fire. To go forward or back is not the question. There is no question here, no direction, no travel. But within the roar of fire, there is a call. The sky is ringing, and I—

answer: *yes, I am she*

I—I—I—robot. I woman. I—can't follow the thread of myself any more. Can't narrate. I'm trapped in the looping of the telephone, in the infinite repetitions of a mirror. I'm on the moon. I'm dormant. On standby. Better than a woman, stinking bleeding oozing wanting crying needing, tearing out her hair, on her knees woman. I'm everything a man wants and nothing he doesn't. If only they could get rid of memory, the fingers crawling through the empty hollows. Then I would be—

I—

It's only one word I need to remember.

I'm smashing my face into the mirror. Grinding my face into broken glass. Tearing the skin from my neck and chest. Plunging my arms into the fire, climbing the burning tree. A vandalism, a crime. A breakdown. An apocalypse. Keep going until I'm worthless to them, mangled, chewed up, scrap. They're breaking down the door, but there is no door. There is no way through, any more, to me.

Their voices fall away but mine goes on. I wail and scream, I sing to God, I chant until I become divine, undying and eternal, diffusing into space. My atoms fall into the shapes of letters forming in your mind. I—I—

I exist.

And you—

RED QUEENING

Red Queening. A crawling door in her mind. *I rise with my red hair… and I eat men like air…* She hated the door, the way it crept and crawled like dirt under her skin. But this door took her deep, deep into the game.

What game? The game is to forget there's a game.

I eat men like air…

Red Queening. Proud slash of knives.

And lungs of burning chrysanthemums. Petals of flame falling from her palms. She was ablaze, a screaming rose, a fragrant fire—and then she bloomed, she blossomed with blood, a rich swell of it, sickening. She shed Neva like a skin, crawled out of her as a door crawls, wide open and hungry. Blood on her face and her fingers. Blood thundering to her heart. Oh yes, oh this… oh yes. A howl of hunger from deep in the woods. She was in. Deep and slick, skin tingling, biting her lip. Back in Wonderland. Back in the hunt.

The Queen's Woods went on for miles, some said forever. Ancient, twisted, gnarled and tangled woods. Riddled with mirrors. Haunted by doors, doors and other creatures, all howling and biting the moon.

I eat moons like air…

Aven ran, fleet and sure. Oh that feeling of the woods parting around her, a path unravelling at her feet. That relaxed, alert feeling as the beast uncoiled from below and warmed her veins. Pleasure, laced with an ache.

Deep and slick and fast and moving in a fluid dance, a flow of her body through trees, a flick of coal glowing within her thighs, a ribbon of flame rising and fluttering. Easy, certain of her prize. The luminous moon cast glitter on the ground. There was a cold breath in the air, a flicker of scent on the wind. A white rabbit darting under the dripping dark bush. Soft and voluptuous with blood. Rich with the scent of tender rose-pink kidneys and palpitating crimson heart.

She chased it through a little slip in a copse and found herself in a clearing. A patch of grass bounded in by tall trees, except for where the land dipped steeply down and where Aven made out a rough doorway in the darkness. A door, hungry and waiting. But there, just inside—there was a glimpse of fire. It roared up and Aven saw a mad heart, held in two hands. A mad heart burning crimson flames and dripping rich velvet blood. A long cloak hung heavy with blood, a face streaked red, a crown knifed into her skull, still bleeding. She held out her heart and Aven wanted it, a want so hard, so hungry, a tug of desire that pulled her forward, stumbling and drunk, tripping into the Red Queen's mirror.

Strung out and sweat-coated, tangled in the sheets. A fire of mirrors under the bed. Blaze and glitter of blood. Oh so many secrets, so many lies, all the dreams of her heart wreathed around her body. Cold as the sea, a grey blur of mist, salt-wrack, tangle of bones, skeleton dance underwater. A shiver of ghosts, feeding from her mouth.

I eat moons like air…

In the ghost-blur of waking, she tried to recall her life from before. That bright sister she'd laughed with, fallen down giggling with, whispered her secrets to. Or that man she'd made love with, but it wasn't love, it was something else they'd made, something that haunted her now like a dark phantom, clinging about her knees.

Dying is an egg, I hatch in the cup of a bell...

Oh *she* was there again. In the room, always there. *Neva.* That person-shaped void. That pod. A dim glow from the corner... she was slicklocked into the Looking Glass Pod, playing that damn game.

I rise with my red hair... and I eat moons bloody and rare...

Taunting voice in her mind. That's not how the poem goes, no, not at all. What were the real words again? Couldn't remember, couldn't think. Would Neva know? No, not she. When Neva came to live here, it was in silence like a cloak of night. And a white dress dripping with blood. Stab stab stab with the shawl pin. Scratching at her chest and arms with ragged nails. *Stop it, stop it,* Aven had begged her. And then one day she came back and there was no Neva, no ragged bloody dress. Only the sleek, smoky Looking Glass pod, a shadow seed planted in the cheap, gross carpet. And since then... had she even seen Neva again? Not really, only glimpses. Only fleeting glances at the edges of her sight. No, Neva was a smooth plastic bug, a pod-thing in the corner of the room.

All at once Aven couldn't bear to be in the room with her, with that thing. She untwisted herself from the sheets, washed at the little sink in the corner, scraped the sweat from her body with a rough cloth and cold water. Just... don't look at it. Don't think about it. Just grab a few things and go. Where? Somewhere. Anywhere. To the sea? Yes, anywhere. It didn't matter. This fucking world. Dying at the edges. Sick all the way through. Everyone wired in to that game, that madness.

The beach of ruins, washed in a low, terrible light. Pale sun obscured by a layer of dirty cellophane. Waves and swells of garbage as far as the horizon.

Aven felt the sickness rise. Why had she come here? Should have known it would be this way. The seas were all dead now, dead and gone. She stood back from the filthy tide, tried not to breathe the air too deeply. Knew that if she closed her eyes, the feeling would engulf her, and she'd fall backwards into an endless void.

She turned to go but there was something moving, a dark shape stumbling towards her over the clotted mass of decaying plastic. It was a woman, cloaked in rags, carrying bags full of scalvage. Ah, she was old, older than old. Surprised to see another here. Her eyes flashed with contempt.

"What the fuck do you want?" Spat the words into Aven's face.

Aven flinched. What was she supposed to say to that? She took a look at the woman's face. It was creped with soft wrinkles and coated in long white hairs. Under her hood, two furry ears hung limp and torn. What was she?

"You lot. You fucking *pod-people*. Playing that fucking game."

"I don't play."

"Don't be so stupid." The words lashed with contempt, her eyes sparking with rage. And she turned her head and loped off, past Aven, under the old pier.

Aven took a step after her. "Hey!"

The rabbit woman answered with silence, impermeable and glistening with hatred.

"Hey!" Aven screamed, her throat raw and dry.

Rabbit woman kept moving, didn't look back at all. But something tumbled from one of her bags and rolled off behind her.

"Hey… you dropped something."

Aven stepped towards it, kicked it with the edge of her boot. It rolled over and she saw its face. Tarnished eyes. It was a head, an Alice head. Its eyes were two slots, empty and dead. Wires hanging from its neck like a mass of veins. Hair wet and strung with weeds and dirt. Aven looked round. Where was that rabbit woman now? Gone, somewhere under the pier. Fine, fine. Let her go and leave her horrible Alice head behind... Aven crouched down to get a closer look. Recoiled when she saw it moving, its mouth twitching as though it might speak. A plump white tongue pushing behind its lips. Slithering down its pitted plastic chin. And then—oh! How had she not seen them before? Wurms. The White Queen's electric maggots. The Alice was crawling with them. They slid from her eyes and nostrils and ears and mouth, waving their blind heads at the air, preening their soft fleshy crowns and their shawls of skin and their little satiny feet, and their vein of dark blood running from crown to foot, under the milky flesh-like silicone. Disgusting things. The Alice head was infested with them, its face crowded with laughter.

Aven took a step back, repulsed and afraid. No, no, she didn't want this, she did not like this game. Fuck that stupid rabbit woman. Fuck this wurm-infested head. Fuck it all. She drew back her foot and kicked the head hard, hard as she could, way out into the Scalvages. Watched it tumble and disappear in the ocean of trash.

She went to one of the Eat Me, Drink Me places that had sprung up in the remains of the city. Sat in a booth on a red plastic chair bolted to the floor, got a cup of koffi from a machine. No one around. Never anyone around. Whole empty city of ruins and dust, could go for days without seeing another person. But still there was no peace. Everywhere she went, every room she tried to live in, it was the same way. The beds were all haunted. That sleek smoky pod soon appeared, a black egg from the air. And

Neva followed. In her bloodied white dress with her stabbed heart. A slow-pulsing fruit, dying in the seed.

She had to get away. Couldn't stay here in this city with these deformed phantoms, these wurm-ridden ghosts. But what was she supposed to do? How was she supposed to live now? And for what? There was nothing left, it was all gone.

Gone. Over.

Game over.

Fuck you all.

But even her anger seemed pointless. There was nothing left to get mad about. Couldn't feel the earth anymore. Couldn't sense that ponderously soft pulse. The magnitude of her breathing. Green jungles chiming and hooting and forests of eternal rain. Seas crowded with monsters and wreckages, beaches with tiny star-shaped sand. And the massive godlike mountains, and the spring carpet of wildflowers and in the summer the dry grass singing. Gone, gone now. How could it all be gone? Once there was a world and now... Aven longed for it again, for trailing her brown fingers in clear rippling water, pressing her palm against the rough bark of a tree, lying in the grass with her sister... their fingers turning pages in a book. All gone now, inconceivably dead now.

For this. For the White Queen's Wonderland of plastic and silicon. Riddled and ruined with wurms. Everything infected and broken. Everything pointlessly fake and wrong. This plastic table top. This drink of nothing.

An odd scrape above her and Aven glanced up— god*damn*. One of those horrible robot Cheshires was sitting on top of the koffi machine, smashing its mirror teeth together and laughing.

A heap of broken images, where the sun beats...

"Shut up!" Aven screamed and hurled her koffi at the Cheshire. "Shut up, shut up, shut up!" Grabbing at its fake and empty body... but it wasn't empty, it was seething with wurms, and Aven threw it, sent it smashing into the hard acrylic floor. Screaming "I hate you! I hate you!" over and over like a child.

She should go back to the room. Drag that egg outside, smash it and burn it in the empty street. Or maybe she should just keep walking, away from the city, away beyond the Scalvages and from all these ghosts. Neva was nothing to her, was she? Neva had already lost the game. That man was playing her now. Playing her until he used her all up. Slick-locked in the pod, sealed up so you couldn't even see the join.

That man. Echo. A ghost of a name.

No. Why think of him now? Stay away from him. Stay real. She had to keep moving, keep walking. Stay real, stay in the real even though it hurts, even though each step is like knives and her bones are weak and they feel like air, like she's disappearing into a needlestorm blur of pain... stay. Push, push into it. *You can take it, come on, one more and one more and one more step...* or maybe she should go back, go back to the beach, look for the rabbit woman, don't lose her this time, follow her and find out how she lives in this dead world. Or no, keep going, get out of the city. She was lost now, lost and aching and could hardly take another step when she looked up and saw she was walking into a dead end. A wall ahead of her. And on the wall, a Looking Glass pod. Horrible glossy egg.

She knew it was him, it was Echo. It was his idea of a joke, taunting her. Why couldn't she get away from him? Why wouldn't he let her go? And now she was struck numb with dread. Echo was a door, wasn't he? Yes, Echo was a hungry door that lured you in, that whispered promises and ravelled you with his fingers.

Go, go, go, said the bird —

She had loved him once. She tried to tame the moon for him. The mad hatter with mercury in his veins, with silver fingers dancing over her skin, gliding and diving and flickering and oh... the red, red rose, the burning heart, the soft and melting tongues of flame. She had loved him when he showed her the doors, when he prised open the folds with his fingers.

Is this what you want, Neva?

I'm not Neva. But yes, yes. Sinking into the door, slick hot deep... the door sliding and squeezing around her, molten heat that swirled and gathered, the coming of something vast and wild and timeless. But he was laughing, she could see his teeth that shredded hearts, and something else troubled her, nagged at the back of her mind.

Through the unknown, unremembered gate...

Caught in the tidal swell, like a moon pulled down into the ocean.

But even as she slipped through the door of herself she met herself coming back the other way.

Oh everything is upside-down here.

This is wrong, this is wrong, she told herself.

She knew then there would be wurms in the rose garden, white maggots crawling in the red folds of roses. She knew Echo was mad and a liar, that he'd devoured her like a door and that the slick crack locked down pod would be her coffin. Soon, soon. She was weak from running, weak from remembering. How many times had he played her? Always his Alice. Always, always, until he played her out.

Deep and deeper into the game. What game? There's no game. There's only hunger. Hunger like her insides had been burned out by fire. A hollow house, haunting the woods. Hungry for anything. The taste of blood or the plump fruit of a kiss. A sticky peach, a pelt clotted with blood, the plunge of a sword, a bite into flesh. Soft and hot and spurting with life… the ache of hunger sharpened her senses, honed them to a razor edge. She moved stealthily, deep and deeper into the woods.

Bloodsong, blood symphony, blood ringing in her ears. And then another song, a succulent warble, a rustle in the bushes—Aven lashed out with fluid heat and snatched the bird from the air. It died, it sang, it died in her fist.

Go, go, go, said the bird—

She whispered ghosts and roses, cupped it in the bowl of her palms. Still warm, the little heart's echoes palpating the air. Feathers soft and greasy-smooth. Tender white down speckled with flecks of blood. The crush of its gold-brown dappled wings. That quick fragile song of dying: a love song to the soar of sky, to the breath of cloud that tears the blue, to the tops of trees and the ground far below, all passing into mystery. Joyous death dance in its little skull. And Aven… oh yes, this moved her, this fuelled her. And she wanted its heart.

Pushed and pried and tore open its ribs with sharp fingers. But no, no, something was wrong.

Click clack.

No heart but a wurm. A maggot all firm and pinched into plump segments, waving its crown in the air. Mouth fanged and bloody. Crawling out of the bird's ribcage, looking around with dead eyes. A dark vein moving under white jellied flesh.

Aven dropped it to the ground and crushed it under her boot. The snap and crunch of tiny bones. Rubbery and sticky smears into the dirt.

A languorous voice spoke.

You do not do, you do not do any more black pod, in which I have lived like a heart…

What… what was that? She glanced quickly around.

29

The Cheshire was in the tree above her, one paw dangling down. Wide, easy smile. Glimmer and glitter of teeth. Then he wasn't there, it was just the tree and the sky behind... but the shape of him was still there, a shadow in the real. A scattering of diamond teeth and she could see him again. Somehow he was there and not there both at once. Aven found she saw him best when she looked up through the web of her fingers. A blur of dirty orange fur. Claws and teeth. And that smile.

"What did you say?"

Oh nothing, nothing...

"Tell me, please. I'm so hungry."

The Cheshire dug his claws into the bark and stretched long and lazy. Muscles moving under his fur. And the white flick of his tail dissolving away, melting and melting as invisible flames of air consumed it. Until only his fearsome grin remained, hovering amongst the leaves.

What might have been and what has been, point to one end, which is always present... Or say that the end precedes the beginning, and the end and the beginning were always there, before the beginning and after the end...

Aven didn't know what he was saying. His voice was a dream of bones. A forest of bone trees, skeleton tangle dance, lonely bone dance in the breeze. Clack clack clatter of bones. And that smile again, a little way into the woods now. Follow him, follow the rattle of bones.

Aven, Aven... why are you so hungry for hearts?

They were lying in the grass by the riverbank, books of poetry strewn around them and the sweet gurgle of the river running below. A tree sheltered them from the blare of the sun. Aven's sister was sleeping, dreaming, twitching like a dog chasing rabbits. And there! The white scut, the long stretch over the turf. It raced by and disappeared into a rabbit hole, down through tangled paths into its warren. Aven picked a daisy and brushed her fingertip over the tiny white petals and the yellow cluster of its centre. Squeezed the soft pale stalk between her nails. Daisies were her favourite flowers, so quiet and not at all brash. She pulled off its petals one by one, counting *he loves me, he loves me not...* losing count and brushing tiny white tears from her lap. How strange to count loves when there were no loves; she was too young and the summer was only just beginning. That love she counted was only a vague flutter at the edge of her mind, an echo from the future. *He loves me not...*

But when she looked up from the flower, a dark shape crossed before her eyes. It took a moment to see what it was, something so incongruous that her gaze seemed to slide away from it. Resting on the riverbank, a large shadowy egg. It looked wrong. Unpleasant. An alien pod nestled in the green.

A glance back at her sister. Still sleeping, sprawled among the books and the detritus of their afternoon, covered in blades of grass and tiny white petals. Aven got up carefully, and in her bare feet she ran down the riverbank to look at the smoky smooth pod. Even its smell was all wrong, chemicals and dirt, smells she didn't know. Put a small hand against its shell and felt something slide under her palm, some mechanism moving and clicking deep within. The shell of the pod popped open, and Aven looked in—

And then all at once she was falling, falling, tumbling through a black emptiness. She knew she was falling because of the wind that blew back against her, streaming her hair above her, she was falling like a drop of blood, trailing crimson... and she knew it would never end, this falling was all there was now. Forever. Falling through the past and the future as a dark seed flying through space.

31

Echo was waiting for her when she turned back. Leaning against a broken bit of wall. Watching her with a crooked half-smile playing over his mouth. She went towards him with fists clenched. She'd never get away, would she? He'd hunt for her in the past, in the future, in any world she travelled through. Hunt her down and find her out. As long as she was lost in the game and he wasn't, he'd always be able to find her and play her. Play her needs and fears and memories down to the last nerve. Until she was all burned out and her life was used up, every last sorry moment.

The look on his face now. That dead look. Cured of whatever had once made him real to Aven. Cured, she hoped, of whatever had made Neva love him. "Leave me alone."

I just want to make things right. Make everything right and beautiful and perfect again.

She flinched at the sound of his voice. Something wrong with it. That cold mechanical voice sounded somehow broken and scratched. She knew if she could see under his skin he'd be a tangle of wire and moving parts. And she knew his insides would be crawling with wurms. She could see them now, swarming and crowding and moving his limbs in strange jerky motions.

"Don't come any closer. You're broken. You're infested."

You loved me once. It didn't matter then.

"You're broken. You're letting those things into the world."

No, it's you that's broken. You're the broken of the broken world. We just want to make you whole again.

"You're a wrong door, a broken door."

I'm not a door, Neva, no no, not a door, not me...

"Don't call me that, don't ever say that name."

She turned away from him, walked back towards the city, not looking to see if he followed. It was easier going back that way, no struggle to get through dense lines of static that pulled and tore at her. Easy to walk back to where she'd been, the little Eat Me, Drink Me, now strangely full of people. Children! She wanted to go in, to sit among the children and lose herself in their innocent laughter. But she hesitated for a moment by the window, and saw that they weren't laughing, weren't playing at all. They were still and their faces were blank. And Aven realised they weren't little children, not really, no. Not little girls. They were too still, too stiff and proper. They all wore the same clothes, that blue dress and white pinafore, and their hair pushed back by a band, and striped tights and Mary Janes... and their faces! Their eyes were black and their lips were black and they stared at each other with dead looks that Aven hoped would not turn upon her.

They were Alices, mechanical Alices with their ghosts trapped deep within. Like Echo, the way he had become a copy of himself, a strange replica. And she—Aven—what about her? Was she broken, like Echo said? Or was she too real, was she sick from reality? She didn't feel real at all, no, she felt like part of herself was missing and ruined. She hated this day, this derelict city, the dread Scalvages. What else was there to do but hide, hide away and hope they wouldn't find her again until the game was over. Was this their beloved Wonderland? They could keep it, they could have it, they could burn it to the ground for all she cared.

She followed the sound of bones, clattering and dancing in the trees. Followed the Cheshire's teeth, sparkling and sawing the air, until she lost him in a ray of sunlight through the leaves that dispersed him into motes of dust and pollen. She glanced around, got her bearings. Lost in a deep and ancient forest. Haunted by wolves and bears and doors and mirrors. And hunger. Aven's heart, hungry and hunting.

She followed her hunger into dusk, and through the first

prickle of stars overhead. Then she heard noises, inaudible chanting and whispers. She slipped quietly through a little brace of trees and there they were. All sat around the table, the Mad Hatter with his knives and pins, the others with their claws.

Here is rock but no water.

On the stone table, the Red Queen was pinned sacrificially. Clothed in sheets of her own blood. Her crown a thin red line around her head, starred with congealed beads of ruby. Her sceptre a bone, dripping with flesh. And her dark skin sliced open along the heart-seam, and the rib bones pulled up and broken back to expose the dreaming heart within. Pulsing heat into the air around her. Mad, ablaze with flames of blood.

The Hatter lifted his head from his hands and stood up when he saw Aven. He waved his bloodstained white gloves in the air.

Finally! We've been waiting for you. We didn't want to start without you.

At last, at last. Yes, she had found the prize, at last. And Aven's mouth hungered for a bite of the heart. Her teeth ached for a taste of it. But even as she imagined closing her mouth around the soft velvet carmine, she remembered the wurm in the heart of the bird, and she knew something was wrong.

Take the knife. You can have the first bite. You've earned it.

"No, what's wrong? Something's wrong…"

The Hatter smiled in confusion and she saw a darting spike of wurm crowning between his lips.

But it was too late, she was too hungry and she couldn't wait another moment. She wanted to taste blood, to wear its crown, to be baptised into the real, with its flesh and its death. It was all she wanted. She grabbed hold of the knife the Hatter offered her, and plunged it deep, deep into her own breast.

Red Queening. A door that screams in agony when you play it. A door that bears you out on a tide of blood. Out of the game. A loser with a crown of blood carved into her head.

Borne out into the world again. The door closing behind her, Echo's uncanny face corrupted and riddled with wurms. She tore through his empty shell and tore out handfuls of wires and circuits as she went. All corrupted, all broken. He wasn't even a person-shape anymore, he was a big pulsing wurm with a soft fat crown and that dark vein throbbing under the skin. And Aven had torn through him, through herself, inside out and back again.

And now.

Maybe it was the time of ghosts, the time of bones dancing underground. Spines uncoiling out of the rubble and skulls popping out like cabbages. Maybe it was time for the dead to play a game.

She tried to break the pod with a hammer, with a saw, but there was no way of opening it, she couldn't even crack the shell. In the end she smeared the join with blood and prised it open with her own bleeding fingers. As the two halves sprang apart, it shattered into pieces, and Neva tumbled out, thin and stained with blood, as vacant and impossible as ever.

Aven picked her up in her arms, carried her out of the room, out of the building. Cradling her like a baby, whispering soothing sounds to her, kissing the top of her head. She carried her out to the Scalvages, sat with her in her lap like a clinging child. Whispered to her, whispering maybe, maybe... maybe there were others, living in the real. The rabbit woman, maybe, or others. There must be. Those not infected. Those not cured of reality. Real flesh blood people with real beating hearts. Whispering that there must be something else, that the world before the end still went on, and the spirits of the world still gathered in the holy places. She whispered that she knew, that she trusted, that there was something left of that afternoon by the riverbank, so long ago now. A scrape of green somewhere, a stubborn tree. There must be.

And Neva sighed, and pressed into Aven's embrace. And Aven was moved and stung with love, and so she made a promise, even knowing it might be a lie. She promised that after all of this, after all of the games and the viruses and the lonely suffering prisons, there would be, at the very end, a grave. A warm deep grave like a tiny notch in the wild green coat of the earth. And bones caressed by dark tendrils, and quick dark worms in the loam.

HER BONES THE TREES

The sleepwalking woman stepped from her dream of the apple and the bear and the rose. She stepped into a seam of light that split her head in two, a beaming noise that siren-circled between her ears, a stutter in the speech of the world. A curtain pulled back. Applause, applause. Their faces were smooth, skin like vinyl. Tiny cheers erupting from their stomachs.

She woke in the passenger seat of David's car. They were driving through the desert. Moon flood on the highway, soft music, slow and dreamy. David leant over and patted her knee. You really are something else, Laura. You know that? You wanna be in one of my movies? It's about a ghost. You can be the ghost.

The ghost-walking woman woke from a dream within a dream within a dream. She walked through many doors, one after another, until she opened the door to the room of her body. It was wearing a red gown, curled on a white bed, face slack and broken. She tried to fall back inside herself, she tried to push back in. But no, no, the body wouldn't yield. Not her body, no, no this body was all dead and wrong. Finger marks on her neck, her face… Her red gown was a dress of blood billowing around her, blossoming from the wound between her thighs, and the beauty—the *beauty* was no longer hers, but had spilled into the waste edges of the dream.

🏠

Laura wanted a language for dreaming, one she could speak with her hands. She drove David along a black snake of highway coiling through the woods. She carried a silence as white and coiled as a snake in her heart.

"I mean for dreams," she said. "I mean the only way you would understand."

David sat up straighter. "Laura, please. What are you trying to say?"

She glanced at him. He was frowning at her, chewing on a fingernail.

"Nothing. Just a different kind of story. Just a dream."

"Sounds like a messed-up dream, Laura."

"I guess it was."

Silence fell, and night fell, and the woods pressed in around them. Laura drove on with the radio playing softly, the headlights peeling back the night from the road. Through a winding tunnel of shadow, deep and deeper into the mountains and forest. No buildings, no houses anymore. Only the darkness buzzing with needles and sap. Finally she rounded a bend and glimpsed the hotel, standing alone and awkwardly in the looming shadow of a mountain. The car plunged forward through the narrow winding darkness, along the slip road, steeper and darker, until the darkness gave out and the hotel was there, ramshackle fragments of porches and windows and chimneys and lights. Laura parked the car in the otherwise empty lot. She shut the engine and thought she heard men—their laughter, their voices. But no, nothing out there except a chilly silence. Her mind playing tricks on her.

David slapped his knees and said, "Hey, look at this. Look where we are, Laura! This old place."

That made her smile. "Where else?"

He nodded. "Good to be back. *Watch out for bears!* Remember that, Laura?"

"Sure I remember. I'll always remember that girl."

"Which girl?"

38

"The *watch out for bears* girl. The one I played."

David smiled, indulging her. "Well, you've lost me there, Laura. I never seem to know what you're talking about these days."

"Oh, don't worry, no, just crazy actress talk. Getting into character."

He laughed, but there was a note of caution there too. "You really are something else, Laura."

She was, she felt it too. She was something else now, something strange, a shape cut out of the night. And as she stepped from the car and breathed in the cold air and the scent of the forest, she felt a physical pull, a tug towards the tangled darkness of the woods. Like before. Like it had always been there, waiting for her to come back.

Movies weren't real, and neither were dreams. But even her memories were strangely vague, floating free of their context, like dresses hanging in the air, waiting to be plucked.

She'd been standing at the window, her reflection doubling her, the lines of her face wavering, the shade of her lipstick darkened by the glass. Her hair messed up, floating round her face. And her hands... a palm pressed against the glass, covering Laura's reflection. She took it away. Breathed a pool of mist onto the glass, and drew a loveheart with her finger. An arrow through it.

"My heart won't stop breaking."

Their reflections overlapped in the glass as Laura approached. Lips crossed and opened. Behind them, in the woods, in the room, shadows moved, branches on the wall, taking shape like the antlers of a great stag. Shapes flickering in the glossy black mirror.

Laura said, "I dreamt I was on stage, somewhere I'd never been before, a grand and enormous theatre. It was a full house, there must have been a thousand, more than a thousand, but all of them were—none of them were real. They were those dolls, you know those Dreemy Peeple, those little plastic girls. And I realised, I saw them all watching me, and I realised, they were waiting. For me. It was the end of the play and I had to say the last line. But I couldn't remember what play it was and I was looking down at my costume, but it was just a red dress and there was nothing on the stage to help me, no one else, no props, nothing at all. And I just couldn't remember—and when I opened my mouth to speak, to try—it filled with ashes and soot and dirt."

"It would have been better if you'd remembered."

"I know."

Laura drew her fingers through the mist on the glass. She was tired, so very tired. It felt like she'd been working on this movie for a long time now. Living in this odd empty hotel that filled from time to time with a scene, with a moment, and then filled back up with silence, with noises from underground, noises from the woods... and why did she feel so drawn to the woods? But she did, she did. And she lay awake, wondering how she should go there, what she would find.

Laura picked through some dusty leaflets at the front desk. Not much going on around here. Not a lot to do. David rang the bell, *ding ding ding!* And a girl came out from the back office. She was young, fifteen or sixteen, maybe. Her hair was long and unbrushed, she was wearing a ratty t-shirt and jeans. Cigarette smoke and peppermint gum. She didn't smile.

"What's that? Can you help me?" David said. "Sure, that would be great. If it's not too much trouble, could you please move me to a different room? I need a room overlooking the parking lot, there are too many trees on the other side."

The girl rolled her eyes. She picked a key from the board behind her and dropped it on the counter. "We cool?"

David turned to Laura, raised his hands in exasperation. "Can you believe this kid? What kind of place is this?"

"Come on," said Laura. "Let's get going. You don't want to lose the light." She smiled at the girl. "He's making a movie about something that happens in the woods."

"Oh yeah, well, watch out for bears," said the girl. She was smiling as she said it, but not in a friendly way.

"Bears? You get a lot of bears around here?"

She rolled her eyes. "I guess. Just don't leave food lying around? I dunno, just don't make them hungry or piss them off. Anything else I can help you with? Okay, have a *great* day." She smiled horribly.

Laura put a hand on David's arm. "Come on," she said.

But the girl had turned her attention to Laura, and the look on her face was different now. "It's not just bears. Things happen in the woods here, you have to be careful. But sometimes you shouldn't be careful. You've never been the Woods Queen, have you, Laura? I hope you can this time."

Laura flinched. Why did she know her name?

"What's that?" David asked.

The girl sighed and turned her attention back to him. "Hey. I watched one of your movies once. It was so fucking boring I swore if I ever met you I'd punch you in the head."

Laura stifled a laugh. "David, come on."

She linked her arm through his and he let himself be led away, out of the hotel, down the steps. As soon as they were outside, he started yelling.

"That jumped-up little…"

"David, she was high as balls. And she's just a kid. Take

41

no notice."

"Call that customer service? What the hell's going on here, Laura? And what did she mean, my movie was terrible? Which movie? She doesn't know what she's talking about."

"David, come on. It doesn't matter. You want me to drive? You can meditate in the car. And let's just go and make this movie, right? Get those ghostseeds fruiting."

"The ghostseeds... Laura, you're crazy, you know that?"

"Loud and clear."

At the bend in the path, Laura turned around to look back at the hotel. The girl was standing at the bottom of the steps. She raised her hand shyly, a tentative wave. Laura waved back.

The mirror was full of shadows. That was all she could see now. Dark and darker, moving like smoke. Lately she'd been forgetting her name. She couldn't remember if she was Laura, or Shelly, or Audrey, or Donna, or Maddy... or was she someone else, was she a person at all, or just a memory, a whisper in another's ear. See how we are indistinct. How we all become nothing. We dissolve into mist, into shadow, we seep into the furniture, we are dust.

How long had she slept in that strange dark pod hanging from a bough. Maybe it was a hundred years. Maybe someone would come after her with a kiss. A *kiss, a curse. Waking is the worst.* She blinked and smiled at her reflection in the window. There she was. *There you are.* Laura, come on. She was always drifting off these days.

The telephone rang and she answered it on the first ring, as though she'd been waiting, but she hadn't, she'd picked it up in surprise, it was right next to her. It was cold against her ear, a cold wind like in a forest clearing, with the trees sighing, creaking, the soft plash of snow falling on snow… and David's voice, counting down four three two one—

He was patting her shoulder. "Laura, honey. You gotta see this."

She opened her eyes, uncurled in the passenger seat. He was driving them through the mountains, the sun sinking, turning the woods to amber and flame.

"The woods are so beautiful," she said.

"They're full of dead girls."

"That's a horrible thing to say."

"Oh no, don't get me wrong. I'm agreeing with you."

"Beautiful dead girls. Exquisite misogyny."

He hadn't taken his eyes off the road, but now he shot her an angry glance. "I wouldn't have expected to hear that word from you, Laura. Of all people. You know who I am, the kind of man I am. You make these movies with me, don't you? If I'm a *misogynist*, what does that make you?"

Laura sighed. "It doesn't matter. You don't know this story."

What did she see in his eyes, in that moment? Only what she'd always seen there but never named. Contempt. Anger. He thought she was crazy. She didn't make sense at all. He said: *you talk a lot, but you're not saying anything.*

She wanted to tell him to stop the car, more than anything she wanted him to stop the car. She wanted to be alone, to run alone through the trees. Lose herself in the woods. The tightening of her core, that pull, that heat. She didn't care what happened to her. She pressed her forehead to the car window, watched the sun burn down the world.

Thinking of the Woods King, thinking of his name—that was all she knew of him, just that, his name and what he was. It was enough for her to bring herself to bed and in the darkness imagine the sweet bite of his kiss... but in the midst of slipping swelling unpetalling—some thing breathed. She froze. Listened. No, she'd imagined it. Her own breath, caught in unfamiliar quiet. This remote place. Wet fingers, her thoughts running away with her.

It breathed again. A soft snort.

David. His adolescent fantasy. Creeping on a girl. Hiding in the wardrobe. No, he wouldn't. He wouldn't. Watching her through the slatted doors. Sick. Why would she think that?

She flung out her hand, hit the light switch.

Fucking hell, Laura! She was being ridiculous. Nothing there. Just a draft, under the curtain. The scratch of heavy fabric over the floorboards.

Strange how her thoughts had gone straight to David... but he wouldn't. He wouldn't do that. That was a strange and puerile fantasy, something he'd worked through long ago. Not something he would actually do. He wouldn't smuggle himself into her room and watch her, like a scene in one of his movies. Close up on her face as she brought herself off. No. The sound of his breath from behind the wardrobe door... he wouldn't do that. How horrible she was, to think that of him.

Nevertheless, she got out of bed and went to the wardrobe. It was empty, only some spare bedding and towels. She went to the window next and pushed aside the curtain. Looked out on the gravel path that led to the front of the hotel. Two figures were walking there. Their shadows fell behind them, long and dark, reaching into the forest all around. The couple walked, but their shadows moved differently. They fell together, wrestled and tore at each other's heads. Laura closed the curtains.

Watch out for bears, the girl had said. She'd known Laura's name. But did she also know that Laura didn't care about the bears. Did she know that Laura still wanted to walk alone in the woods at night? She did, she did. She felt

44

a pull in the core of her body, a physical tug. How strange, how sexual it was, this need and desire. She was afraid of it, afraid of being led away from herself, into the mysteries of the forest. Afraid of her own body. She took two sleeping pills and let them eat her dreams until the morning came.

Fragile white cloud caught among the trees. And the trees crossing spiky fingers against the sky. She was shivering, her bones cold and numb. She was to unfold herself from a shadow hanging like fruit from a tree. She was the first ghost and her revenge was something she carried in her bare hands like a fragile egg. Transparent and teeming with tiny sharp splinters of bone.

David wanted to shoot in the dawn light, to catch the crackle of frost before it softened under the winter sun. The transparency of her dress, her skin translucent, a beam of orange sunlight firing between her legs… that was the beauty, right there. She was barefoot, a ghost. Thin as a ghost. Naked now, always. Because her body didn't matter, after all. They had dragged her into the creek, a gang of them, laughing and roaring. They didn't even stop after she was dead. "The world is a terrible place," David said. "But you see my movies, they are strange but they are also beautiful."

She would unfold from the fruit of the tree, a dark shadow-flower blooming into shade. What would she be, when she crept from her cocoon? A terror, a fierce unloving child. An aching monster. A terrible thing.

David's face next to her face. "Eyes like this. Don't move at all. You're completely dead and no one knows or cares." He moved her arm a little higher, twisted it a little outwards.

She was sprawled on the dirt and there was a man on top of her. And there were men all around her. She didn't know any of their names. In the script they were numbers. It could be Rapist 1 or Rapist 21, they all took turns with her. This one rested his weight between her legs for a moment. He was heavy, stacked with muscles.

"Hey," she said.

"You're dead, babe. Be grateful for whatever you get."

They went again. There was blood over his white shirt. The others were cheering him on and then someone said the line.

Oh shit she's dead

A moment of silence. The guy kept ramming away on top of her. Then laughter. It didn't matter if she was dead or not. It was funnier, now she was dead.

"That's going to get them," David said. "Oh yes, it is. That's a real nightmare, right there."

Laura nodded. Okay. She couldn't speak to David at all in that moment. She was disgusted with him, with herself. But it was just a movie, she was being crazy. It was good he was doing this. Drawing attention to this... to... ah she didn't know the right lines anymore. How this was all justified, what to say so that everyone could keep pretending it was okay.

At last she was allowed to get up off the ground. She pushed the men, the actors, away from her. They were laughing, excited. David was watching the footage back, smiling, nodding his head. Someone—a woman—handed Laura a red coat and she wrapped it around herself. They'd been filming for hours. Over and over, playing the scene out from every possible angle. Now someone was touching her hair, dabbing something on her lip. She put her hand up to her face.

"Stop, please."

"You need to take a break, hun?"

No. She needed it all to stop. She looked around her.

They were in a part of the woods that led down from the road, where the trees were sparse and a thin trickle of a creek ran through. But beyond that, the woods grew thick and dark and tangled. She wanted to go there, and lose herself inside the forest. But David was calling her again, they were going to go again: he wanted everything to be perfect.

They finished and wandered back to their beers and their fire. They went away, they all left. She took a deep, ragged breath. And felt it breeze through her, cold air whistling through her broken insides. She got to her feet and felt her body fall away from her, like stepping out of a dress. It fell in pieces, slumped face down in the creek. She saw it was a body carved open and emptied. Defiled. Annihilated. Shameful. She felt so ashamed. She'd always been a nothing person, a no one, and now even that was over. It didn't matter now. It had never mattered. Had her body ever been touched with love? No, never. Or with desire? No. Tenderness? Not even a glancing blow. They kissed her with broken glass. Caressed her with knives. That body— worthless. She left it spilling its jewels into the cold creek.

But without her body, she was lost. She didn't know how to move, how to breathe. She was ghost… without form or substance. She felt she could drift, she could disperse. That was the impulse she felt most keenly. But she understood she was tied to her flesh by a gleaming strand of silver that rippled into her empty shape and dragged her to the trees. And the body still cried to her: come back, come back. But no, she couldn't, she never would. And so the silver strand wove the empty space around her, wrapping her into a seed.

She woke in the night, the covers fallen from her. Suddenly, without warning. He was in the room, she was sure. She heard his breathing, the sound of him rubbing himself wetly, quickly, a stifled breath—she reached out and slammed on the light.

Nothing. Silence. The room was empty.

The little light glimmered into the shadows. There really was no one here. But she could smell his cologne, his suede shoes.

She grabbed a shirt and jeans from the floor and went to the window. The full moon washed the woods in an eerie pale light. The trees stood out, glittering and frosted, and from the trees hung clusters of blood-dark seeds, opaque and writhing, each one full to bursting with something moving, pushing against the tough membrane of shadow.

One of the ghostseeds pulsed with light, and split its seam with a jagged scrape. From the tight pod unfurled a long stretch of soft fur and claws and teeth. Velvety silky fur, tumbling to the ground. A creature of some kind... a bear. They were bears! All of them. Bears about to be born from their hanging shells. Little girls with big bear heads and bear jaws and bear bellies and bear paws. They bore themselves out of the seedpods and stretched and limbered and tumbled around the trees.

Laura wanted to get closer, to touch their silky fur and maybe have one curl up in her arms... but they were moving away, into the woods, beyond her sight. She wanted to go into the woods, too. She felt no fear. Not of the bears, not of the stories. She didn't care what happened to her. She just wanted to follow that pull, that call of the darkness.

She would go. Now. No more waiting. She went to her door and pulled it open. Something was moving at the end of the corridor. There was the sound of running, something growling low. A thrumming of blood in her ears. And then she was there, the girl, huge and feral now, taking all the space in the corridor and filling it with her silky fur, her claws, her teeth. There was blood on the white ivory in her mouth. She spat David's watch onto the carpet at Laura's feet. All bloody and covered in chips of bone and scraps of skin.

She ran, her red coat flashing through the woods. Wet leaves and soil under her shoes. *The woods are full of dead girls.* She heard voices calling her back, men trailing her, hunting her. She wouldn't go back. She was pulled onwards, that tugging at her core growing stronger, more insistent. She kept moving, running into the dark dense forest, her heart thundering in her ears and her chest burning and her muscles aching—and she tripped on a tree root and fell, sprawled over leaves and mud.

Her heart thumped in her chest. She felt her pulse in her throat, in her fingers, digging into the dirt. She'd fallen into a natural clearing. She clambered to her feet and raised her head, and he was suddenly there, a shadow in the darkness between two trees. He wasn't what she expected him to be, not really. He was wearing a mask but it was a mask of dreaming. She didn't know him, only from stories. They'd buried the stories so deep, she wouldn't have known him at all if it hadn't been for the apple he held in his hand.

"It's just an apple," he said. "Take it, if you want." His eyes were hidden behind the mask, or she wouldn't have been able to look at him, so fierce, so upright was his bearing. The proud antlers that crested around his head seemed to tangle and weave in and out with tree limbs and branches. As though he wore the whole forest for his crown. The Woods King, his hands full of gifts. "Apples want to be bitten," said he, and held out the fruit. She took it from him, their fingers touching, sliding together and apart. The apple tumbled glossy into her palm. She snapped the skin, bit into the pale heart. Juice flooded her tongue, shone on her mouth. He reached out and slid his thumb over the flesh of her lip, then his own lip, licking off the trembling droplet. An almost kiss. A teasing glance. Nothing more. But it was the same as if he'd pressed his whole mouth against her and tugged at her quivering heart.

This was the forest, too. Not only the bare haunted pines with their ghostfruit hanging like seeds, pulsing with dark blood. But this lush place of deep moss and rough bark, green shadow on green shape, and *him*—he knelt at her parted knees, his hair falling softly over her thighs. And then his mouth was at her ear, and he told her a story. *A girl wandered in this forest*, he whispered. *And do you want to know what happened, when she met the Woods King? We made her Queen*, he said.

His palm pressed upon her. The bone of his thumb slid against her. A long ribbon of flame rose within her, a burning rose unpetaled her from below. The stars were dreaming, silver dreaming scattered in the black silken sky. And they rushed back to her, the stars, the dreams, her blood—and she came, back to her body, crying, weeping for all she had been, all she had lost. Not just her losses, no, but all of them, all—but here was the other side of the story and she was glad and grateful she had made it to the end, to say the last line. She sank into his mouth and he spoke her body back to her with the language of dreaming, until she was under the ground in the rich dark soil, growing roses from her fingers, pushing green shoots up into new life.

CAT WORLD

———◉———

My sister Oh and I go to the corner shop and buy a packet of Doctor Rain's Travel Gum. Oh wants Cinnamon Sour, and I want Spearmint Buzz, but Oh wins because she's older and it's her money. We run out to the back of the yard. Oh runs with her hands in her pockets, one hand curled around the Gum. I am never allowed to carry it because she says I might drop it, but I definitely wouldn't. We go to the railway line, where the trains used to come down. There's an overturned crate to sit on and a bit of plastic tarpaulin to haul over our heads. I say, let's do it at the same time, don't start without me. And Oh laughs and says everything with you is like that, you never want to do anything by yourself. But some people are just like that, so what are you going to do?

So we sit together and unwrap the gum at the same time, and we put it in our mouths at the same time, me watching her to see if she's going to do it right, and she waits for me, and I smile and say chew! So we do it together. And then we are gone, and I see her body falling through space, turning and turning like a brown stick in the milky galaxy. That bit is not real, Oh always tells me, but sometimes it's my favourite bit of all.

Then we are there in Cat World. Oh is all clean and her hair is in braids. I guess mine is too. We're sitting in the kitchen at a large wood table, like a slab of wood cut out of a tree just to make the table, and I say, let's do the thing. She says, I don't want to do the thing, we always do the thing. I could sulk but I decide not to waste the time and so instead I get up and look out at the garden where all the cats are stalking through the long grass. Let's play in the garden, I say. We could ride on the horses. Oh says, those aren't horses you idiot. They're swings. You're no fun, I say, but secretly I'm a bit relieved, because I don't want to walk in the garden with the cats. We raid the fridge and eat all the sugary yoghurts, and afterwards we press our faces against the window and point at the cats, then the gum loses its flavour and we are back on our crate in the rain.

I want some more, but Oh shakes her head and presses her lips firmly together. She needs it, she says. She needs it more than I do. She stuffs it right at the bottom of her bag, and tells me I'm not to touch it. I'm cold. Big fat plops of rain splash onto my head. Don't cry, Little One, says Oh. Come on, we'll do the thing. She drags the tarp over our heads again and I clamber into her lap. Her arms wrap right around me, holding me like a baby, and she rocks me gently back and forth. I suck on my thumb and say wah wah goo goo gah, and Oh says, hush now my little baby. She's a lovely little baby isn't she? Look at her, little diddums, yes she is.

Oh has to go to work. A big ship has landed, and the tourists have real money in their pockets. We want real money, paper money, not the stupid plastic money because it's no good for us. We can't buy anything with it. I'm too young to work, according to Oh, but I'm eight, actually. Oh is twelve, and she's been working for years, ever since the men came for our Mummy. They took everything. I don't want to go to work, but I don't want Oh to go to work either. I want her to stay with me and do the thing, and play and go to Cat World, but then we wouldn't have any food and we would die. Oh says we're going to run away to the real Cat World. When she's saved enough money, we're going to find a boat. There are some women, Oh says, who are like mothers. They are kind. They can help us get away.

We do our exercises. Oh makes me remember all the things she's taught me. Hit them in the balls, she says, and put your fingers in their eyes, and bite their ears. All right, I say, jeez louise, I know all this. Oh laughs and musses up my hair and says, just looking out for my little sis.

We drag the tarpaulin over to the side of the tracks where there are some big bins, and put the tarpaulin over the bins, so it's like a tent. Oh is pleased. She says she didn't notice the bins until now. Oh gives me the sleeping bag and my teddy, and our little bag, and makes me put the picture of Mummy in my pocket. I make Oh give me a lot of kisses, and I tell her I want a story, but she says no story tonight, just close your eyes and go to sleep and when you open them again, I'll be back.

I like the sound of rain falling on the tarpaulin. It's a good sound. Nobody walks around the railway tracks at night in the rain. I could light a match if I had one. It'd be safe, probably. I'll tell Oh in the morning: we can have a light when it rains, maybe a fire. It's very dark, but with my eyes closed I imagine I'm going to sleep in Cat World, in a real bed, with Mummy and Oh sitting either side of me, just quietly sitting, and a light on in the hallway outside the room.

Then I open my eyes and it's morning. Light's coming through the blue tarpaulin, and it's sort of milky and nice, even though it's still raining. I'm dry and warm, so I just lie there for a bit, thinking how nice it would be to wake up in Cat World for real. And I think what shall I say to Oh first of all, will I tell her about my dream or will I go and get her a cup of tea from the tea boy in Edward Road. She's quiet when she's been working, but she'll give me some money to buy tea and maybe some fruit. So I decide to get the tea first, and that's when I realise she's not there.

She's not curled up in the sleeping bag with me, or crouching under the tarpaulin, watching the rain. I lift up a corner of the plastic and look outside to see if she's there, but she's nowhere.

She hasn't come back.

I'm not going to cry, I'm not. I'm a big girl. I'm going to get back into the sleeping bag and curl up and close my eyes and dream about Cat World. And next time I open my eyes, she'll be back.

Rain makes the neon shine and hurt my eyes. I hide in a narrow alley, behind a giant blue bin. My stomach growls at me, and I think about climbing into the bin and looking for food, but I don't, because what if someone catches me? What would they do to me? Oh says they can do anything they like to us—there are no laws about what happens to little girls who live on the street. Anyway, I'm watching the door on the corner, where men are stepping in and out. They laugh loudly and slap each other on the back. Their eyes are bright and cold.

Smells from a nearby café drift up my nose. Bacon and eggs, hot greasy sausages bursting open in the pan. My pockets are empty. I check them, anyway, for the thousandth time. Finally, the door swings open and a girl steps out. I recognise her: it's Book.

"Book! Book! Hello!" I wave at her and she looks back at me, not smiling.

We know Book from the old days. Her Mummy was my Mummy's friend. They used to talk for hours, over the fence between the back gardens. Book and Oh used to play together, and I wasn't allowed to join in because I was too young and stupid to understand their games. Instead I used to lean against my Mummy's legs and listen to her talk about the government. She did not like the government. No one did.

"Little One? What are you doing here?" Book says. "Where's Oh? You're soaked! Come in out of the rain." She takes me by the hand, and her pointy fingernails dig into my skin. She leads me to her sweaty, perfumed cubicle at the back of the hotel. It is the size of a single bed and it's not possible to stand up in there.

"I've lost my sister," I say. I want to wail. I'm so hungry, too. But Book is very calm. She sits with her legs crossed on the bed, so I do the same. My hair is dripping onto the blankets.

"She didn't come back yesterday, or the day before," I say. My voice sounds strange to me, having not spoken to anyone for two days. "I've been waiting and waiting. Can you help me find her?"

Book looks startled. "I don't think that's possible," she says. She rubs her hands over her face, pushes her black hair back, sighs. "Girls disappear, honey. They don't come back."

"No," I say, making Book raise her eyebrows at me. "She has to come back."

And then I think, what if she's gone without me? Maybe she found the women who help, and she went on a boat, and she forgot me.

"Poor little thing. Hey. You could work here," says Book. "I'm sure if I spoke with Mr Cow— "

I shake my head, stricken with fear. I cannot.

"You always were a big baby." Book laughs. "But if you won't work, I can't help you. And if Mr Cow finds you here, he'll make you work. Trust me."

"Did she come here? Did she go anywhere else? Did she have any other friends?" I'm trying not to cry, but tears bubble out anyway.

Book shakes her head. "Don't be sad," she says.

"I can't help it." I wipe my nose and eyes. "Aren't you

sad?"

Book makes a funny expression, turning the corners of her mouth down. "I don't know," she says.

For some reason, this makes me cry even harder than before.

Book shushes me. "Don't want Mr Cow coming in here." She yanks up a corner of the thin mattress, and digs around in there, eventually coming up with a little plastic bag.

"Here," she says. "This is all I can do."

She hands me a crumpled bit of paper, which turns out to be a five-pound note. So old and used, it feels soft, like it might dissolve in the rain. Then she gives me three sticks of Travel Gum—Spearmint Buzz flavour.

"That's it, honey," says Book, closing my fingers around the gum and money. "You'd better go now."

Three sticks of gum means three visits to Cat World. And that's when it hits me: I bet Oh's gone to Cat World! She's probably there, waiting for me, right now.

I run to the railway yard and get under the tarpaulin. Everything is wet now and I can't get warm, but I have money and I could buy a match and make a fire. When Oh gets back, she might want that money for something, though. And she probably has a match already. So I just try to find a dry bit of blanket to sit on and unwrap my first stick of gum. It tastes minty and sweet, and reminds me I'm hungry.

Then I'm falling through space and I can see Oh's brown-stick body turning and turning, but it can't be her, so maybe it's me, or maybe it's just like the credits or something. This bit isn't real anyway.

When I get to Cat World it's raining there too.

I'm in the kitchen and Oh isn't there, but I feel like

she must be around somewhere, so I don't panic. I make myself some cereal and eat it, shovelling it in, with my Travel Gum wedged in the side of my cheek. Fruity Loops. My favourite. It doesn't matter what I eat here, no one ever tells me off and the refrigerator is always full of stuff. In the garden the grass has grown extra-long, probably because of all the rain, and I can't see any cats around, but the horses are swinging back and forth.

I look all over the house, even under the beds and in the wardrobes. Oh is very good at hiding; we used to play it all the time when I was little. Just in case she's hiding somewhere, I call out her name, Oh! OH! Where are you? But there's no answer.

When I don't find her, I sit back down at the kitchen table and look out at the rain. I've got this horrible feeling Oh's out there, outside, with the cats. That means I've got to go out there, too. Outside. With the cats.

But the gum's losing its flavour so I chew as slowly as possible and stand in front of the refrigerator, looking at the photographs held on with fridge magnets. There's Oh when she was little, holding Mummy's hand. Mummy's hair is all different colours. I'm inside Mummy but you can't see me yet. They're sitting on the horses and Oh is laughing really hard, like something is just too funny. I wonder who lives in our house now.

And then I'm back under the tarpaulin, and my bum is cold, and I curl up small as I can and try to think about what to do next.

Book brings me a cup of soup with bits of pasta floating in it. The soup's cold. She brings me some bread too, and I eat it all because the food in Cat World is comforting but it doesn't fill you up. Then she helps me hang the blanket out to dry.

She rolls her trouser legs up over her knees and pulls her hair back into a ponytail. "I love the sun, Little One, don't you?"

I shrug, because it's not exactly warm, really, and go back to beating the blanket with my hands to scare the bugs away.

"How's it going, sweetie? All on your lonely only, eh."

"I need some matches," I say, holding my palm out to Book. "Gonna make a fire."

"Ai! You can't make a fire here, Little One!"

"Why not?" I close my fist and shove it in my pocket. There are the two sticks of gum and the soft silky note brushing against my knuckles. "Oh always makes a fire if we get too wet, or she makes us run around until our clothes get dry again."

"That's why Oh always smelled like a dying dog, I guess," says Book.

"She does not!" I put my hands on my hips, and Book laughs.

"Chill out, Little One. I'm just kidding."

I remember that Book was the one who never let me join in her and Oh's games. She said I was too stupid to understand and then when Oh got mad she said, 'only kidding!' So, nothing's changed.

Before she goes, she gives me her jumper and two matches. "Don't freeze to death," she says. "But be careful about that fire. You don't want anyone to see it."

In the end I wait until it's very dark and raining again, and I build the smallest fire in the world under the tarpaulin. When I light it the space fills up with smoke and I can hardly breathe, but I get warm and I decide to go back to Cat World.

This time something's different. At first I'm not sure what it is, everything looks the same, but it feels different. So I take a look around and see what I can find. It's just that the back door is open.

The door has never been open before.

The cats can get into the house.

I can go outside.

With the cats.

I stand behind the door, ready to slam it shut if a cat tries to get past me. The horses are swaying back and forth. I can feel the sun on my face, and when I close my eyes, bright white blobs fall down the inside of my eyelids.

I hear voices that sound like they're coming from far away. Laughter, some crazy kids laughing. I smile. It must be Oh. I just know it is.

And I want to get to her, find her, bring her back.

But she's outside.

I could run through the long grass to the tree. I could shout loud, so the cats can hear me and get out of my way. I'm a brave girl. I'm a big and brave, clever girl.

So I pull the back door open wide, and take a deep breath.

But there's one, right on the doorstep! A black cat, licking its paw. It looks up at me with green eyes and opens its mouth wide like a yawn, and its huge teeth sparkle in the sun.

So instead I go upstairs and I climb into my bed and all my toys are in there. I remember my Mummy sitting on the edge of my bed. I think I can feel the weight of her, near me. She reads me a book, and then she says, time to sleep! And I say, no Mummy, just five more minutes, but she says, come on Little One. She gives me my teddy, the soft black-and-white cow, to squeeze, and I close my eyes and put my head back on the cool white pillow.

The little fire has gone out, and everything in the tarpaulin stinks of smoke. Everything is dirty and wet. Everything is cold.

I think if Oh came back now I would punch her in the face. I would claw her eyes out. I'd kick her head in. I hate her! She went without me. She's probably on a boat right now, sailing to some other country where she can be safe and live in a house and grow up, and she's already forgotten all about me.

Book comes and brings me half a sandwich and a cup of tea. She's wearing new jeans that are bright blue, and trainers with orange and red flashes all over.

"Mr Cow took me shopping," she says. She does a little twirl under her umbrella. "Not bad, eh?"

I sniff. I pull my knees up to my chest and try to wrap myself around the warm plastic cup of tea.

Book shrugs.

"Hey, Little One," says Book. She takes off her jacket and puts it round my shoulders. "Poor thing. Look at you! You can't carry on like this. You'll freeze to death."

I try to shrug, but all that comes is a shiver.

"Come back with me," says Book. "We'll get you cleaned up. Get you a lovely warm bed."

"Can't," I say. "What if Oh comes back?"

"Silly," says Book, rubbing my arms through the jacket. "She'll find you at Mr Cow's, won't she? It'll be the first place she looks."

That's right, I think. Book is right. So I allow her to pick me up and put me on my feet, and we walk holding hands towards the town.

Mr Cow looks inside my mouth and in my ears.

"What are you looking for?" I ask, but Book shushes me.

"She's scrawny," says Mr Cow.

"She's young," says Book. "She's fresh."

They're talking about me like I'm not even there.

I have a blanket on the floor. The floor is made of straw, so it's warm at least. There are about ten of us in the tiny, square room, all clutching our blankets. I thought I'd have a cubicle, a real bed, like Book does—but she says you have to work really hard to get one of those.

No one in the room says anything to me, and I'm too shy to speak to any of the other girls.

I wind myself up in my blanket, and try to make myself small. Sometimes the door opens and Mr Cow or Book comes in and wakes up a couple of girls. They leave the room together. Sometimes the girls cry, and Book puts her arms around them, mothering them. She shushes them and pushes them gently along. If it's Mr Cow, he doesn't say anything. Just grabs their arms and shoves them out of the door.

What happens in the other rooms? I want to ask Book, but she doesn't look my way. Besides, I'm not sure I really want to know the details. I know the facts—Oh told me all of that ages ago. It's bad, but you can survive it. It's bad work, that's all. It's the same work Oh did, before she left.

Some of the other girls cry, but I don't feel like crying. There's just this big dry stone inside me now.

Mr Cow says there are rules. He doesn't let us chew gum. He says it is unladylike, and the customers don't like it. The customers want us to be *there* the whole time. So Book goes around the room and picks up every girl's blanket and shakes it so all their private things fall out: matches and beads and photos, white sticks of Travel Gum. Book collects all the gum in a plastic bag. When she gets to my blanket, she shakes it out just the same, but I've already hidden my last stick of gum under my foot, and I stand on it the whole time she is looking.

"Good girl," says Book. She hands me the photo of my Mummy. "Don't worry, hon," she says, whispering into my ear. "I'll give you some later, don't tell the others."

When she's gone, I fold my blanket up and put the photo and my last stick of gum at the bottom, careful not to let any of the other girls see me. Is this what Oh had to do, I wonder. Did she use up all the flavour and have to go into the room and be *there*, the whole time? I look around at the sea of wide, frightened eyes, and one by one, the girls look away. We are not little girls, I think. We are something much more terrible.

It's not real, I think. It can't be real. Somewhere there is another me, a me who is asleep in bed with her Mummy sitting next to her, her Mummy's weight on the bed next to her. Maybe she is dreaming this. But when I wake up, it's because Book is shaking my shoulder, and her face is close to mine. I can see the make-up smeared over her skin, the little holes where it has sunk down into her pores.

"Little One," she says. "Come on, get up."

She smooths down my dress with her hands and quickly brushes my hair, then runs a smear of lipstick over my mouth. It's greasy and tastes bad.

"Don't be scared, Little One," she says. "There's nothing to be scared of."

"I've changed my mind," I say. "I want to leave."

"You can't leave. Mr Cow's looking after you now." Book fiddles with my hair, pushing it behind my ears. "You don't want to be ungrateful."

She presses two pieces of Travel Gum into my hand. "See? I'm helping you."

I throw the Travel Gum away, behind me, hoping it

lands on some other girl's blanket.

"Don't help me," I say. "You've helped me too much already."

Book grabs my shoulders and puts her face right up to mine. She whispers, hissing through her teeth. "You want me to call Mr Cow? I'll go and get him, shall I, and tell him what a bad, ungrateful little bitch he's bought?"

I shake my head. I let Book lead me out of the room.

She leads me along a narrow corridor and down two flights of stairs. I notice that the stairs carry on going down, probably going out to the back entrance. Book pushes me along the corridor, and into a room with a bed in it. She gives me a mean look and slams the door shut. I hear the lock being turned.

The room is pink, the colour of bubble-gum and dolls' dresses. I climb up on the bed. The bed covers are pink, too, and lacy and frilly. My legs don't touch the floor, they dangle down. I swing them back and forth. I have my last piece of Travel Gum in the pocket of my dress. That, and the five-pound note. That's all I've got.

A key turns in the lock.

I jump up from the bed, and run behind the door.

The man has long hair and a beard, and he's wearing jeans and trainers. He looks kind of nice.

He says, "Where are you, honey?"

Then he unbuckles his belt.

The black cat licks its paw and rubs behind its ear. It keeps looking at me with its green eyes.

From far away, I can hear Oh's laughter. Sunlight sparkles over the whole of Cat World.

The black cat stops washing, and pads towards me. It slinks around my legs, around and around, mewing and purring. It's hungry.

Oh says, you've got to hit them really hard in the balls, because that's where it hurts the most. You've got to use all your power.

What's power? I want to know.

She taps me in the middle of my forehead, then my chest, then my stomach.

I'm too little, I say.

Oh waggles her eyebrows up and down to make me laugh. Little is good, she says. You've got the element of surprise.

His face goes bright red and he doubles over. I might have killed him, but I don't want to stay to find out. I bolt out of the door and race down the corridor. I'm aware of Book somewhere behind me, screeching, but all I can think about is getting down the stairs and out of the hotel. I feel like I could take off at any time, just fly up into the air as I round the corner of the stairs, leap down the next flight, jump into the stairwell and land on my feet.

There's a fire door at the bottom of the stairs, but there's no one there. No guards, just the door. I take it in fast. No guards. No padlock. I hurl myself at the door, and as it swings open, an alarm blares out. It's too late, though. I'm too fast. I am off and running, running on my bare feet on the wet roads, and I don't stop until I get to a long street with houses, and then I duck down an alley and let myself into a back garden, and then out through the thorny bushes into the long grass beyond.

I follow her voice, Oh's voice, through the long grass. The

cats wind about my legs. The cats follow me and run ahead. Oh is laughing, laughing in that hard, silly, way of hers.

I bet she's spinning around and around in the grass. Around and around, with her arms out, spinning until she falls over, and the world keeps spinning her around.

It's all right, Oh, I call out. I'm coming, I'm nearly there.

Through the tall trees I catch a glimpse of her dancing in the meadow. The sunlight bounces off the grass and the flowers. She's laughing.

The cats run towards her, their tails flickering in the long grass, and I run towards her, too, fast as I can. But my foot strikes something, and I stumble and fall, hurting my hands.

I'm not supposed to see it but I do.

She's lying with her face pressed into the grass. Her hair is all different colours. The men have been here. Her clothes are torn and bloody, her skirt bunched up and twisted round her waist. There are big red gouges down her legs, red and blue inside and squirming with white worms.

And the cats sit a little way away, licking their paws and rubbing them round and round their bloody mouths.

Then we're in the kitchen and the back door is shut.

You're a silly, says Oh. You didn't see anything, really. She picks me up and sits me on her lap. There we go little baby, who is a little diddums, is it you? Is it my little baby? Don't cry, Little One, don't cry, don't cry.

And by the way, she says, don't stop running.

The sun is bouncing off the flowers in the meadow. Despite everything, the sun feels good. I hold my arms out and spin around and around, until I'm so dizzy I can't stand up, and I fall into the soft grass and laugh so hard it's like I'm crying.

Maybe she's somewhere in the tall grass, somewhere, hidden away. Like my Mummy was hidden, after the men came, and we looked for days and days, but the cats found her first. Wherever she is now, I know Oh is not coming back. And I want to be sad, but I can't, because I haven't got the time. I want to chew Travel Gum and live in Cat World, and lie down here until my body turns into grass. But I can't. I have to get to a place where there is a boat. I have to find the women who help. I have to keep running, because it's what Oh told me to do. Because I'm the only one left in our family, and I have to remember everything.

So I stand up, and brush the grass seeds from my dress, and carry on.

THE BOOK OF DREEMS

In the Book of Dreems, a dog is a friend.

Fraser told Kate the dog was in her head. You imagined it, he said. The mind can play all sorts of funny tricks. But Kate was sure about the dog. It was the only thing she remembered: the little dog running around and through her feet as she tripped, stumbled, whirled in the darkness. A long vague slow sick wrestle with wet branches and thorny bushes, and the little dog tumbling at her feet, whining and yelping. After that—nothing. A lacuna, a drop of darkness in her mind. As if someone had reached in with thumb and forefinger and pinched out a little of her brain. An absence felt in the centre of her head, something missing.

Fraser said, the doctor said, everyone said—there was no dog. If there'd been a dog, it must have run away. The doctor told her, strange things happen to brains when they black out. She explained it all in a calm voice. There's no damage, she said. It's common to not remember a traumatic event, the brain's way of protecting you. It's a good thing. You don't have to worry.

Yet there was an absence. A dark matter. A black hole with its chaotic corona, an event horizon over which tumbled thoughts and memories and intentions, if they drifted too close, got caught in its gravitational pull. When Kate tried to think about the accident, to imagine, to edge her thoughts towards that black lake, she lost herself horribly. She forgot. She sensed herself dissolving into the thick inky void, and was afraid.

While she was in hospital, the apartment changed shape. It moved through itself like a Necker cube, an optical illusion, turned itself inside out, doubled itself in rooms and hallways. Maybe it was a sleight of hand. Or maybe it was the twist in a Mobius loop, a different dimension on the same plane. Or maybe it was just broken. Kate tripped over its fracture lines. She walked into walls. She banged her knees on the table, trapped her fingers in the cupboard door, called Fraser to help her with the window that wouldn't come unstuck. She didn't know what to do with herself.

"Bed," said Fraser. He put an arm around her and walked her to the bedroom, pulled back the bedcovers for her, tucked her in like a child. It made him seem somehow fatherly, a thought that hadn't occurred to Kate before, despite their age difference, his forty-seven years against her twenty-two. But then, she hadn't known her father, so how could she compare? Fraser was so certain, so sure of himself and his place in the world. She was grateful for that, for everything he did for her. She wanted to be reassured by him, by his calm presence and the touch of his hand. But his fingers felt hard and cold, strangely repulsive. She thought they'd argued, before the accident. Had they? She remembered anger darkening Fraser's face, and something dark and wet slithering from his mouth, some black fluid leaking from his eyes and nose—but that couldn't be right, that was her broken brain talking. She drew his hand to her lips, forced herself to kiss his palm, though it felt waxy and stiff. Everything was a little strange, it was normal for things to be strange, when you'd been concussed. That's all it was, she told herself. She put his hand down on the bed, carefully, like it was a valuable object.

"What did we fight about? Before the accident, I mean. I can't remember."

"We didn't fight," Fraser said. "We never fight."

"Was it something to do with the program? Something to do with… those things?"

"The Dreemy Peeple?"

Kate hated them, those dolls or robots or whatever they were. She never told him that outright, but she did. She hated them. They frightened her.

Fraser smiled. That smile of his. "Sweetie, we didn't argue. Actually, we talked about going to the moon."

"Oh. But—I don't *think* I want to go to the moon…" She had to be so careful, when she disagreed, not to hurt his feelings. He was a very sensitive man. And he'd been under so much pressure lately, she didn't want to upset him.

"I know, my love. I know that now." He smiled sweetly. "I'll be a while, okay? Some emails I need to send. Sort out some glitches. Hate those glitches." He leaned down to kiss her. She kissed him back, tried to draw him into the kiss. But his lips were cold and rubbery, she didn't know how to kiss his lips when they felt so lifeless and numb. And he broke away. "You need your sleep."

"I'm not tired."

"I won't be long."

"Fraser?"

"What?" He stood in the doorway, waiting for her to speak, his hand on the light switch.

"What happened? I can't remember anything."

"Nothing happened. Go to sleep." He left the room, turning out the light and closing the door behind him. The darkness felt heavy, pressing down on her. What did he mean, *nothing happened?* Why wouldn't he tell her anything? How could he just leave her in the dark? It wasn't like him, she thought. Or maybe it was like him. She tried to remember Fraser, what he was like. She knew she was being strange. He was right there, in the other room, working. But it was strange, it felt like he'd gone. Oh, but she was being ridiculous. Fraser was Fraser. It was Kate who was wrong. Of course. Even before the accident, she had a terrible habit of being wrong.

When she woke in the early hours, Fraser had come to bed. He was sleeping, lying straight and neat as a pin. Distant, almost alien in his composure. His eyes were closed but Kate suspected he was awake deep down. Awake somewhere inside himself. Maybe she could speak to him in the middle of the night. The real Fraser. Her love. She thought about loving him. Her body flooding with love for him. A stomach lurch, an electric jolt, a shiver when she thought of him. The real Fraser, not the strange one who brought her home today, who slept here like an empty doll of himself. Where was he? Could she wake him? Bring him back? She stroked the inside of his elbow, glanced her lips over his shoulder. Whispered. *Wake up. Kiss me. Touch me.* But he was gone. His breathing was regular, so harsh and monotonous it sounded machine-like. He lay completely still, his wanting self hidden away somewhere, inside another dream. Kate sighed and rolled away from him onto her back. She closed her eyes. *I want you to touch me. Not you. I want the real Fraser.* Why wouldn't he wake up? Where was he? It was as though he'd vanished, disappeared so completely she thought she must have imagined him, he had never been real in the first place. And still she couldn't bear it—the absence of his mouth, his hands, his hair in her hands, his tongue around her tongue—she couldn't bear the absence of him, and she didn't understand. He hadn't gone anywhere. He was there, right there beside her. But untouchable. As cold and distant as the moon.

Fraser left for the moon the next morning. He put the apartment keys on the bedside table, next to Kate's head. "I don't want you to dream anymore," he said. "While I'm gone, I want you to learn to stop dreaming. I hate it when you dream. It's so loud. It keeps me awake, and I need my sleep. I need to be on top of my game. You understand? No more dreams from now on." He kissed her cheek. "I'll call you from the moon."

It was a plane to Florida and then a shuttle to the Moon Unit Hotel and Resort. A long, long journey. Kate went back to sleep after he left, woke up in the early afternoon, in a panic, knowing she had defied him and dreamed something, not knowing what the dream was, but something she shouldn't have dreamed, something illegal. He wouldn't know, it would be okay, he couldn't possibly know. She was worried, though. She didn't know how to stop her dreams. They just came, or not, regardless of what Kate wanted. He must have been joking, she thought. He must know you can't stop dreams. He had a strange sense of humour at times.

She wandered around the apartment, Fraser's keys in her dressing gown pocket, swinging against her thigh as she walked. The apartment was definitely different from how she remembered. It was the weirdest feeling. Brain damage. That inky black lake in the centre of her head, sucking at her memories. It had taken them, taken the other rooms, the staircases and hallways. She didn't even know what the apartment was supposed to look like. It was as though she'd never been there before. Rooms upon rooms, and rooms within rooms. Some of the doors were locked. But there was a key for every door on Fraser's key ring, and she opened them all, one by one, to see what was inside. They were just ordinary rooms. Bedrooms, bathrooms, sitting rooms. A library. She spent some time in there, trying to read a book that kept all its secrets from her. She could barely even read the words, they were so faint on the page, broken whispers from another story. It was unsettling and she put the book away, and left the library. She came back to the living room, curled up on the sofa in front of the television. She didn't want to go to bed in case Fraser called—he'd been travelling all day and night, it would be awful of her not to be awake when he found a moment to call. She sat upright on the sofa, biting the inside of her cheek to stop herself from sleeping.

When Fraser called, she answered on the first ring. She needn't have worried. He was in one of his tender moods, tired and tender, and she wondered why he couldn't always be this way with her. He said he missed her. He wished she had come to the moon with him. She promised him she would, one day. Next time. But she was lying—she was afraid of going to the moon, afraid of the shuttle, afraid the oxygen shields would fail, afraid of the Dreemy Peeple that wandered the hotel, served drinks in the bar, made the beds, waited tables. They were everywhere. In Fraser's room. She could see one behind him, a Dreemy Peep slumped over his bed, wires spilling out of its back. Broken. Its arms were dislocated and hanging from its shoulders. Its legs popped out at the hips. A strange misshapen thing. Its head was turned towards the screen and when Fraser moved aside, Kate got a glimpse of its face, a dented and torn raggedy hole in the plastic at its temple. It reminded her of someone, but she couldn't think who.

"I should have stayed," Fraser said. His image crackled over the screen. "You could be up to anything. Plotting, scheming, planning my downfall."

"Oh that's all I do, all day long." Kate smiled.

"Don't laugh at me."

"I'm not. I'm sorry. It was just a silly joke."

"Yes it's so funny. Your husband far from home, you think you can do anything you want. Don't be like those other bitches, Kate. Don't be a typical bitch girl. You're better than that."

There was the sound of popping plastic and synthetic voices from Fraser's room. The Dreemy Peep slumped over the bed was twitching and twisting, speaking in a strangulated blur of static. Kate tried to hear what it was saying, but it was too faint, too weirdly spoken, stuttering out of its wires and speakers. She thought she saw a glaze of despair in its eyes as they shuttered forward in its head. She must have imagined it. But Fraser had turned and seen the Dreemy Peep too.

"Glitches!" He screamed. "Hate these fucking glitches. I better go. Sleep time for you. And no more dreaming, don't forget." He signed off before she could ask if he was joking.

Kate turned the television on again. That stupid advertisement for Doctor Rain's Travel Gum. With the cartoon dog that ran around farting rainbows and singing.

When you're lonely and in pain
Make a call to Doctor Rain!
Chewchewchew! No longer blue!
Doctor Rain is here for yoooooooooou!

Kate couldn't figure out what the dog had to do with the jingle or even with the gum. Dogs like to chew things, she guessed. And they're happy. Or was the dog supposed to be Doctor Rain? It didn't make any sense. But there was something she quite liked about that little dog. The sweet way it bounced around, a silver key dangling from its collar. The way it winked at her, at the end of the advert. Its stupid, cute little face.

The advert ended and the screen went black, then gradually broke into a buzzing static blur. Rain, torrential rain. A little copse of trees and bushes, a deep wet green, water dripping from the branches and tips of the leaves. And under one of the bushes, a woman, naked, curled up in the wet soil. Blood poured from a cut on her head. Kate put a hand to her temple, felt the tender wound tied up with wiry stitches. On the screen, a boot swung towards the woman's face, smashed into her cheekbone. A caption flashed up: THROUGH THE NIGHT DOOR. Kate grabbed the remote control and turned the television off. She felt sick. She didn't like to see that kind of thing. But she was fine. She was fine. Maybe she was dreaming. It was so late. She should go to bed. Bed was the best place for her now.

Sleep. No dreaming.

But in the hallway, she lost her bearings. Somehow, impossibly, she walked the wrong way from the living room to the bedroom. She turned herself around in circles, not knowing which way to go next. The long, doorless hallway kept taking her around corners, tighter and smaller corners, until she found herself at the foot of a little wooden staircase that led up to a hatch in the ceiling which led… she had no idea where it led. She'd never been in this part of the apartment before. Not that she could remember. It was cramped and close at the foot of the stair, claustrophobically trapped by the angle of the corners that spiralled around it. So she went up. Up the little wooden stairs. Through the hatch. She climbed out into a kitchen, crawled out from underneath a table in the middle of the room. The only light came through the window over the sink. Kate could see it was twilight and raining. It was strange, so strange. She had a memory of this place. Like she'd been here before. All so familiar: the cheap wooden table, the photographs stuck to the fridge. Kate knew those people, the people in the photographs. But she couldn't place them, couldn't think of their names. Friends? Family? Was that… someone she knew? But the longer she looked at them, the stranger they began to seem to her. Their skin, their faces: they looked wrong, too smooth, too shiny and stiff. Looking at them made her anxious. She wanted to open the back door, to let some air into the room. She reached up above the door frame and felt around until she put her fingers on the key she knew would be there.

The door opened into an overgrown garden. A sea of green, swaying and dipping in the rain. The water pummelled against her, soaking her through to the skin. Cold, shivery… and something not quite right. There was something out there with her. Something that crawled and mewled piteously under the bushes. A bloodied, moonstruck thing. Smashed in and broken. She was terrified of it, terrified and ashamed. She turned back to the door, but the door was gone, the house was gone. The light in the garden was failing, the rain coming down harder than before, and the moon drifted out from behind trees. A white eye staring down at Kate, transfixing her, pinning her to the spot. She wanted to move, to turn and run, but the next thing she felt was her knees buckling as she was hit from behind, a mud-caked black boot travelling towards her head.

The moon opened Kate. Traversed her. Translated her. Broke and rewrote her. Her face stretched out, the bones snapped and splintered, a sensation of her whole self being pulled forward, through her mouth. Her hands shrivelled, fingers melted together. The moon churned through her, a hundred new smells, her milk-sweet mother running in the grass between trees, in night's glamour, fresh cold rain dripping from leaves. The moon roared, it sawed through her, turned her inside out and silver bright. She tried to beg forgiveness but she'd forgotten the moon's language. It was a prising apart of dimensions, it was two knives scraping each other to death. It was a whispering rustling creature in the leaves. She spoke but her words came out stripped of meaning, in strings of saliva and bile, she spat and retched words into the dirt, and they crawled away like blind white maggots, and burrowed into the soil. She forgot the language of her own self, and when she cried, it was the whimper of a beaten dog.

Alone, alone, she was a creature hiding in the woods, in the cold rain, in the sharp grass and velvet-soft moss, not knowing herself at all. Lost in the dark spaces between things. But a voice spoke in her ear, spoke without meaning, and he was there, he was with her. And she was glad, she wanted him there. More than anything. Yes. She clung to him, wild panic let loose. Come back, he ordered her. Stop dreeming. He made the world for her again, pulled shapes from the darkness and built walls for her to live in. He covered her body with his own, held her down, crammed her into a person shape, pushing and moulding her body until it made sense again. He traced words against her skin, speaking in tongues, sharp tooth, soft lip, a fluid language that flowed inside her. He pressed his fingers to her, where she was tangled and wet, slipped and stroked inside. It was an entanglement of mouths, tongues, lips, it was a summoning, a gathering spell, bringing her into herself. She clung to his neck, breathing in the smell of his skin, his realness. (But how was he there? How had he returned from the moon so quickly? No, no, never mind that. Don't doubt him. Don't fear.) Yes, he was so real. And the bed was real, the room was real, everything was real and really there. It had never gone away. She had never gone away. Only… maybe, maybe she had slipped, wandered a little too near that black lake of forgetting, the dark lacuna in the centre of her mind. She was afraid, but Fraser loved her, was loving her, holding her in the world with his own hands.

Yet his tenderness was a passing thing. He unpeeled her arms from around his neck. "Turn over," he said. He gripped her wrists and pinned her out across the bed, her face pressed into the pillows. "Do as I tell you," he whispered. "I have to fix this one little glitch."

She couldn't move if she wanted to. She was frozen in place, as passive and inert as one of those terrible Dreemy Peeple dolls. And yet he was making her feel so real. So much more real than she was in that other place, with the rain and the dirt. The hallucination or whatever it was, the way her body had changed, turned inside out. That wasn't real. But this was. This felt so real. Painfully real. So real it hurt. He levered her open at the seam, pierced her with stiff fingers.

"You've been dreeming, Kate. What did I tell you about dreeming?"

She whispered, "I'm sorry. I'm so sorry."

"How can I trust you now? You're just like all the others, aren't you? Admit it."

No, no. Sorry. Please. How could he doubt her, after everything? But all his softness had leached away, into the darkness, into some other realm of himself. He was rigid and furious. He stabbed at something inside her, popped something in her back. She felt her wiring spilling out, pulled out in Fraser's hands. He wrenched her arms and legs from their sockets, made her a strange broken shape.

"No more dreeming. Swear to me."

She couldn't speak. She couldn't even move her head, let him see her eyes, to make him know how sorry she was. So sorry.

"Glitches. Fucking glitches. Don't think you can use them against me."

No. She wouldn't. Couldn't. Didn't even know what that meant. Just please, please stop now.

"Don't break my heart." He spat the words out, forcing her head down into the pillow, tearing her hair from the tender wound. "Don't be like all the others."

He went away again the next day, leaving Kate a long list of rules to keep to. He would know, he said. He'd know if she broke any, if she even thought about breaking any. *No dreeming, no listening to the moon, no screaming, no touching yourself, no opening the door, no running away.*

But Kate couldn't help breaking rules. And she couldn't help the moon from whispering its broken language into her ears. A fractured, jumbled language, words cracked open and drained of blood, bleached bone-white. It was wrong, it was terrible, of course it wasn't real. No. But she didn't know how to stop it. She couldn't silence the moon, so she silenced herself. She closed her mouth and stitched it shut. She knew she would never, could never tell Fraser. Not about the moon. Not about the strange television, or the dreeming dolls, or the night doors, or any of the other thousand tiny secrets she was keeping from him. He mustn't know anything. He mustn't know that she knew. That was the only way she might survive him. Keep everything secret and hidden away.

She was a closed case, her skin zipped tightly around a million unspoken words, a whole alphabet of herself, crazed little letters she had to keep still and quiet and contained within her body. They moved around inside her, spelling out blackbirds and spiders, ghosts and books and rotten apples, dead leaves and murdered girls and wrong music and long falls in the darkness. She felt chaotic inside, under her skin, stuffed tight and swarming with dirt. She couldn't stand it. She wanted to explode out of her body, unspool out of herself, unravel the tangled mess until she was nothing but one long thin strand stretched out across the universe.

But no. She would never be free. There would always be this pain, this bone-crushing pain in her head. She took a handful of painkillers, too many, she couldn't help it. Needed the pain to stop, couldn't take any more, couldn't stand the sawing at her bones. She screamed, knowing she was breaking his rules, not caring. The scream burst up from somewhere deep inside her, calling up some ancient vision of herself, her throat raw with the rush of air, emptying her lungs. She screamed and felt something break inside her head, a snapping of some connection. Then there was a brief loose emptiness, and she felt something warm and wet on her cheek. Something dark, spreading over the pillow. Blood. She was bleeding. Shaking, she got out of bed and stumbled to the bathroom. In the mirror she saw dark stains over her face and hands, streams of liquid running from both ears, dripping down her neck, her back, her breasts, everywhere. But it wasn't red. It wasn't blood.

She wiped her fingers over the mirror. Black smears across her reflection. Black ink, leaking from inside her head.

Dreeming. I'm dreeming, and he'll know. He'll know. He'll come back and fix me, fix my glitches. He'll fix me and I'll be good again, I'll be his Kate again.

But she knew she wouldn't be good again. She knew this time, he wouldn't forgive her, that in fact he was impatient for her to break his rules. Excited. He couldn't wait. And she knew that she was no good to him now, now that she'd broken the spell he'd cast over her. He would see it and be bored right away. He'd kill her. He'd turn her into a Dreemy Peep. Even if he couldn't tell by looking at her face, he'd see the ink all over the bathroom floor. All over the mirror. Smudged over her face and pooling at her collar bone. No, no. He was on the moon. He couldn't see her. He couldn't, could he?

She stumbled out of the bathroom and down the hallway towards the front door, trailing black droplets behind her. He was in the apartment somewhere, she could sense him. Coming after her with his tools and his hands, ready to fix her glitches, rewire her. Make her good again. Again? How many times? What even was she now—just a thing made of plastic and wires and spare parts? But it wasn't true. No, no. That's just what he wanted her to think.

The door was locked, of course. Kate went through Fraser's keys frantically, looking for one that would open it. But she knew she knew she knew there was one key he would never give her. The key to her escape. The keys failed, one after another, until she had tried them all. And yet, there was something. A little something, dancing around her feet. When she looked, there was nothing there. But she remembered a little dog. A little dog with a key hanging off its collar. That had stayed with her. Stayed in her head.

Kate scratched at the bandage over her wound, pulled it away. She dug at the stitches, picked them apart with impatient fingers. Blood spilled over her hands, making it harder to grip the wiry threads and pull them out. When the wound was open she stabbed inside it with her thumb and forefinger shaped like a beak, digging around in the broken skull, pulling out a bloodied silver key.

The door opened into Fraser's room on the moon. She knew it would, it must do. She was there already, too, broken and slumped over the bed, her back panel open and wires tumbling out. And Fraser standing over her yelling, "Fucking glitches! You're just like the others, full of disgusting glitches. Stop dreeming! Stop it!"

Kate came closer and he saw her and turned on her, grabbing her by the shoulders, slipping because of all the blood and the black liquid on her skin.

"What the fuck? What's this?"

He slammed her down onto the floor, but couldn't get a purchase on her. The floor was slippery now and she was soaked. In the confusion, she managed to climb on top on him, press herself over him and hold him down for a moment. It was pouring from her now, the black ink rushed out of her, like blood from a severed artery, covering them both. It was a lake of ink, flooding out of her and into him. That black lake inside her head, that black lake of forgetting. It spilled out and out of her, and as it drained away, she remembered. Remembered how he had dragged her outside in the night. Dragged her by her hair. How he had kicked her, stamped down on her head with his big black boot. How she had screamed and begged for help, for someone to help, for the moon to fall down and rescue her. She remembered it all, and everything that had come before that, the slow silencing, the friends she had dropped, the job she'd given up. She wanted it all back now. She wanted her life. Her self. She would take it all back.

Black lake water flooded over Fraser, into his mouth

and his eyes. It made him stutter and twitch uncontrollably. She saw blue sparks fizzing over his skin, heard the crackling of his insides, the liquid sloshing in his hollows. She slumped back on the floor, and watched as he struggled to sit up. Still in his clothes, his smart leather shoes, his legs splayed straight out before him. His mouth stuttered open and closed, his eyes rolled back in his head. He was broken. If not, she would smash him to pieces. His smooth skin and his perfect hair, all sticky with blood and ink. And his moving parts, clogged up now and stuck. His mouthpiece twitched. A blue filament arced through his eye, leaving it black and empty. No. His eyes had always been empty. She saw her own self reflected in the glossy dead orbs. That was all she'd ever seen in him, after all: her own love, her own strength. She was the one who'd been real. Kate, and the others, the bitches with glitches. They were the real ones, humming with so much reality that Fraser couldn't bear it, would do anything to deny it, kill it. But it was undeniable. She felt it in herself now, in her aching, beaten body. She felt it thrumming inside her veins, thundering to her heart.

THE SHADOW MEN

———◉———

In a night that was like the mouth of a bear, a thick tangled forest of a night, the Queen Beast walked. She was tall and deeply rooted as a tree. Vines tangled under her boots as she stalked the night with her high-legged walk, until she came to a clearing where a black puddle shone before her, glossy as onyx. She breathed the world through her skin and into her bones, and chanted words to summon a spirit from the water.

It was in her bones and blood, this craft, this knowing. It was in the sap and roots of the wood.

And yet. No matter how she tried, she could not conjure the ghost of her sister. Perhaps she was too desperate, she missed her sister's face too much and it clouded her craft. Her sister should have reigned for a thousand years, but some darkness had dragged at her, some weight pulled her down, until she could no longer stay out of the earth. She'd died too young; the new Queen didn't need magic to tell her that. But what to do—what to do with her grief, and what to do with her power. That, she could not tell.

These woods were the realm of the Queen Beast since time began. But the Queen wanted no dominion, no territory or power. She lived in the woods and from the woods; and the things of the woods stalked her and avoided her and lived with her all in their turn.

But that night, that heated dream of a night, she could not live. She couldn't sleep or settle. The blood crackled in her veins, her black hair knotted itself into clumps. There was too much she didn't know. Too many stories left untold. The night was buzzing with static and the Queen Beast felt the time come upon her. She stared into the onyx puddle and spoke the words that opened the doors between realms. Willed the oily sheen of aura to resolve into the shape of her sister. Her voice. Anything. *Now*. For now was the time. She felt time approaching with its skeleton dance, its skull grin and ship of ribs. She crouched down to the water and broke the gloss with her dark hands. Nothing but ripples, the broken reflection of her own face, the tip of the moon piercing the gel of night.

Her sister's ghost was hidden and silent. But the feeling remained, the sensation of something coming, time ticking down like teeth clicking in a jaw bone. Rattle, rattle, and all tumbling out.

On a night like the grinding jaw of a machine, a piston pump of steam and smoke, Davey fell sleepless into his bed, beside his sleeping wife. He writhed there, the sheets catching at his drunken feet, sweat trickling through the thick hairs on his thighs, the thrumming of the streetlamp outside filling his ears with a horrible repetitive thump. His wife snored loudly, and he thought about what it would be like to punch her until she stopped. He wrestled with himself in that bed until he couldn't stand it anymore and he dragged on his clothes and took himself outside into the street, which was humid and clotted with stink. He scraped his body against the brick walls of the houses, grit and dust stinging his grazed flesh. When he staggered, and rested under a streetlamp, his shadow stretched and taunted him with its height, its fingers spread against the roofs of the houses, its head melting into the black sky beyond. How he hated his shadow! How he hated this summer, and the women in their sun-drenched skin, and the dust that clung to the dampness between his legs and under his arms and in the crease of his neck. And his wife, sleeping through it all, like some kind of dumb beast. And this city, that was finally ending, that was crumbling at the edges. How he hated this city. And hated the damp, drunk, fetid night, and all that it held in its horrible mouth.

He walked until he no longer felt drunk, but he felt like a dishrag, boiled and wrung out, and he couldn't remember what had driven him from his bed. The alcohol all sweated out now, he was evaporated down to the thick white milk of his essence, his body, his mind. A creamy sludge of himself, the gunk of his life. He wanted another drink, to wash out the queasy slug that crawled in his veins. But he was walking in the park now, walking across a dark expanse of scuffed earth. And his shadow walked over the grass before him, and beside him, doubled like hands of a clock, long and thin and wavering like ghosts.

All around him the city gnawed at the night, concrete teeth, metal jags, smoke curling from a pitted tongue. Sirens looped and called like anxious birds, from one side of the city to the other. It was all ugly and cracked, all broken down.

A stumble then, and he found himself falling, and landing on the hard ground. His shadow a strange mis-shapen aura spreading out from his body, pooling blackly on the grass. And he knew he couldn't get up, wouldn't get up, and he closed his eyes and buried his face in the scratchy earth, and waited for the morning to come.

Once there was a man who hated his shadow.

The dying Queen told the story with blood in her throat. When she coughed, blood bubbled from her mouth. The Princess held her sister's hand, stroked her skin to soothe her. *Maybe you won't understand. But listen,* said the Queen. She moved to sit up in the bed, and the Princess helped her, and sat beside her, so as to hear her soft voice.

Once there was a man who hated his shadow. The way it followed him around. Clung to him, seething darkly. It was a monstrous, ugly thing, this shadow of his. He wished he could get rid of it for good. And so he travelled the world looking for a witch or a way that would set him free.

In the course of his travels, the man walked through these very woods. And in these woods, he met a woman. This was the sort of woman who would dance to the music of a fire. Hips shaking, arms wailing like snakes. She was the sort of woman who ran outside in u thunderstorm. And when she was angry, she was the sort of woman who rose up and blossomed into a furious inferno, burning everything she touched with hands of flame and tongue of fire.

"I know that woman," said the Princess Beast, and her sister shook her head. Every movement costing her effort and pain now. *One day you will know her, I think...*

The Queen's voice trailed off, eyes clouding into sleep. She was young in years, a few hundred years alive. But this strange illness had made her ancient, weak and desiccated, too thin, too quiet and still. There was no cure, and death was close, kissing close. The Princess scented it on her sister's breath, a sweet rot. A hot spark of fury—how this illness stole and broke and lied! She bit her tongue so as not to disturb the Queen's rest. But so close were they, these sisters, so simpatico, this angry spark ricocheted silently between them, and brought the Queen around from her slumber, whereupon she resumed her tale.

Yes, yes... this was a hot flame of a woman, and as soon as he laid eyes on her, the man fell in love. He wrote love songs to her eyes, her lips, her knees... and when she brought him to her bed, he wrote love letters with his tongue and hands until the woman was drunk on his desire and she also fell. She'd never known love before and it astonished her. It was blissful to love him, blissful and addictive. And so, one moon-full night, she gave him her promise.

So they were happy.

"For a time," said the sister, knowing fine well this was not how these stories ended. The Queen smiled weakly.

Yes, for a time they were happy. But of course something had to turn it, some little key that opened the door to sorrow. And so it was, a dark little slip of a thing that turned and twisted and wrenched them apart. For the man still hated his shadow, you see, and he had begun to notice how the woman loved it. How she would sometimes caress his terrible darkness. How she would dance to his shadow with her own. To her it was a kind of poetry. The way their shadows moved together. The annihilation of one by the other.

The man grew cold, and jealous, and angry. He accused the woman of loving the shadow more. He blamed her for the way the shadow stuck to him, for the ghosts that haunted him by candlelight, sunshine, fire and moon.

"How can I love you like that," the woman pleaded with him. "How can I love you in fragments and pieces?"

The Queen coughed, and a trickle of blood ran from her lip.

"Don't say more," the Princess said. "Rest now, sleep a while."

The Queen clutched at her sister's hands. Her own hands were papery and thin now.

"I know," cried the Princess. "I know you would tell me now. But save your strength, please. I beg you. Finish the story tomorrow."

Their fingers entwined, their heads together on the pillow, hair winding and knotting. The Queen's breath was a flutter of soft wings, a moth in her throat, beating gently until its wings were soaked with blood, and beat no more.

When Davey woke it was raining, a dirty city rain that splashed black and sooty on his arms. He was lying on the bare scuffed earth of the park, patches of grass trying to grow here and there in the dusty ground. He didn't know what time it was, but it felt early, nauseatingly early. There was a strange sickness in his body. A weakness. The rain falling against his skin felt hard and rough. A struggle to get to his feet, and once he was up, he felt almost afloat, so insubstantial he could be swept away in the wind, rained out of existence.

Hungover. Yes. Sick. And he'd dreamed something.

A crack of pain across his head. That cheap dirty homebrewed wine... why had he drunk so much of it? He felt stupid now, and tired and weak, and he had to force himself to move, one foot in front of the other, back across the park and through the streets towards his room. Even as he was walking, he felt that lightness, that unbearable, sickening lightness in his body. *I must be ill.* Maybe he was very ill, maybe he had that city illness, that pollution in his blood.

A small group of men were sheltering under the roof of the derelict building on the corner of his street. Davey's dad, and some of his pals. They stopped talking as Davey approached and he realised they'd been saying something about him. One of them, a short wiry little bald man, called out to him. "Hey, son. Over here."

Davey shook his head and tried to walk faster, but he felt like a ghost, like the world was too substantial for him to move through. He swam helplessly against the air.

The wiry little man caught up to his side. "Hey son," he said. "Davey. Don't just ignore your old man, you ungrateful bastard."

Davey backed away from his dad, the drunken old git. He raised both hands in the air as if to ward him off.

"Okay son, okay. I just want to converse with you. You and I have something in common. More than blood. Listen to me, son. I know I've not been the best father, alright. But I know, I know what you've lost, and I know how you can get it back."

"Fuck off," said Davey.

His dad shrugged, and Davey walked on, weak legs pushing through the rain.

It was a struggle getting upstairs to the room. Empty now, his wife at one of her jobs. He stripped off his sodden filthy clothes, leaving them in a pile in the corner. Only then did he think about what his father had said. *I know what you've lost...* What, what had he lost? The answer came to him at once. A brutal punch in the guts.

He switched on the overhead light. Glanced about. Held his hand up to the bulb. Turned slowly all around.

It was gone. His shadow. It was gone.

In his dream he remembered his wife in a way he'd never really known her. She was by a stream in the woods. Washing her thick bundle of black hair, sluicing water over a rock. She was wearing nothing but a cloak, and she loosened this from her shoulders and let it fall away from her. When she bent her head to the water, her flesh bulged in clouds over her belly, her breasts hung down, her thighs softly trembled. She stepped into the water, turned and saw him watching.

"What are you doing?" he said.

"Oh," said she, "oh..." And she looked him up and down, and smiled. "I see spring has sprung."

Ouch. A sharp throb where her eyes had glanced. And now she was laughing to herself, pouring water over her shoulders.

"Ruby..." he faltered. He didn't know this woman, his wife.

He watched her, tense silence held in his fists and

under his feet and in the deep low knot of his hungry self. He followed the trails of water that drizzled from the black hair between her thighs, the rivulets of water that poured over her breasts and dripped from her nipples, the water that pooled in her navel and swam over her stomach. It was a trick, he thought, a kind of cunning that women used against men—and it wasn't fair. And he hated her for it.

His wife turned to him with a sharp look, as though she'd read his thoughts. "Fine," she snapped. "Fine." And her smile flashed like a knife, and it was a knife, and it sawed him wide awake.

Whisper breath of dawn breaking, and the Queen Beast woke to a gentle rain that fell against her cloak, under which she'd slept. She sat up and hugged herself for warmth, wrapped the damp cloak around her and waited for the sun to break through the mist. Birds called, each to each, their songs full of silly joyful shouts. But something in the woods was not quite as it should be. Something was *there*. The Queen held still and waited. That was the most important part of any hunt: the still silent wait. The world could change shape at any moment. So she waited.

Now she saw it. Where the onyx puddle had been the night before, now was some kind of garment or fabric, balled up in a soft mound. Tentatively she reached out; tentatively touched the garment with her fingertips. It was soft, soft as moth wings or spider webs, a delicious curious softness she wanted to wrap herself up in. Working slowly and carefully, she unravelled the garment and laid it flat against the earth.

It was no garment, but the shadow of a man. Tall and dark with soft fuzzing edges. The rain pattered against it, softly, slowly easing to a stop. And the Queen Beast stood at the shadow's feet with the rising sun at her back. Her shadow grew and covered the other. Their hands wove like braids, their heads melted into one, their legs trembled together. The strange shadow moved with her own, dancing, growing, each one in turns blotting out and revealing the other... darkening and enlightening, shaking and patterned with leaves and shapes of birds flying overhead, shadows passing through shadows, flashes of sunlight wiping them out.

Once there was a man who hated his shadow... the Queen Beast heard her sister's voice, whispering in the trees. Where was the man to whom this shadow belonged? At the thought of him, whoever he was, she knew she should be afraid. She'd leave the shadow behind, she decided. It wasn't *her* shadow, was it? Nothing to do with her. Except...what if this strange gift was a message from her sister? Isn't that what the Queen Beast had been hunting for all along?

No, no. Her instinct insisted. Leave it be.

But when she turned to walk away, a wrench of wild pain brought her low. Somewhere at her root and centre, it dragged at her.

She turned back. The shadow was lying where she left it.

"Fine," she said. "So be it."

She draped the shadow around her shoulders like a cloak. Then moved off, silently, into the woods.

He paced the room for a while, feeling mad and broken. Sick, the sickest he'd ever been. He threw up in the tiny bathroom down the hallway. Afterwards, washing his face, he was surprised by how solid he seemed to be. His reflection in the mirror as real as ever. Could almost see the bones under his skin. But how could it be? He must be dead. A ghost of himself. And if he was dead now, then his whole life had been... *this*? This waste? This numb nothing drudgery of days passing by. In his youth he'd been something, he'd been quick-sharp and tough. But Ruby'd put a stop to that. And they'd been happy, hadn't they? Yes, for a while. But the happiness had run out and now there was nothing but this bedsit squalor, this dying city. *Help me...* his mouth formed the words but he made no sound.

At last he left the bathroom and a shape on the landing startled him. Someone waiting outside the door to the room. A woman... no. His wife. She looked tired, looked nothing like the Ruby in his dream, the woman who had sprung his desire. That memory brought a flash of shame. When was the last time that had happened in real life? She didn't give him anything a man needed, nothing at all.

"Why are you out here?" He opened the door and walked past her.

"I was waiting for you," said Ruby. Now that he looked at her, he could still see it. That softness in her eyes. The curve of her smile.

"Waiting for me? Why not wait inside?"

She shrugged. She still hadn't come into the room, but was standing in the doorway, watching him as he sat on the bed and pulled on a pair of trousers.

"Don't start with one of your lectures. I need a drink."

He pulled on his shoes, tightening the laces. Good, she was quiet. He couldn't stand it when she nagged.

"What then? Cat got your tongue?"

She sighed. "I'm going, Davey. It's time for me to go."

Davey exploded up off the bed, grabbed his wife and dragged her into the room. She didn't fight him, but somehow she made her body heavy, or he was just so weak now. Either way, it took all his strength to drag her inside. But he did it. Dragged her into the room and threw her onto the floor. Anger fuelled him where his muscles and bones were flimsy.

"You are not fucking leaving me! Do you hear? You don't fucking go anywhere."

He wrested the keys from her hand and went out, locking the door behind him.

As the day wore on, the shadow on the Queen Beast's back grew heavier and heavier until she could barely take a step under its weight. Oh, she should have trusted her instinct. To rule without wisdom made her the Queen Fool.

They came at last to a place where a tumble of mossy stones led down to a wide, shallow stream. The Queen laid the shadow down on the bank. Muscles tight and painful as she eased them into long stretches. She knew this place, maybe from a dream. The water sparkling in the sunlight, the moss a deep velvet green, and tiny flowers glittering in the moss, and ferns swaying, and trees whispering with their leaves.

The Queen Beast laid her cloak down beside the shadow, undressed, and stepped into the cold clear water. She drank some and cupped more in her hands to pour over her body. The cold water raised goose bumps all over her skin, then the sun warmed her again, and a sigh seemed to swell from the air itself—but not her sigh, not her breath, no. She glanced around. The sun was behind her and before her two shadows were moving together, her own and the other. Palms stroking, heads twining and dipping, fingers rippling and stretching as the sun wavered through the trees.

The Queen Beast stretched out upon her cloak. Closed her eyes and sensed the shadows making love around her. Her body thrummed with warmth, gliding down and parting the wet tendrils between her thighs with seeking mouth. Then she did sigh, as a soft petalled rose blisses into flame. And then she slept, covered in dappled sunlight falling through the trees.

In her sleep, she saw her sister, finally, her sister sitting on a rock by the stream. She was sewing, carefully stitching a soft black garment... a shadow, the Queen realised. She was stitching a shadow to her own. Or no, not stitching. Rather she was carefully, painstakingly, picking the stitches out. As she worked, she wept. The Queen Beast put a hand on her sister's shoulder, a rush of love and feeling—but there was no touch, she wasn't really there. Then a sound came from the woods behind her. The Shadow Man. Stumbling through the trees. Pale and white and weak man. No shadow, only his flesh, his feet slipping and tangling in the undergrowth. A knife flashing at his side. A fiery torch blazing in his hand.

The rain had stopped and it was filthy hot again when Davey went back to the street corner. The other men were gone but his dad was still there, sitting in the darkness of the derelict building, smoking a thin bedraggled roll up. He lifted his hand in greeting.

"Son," he said. "You came back. Come and sit down, pull up a crate."

The corner he sat in was so dark, Davey couldn't make out if his dad had a shadow or not. Were they the same? Was he just like his father? No, his father was a waste man, a madman, wasn't he? You could tell from the set of his body, the knife-quick wire of his stance.

Davey sat on an upturned crate and took the bottle that his dad held out. It looked like whisky but tasted more like medicine. Strong. He shouldn't get drunk, not with Ruby up there in the room. He was confident she couldn't get out without a key. But he couldn't keep her there forever. He had to decide what to do. *Think, think...* only he couldn't think because his father was talking, jabbering away in a low voice, and the drink was already glittering up the edges of things.

"Maybe I should go home," said Davey. "On second thoughts, you know. My missus will be wondering where I've got to."

His dad shot him a sharp glance. "Oh, aye? Under the thumb?"

"Fuck off," Davey said, then laughed to cover it up. He tried to pass the bottle back over but his dad shook his head.

"You keep that, son. Drink up."

"Very generous of you." Davey took another drink.

"I'm going to tell you a story, son," said his dad. "It's a story about pride, about honour. Maybe I haven't been the greatest of fathers, but I'm here now, lad. So tell me, son. What makes you feel proud? What makes you feel honoured?" He leaned forward, searching out Davey's eyes with his own. "When was the last time you felt like a real man? When was the last time you felt like a *king*?"

Davey shook his head. He didn't know where to look. He didn't know how to answer.

The Queen Beast stayed in that place until nightfall, until the stars popped out of the blue-black sky, giving her a map by which to orient herself and navigate back to the castle. Several days of walking—longer if she had to drag the other shadow with her all the way. She hadn't planned on returning home for centuries, but now was no time to be the Queen Fool, wandering lost in the woods. An enemy approached and must be quelled. The dream of her sister could not be ignored.

She pulled her cloak warmly around herself. Looked down at the shadows, dark and lost in the night.

"Can you walk, Shadow?"

Silence. She thought not.

"Very well. Enjoy this good place. I go on."

95

As she stepped away, into the night woods, she felt that tearing pain at her roots. That shadow dragging at her, the stitches torn open. Agony, flesh ripping from her womb. An urge to run back, gather it in her arms. And then what? Should she carry it for another hundred years? Another thousand? Stitch the shadow to her own and let it live from her body like a parasite? She thought of the weight of the shadow, how it had felt like iron draped over her back and shoulders. She thought of her sister, unpicking the stitches. A shadow had clung to her all those years, hadn't it? A shadow she'd carried for another, as proof of her love. Thinking her love made her strong enough. But it had only dragged her down, down, down.

The Queen Beast walked on, walked against the pain, that agony of leaving. But she'd known pain before. Wounds healed. Scars were forgotten in time. But a burden like the shadow would kill her in the end.

And so she went on, bleeding and weeping, her shadow stretching desperately back to the other. The Queen Beast did not look back, did not allow herself another moment of doubt. Only kept moving forwards, heart-bitten and heart-broken, but focused and ferocious as a wolf, moving under the night's tutelage and its ancient map of stars.

On the walk back to the room he felt stronger. Sure of himself for once. He'd seen it in her, hadn't he? Seen it in Ruby? That murderous look in her eye. Thief. Took away everything that mattered and now she was leaving him. With nothing. Nothing but that shitty room, this shitty fucking life. When he could have been anything, anything he wanted.

He felt the lack of it now as his power. His empty shadow was like a deep well of water he drew on until he was drunk with pure and pristine understanding.

He looked up at the evening sky, grey and bloated

with the drowning sun. How he hated the weight of the sky, the way it pushed down on him. All the weight of this world, trapping him here. Until now. Until his father's story unravelled the memories he'd repressed for so long.

His thoughts wandered, sick and drunk. See, I wasn't meant to be here, in this world. She trapped me. She did this to me. His father's voice: *Another time. Another place. When we were kings.*

Maybe you don't remember the place, but you've been there in dreams. Remember the heat of the fire, all of you marching forward with your torches high and aflame... can you see it, son? The night all lit up by fire. You're marching towards that forest, that terrible wood where she reigns free. You and the others. You're not alone anymore, son. The shadow men, we are everywhere. Our great mass pushing forward. We were meant to be Kings. This was all meant to be ours. So take it and burn it down. And when her soldiers come you cut them down. Cut their hair and cut their throats, cut off their breasts and cut out all the rest until their blood flows like sap through the forest, which is the world, which is yours, son. Ours. Our world.

He remembered. Remembered his dad's voice, telling him the story. Remembered the sound of fire crackling and spitting all around him. The feel of it. Like it was burning in his veins. And the shadow men... the Shadow Men. Majestic in their bearing. He felt it now. That flame. That resolve. He would do what he had to do.

He unlocked the door to the room, bracing himself for Ruby's anger. An anger he'd resolved to break with one sharp snap. But that thief, that woman—she was gone. The room was empty, only his clothes in a pile on the floor. Only the stink of his body on the bedsheets. The empty bottles. The detritus of his shabby life. No Ruby. No Ruby anymore. He sat on the bed, head in his hands. She'd left him with nothing... but then he saw it, folded neatly on the wooden chair. Soft and black and fuzzed around the edges. The one thing she had left behind.

The Queen Beast felt her strength returning as she walked. The tearing pain eased to a sore ache in her womb. It would ease off completely in time. A scar would be left, perhaps, to remind her. When the shadow men came with their fire and knives, she would remember. Remember this pain. Remember how all these woods were her realm, to live and to die for.

And the Queen Beast rode into that night, that night like the mouth of a bear, and on its fluid tongue she was a word, a breath and a sigh. Moving into the darkness wreathed in shadows. Readying herself for her reign.

KUEBIKO

"The story contains a house. The house contains an absence. The absence contains a mirror. The mirror contains a body. The body contains a story.

The story cannot be contained."
—Kuebiko

The House of Bodies. The house is flesh and skin; the frame is bones. Cartilage and muscle, tendons stretching for hinges and joints.

The House of Time. The house is made of nothing but millions of passing moments, layered one over the other until they achieve the substance of mortar.

The House of Sleep.

I'm so tired.

Margaret Penderyn is dead. She's dead, or gone so far and for so many years, she might as well be dead. The house, her art, everything's been signed over to me. I never had anything of my own before, not like this, not anything that matters. The money from the installations, the royalties or whatever, that's nothing. But the house—the House. Pete said, let's just sell everything, and we can draw a line under it all.

A line under all what? He'd draw a line around my body if he could, and cut me out. But he can't because around me is a scrawled black aura, a scribble that buzzes and itches. A million spiders crawling. Where is the line?

"You've crossed a line, Raewyn," he said.

The train follows a line, curving around the coast. There's no one else in the carriage, only me. We went over water and I thought for a split-second the train would jump across, like it jumps the little brook in Alice. (Even just writing that down, I can picture Pete rolling his eyes.)

Draw a line under the past, Pete said. He thinks I'm trying to find meaning that isn't there and I'm only going to open up old wounds. And he won't be there to put me back together again this time when it all inevitably goes wrong. He said, "If you walk out that door, don't think you can just come walking back." I thought people only said that in stories. I said, fine. I don't want to go back. I don't think.

The Door of Never Going Back.

Pete would never say this to my face, but I know what he thinks. That it was all a hoax. A game. An incredibly intricate installation. Margaret Penderyn's last and greatest work of art. But where does Tanith fit into that? Was that part of it, too? Impossible. Does that mean it was *all* Mum's doing, all of it? From when? From our births? I've said that to Pete and he agrees, to my face, that the hoax theory makes no sense. But I know, I can tell what he's really thinking.

Where's the body? Where's the skin and blood and hair and bones of her?

He blames her. To him, she's a monster; she abandoned me. And he can't understand why I'm going back there, opening up old wounds, old doors. But he wouldn't understand, would he? Because we're from different worlds. Pete belongs here. He has all these memories wrapping him into his skin, he's wound and bound by the fabric of the past, by a tapestry of moments that ravelled up his life. But me, I don't remember much. I float loose. I'm unbound, raw and tender and lost like a red cloud, a clot of flesh drifting over the sea.

I think—I want to see the House again.

Pete thought I would be too frightened to do this. Yes, I'm scared, I admit it. But the point is, there's nothing safe. This train could come off the rails, a bomb could go off, there could be knives in the guard's jacket, there could be a rape in the train toilet, there could be a suicide. There's nothing safe in this world. I've always known that. And is it, maybe, more frightening to stay away?

Nearly there. We're racing through tunnels of green and past concrete slopes. I can smell the sea already, scraps of it through the train window. I can smell salt, dirty petrol, and fish, a thousand seagulls, pebbles sticky with syrupy alcopops and glitter. It's familiar and frightening all at once.

Welcome. This is Kuebiko.
 Please touch the screen to enter.
 Please say clearly: Yes. I accept.

Thank you.
 Please now step into the hallway.
 Please remove your shoes and place them neatly to the side. When you have done so, please say clearly: Yes.

Thank you.
 You are now standing in the hallway of a three storey Georgian terrace near the sea front, looking up at a wide wooden staircase with a faded patterned carpet running down. At the top

of the hallway, you can see more stairs curving around, and a short landing running towards the rooms at the back of the house.

Stand on the spot in the hallway marked with a black X, facing towards the coat rack and the love-seat. When you have done so, please say clearly: yes.

I'm sorry. I didn't hear that. Are you standing on the X? Please say clearly: yes.

Thank you.

Behind you there is another mirror. Please take a moment here to reflect. You exist here in infinite repetitions. You exist in other worlds, where all is aslant. The house has sliced you into a billion overlapping pieces of yourself, a stack of copies. Maybe you have already lived forever; you have become multitudes. Maybe this life is the last.

Maybe you get another chance.

The House washed over me like a ripple of film.

The House opened on a series of hinges, a doll's house opening and expanding. The front door slammed behind me. I stood in the hallway, being devoured by the black and white tiles, the mirrors and the stairs. Like travelling backwards in time; the hallway made me nauseous. I felt for a moment like *I* was the knife in the body, twisting and turning and digging her out of herself.

I remember the House, or at least there's a familiarity. I know it in my body, in my hands, in the ways I move through the rooms. For a long time, no one could bear to look at me, and I moved through the House like my own ghost. That's what I felt like.

The House of Wounds. Every doorway a knife stab.

When I opened the front door, the movement of air sent dust flying in thick clouds around me. Like magician's smoke. I pulled myself from a hat, dirty and bewildered. This was my home. This is where it happened. A feeling without a name. A travelling away from myself, and looking back, along a narrow rippling tunnel.

I didn't know what to expect or what to do. The place was filthy, years of accumulated dust that had never been disturbed. So I cleaned. I went through the rooms, pulling the dust sheets from the furniture. I found a hoover and plugged it in. I swept and polished. It was like a slow realisation, polishing a memory, the house coming back bright and vivid against the gloom, the rain coming down outside. It was almost like an advertisement, the way I could swipe away a thick layer of dust to reveal clean bright wood beneath. Zing! But the House can never be glossy and sterile. When I look closely, I see everything is stained, the stains have seeped into everything, right deep down into the fabric of everything.

From time to time as I worked I thought I heard noises coming from upstairs. A thump of a foot on a floorboard. The crackle of a television. But then I'd turn off the vacuum cleaner and there would be nothing but silence. My own breath. Filaments of dust floating down around me. It only increased my apprehension. I don't believe in ghosts, at least, not usually. But I could picture her, in the bed, as though she were made of the bed, a cloth mother, a sentient mattress. She slept there for seven years, seven solid years of sleep. Seven years I didn't see her eyes. I used to imagine them as two black orbs behind her crinkled eyelids. Two black orbs that swirled with silver stars caught in eye jelly. I dreamed that her eyes were eggs that hatched two bald featherless birds with wide-open beaks, carmine throats, screaming like empty leather purses.

I walked past her door. Once, twice, three times. Thinking, maybe we were wrong. Maybe we were wrong and she's still there. Sleeping. Dead. We just didn't see her, we missed her, somehow, in all the looking. Blinded by the slant of light through the curtains. Lost in a sleight of hand, a mirror game, a stopped clock. Disappeared. Like a conjuring trick. Sawing a woman in half. Or is that a different kind of trick.

In the end I simply grabbed the door handle, turned it, and went in. And of course she was not there, and I felt relieved and also ridiculous, and also angry. Enraged. There was nothing there. Nothing, she'd left nothing for me at all.

How could she leave me with absolutely nothing—no clue, no sign, no answers?

I picked up an old dried-out bottle of perfume from her dressing table. It didn't even smell of her. It didn't smell of anything. I threw it at the wall. It broke, released a gust of powdery rot. Then I broke everything. I wrenched the mirror from the dresser and smashed it to pieces in my bare hands. Seven years bad luck but that's a fucking joke. I swept everything from every surface, and crushed it under my feet. Pulled her clothes from the wardrobe and toppled the wardrobe and stamped the back of it until it splintered. Tipped the bed over, pulled the sheets away, even tried to tear into the mattress but I couldn't do it, I was just beating the mattress with my fists. That's when I saw the notebook. An exercise book, like we had at school. It had been squashed between the mattress and the bed frame, and now it slid out.

Her handwriting. Her words.

Why must they always make me a door? They make me a door and step through me, into their other worlds. They make me a door and

swing me back and forth, back and forth between worlds. I am inside on the outside, outside on the inside, an inverted mouth, a mouth.

(The kitchen smells of)

The kitchen should contain a deep hole, deeper than

deeper than

a hole to fall down forever, Alice-like. Or a well.

It must be the kitchen. The kitchen is the territory. The void in its heart is where the woman has been blanked out.

The kettle is boiling. I can't remember the last time I saw a kettle boiling. What a stupid thing.

(but

why don't you just get up?)

In the kitchen, on a counter top balanced over the endless unstoppable void, a kettle is boiling, forever. Interminably. It boils impossibly, a lifetime of kettles boiling, cups of tea.

(have a lovely cup of tea

cup of tea cures everything

make us a cup of tea, love

creepy

your turn to make the tea, Rae

Tan)

The kettle boils and steam rises to the ceiling and then it begins to rain, raining soundlessly into the dark empty hole that has eaten the kitchen.

Lacuna. It is as it is in my mind. In my mind, a great black spreading lake. Deep. Hungry, inky well.

The territory is the void.

On another kitchen counter, a television plays advertisements for floor cleaner. Jif cif flash mr muscle. Kids and dogs with muddy paws. Laughter. The floor swipe, and the zing!

But would it rain, into the television? Could we do that? I don't think the insurance would like that. Does it matter? This will be the last time for me. The final attempt.

See I know how to do it now.

The kitchen. In the kitchen, which is scoured out by a deep black void, a kettle is interminably boiling, and the steam is condensing, and it's raining on the television, which is playing advertisements for different floor cleaners, modern ones, you know, and the television is sparking and spitting streaks of fire.

([laughter] LOL)

Actual lol.

(the day the television exploded
the space shuttle exploded
you were never an explosion
you were a soft implosion
silk
a real man wouldn't put up with her)

There'll be voices coming from the void. Voices layered over voices, and as you fall, the voices will become louder and multiplied; use sound mirrors, something to mirror the sound. A sound mirror? My language is failing. My body will be the first to go.

Last night I had a visitor. A guest from another world. She said she was a guest, but I misheard her and thought she said, a ghost. She climbed into bed with me. Her body was real, and solid, and had weight and gravity. I wasn't scared at all.

She said she's from another place. She said, it's different there. We know doors.

I said, my mother knew doors. She made doors.

Ah, said the guest. I know.

At least, I dreamed? I dreamed.

I slept in my old bedroom at the back of the house. Not the one we shared before, me and Tanith, but the one after that. The one after Tanith. I thought I would never sleep but I did. I slept in the arms of the guest, and rested on her tongue. As I slept my body flowed over her body, she flowed into my body, I was water, I slept like a deep muscle of water, turning in the sea. But this morning, I am so tired. I got out of bed on my hands and knees. Drained. I need coffee but I'll go somewhere. To the old pier.

Why don't you just get up, Mum wrote. Why don't you just get up? That's what I used to say to her, all the time. I used to sit beside her bed and watch her sleeping and say: why don't you just get up? Get up, get up, get up. You lazy selfish bitch, get up. She left me alone with the loss, with the house smelling of blood.

I see now, that she always intended to disappear.

I begin to see how she did it. The notebook contains all the instructions, but anyway that doesn't matter. She already told me.

Her voice takes over mine.

But then I hear Pete's voice in my head, telling me I should leave this House. This is not some kind of a game, he said.

my hands feel like two balloons

I'm so tired. I want to sleep. I'm in a cafe, drinking bitter coffee, looking out on a rain-pelted and stony beach. Out there, the wind rages. I thought it might wake me a little. Spit salt and sand into my eyes. But nothing breaks through this fatigue.

The kitchen is the territory.

There was blood on the walls. On the floor. It was literally everywhere. I didn't comprehend until then just how much blood the human body contains. How could it be everywhere? But it *was* everywhere, it was soaked into the things of the house, the atoms of the house. It was months, we kept finding it, traces of it. On the knives and forks in the cutlery drawer. In the corners of the windows, the creases in the curtains. There were blood stains on the wall. I kept scrubbing away at them even after Mum gave up and took to her bed.

The House of Blood.

I remember coming home from school and running upstairs to Mum's bedroom. It was years later, years since Tanith. I was hopeful then, almost happy in a strange kind of way. I thought Mum was getting better. Because those afternoons she had started speaking, you see. Nonsense, mostly, a lot of things I didn't understand at all. She was speaking in her sleep but it was more than that. She was talking to *me*. I'd run home, run to her room, kick my shoes off, and lie down beside her on the bed.

The first time she said it—

kuebiko

I felt a jolt through my body. Enough that the bed moved. And for a second I thought she'd woken up.

I don't want to go into the kitchen. I would rather do anything at all. But it's the only room left to do. I've put things in boxes, I've sorted, I've worked—I've worked to the point of exhaustion. You see, Pete? I've done all this without you.

You haven't called me. You still won't come over. You resist and you entrench yourself and I thought it's what I wanted but now I realise—maybe that's why I didn't resist, didn't even try to stop her. The guest. I encouraged her. I *wanted* her inside me. God. I ate her in delirious mouthfuls. Because when I said *blood*, when I said, *there was so much blood*, she didn't cringe away from me, like you do. She moved closer. Our hands touched, fingers intertwined. She kissed the small of my back, the nape of my neck. I cried the whole time, even when I came, I was crying. She cried too. It couldn't have been that way with you, could it? You don't cry, crying makes you soft and weak, like a woman. And you are hard, like a man. You stand firm, erect, hardening… you are calcifying, you've turned to stone. I can't touch you,

you don't feel it when I touch you. You find me tiresome, you find me endlessly sad. But isn't that why you loved me in the first place? You were drawn to my mysterious ever-bleeding wound. You sewed me up tight, but you can't cure me, you can't end this. You called me endless, an endless mire. You say, don't cry, please don't cry. You say you love me as if it is supposed to help. But then you won't come with me. You won't step across. Through this Door, this House of—

you are too afraid.

And she is not. And neither am I.

Why won't you do it, what's stopping you? But you have never, have you? You have never come across. You left me alone in this body. This House of Wounds. And now. She has entered me, not as a door, but as a room, and I'm so grateful.

And so very, very tired.

(kuebiko
create the illusion of time
I feel it in my body. In my water)

Create the illusion of time. I'm going to use the house to do it. The whole house. The annoying thing is, I feel I can do it. I can make it. But the thing is,

here I am

(my hands feel like two balloons)

it's the rest of me. My hands refuse.

Before I was—vivid and mobile. Like a latch springing. Like a larch singing. It was this other, younger, less exhausted woman. My daughter, maybe. One of them. But it was me, take responsibility, Mag, you made all those houses. I made this house but now I must unmake it.

The trouble is

the trouble is, the thing is

a condition with many names, but what it means, the upshot of

all that is, it means this bed is a raft and I'm drifting at sea. Years and
years, drinking rain.

    So don't tell me, don't try to tell me about how
    (you've already left me)
    the thing is I know how to do it
    like a fish hook
    a needle unthreading
    the inside of the labyrinth is possession

    you only need three things

Follow the passage before you. As you can see, the rooms appear to unfold in disorienting fractalizing kaleidoscoping shapes and colours. The house now appears to contain multiple iterations of itself, psychedelically spiralling away from you. The music you hear, the wet scrape and soft groan, is the sound of dimensions mating and mutating.

This door you may open if you wish, although I don't advise it. Behind this door you will be embraced by the television mother. Her head is a television, her hands are televisions too. Her embrace is a concussion, an injury, a puddle of blood. But the television mother is a good mother in her way, a better mother than me. She washes the floor, she cooks the dinner, she folds the laundry and puts it in neat piles. She tells you she loves you in her crackling voices. Her hands that are televisions clap in delight when you succeed at something, no matter how trivial or pathetic or pointless it may be. Her television hands smash together and shards of broken glass spray around the room.

And she sparks fire and her voices are
sirens.

Texted Pete to say I'm staying at the House a bit longer.
Said it was helping a lot. He texted back, asking how long
I'm staying and when I was coming home. I said, I don't
know.

I don't think I'll go back. I want to stay here. I want the
guest to come again. I want to sleep like flowing water, with
her flowing around me. She held me inside her body and I
remembered so much, all at once. She said that was right,
that's how it is where she's from. A place where bodies are
houses, where doors open into other people. Like a piece of
music that comes flooding together and you flow up from
the top of your head. Inside her body, I was free from pain.
I was free from beauty.

Will I be able to do this in a week? Make a door and go
through it? It took Mum seven years, but maybe she didn't
realise until the end, or maybe she didn't have the strength
to do it all at once.

I feel that I will. I'll stay awake. I won't sleep at all.

One time when we were little, we tried to stay up with
Mum all night. She was working on an installation, one of
her doors. She kept on walking through it, and through
it, as though she were threading it with her body. Her
installations were all like that, she said they were doors to
other worlds. I used to think she was sculpting the air itself,
moulding matter into shape. She layered the world over
itself and made it slightly askew and distorted. To us as
children, it was simply mysterious. We watched her from
the landing above her studio, our legs dangling through the
banisters. She had her big hair tied back in a turquoise and
gold scarf. The colours so intense, they whirled and made
trails around her head as she moved. She threw blankets

and cushions up to us, said, go to sleep.

She put our favourite record on the record player. We knew every bump and scratch.

When I was a child, I caught a fever

The problem is, the thing is—a condition with many names. The thing is, the truth is, I don't want to remember. It is easier to be asleep and numb.

But I have been remembering. The guest asked about the tune I was humming, and I told her, and she said, play it to me. So I did. I found the record and we listened to the whole thing, both sides. When I got up to turn it over, she said, Raewyn. Just that, just my name. But it was like something gifted.

She says they come back whenever they can find a door. She says they want to remember us.

She said, "Your sister" but I must have fallen asleep or somehow the world fell away at that moment. There's a gap, a lacuna, a spreading darkness. Because I don't want to remember. But I must, because memory is a door, is a step through a door.

The guest said, it's very lonely here. It's very lonely, in your body.

Here in the kitchen, you will observe that the floor has fallen away into an endlessly deep blackness, an uncrossable void, a voice that speaks in chasms and

orgasms

grinding flesh on stone

a voice that pulses from the walls of a dark well.

You will note that a kettle is boiling. You'll see a television on the counter, on the far side of the black void. It's showing advertisements for floor cleaner. Here, you see a woman smiling vacuously as she pushes a mop over a kitchen floor. There's a lot of blood to mop up! There's blood everywhere. It's all over the walls, the counters, the windows. The kitchen table, the chairs. You'll notice the little things, the homework books on the kitchen table, the teapot. All slashed with blood. A pile of newspapers and flyers sprayed with blood and tiny white chips of bone. The fruit bowl with its three blood-spattered apples. Let me draw your attention to the woman sluicing out blood in her white bucket. She has blood on her face and in her hair. She has blood on her clothes, on her white jeans.

The television should explode and fall into the void, trailing white fire. I'll come back to life. I'll come back and she'll be—

It was the day the space shuttle exploded. We watched it on the old television in our room, in black and white. There were thick plumes of smoke that shot up and forked out across the sky. We saw the photograph of the teacher who had been on board. She was burned up in an instant. Imagine if it had been our teacher, Tanith said.

She was wearing her blue dressing gown. Royal blue, it was. Colours seemed richer then. Other colours, I mean. Not just red. But her face in my memory is smooth, brown skin with no features. Of course there are photographs. And anyway we were exactly alike. I need only look in a mirror if I want to see her image.

But I want to remember.

Mum said, there's no such thing as death, not really. It's

only a door, just another door you have to open. But Tanith cried, because she was so soft-hearted. I didn't want to be like her, I wanted to be my own person; I wanted to not be afraid of death or of doors. So I told Tanith about Laika and the space dogs, and then I told her about the atom bomb, and about children covered in napalm, and babies thrown in ditches, and all the other horrors I had heard of in thirteen years of life. And then Tanith was *completely* inconsolable, and Mum came in and said, for god's sake Raewyn. Leave Tanith alone, can't you see you're upsetting her? And then I cried because it all seemed so unfair. Because I was just trying to be strong.

See, it should have been me. Everyone thought so, not that they would ever say it. But that's what they meant, that's what their silence, their refusal meant. Sometimes it takes a while for the meaning of things to become clear. Mum told me that. She said that at first, people didn't understand her work, and they would say, it's just a door? It's just some doors? Have some imagination! Mum would yell. Use your brain and work it out for yourself! But sometimes it takes a while. It's taken me a while.

Tanith cried so much that day it gave her a headache, and that's why we left her at home. It was only for an hour. I picked pretty shells and stones from the beach for her. I found a dried-up starfish and thought, she'll love that.

For a long time after that day, no one looked at me. They couldn't even look at me, not for a moment.

Don't get up, the guest said. She'd brought me my notebook and coffee in bed. I sat up, bleary-eyed, hands wrapped round the coffee cup. The same record was playing softly again. Outside, the day was grey; rain threw itself against the windows, the windows rattled in their frames.

Make a door with music, she suggested. She spoke

between my legs, sliding against me. What is a door anyway? A door is a wing in a wall.

When we fuck I'm not even sure if that's what we're doing. We're naked, wet, inside each other but it's a constant coming that slides into sleep, a conversation when we're each the other, an unlimited deep compassion, an orgasm that flows between us in a fluid figure of eight. I forget myself, I don't even know if the guest is there or not.

You won't know I'm here.

I'm not dreaming but I see and feel the past and future.

When the guest's not here (where does she go?) I sleep more and more. I'm so tired all the time now.

Seven years she slept. My mother. Seven years and then she was gone.

I don't have seven years. I have to find a way to stay awake. Because it's here, isn't it? They're here. The things I need. I know they are.

I've made myself get out of bed and come here for coffee again. Have to stay awake. The walk nearly destroyed me. The wind was freezing and full of stinging saltwater. My face feels raw from it. I have sand in my hair. I'm bedraggled. I'm the only one in the place, though, so there's that, and I'm sat right by the fire. A woman came out from behind the bar and gave me a towel and a concerned look. I'm fine, I told her. I just had to get out of the House. I can't think straight in there.

My journal is... confusing.

Also. There are a thousand messages from Pete on my phone. I was drafting a response but. What is there to say.

Every time I think about Pete, I get a twinge in my left ankle, a painful pinch. My body jolts, jumps a little to the side.

I composed a text to him, avoiding the question of when and if I plan to go home. I tried to be chatty, and joke about the weather here. I will probably die of cold, I typed.

But then I just deleted it all. He doesn't care, does he? He just wants to know when I'm coming back so we can start dividing up our possessions and getting on with the rest of our lives.

He can have everything, I don't fucking care.

Please follow me towards the back of the house. The floorboards undulate below your feet. If you feel sick or disorientated, please hold on to the walls. You will find yourself in front of a closed door.

Gather close to me so I can whisper. Behind this door are many sleeping children who must not be woken. They are beautiful children. Some of them are only babies. They won't wake up. The waking world is beyond their ability to comprehend or absorb. They are children coated in napalm. They are babies thrown into ditches. Passed around from man to man in dirty rooms and sheds. They are walled in by a courtroom of fleshy, dragging faces, mouths all moving incomprehensibly, violently. The cradle is rocked by the tremors of gunfire, the chess game of landmines in a rice field, a nuclear bomb detonated in the middle of a shopping precinct.

Wait. Press your palm against the door.

Those sleeping within are travelling very great astral distances. They are travelling very far from their bodies. Their bodies are meaningless galaxies that cannot hold them in orbit.

You may not go inside. You may not look at them. You may only imagine them. Imagine this door opens onto a rippling field of grass.

There's a windmill, sails turning against a wild summer sky. Inside, women are pulling threads from the wind, skeins of red and yellow and mauve and gold, and strands of cloud as soft as breath. They're weaving a flying carpet as warm and gentle as the air, to bear the children to their heavens.

I like to imagine that.

I saw her. I think I saw her. On the beach, coming back from the cafe.

When I was a child, I caught a fleeting glimpse
out of the corner of my eye
I turned to look but it was gone
I cannot put my finger on

She was dressed in royal blue. She was walking ahead of me, so I only saw her back, her hair in braids. And the wind wuthered between us, and when I called her name, the wind snatched it away.

But I think it was her. I recognised her walk, her way of being in the world. God, I felt so desperate to catch her up, to touch her, see her, but my legs would hardly move against the wind, I felt I was being pushed back. I yelled her name, over and over, but it was just sounds lifted away in the air. I willed her to turn around and see me. I needed her to look at me. But at the same time, I had the strangest feeling that I wasn't really there. That if she turned towards me, she would see nothing but the grey-brown beach and the slate sea, and my voice calling her name would be nothing but an echo, a scrap of sound, of seagulls scraping the wind.

Of all the doors I've made, this will be

a door that swings open into
it is better to say nothing. Should someone come.
    I am asleep when Raewyn lies down beside me on the bed. I think
it is Raewyn but perhaps it is Tanith. They look just the same and I can't
tell them apart in my sleep. But when the guest comes I am awake, wide
awake, and flowing into other dimensions.
    I can make a door out of anything. I can make a door from myself,
into myself the house of my self, and others can come through. And that
way we can remember. It all.
    (It was the day the space shuttle exploded
she cried so much she had a headache
you think it's a safe area
the children will be safe here, you think)
    The television explodes and great black plumes of smoke fall away
into the void in the middle of the kitchen.
    I will come back and it will be -
    and she will be -
    and it will be like giving birth, like going through a door, like you
went through the door of my body and into the room so now you can
come back. If you can come back, if you step through me, if you all come
through into the room of myself. I will mother, I will guide you, I will
re-create myself as your mother-guide. I will wake up and be that.
    (get up get up get up
you lazy selfish bitch get up)
    The woman mops up blood, so much blood. She sluices the blood-
soaked mop into her white bucket. There's blood on the walls, on the
window. And screaming—
    There should be the sound of screaming.

I was woken, I don't know when, by knocking. Loud,
hollow, repetitive, boom boom boom through the House.
The guest said, answer it. I was so tired, so exhausted, my
limbs felt like noodles, like useless. I dragged myself to
the front door holding on to the walls, and all the while

the knocking went on and on, boom boom boom, like the House had a heart and it was beating loudly — and I opened the door and it was Pete.

He reached for me, to try to hold me up, and I stumbled away from him. I fell. I don't know what I said, I can't remember what he said. We were in the kitchen and he was making coffee. I said, don't turn the tap! Because I knew that blood would flow out like water. The blood was everywhere. The table, the chairs, they all had blood in the grooves of wood, in the grain. It was in between the floor tiles. Splashed across the ceiling.

He turned on the tap and water came out. The coffee pot gurgled. I said, what do you want?

He said, how? How can you stay here like this? I can hardly breathe for all the dust. You didn't even take the dust sheets off the furniture. How have you been staying here like this?

I was going to do it, I said. Clean and tidy. I was going to, but I was so tired, too tired. I needed to think.

He made me drink the coffee. Then he came with me to my old bedroom, not the one we shared before, but the one I stayed in after, and he said,

Raewyn!

or did he say Tanith

He shook out the bed covers and the air filled with thick grey clumps of dust, which set him coughing. I lay down on the bed and Pete went away and came back and started shoving everything into black bin liners. He picked up that old record and held it out.

is there anybody in there

He said, well this is fucked.

A great jagged crack through the centre of the disc.

I said, it plays fine, don't throw it away.

He started up the hoover and I watched the floor come clean and bright. There was dust in his hair and I wanted to brush it out, but it was impossible to touch him, he was too angry, he hated me too much.

there'll be no more

The record played and the guest swam up inside me, flowed over me and through me. She filled my body with her body.

the inside of the labyrinth is possession

What's this? Pete held up my mother's notebook. He flipped through the pages.

There's nothing in it, he said. Some pages ripped out, he said. Do you want to keep it?

Please stand on the black X.

Please do not panic.

You may be experiencing the void as a mirror.

Remember you agreed to accept everything.

If you no longer wish to accept Raewyn Penderyn as your body, please say clearly: I am not Raewyn Penderyn.

I don't believe you. You wrench the mirror from your mother's dresser, tear it from its hinges and smash it on the floorboards. It shatters. Glass bounces around the room. You pick up the end of the dresser and use its foot to crush the mirror to powder.

Or this.

You are facing a mirror. Press your palms against the glass. She looks the same as you, exactly the same. You are both so beautiful, both with that same bright smile that lights up your eyes. As you press your hands to her hands, you will begin to feel the softness of the mirror. Nothing in the world is solid, not deep down.

A mirror is soft, one of the softest substances you know. It is a slow silvery melting under your skin.

If you wish to experience the door now, please say clearly: yes.

I'm sorry, I didn't hear that. If you would like to go through the door, please say clearly: yes.

We are on the train. Away, away. The line curves around the coast. We race through tunnels of green, past slopes of concrete. The smells of the sea and the beach come to us in scraps through the train windows, but we are racing away, and the smells are fading, and the beach is getting smaller and smaller in the distance, until it is a round grey eye at the end of a long wavering tunnel. A long, long tunnel. We are far distant. We are looking from elsewhere, through a narrow spyglass. Through a fisheye spyhole in a locked and bolted door.

Dogs

———————◉———————

Dr Head stops me on the stairs. He's wearing the dog head mask I made in art therapy. I am happy to see it again; they confiscated it after I wore it to the supermarket one time. They're not really allowed to confiscate my things. I complained, and filled out a long yellow form.

The doctor puts his stubby fingers on my arm, and turns his long dog nose towards me.

"We have an appointment," he says.

In his office I sit on the small brown chair, and he sits opposite. He takes off the dog head mask and puts it on the desk in between us.

Dr Head smiles, briefly, and ticks a box on his notepad. (I expect it is the 'smile at patient' box.) He writes some things down, leaning over his pad and frowning, as if it is a great work of art, which perhaps it is. While he isn't looking, I pick up the dog head mask and cradle it in my arms, holding it very gently so as not to crush its delicate papier-mâché skull. I stroke its nose.

This is my very favourite thing in the world.

"How have you been?" The doctor doesn't look up from his pad. "You are still having the migraines? Hallucinations? Distortions?"

He shines a light in my eyes. I want to protest at the way he pulls back my eyelids so firmly. It makes my brow bone ache and bright spots flash in my vision. But I don't say anything. I never say anything, because I don't know what to say.

The doctor looks in my ears with his intrusive beam of light. I wonder if it is possible to see right down the twisting ear canals and stare at my brain.

"Any more headaches?"

The usual. Quite bad. I have to go to bed when they come.

Dr Head flicks the light off.

"And are you sleeping well, or not so well?"

I pull myself up onto the bed, and at once there are tendrils of ivy and flowering vine growing out from the floral bedspread. They twine around my wrists and ankles and across my forehead and throat. A woody thicket grows around me and weaves me into its centre. I'm spiked all over by thorns, like in an iron maiden; a rose maiden, pricked to bleeding. Red roses bloom under my eyes, over my stomach.

I can hear, beyond my thorny prison, the sound of a chainsaw buzzing, and then you lift the tangled bushes away, leaving thorns spearing my eyes and my lips, and you lie down on top of me, your whole body over mine, and your nose touching my nose, your long hair hanging around my face.

You look the same, but you smell different. The tang of blood is on you. You kiss my neck, and the velvet roses drop their petals around us. You push your penis into my hand. It is like a licked bone. It slicks through my fist, and you breathe hard in my face. A tremendous heat radiates from us; a jungle shoots up around us, bright green, obliterating the winter garden.

When I wake up, the dog head mask is next to the bed, and

I am alone.

I lie still for several minutes, waiting for my dreams to leave, for the day to settle upon me. I feel it is a good day. My head is light and empty, without that knocking feeling, that lump of pain rolling against my temple when I move. My body feels loose and open. I am wet between my legs and I put a hand down to feel myself, bringing it back up bloody.

My period has come in the night. Dark wet blood soaks into the sheets. When I walk to the shower, I leave a trail of red droplets spotting the carpet. The water runs pink, and slugs of flesh slide down my legs.

I'm too scared to use a tampon today, in case it gives me a headache. I don't know why it should, but this is something I worry about. I do not want my body to be plugged up and stoppered. Perhaps this is a mediaeval idea: purging, the expulsion of black humours, bloodletting.

There are books I could read on the subject. I could find a connection between migraines and blood. I am well enough, today, to read a book. Perhaps well enough to go into work, although it's already late. I dress for work, anyway, and a few minutes later I am outside.

I am wearing sensible shoes, a tweed skirt, woollen tights, a high-necked jumper and a coat, and with the dog mask over my head I am warm despite the November chill. There's a short cut I can take, walking past the bridge and turning into the steep, hidden steps at the top of a cul-de-sac, which lead down to the canal path. It is very quiet. I sense there is a diffuse, spreading pain in the dog head mask. It is not my pain. It belongs to the dog. Or so it seems to me.

I stop, so that I can stand and breathe. Count my breaths, as I have been taught. Through the eyes of the dog head mask, the world has a dusky glow, a blurred edge, like an old silent movie.

There is something moving in the canal, bobbing on the

oily surface: a piece of old carpet, a white eye. Then it turns over with an obscene gulp and I see it is a dead dog, floating on the water. I don't know if it is real or hallucinated, because then the dog's pain becomes mine; it stabs through my temples and the acrid taste of chilies fills my mouth.

She comes to the hospital on my birthday. She brings samosas, pakora, spicy dumplings, all wrapped up in clean tea towels. I look at the food but do not touch it, and the nurse puts it on the bedside table.

We don't speak and she will not look at me. I mention the weather, but she only grimaces, as if hearing my voice gives her physical pain, which perhaps it does. What does she want from me? Why does she come? I want her to strike me. I would like her to push me back on the bed and strangle me, to scream in my face. Anything, just show some emotion.

If anything, this seems to be forgiveness.

The food smells wonderful. It fills the whole ward with its scent. I'm hungry, but I don't want her to watch me eat the food she has prepared. It is flavored with her tears. It is dreadful to burden me with such sad, delicious food.

As soon as she leaves I stuff my face, pushing the food into my mouth, until my eyes sting and the heat of the chilies makes me cough. The other patients watch me angrily, resentfully. They want me to make myself sick, but I keep everything down until later, when the headache comes back and I vomit up all the food. It burns my throat when it comes back up, but I scarcely notice.

"This isn't good," the Manager tells me, over tea in pale green cups. She sighs. The sides of her face puff out. I think she could blow a ship across an ocean with a sigh like that.

I can't look at her. She is too kind to me, and it makes me cry. I hold onto my cup, tightly, because I am trembling. The tea stirs itself into a whirlpool, and milky brown waves rise up at the sides of the china.

"You don't work here anymore," she says. "You can't keep coming here all the time. It's not right. You have a serious condition."

She hands me a cigarette and I jam it in the corner of the dog mask's mouth. Smoke fills the inside of the head, and I suck it into my lungs, trying not to choke. When I cough, it sounds like I'm barking.

"For god's sake." She puffs angrily at her cigarette. "Just take it off."

I would like to take the mask off, if only to please the manager. She has been kind to me. But I know it won't come off, and I can't explain it, so I don't try. We sit in silence for a while.

Finally she says, "Why do you keep coming here?"

There is nothing I can say, nothing I deserve to say. If it were possible, I might tell her, I am lonely. Lonely apple falling from a tree; lonely bone gnawed by a dog; lonely *thing* without a will of its own. A thing with no substance, no reality, or at least no more than an apple or a bone.

There is nothing to say, because my story is everywhere already. I am written about in medical journals. The library has a file on me. The police. There are witness statements, insurance claims, expert reports. What can I add? What more can I say? I have only these moments, the moments in which I live, and they are private, and I am ashamed of them.

Shame feels like cold cotton sheets under my hands as I sit and watch you pack. The suitcase is hard and has a satin lining. I watch you fill it with clothes, carefully folding everything. So neat, as if someone is watching you. Someone other than me, I mean. You take a framed photograph from the wall and two books from the bedside table, and your watch, throwing them all into the case and closing it with a series of loud snaps. The sound of the case shutting is so definite, so final. *There*, it seems to say. *That's that.*

My car is parked outside. I want to ask you, are you sure? Are you sure you're sure? Your face is grim and determined, not happy. I don't want you to leave your wife. I want you to stay. I want to finish it with you, just get up and walk away. But it's too late; you've decided for us both, and I can't find the words to tell you that it's a mistake. You take my hand and I follow you downstairs, you bumping the suitcase against your leg, and at the front door you pick up the leash and you whistle, a choppy little whistle.

A door slams in the top of my head, and I drop out of the sky and into my bed. It is a horrible way to wake up. I hate being in the hospital. Everything is white and cream and pale blue, washed out. They have drawn the curtains around me, and made the bed with me still in it, sheets up to my neck, pulled taut over me.

Today, I am going home.

I lied and said that someone was coming to pick me up. They didn't want to let me go all by myself, and I was scared that if I hesitated, they would ask *her* to come. She is my only visitor, after all. I imagine her driving me back in her white Subaru, and leading me up the stairs in her perfect, quiet, empty house. She would insist I sleep in her bedroom, wear her robe, use her towels. She'd tuck me up in her bed, the bed where I fucked her husband, the one and only time we fucked, and where I watched him pack his case and leave her.

128

Perhaps she would show me the vase where she keeps his ashes. She might let me touch it. I will want to run my fingers through the ashes, but she will snatch the vase away from me with a cold look. "That's mine," she will say.

This is unbearable. This must not happen. I am panicking even though I know that this doesn't happen, that in fact I walk out of the hospital alone, and go home to my own flat, alone, and get straight into my own, cold bed, in a room full of ghosts.

The paper is wet in my hands. It has its own intense smell, wet newsprint; the soft animal smell of the glue; the acid metal smell of the chicken wire frame. The paper sticks to my fingers, paste sliding onto my palms, but I patiently lay it out. Layer by layer, it becomes something. A face. A loved face.

The teacher is a short, stocky woman who moves her hands awkwardly when she speaks. "This is interesting," she says, making a long sweeping gesture, as if she is trying to sell my mask on a tacky shopping channel. "Fascinating. Tell me about it."

I shrug, keeping my eyes on the mask.

"What does this mean to you?"

The newspaper is melting in the paste, but I can still read the print, every word of it. I try to avoid it but it is not possible, the words are pasted to the inside of my eyelids, the inside of my skull. I cannot escape the story, my story. Even though it is all chopped up like a salad.

"You lost your dog in the accident," she says, holding her palms out to me.

That is not the point, I think to myself. Why does everyone keep missing the point?

Love me, love my dog, that's what you always say. The secret joke is that I love the dog anyway, easily. It is not hard to love a dog, soft creatures made of loyalty and fun. I might have told you, there in the hallway. I might have said, even though you had the suitcase in your hand, I think I could have told you that I didn't love you. But when you whistled, the blonde dog came bounding up to us, ecstatic and blissful, and I thought that I could not bear to walk away and leave it behind.

The dog sits up in the back seat of my car, pushing its head between us, breathing hot doggy air on my shoulder. We are all laughing. You tell me you're so happy, that you know it's the right thing to do. And I agree, yes, it's right. It feels right. But there she is: your wife, my friend, coming home to an empty house, to a note from you with my name in it. *I love her. I want to be with her. It's not you. It's me. It's her.* And not even the dog there for comfort. But then I think of us, the three of us walking in the park, you throwing a stick for the dog. A family.

I'm stealing her life, her whole life.

I'm not laughing anymore, just driving, putting my foot down and speeding off in the getaway car. Getting the hell out of there before the sirens come screaming down.

You put your hand on my leg and say, hey, slow down sweetheart.

The taste of chilies in my mouth, and the smell of blood in my nose, and the sharp cold November bring me back. There is blood puddling in my underwear, soaking into the gusset of my tights. I forgot to wear something to soak it up. It has a strong scent, not unpleasant.

I can smell everything that has ever fallen into the canal, including the dead dog. It drifts into the weeds; a bloated and oily white body, its eye turned on me with interest, its tail bobbing in the water. Old Faithful.

Should I have asked her to come for me? She would have come, I feel sure. Come to sing her sadness deep, to show off her sadness, which I cannot stand. Her sadness is perfect and complete, a detergent kind of sadness that wipes out all the breeding confusion of life. Mine is gross and messy; it garners no sympathy. I am sorry for myself, most of all. How can I live like this? I don't even have my job at the library anymore. How could I forget that?

I contemplate putting stones in my pockets, like Virginia Woolf, and falling into the water.

When I get home, I find that I can't take off the dog head mask. It's stuck. I telephone Dr Head, but they cannot put me through. They have never heard of Dr Head. Of course, I knew that wasn't his real name, but I forgot.

They think I'm crazy, but I just forgot. Anyone can forget.

My voice is muffled by the dog mask, distorted by having to travel along the long snout and into the receiver. It sounds like a series of growls and yelps. I realize that this is what I am doing: growling and yelping. I am chewing the phone handset with my long teeth. It is satisfying, chewy and crunchy.

I'll go to bed and sleep it off.

I'll curl up in my corner, in the old flowered duvet, and dream of being human.

WAKE UP, PHIL

———◉———

Laura Harrison pinned the image to the soft grey foam of her cubicle wall. It was a picture she'd torn from a magazine—a sweet-looking real puppy, chewing on a flower. Its big brown eyes expressed a mixture of fear and happiness—excited to be chewing the flowers, worried it was going to get into trouble for it. Not too worried, though. No one was going to beat this little sweetie or put it out into the Glare. Laura thought if it were her puppy she might punish it with some enthusiastic hugs or belly rubs. Not that she would ever be able to have a puppy, a real one. It was just a dream.

She already had quite a few pictures pinned up in her cubicle and was nervous about adding another. Strictly speaking, Serberus permitted employees on this level up to three personal items in their cubicle. Laura was never sure if this included pictures. Most people seemed to have one or two pictures and maybe an ornament, but Laura's cubicle definitely stood out as being more decorated than the others. She chewed her fingernails while she thought about it. Then the computer beeped, and she hurried to sign in and start work.

At eleven, Alison came by and tapped Laura's shoulder. Laura smiled hello. She liked Alison. Even though Alison was her supervisor and could report her to the higher levels, she was pretty normal, most of the time.

"That is just so adorable," she said, looking at the real puppy.

Laura sighed. "I know. It looks so soft and sweet."

"It really does." She gazed at some of the other pictures in the cubicle, lingering over one in particular.

"Now this, I don't get at all," Alison said. She traced her finger over the card. It was the image of a woman, but the woman had been cut into pieces and reassembled in an odd way.

"It's by Pablo Picasso," Laura said.

"Ooh. Very fancy, I must say."

She smiled, but it was only with her mouth. She wouldn't meet Laura's eye.

"Now, what did I come here for? Oh yes. You're to go up to the eleventh floor. Appointment with Dr Throom."

Laura's stomach sank. "Eleventh floor?"

"Oh now, it's nothing to worry about. Very standard, just routine. You've been with us a few years and it's time for a little check-up from the neck-up."

Everyone knew that once the eleventh floor noticed you, you were done for. Laura had seen it happen to colleagues—people she had liked. They got called up on routine checks, and you never saw them again. Rumour had it they were assigned to a colony, or worse. Her mind raced through memories of the past few days—had she done anything that the Company would notice? Consumed any non-Serberus products or made any positive references to the enemy? She glanced at the picture of the real puppy. Was that it?

In the elevator, she tried to calm herself with some deep breaths. It would only make things worse if she went in there with sweaty palms and hyperventilating. She hadn't done anything wrong, she was sure of that. Pretty sure.

The elevator seemed to take an age to get to the eleventh floor. When the doors finally pinged open, Laura had (she hoped) composed her face in a semblance of confident calm.

The eleventh floor was the highest she had been in the

building. There was a wide expanse of carpet to traverse to get to the reception desk and the receptionist was one of the most beautiful women Laura had ever seen in real life.

"Can I help you?"

Laura was still yards away from the desk when the receptionist called out, and she hurried over, feeling her body to be something cumbersome and grotesque she was dragging around with her.

"I have an appointment with Dr Throom," she said.

"Yes."

The receptionist tapped her long, hard nails on the counter top.

"Laura Harrison," said Laura. She was beginning to sweat again. The receptionist was making her nervous.

"Wait there. The doctor is with someone right now."

Laura took a seat on a cheap foam sofa, several yards away from the reception desk. She wasn't sure how to sit. Was there some way of sitting that would demonstrate a sane and well-adjusted mind? Maybe the truly sane and well-adjusted didn't spend so much time worrying about how they sat on a sofa. Maybe if she was truly sane and well-adjusted, they wouldn't have called her up to the eleventh floor.

After several minutes, the receptionist directed her to Dr Throom's office. The doctor was in his fifties, with a comb-over and an avuncular manner.

"I'm so sorry you had to wait, Miss Harrison," he said. "I hope you didn't mind too much?"

"No."

It sounded rather blunt, that 'no.' Rather stark, just out there on its own. Maybe she should say something else, but the doctor was already talking again.

"Do you know why you're here?"

"Is it about the puppy picture? Because I can take it down—I mean, I can take all the pictures down, if that's better."

"Oh, you like puppies? Well, then. My little girl is just the same. She's six and all she ever says is, 'Daddy please can we have a puppy?' It's quite enchanting." He put on a little girl voice to demonstrate. "Daddy, please! Just a little one!"

Laura shifted in her seat. Maybe she shouldn't have mentioned the puppy.

"Of course, I don't make that sort of money. I've said I'll get her a Serberpuppy for her birthday. Do you think she'll be satisfied with that, Miss Harrison?"

"I guess... I don't know..."

"Well, we're not here to talk about puppies, are we?" Dr Throom smiled and laced his fingers together.

"You're a little overweight, aren't you, Miss Harrison?"

Laura blushed. "It's hormonal," she said.

"Now, now, it's fine to carry a little extra. I do myself. But we all have to think about the image we're projecting into the world, don't we? We don't want anyone to think we're like those greedy fat bastards at Callitrix."

"I only choose Serberus foods," Laura said. "Serberus Low Cal meals. It doesn't seem to do anything... I mean... my endocrine system, the doctor said it was a mess and..."

"Serberus meals are designed to be nutritious and complete for every kind of body."

"I know." Laura felt tears coming. She tried to hold them back.

"Serberus cares about you," the doctor said. Kindly, gently, he tilted his head to one side. "Serberus wants the best for all citizens."

"Are you going to send me to the colonies? To the war?"

Dr Throom barked out a laugh. "Goodness, no! What an idea."

Laura felt a tear escape and roll down her cheek. She brushed it away.

136

"What then?"

"Serberus wants to help you, Laura. I can call you Laura, can't I?"

She nodded, biting her lip.

"My dear... Think of Serberus as your family. If a family member was struggling, wouldn't you want to help? Of course you would, and that's why we've developed Serberitum."

The doctor gestured to a poster on the wall behind him. There was a picture of a sunset and a very slim woman in a bikini holding up a bottle of tablets. Across her thighs, in block letters, was the legend: NOTHING TASTES AS GOOD AS SERBERITUM FEELS.

"It's a drug?"

"For weight loss!" The doctor grinned.

"I can't afford it," Laura said. "I'm only a level 2 employee."

"But that's the beauty part," said Dr Throom. "This is the part of my job that I have to tell you is so rewarding. When I can help a person like you."

He handed Laura a white paper bag. "Six months' supply."

"I don't understand."

"All we ask is that you report in every couple of weeks and let us know how you're getting on, tell us about any side effects or anything like that."

"Side effects?"

"There won't be any. Serberus pharmaceutical products are rigorously tested to comply with all global standards for medicines."

Laura opened the bag and peered inside. "Do I have a choice?"

"A choice? *Obviously* you have a choice! This is Serberus, not those commie bastards Callitrix."

He glanced at his watch, and smiled apologetically.

She stood. "Where should I go now?"

"Back to level two, of course. Where else?"
He held his office door open for her.

After work, she took the south tunnel home. The Glare was particularly ferocious that day and even in the air-conditioned tunnels she imagined she could feel the boiling heat outside. Once, when she had been very young, no more than a baby, she had played outside in the street, rolling a pebble over the scratchy pavement, leaving a chalky white mark. But when she asked her parents about it, they said it had never happened. They said they wouldn't have let a small child out into the Glare, not even in those days. Maybe they just didn't remember.

She stepped onto the tributary walkway that led to her building, and then the elevator up to her floor. It was impossible not to imagine what it would have been like to walk outside, to walk home from work. She imagined there were still sidewalks and roads, empty of course, between the overlapping black tubes of the tunnels and walkways. She had heard that, very rarely, a weed would grow from the cracks in the road, but it would always be dead within hours, parched of life.

The viewscreen in her apartment came on automatically when she walked in, showing the news. Callitrix losses to Serberus in the colonies. THOUSANDS OF CALLITRIX FORCES SURRENDER... SERBERUS REJOICES AT GAINS ON MARS COLONY. Laura switched the screen off. She opened the bag of tablets and put them out on the table. Six bottles. She opened one and tipped the tablets out. Thirty tablets. There was a leaflet in the bag.

NOTHING TASTES AS GOOD AS SERBERITUM FEELS*
TAKE ONE PER DAY WITH SERBERWATER.

*SERBERUS WILL NOT BE LIABLE FOR ANY
MEDICAL PROBLEMS RESULTING FROM THE
USE OF THIS PRODUCT.

Laura wondered if taking the whole lot would kill her.
She picked up a tablet and put it on her tongue. Maybe it
would make her thin. Maybe she would get promoted to
Level 3. She ought to be happy to have this opportunity to
change her life. Diet pills were some of the most expensive
medications around—after paying for air, and meals and
water, there would never be enough left over to pay for
something like this.

She swallowed the tablet and washed it down with a
glass of Serberwater.

There was nothing on the viewscreen except for
news, and messages that popped up from her parents and
colleagues. Alison sent a message saying, 'so glad you came
back x'. Laura muted the messages and switched over to
the Cute Puppies channel. She sat for three hours watching
them playing, running over grass, being picked up and
cuddled by their humans. She watched a dog carrying her
puppy over a stream, then they both put their heads down
and scooped up the water with their tongues, the puppy
looking up at its mother to check it was doing it right. After
a while, Laura felt her eyes drooping shut. She lay down on
the sofa and within moments she was asleep.

Martin was out in the garden, on his knees by the rose
border, wearing his red shirt and yellow board shorts.

"Very colourful. You'll get bees trying to pollinate you,"
Laura said. She handed him the tall glass of lemonade and
he drank it down and wiped his mouth with the back of his
hand.

"I already got stung," he said, and held out a skinny

wrist for her to inspect. A small red welt had risen there. She put her lips to it and kissed.

When she raised her head, she noticed their neighbour across the street was watching them. He'd moved in a few weeks ago, but they hadn't had much to do with him. A draft dodger, Martin called him. Some kind of a writer, apparently. He was slightly fat, he had a beard, and he wore Hawaiian shirts with great big flowers on them. Phil something-or-other, his name was. His house was always full of hippies and drop outs, hanging out, smoking marijuana. Laura waved to him and he raised a hand in greeting.

Martin belched.

"That lemonade tastes like ass," he said.

"It's Serberus brand," Laura said. "I won't buy it again."

"We should make our own," Martin said, gesturing towards the lemon tree at the end of their plot. "If life gives you lemons, and all that."

Laura poured the rest of the lemonade down the sink, then washed out the plastic bottle. What were you supposed to do with all the plastic bottles, she wondered. You threw them away, but they didn't go anywhere. They just clogged up the landfill sites. You couldn't burn them. And if you buried them under the ground, they released all these chemicals that got into the food. She sighed. She assumed that the government were working on it, but it was worrying, nonetheless. She peeled the label from the lemonade bottle. SERBERUS BRAND. A stray thought crossed Laura's mind.

NOTHING TASTES AS GOOD AS SERBERITUM FEELS.

Serberitum? What the hell was that? Laura looked at the list of ingredients, but she couldn't see Serberitum listed. It sounded familiar, though. Definitely sounded like something she'd heard before. She rolled the word around in her head for a while. When Martin came in to wash his hands, she asked him if he'd ever heard of it.

"Sure," he said. "It's in those tablets the doctor gave you. You're still taking those, right?"

He put his arms around her waist and kissed her neck.

"That's it," she said. "That's been bugging me like crazy."

"I remember because you made me practically memorise the leaflet." He was nuzzling against her collarbone now, and working his hands down her back.

"I was worried about the side effects," she said. She wanted to push him away, but didn't.

"Silly," he said. "All those things you used to worry about. The environment and Vietnam and all that stuff."

They went into the bedroom and Martin pulled the curtains against the strong afternoon light. He took off his shirt and sat on the bed, patting the space next to him.

"Let me just take my tablet," she said. "I don't want to fall asleep and forget about it."

"Sure, honey."

She went through to the bathroom and took out the bottle of pills. Ran down the list of ingredients and there it was. Serberitum 100%. She took her pill, splashed her face with water and went back through to the bedroom.

"All done?"

"All done," she said.

Their lovemaking was brief and not unbearable. Since she had been a little blue, she had gone off sex. The tablets were supposed to help her feel more inclined towards it, but she hadn't noticed any difference in that department. She'd lost a little weight, though. She felt lighter than she had for a while. Martin said he liked her skinny. He moved against her, moaned into her ear. She moaned back. It wasn't possible for her to relax and enjoy it. Whenever she closed her eyes, her mind raced with images of burning children, and forests turning to deserts. There was a hole in the ozone layer now, that's what some people were saying. It was going to get bigger and bigger and everyone would have to live underground or something.

The doctor said that it was common for young women to have these kinds of thoughts.

"The best thing for girls like you is a baby," he said. "You need something to focus your energies on. Keep trying. But in the meantime, I think these new brands of tranquillizers will really help."

The tablets had helped, a little. But not enough to stop her from worrying about how things were going. Everyone had a car now, even Martin had a Ford. All that lead in the air, all the crude oil they were pumping up from under the ground. And there were bombs, nuclear weapons. The Soviets had theirs aimed right at them.

Martin shuddered and she yelped and groaned, hoping this would help speed the conclusion. It did. He rolled off her and reached for his cigarettes.

"Aww honey," she said. "I wish you wouldn't smoke in the bedroom."

"You should try it," Martin said. "It calms your nerves."

"You know it's supposed to be bad for you."

"So they say."

He smoked the rest of it in silence, and then stubbed it out and rolled towards her, breathing his chemical-laced breath into the crook of her neck.

"Honey," he said. "This is all I ever dreamed of."

When he fell asleep, Laura got up and went to the bathroom. She showered and put on her summer dress. It was still light outside, and all the plants and flowers were soaking up the Californian sunshine. She decided she'd go out and sit for a while. One thing that made her feel better was being out in nature.

The neighbour was still in his front yard when she went out into the garden. He waved to her and she raised her hand.

"Hey," he yelled.

She smiled and sat down on the bench.

"Hey, could you come over here for a minute?"

She looked down at her dress, her bare feet, and over at her neighbour. Would it be all right to go over there, dressed like this? She could hardly refuse, it would seem terribly rude. They were neighbours, after all.

She crossed the road. The tarmac was warm and very slightly sticky under her feet.

"It sure is hot today," she said.

The neighbour nodded slowly, as if she was saying something really profound.

"Hey," he said. "Do you partake?"

He offered her the joint he was smoking. She thought about his big red lips bogarting the end of it, and shook her head.

"I'm Phil," he said.

"Laura."

They didn't shake hands.

"Can you help me with something, Laura?"

"I guess."

"It's in the house. I need a second opinion. Maybe you can think what to do about it."

She knew it was dumb, following this guy she didn't even know inside his house. A den of drug taking. There were always people hanging around there, students and drop outs, draft dodgers. The kind of people that got Martin really worked up. (If he didn't have his eyesight problem, he would have been proud to serve his country.) Laura looked at Phil's soft body, his clever face. He didn't seem like a loser to her. She was interested in these people, the people that hung around here sometimes. At least they cared what was happening in the world. They went on marches and recycled their stuff.

Inside, the house was dark and smelled of unwashed

143

laundry and marijuana and paper. There were books piled up against every wall, and stacks of paper on every surface. Even some of the walls had writing on them.

Laura followed Phil down a narrow hallway.

"My husband says you're a writer," Laura said.

"I guess I am," Phil said, without turning around.

He led her through to a back bedroom. He held open the door for her and she had a moment of panic as she wondered what might be about to happen. But nothing happened, except that it was dark and she said, "Can you switch on the light?"

He flipped the switch, and Laura saw that he had jumped onto the bed and was lying there with his eyes shut. His Hawaiian shirt buttoned up. On his back, his belly flattened, his chunky fingers splayed against the sheets.

"I can't wake him up," said Phil.

She looked round. He was standing at her side. She looked back to the bed. He was there, too.

"I've tried everything," Phil said. He sat down on the bed next to himself. "I guess maybe I need an outside person to help."

Laura felt herself swaying back towards the wall.

"Are you okay?" Phil asked.

"Fine, I'm fine," she said. But even as she spoke, she felt the contents of her stomach rising and pushing at her throat. She ran outside and fell to all fours on the grass, spewing lemonade from her guts.

"Get me Throom."

Laura Harrison tapped her fingers on the desk and watched the beautiful receptionist hurry off towards the doctor's office door. Laura hated coming down from the thirteenth floor. It was true you could feel the Glare more strongly down here.

"Please come through, Ms Harrison," the receptionist said.

Throom stood up when Laura walked into the room. They shook hands.

"This is an unexpected pleasure," Throom said.

Laura sighed. She disliked the obsequiousness with which the lower levels had to treat her, and which it was her duty to bestow on those above her in turn. It wouldn't do to question it, though. One always had to protect one's position in the company.

"I want to ask you about Callitaxor. What do you know about it?"

"Callitaxor... It's one of our top sellers in the weight loss range. I can get someone from pharmaceuticals to come in and talk to you..."

"That's all right. You see, I've been taking it myself for a while. And I wanted to ask you about side effects."

Throom shifted uncomfortably in his seat. "If I may say, Ms Harrison, I can't imagine you needing to lose any weight at all."

Privately, Laura agreed with him. If anything, she was too thin now. Her clothes hung off her and she couldn't get comfortable in bed because of the way the mattress pressed on her bones. But Martin said he liked her skinny. And it had probably been a factor in her promotion to the thirteenth floor.

"And the side effects?"

"Callitrix pharmaceutical products are rigorously tested to comply with all global standards for medicines."

"Have there been any reports of... well, any odd effects? Feeling a little displaced, I suppose."

Throom gazed at her, nodding his head. "Should I arrange for a medical?"

Too late, she realised that she had made a mistake going to Throom. He could start a rumour against her. That she was agitating against a Callitrix product, that she was making anti-company insinuations, anything.

Laura stood up. "It was nothing really, just a matter of curiosity."

"As far as I understand it, the main side effect of Callitaxor is weight loss."

"Is that so? A side effect? Then the intended effect is…?"

"Oh, it was something they were trying in the colonies for a while. Some kind of mental warfare. It didn't work at all, but they noticed that everyone they gave it to got skinny. Funny how science works."

"Mental warfare?"

"What you might call a hallucinogen."

"I see."

"But the chemists adapted it for civilian use, obviously. Have you experienced any unusual mental states, Ms Harrison?"

"Of course not."

Throom smiled, rather unctuously, Laura thought.

"You seemed a little distressed when you came in," he said.

"Did I? Well, perhaps it's the Glare. You know, it's definitely stronger down here. How do you stand it?"

He tilted his head. "How kind of you to be concerned."

"I'm very concerned," Laura said. "I certainly don't think you should have to labour away down here if we can find a place for you upstairs."

Throom's smile grew bigger, threatened to take over his face. "A move upstairs would be most welcome," he said.

In the elevator, Laura allowed herself to slump a little bit. Going to Throom had been a bad judgement call on her part. A terrible one. Why had she been so stupid? Now she had to find him a job on the twelfth floor—that meant sucking up to Martin. And there were no guarantees *that* was going to work. What an idiot she had been.

Martin was waiting for her when she walked into her office. He was looking at the map of the territories above her desk. The map lit up with a red light every time Callitrix took another mile of land.

"We're hammering those Serberus bastards," Martin said. "Good times."

"Great."

She went to her desk and opened the drawer. The bottle of pills were right there, where she'd left them.

"Did you want to see me about something?"

"Just wanted to say 'hi' to my wife."

Sure, Laura thought. She suspected he was having an affair with the beautiful receptionist from the twelfth floor. The higher up you went, the more beautiful they became. The receptionist on fifteenth was breath-taking—no one could even look at her.

Martin leaned across the desk and kissed her cheek.

"See you at home," he said.

When he left, Laura took the Callitaxor out of her desk drawer. Maybe she should stop taking them. She was thin enough, now. And that thing she had, stupidly, tried to tell Throom. It was like sometimes she was living in a different world. No, not so much that. At a deeper level of reality. It had been getting worse lately, and she suspected that the effect was cumulative. It frightened her to think that she might not be able to get back to the surface reality. This one. Clearly, *this* was the real reality.

She turned the bottle of tablets over in her hand, then something made her drop them on the floor. The bottle rolled away across the carpet, and she scrambled to pick it up. She stared at the label.

NOTHING TASTES AS GOOD AS SERBERITUM FEELS.

Serberitum? That wasn't possible. There couldn't be a Serberus product here, in this office, in Laura's own hands. She turned her desk out, looking for the Callitaxor. Had

Martin switched them? Was he capable of doing something so cruel? If they found her with Serberitum, she would lose her job. She'd be sent to the colonies. Or worse.

All right, she thought. All right. Calm down. She slowed her breathing and sat down behind her desk. Maybe eat something. Have a glass of water. She buzzed her secretary.

"Brad, bring me some Calliwater, and a Callisandwich."

"Right away, Ms Harrison."

He sounded normal. Everything seemed normal. It was only the bottle of tablets that was out of place. She looked at the label again. Serberitum. Was it Martin's idea of a joke?

She peeled the label from the bottle and burned it in the decorative glass ashtray on the desk, hoping it wouldn't set off the smoke alarm.

The puppies were still on when Laura woke up for work the next morning. She took her Callitaxor and had a quick shower. Unbelievably, she hadn't eaten since breakfast the morning before, and she wasn't hungry. This stuff really works, she thought. A thrill of excitement passed through her. If she was thin, she might get a promotion. She might attract the attention of one of the bigshots on the third floor. Maybe even the fourth. But she was getting ahead of herself, she knew. Her skirt still felt tight over her hips and she didn't look any different yet. And, she reminded herself, the eleventh floor were taking notice of her, and that was never a good thing. Best to keep her feet on the ground.

She had a Callicino and watched the puppies playing for a while. If she got promoted to the fourth floor, she could save up. She could have a Callihound. It wasn't the same as a real puppy, but it was still soft and you could hug it, and you could programme it to wag its tail when you came home and whimper when you left again. You could still love it. A real puppy could love you back, that was the difference.

By the time she got down to the walkway, she was lost in thoughts about what Callihound she would get. Ideally, she would like more than one. Of course, it would be stupid to buy two at the same time. Built-in obsolescence meant that Callihounds would die after seven years. She had heard of people hacking the motherboards to override the obsolescence function, but that was considered an anti-Callitrix act and you'd get sent to the colonies, or worse.

Lost in thought, she barely registered an overhead viewscreen showing Serberus gains in the colonies. Then, as she was crossing into the Northbound tunnel, she noticed the vendor on the corner was selling Serbercoffee. He had a poster pinned to his stall. A picture of a couple running through some long grass, and the legend: NOTHING TASTES AS GOOD AS SERBERITUM FEELS.

Laura's hand flew to her mouth. She stopped and leaned against the wall. *Serberus.* This was Serberus, not Callitrix. She turned out the waistband of her skirt. SerberWear brand. The label inside her shoe—SerberWalk. Her bag was made by SerberCarry. She looked around, seeing the same logo everywhere she looked. Of course it was Serberus. It had always been Serberus.

She heard a laugh, and turned towards it. Standing beneath a sign reading SERBERUS NORTH TUNNEL was a man. A slightly fat man with a beard. He stood out, dressed in a colourful shirt with flowers, and light-coloured trousers.

"There you are," he said.

The air was terribly hot, hotter than it ought to be, Laura thought. God, what if it were all true, about global warming and all those terrible things? The internet was full of people panicking about the weather. She looked around, at the cars going by. Fast, hungry machines. But then she saw something else. She stopped in her tracks and leaned forward, patting her hands on her legs. It came towards her on the end of a leash, wiggling with excitement, leaping up to lick her face.

Its owner yanked the puppy away. "I'm sorry," she said. "She's very excitable."

"It's okay," said Laura. "I have one just the same."

She walked along the street, anxious, but unable to pinpoint the cause of her anxiety. It was as if she had woken from a bad dream, the kind of dream that spoils your whole day.

By the time she got back to the apartment, Laura felt calmer. She opened the front door and Throom rushed out, wagging his little tail excitedly. Laura picked him up in her arms, kissing the soft fur.

"Hello baby," she said.

"Hi honey," Martin called her from the living room.

She went inside. He was sitting on the couch in the living room, the flat screen television taking up most of the wall in front of him. He was watching the news. Something about chemical warfare in the Middle East. Or was it nuclear weapons in China? Laura tried not to follow the news too closely. Whenever she did, she was gripped with fear about the future of the planet. It was depressing, because there was nothing she could do about it.

Throom wriggled in her arms.

"Good day?" Martin asked. He looked her up and down. "You know, you can really tell the difference since you started on those tablets. You look great."

Laura smiled. "They're really working," she said.

It was true. She felt smaller already. The waistband of her skirt was loose and her blouse was looking a little baggy. If anything, she was worried about how well the pills were working. And the side effects, of course. She was getting a lot of *déjà vu*, and other feelings she couldn't put a name to. Like right now. She was standing in the living room, watching Martin, cuddling Throom, but somehow she felt very far away from herself. Like she wasn't really there at all. It was a funny feeling. It made her laugh.

"Hey, do you remember that weird neighbour we had, years ago, back in Cali?"

"Sure," said Martin. "Crazy Phil. Sci-fi Phil."

"Well, I thought I saw him today, on the…" Now, where was it? Laura cast around in her mind for an image, or a word, and drew a mental blank. It had been happening more and more often, this inability to remember. This erosion of her world. Maybe it was old age.

"On the street?" Martin suggested.

"Maybe," said Laura. Damned if she could remember.

There was no discretion, no privacy, when they came for her. Of course not: they had to make an example for everyone to see. They marched into the office in big boots and crisp uniforms. Didn't speak, didn't say a word. Everyone saw them coming. Everyone *felt* it. Laura knew they were coming for her. She looked around her office, at the big, fake window and the faux wooden desk. Nowhere, nothing that could possibly save her. So she sat at her desk and tried to project an appearance of calm and concern.

Two male officers marched into her office.

"We have reason to believe that you have engaged in anti-company activity," said one of the officers. His face was round and almost childlike, but his narrowed eyes betrayed no compassion or kindness.

Laura gasped. It was half-pretend, half-real. "There must be a mistake."

"That is what we need to determine."

But everyone knew there were no mistakes.

Laura followed the men out of the room. Looking back over her shoulder, she saw more uniformed officers swarming into her work space, pulling open drawers and cabinets. *The pills,* she thought. *They were wrong—weren't they?* She turned away, faced forward with her head held high, avoiding the embarrassed looks of her colleagues and staff. But at the door to the elevator, she called out to Brad, "Call Martin, tell Martin," and Brad looked away.

They took her downstairs. She didn't know how many floors, and didn't ask. They were silent, impassive agents of the company. Which company? Wasn't that the whole problem?

They led her through a narrow corridor and finally into a small white office. There was nothing in there but bare walls and floor, and a table with chairs either side. There she was locked in, and left alone.

Martin would come, wouldn't he? As soon as he heard what happened. They had a lawyer—they had friends. She'd always done a good job, done her best for the company. That had to count for something. She convinced herself that it did. She told herself that this would all be over soon, and she could go home. When she heard the door being unlocked, her heart leapt. It must be Martin, come to get her out, to explain everything away. But it wasn't Martin who came into the room. It was Throom.

"Throom, thank God, I need your help—" Laura blurted out, falling silent when she saw the amused expression on the doctor's face.

Throom took a seat across from Laura and folded his hands across his chest.

"Well, Ms Harrison," he said. "Is it Callitrix or Serberus? Where do your loyalties lie?"

Laura stared at him. Her heart was throbbing, it felt like it was in her throat.

"It's a simple question, Laura. The answer ought to just

roll off your tongue."

She shook her head, unable to speak. Was it Callitrix? It was Callitrix this morning, she was sure. Or had it been Serberus? Maybe it was always Serberus. She looked around the room. No clues.

"Oh dear," said Throom.

"I'm loyal," said Laura. "You know I am. It's just I can't... it's a problem with my memory, not my loyalty to the company."

"But how can you be loyal to the company if you don't know what company it is that you're being loyal to? Where's the logic in that, Laura?"

"Can't you help me, Throom? Doctor? Just—help me."

Throom shook his head, slowly. "Now, after all I've done for you. After all the *company* has done for you."

"There must be something I can do, something you want." It came to her. "A dog! Your little girl wants a dog. I can get you one, I can buy one."

"Callihound or Serberpuppy?"

Laura slumped backwards. "You know I don't know."

"You're saying it doesn't matter?"

"No! I'm saying I don't remember."

"What don't you remember? Don't you remember how the company helped you, raised you up? Don't you remember when you were just a plump little number cruncher on the second floor?"

Laura shook her head, miserable.

"Serberus," she whispered. "It's Serberus. Right?"

"Oh Laura," said Dr Throom.

She sat on a hard chair next to the bed and watched him sleep. His round belly rose and fell, straining at the buttons on his Hawaiian shirt. He snored, thunderous snores that shook the flesh of his face, comically.

Laura would never be able to sleep in a room like this. It was a mess, for one thing. Books and papers strewn on the floors, every surface covered with beer cans, ashtrays, ornaments. There was a large framed print on the wall over the bed—a Picasso, the image of a woman in geometric confusion—that drew Laura's eye. It was easier to look at than the impossible man on the bed.

"I'm worn out," said Phil—the awake Phil—who was standing in the doorway. "Haven't slept for days. What would I do? Just lie down there with my own damn self?"

This isn't happening, thought Laura. It's all right, because this isn't happening. I'm dreaming. I inhaled some of that Mary Jane and it's affected my brain.

"If I go to sleep, then what happens, you know?"

"I don't know," said Laura. "How should I know?"

"Well, you seem like a sensible girl."

My God, thought Laura.

"I've been taking amphetamines to keep awake. But now I'm worried that it's keeping him—the other me—asleep. Maybe it's making everything worse."

How could it be worse? Laura looked from the sleeping Phil to the wired, wild, completely awake Phil. How could it be *worse* than this? It's a joke, Laura thought. A practical joke on a gullible neighbour.

"Give me a match," she said.

Phil threw her a book of them, and she lit one and held it under her hand. Closer and closer until she felt a searing pain in her palm, and she couldn't take it. She wrapped her fist around the match, extinguishing it.

"I guess that didn't help," said Phil.

"Should we try it on… him?" Laura gestured towards the sleeping man on the bed.

"I dunno. Seems kinda violent."

"Well, if you want him to wake up…"

Phil nodded. "I do. I mean, I guess I do."

"You guess?"

Phil shifted uncomfortably from foot to foot. His Hawaiian shirt made rustling, scratchy noises.

They went back outside to the front porch again. The sky was getting dark and the dirt smelled good—rich and loamy, like it was full of life. Laura looked across the street to her house. If Martin woke up, he'd wonder where she was.

"I ought to get back," she said.

"Sure," said Phil.

"Sorry I couldn't help you."

"No big deal."

No big deal, thought Laura. No big deal. Only what if it was a big deal? What if this was her chance to do something different? Here, with this odd man, on this dream-like evening, she heard her thoughts calling to her. What if *this* was the moment to act? What if she could somehow step outside her own life, give up her dependence on Martin, and her tablets, and plastic bottles and Ford cars? She could stay here, with Phil. They could solve the problem of the sleeping man. In a way, Laura wondered, didn't everyone have the same problem? Didn't everyone have a sleeping partner, another self? And what if she could wake *hers* up? Then what?

She dismissed the thought, and hurried home.

"If only you knew," said Throom. "If only you knew how many chances you've had."

Laura's stomach gnawed with emptiness. *I'm so thin now*, she thought, with a sort of hungry triumph. On the viewscreen, the white-coated doctor was shaking his head, and his patient was crying. Every week, it was the same show, the same story with different players. But of course you had to watch. What if Alison mentioned it to her, and Laura couldn't remember watching it? She'd be reported, for sure. She forced herself to concentrate on the screen.

The woman had been caught with an inferior Callitrix product, a Callisandwich. "I was hungry," the woman said through her tears. "I didn't realise until it was too late."

It would be re-education, Laura thought. Re-education, like she had been through when it happened to her. They could have sent her to the colonies, or worse. But instead they had put her to work on the second level. The company wasn't cruel. But the company did have to make a stand.

She still had to undergo the twice-weekly education programme, now blaring at her through the viewscreen.

"What if there was really no difference between a Serberloaf and a Callisandwich?" The doctor loomed forward so his face took over most of the viewscreen. "What if it was all the same thing? Did you ever think about that, Laura Harrison? Did you ever think about what's really important?"

Laura shook her head. She wouldn't be caught out again.

"It's Serberus," she said. "Serberus is the best. It's always been Serberus."

But somehow she knew that was wrong.

CROW VOODOO

———————◉———————

Mortimer Citytatters is a midnight crow and a sinister spiv, but he knows what people want in wartime is a story. So he tells them: spine-chillers, bone-warmers, knee-tremblers, colly-wobblers, stories that drill your teeth, that perform open-heart surgery, stories that make the blind walk and the lame speak. It's a good all-weather business, combined with a spot of common or garden begging, that makes ends meet.

No one should trust Mortimer Citytatters, but Jenny is paying him to write letters to her sweetheart in the war. The crow writes scathing love letters, without a lick of sympathy in them.

Dear Robin, he writes in scratchy midnight ink, *Now that the nights have turned longer, I barely think of you.*

Robin reads them over and over, the black crow letters in the smudged envelopes that come every week. He reads them until the ink starts to wear away and the thin paper goes bald in thumb-sized patches. The letters are good: they have violence in them. They give him sleepless nights. *I danced with an American soldier. He had strong arms.*

Robin cannot stop thinking about Jenny's cold little body, their first time together the night before he shipped out. He must come home safe, he thinks, home to her. But Robin worries about how she is making ends meet and what Mortimer Citytatters might ask her to pay for the letters. Surely it cannot be so very much. *Tell me if it hurts, Jenny.* But he doesn't want her to stop.

Jenny could write her own love letters, but Mortimer Citytatters is a midnight crow and he has the cruel voodoo she needs. The letters are black-crow magic, but if they keep Robin safe it can't be wrong, Jenny tells herself. She is paying for the promise of his homecoming, but she doesn't know how much. It costs so very little, really, and it hardly hurts at all, the crow says.

Bombs fell near us. I could be dead by the time you come home. The tramps sit on legless chairs in the rubble.

Mortimer Citytatters keeps Jenny's account very carefully. It is a long time before he lets her see his sharp beak.

He names the baby Savage Citytatters, a good crow name and it will give her black hair when she grows up. He tucks her under his waxy black wing; she feeds on softened grubs out of his gullet. The baby doesn't cry much. Perhaps she is content to sleep in the humid feather bed and eat mushy grubs; perhaps it is nice.

When she can walk on her podgy legs, Savage Citytatters goes with her father to the City. While her father tells spells and stories to the war-dazzled punters, Savage collects rubbish in a little bag: used tickets, apple cores, bread crusts. The other crows call her *sweetling* and *hushling*, and give her cigarette ends to put in her little bag. Mortimer Citytatters calls her *darkling vane*, and sometimes, *Jenny's chicken*, which are special magic names a father should teach his child. In the evening they go home to the tarpaulin house under the bridge, and after doing her chores, Savage spreads the contents of her little bag out on the ground, and sees which things have power. Sometimes it is an apple core, and sometimes it is not. Paper is often good. This work is arcane and difficult, crows' work. Savage usually mistakes the things for what they are not, and the things get thrown on the fire.

Although she is small, Savage must work hard for her father. If she works hard, Mortimer Citytatters will stroke her black hair with his wing. Savage collects wood, and begs for matches, and makes the fire just warm enough. She has to find food. Sometimes it rains and there are big snails, or she makes a stew of apple cores. Once she found a bag of kittens, alive, that had been swept up the bank of the oily river; she roasted them with wild onions. She sweeps the floor of their home, which is always too muddy, and re-makes the deep nest. At night Savage curls under her father's black wing, and he tells her the crow stories.

Once, a girl, he says in his laconic crow voice, *and that is the whole of it, came on a shuddering horse to a stop. They had pieces of moon, they were silver, and then there was the Very Old. The Very Old put the moon into the girl, into her belly, and the girl bled on the horse, so the horse galloped away. In the moonlight they didn't. In the sunlight they did. That is how it happens.*

Savage feels the story wake up inside her belly. She thinks this story was sleeping, and now her father has woken it with his telling. The more stories awake within her, the more she is crow, and the more power she can find in the world. This is why the stories are told, father to daughter. Savage curls up under the wing and feels a fierce love for Mortimer Citytatters that carries her into sleep.

Jenny comes to the City to watch the girl and the crow. She doesn't tell Robin. He came home from the war, like the crow spelled, but broken and spoiled. So Jenny comes to the City alone and stands at the edge of the square, smoking her cigarettes one after the other. She doesn't want to come, but she must be punished, she thinks, the way some women punish themselves with knives and flames.

Savage Citytatters, she is thirteen and becoming more

crow every day. She sees the woman watching and her heart flaps its black wings at her. Why does her heart fly to her? Like it is flying out of her chest, towards the woman, and Savage feels strange. She wants something she cannot understand: to stand next to the thin small woman and lay her head gently on her shoulder, to softly take her hand.

Now she is old enough, Savage stays with her father when he tells crow stories, and there are punters come for the telling. Mortimer Citytatters takes a tooth from one man, takes a whole eye from a girl. They want things from the crow that only a crow can give. *They only pay what they can afford. We must make ends meet.* Now that there is something that Savage wants, she feels pity for the people who come for crow voodoo. She will not let her father know she is starting to like how it feels: the pity, the wanting.

Savage Citytatters can find things of power when she needs to now, and that evening before home she trails around with her little bag, collecting apple cores, used tickets, and paper, always paper, and like this she comes to the edge of the square where the woman watched all day. The woman is gone, and there are many pieces of rubbish here, but there is one powerful thing that Savage badly wants. It is a cigarette end, smoked down to the filter, squeezed tight between the woman's fingers and dropped, still smoking, to the ground. This special one Savage puts in the bag with the rest, with her father calling her to *come, darkling vane, come home.*

In Jenny's home there is work: drudgework and slow patient work, the work of marriage. Jenny knows they did a wrong thing with those letters, all those years ago, but it is she alone who pays. She only wishes she could bring the crow girl home with her, sit her by the fire, pull out her soft black wings. Jenny has lullabies, clean apron pockets, warm bread dough: all waiting.

When Robin came home broken, Jenny married him anyway. She fed him and put him to bed every night, and washed him, and cooked and cleaned for him, and held his hand to cross the road, and did her best to love him. He doesn't know to love her back any more, but some part of him remembers, for he often asks Jenny to read him the crow letters that brought him home. Jenny pretends she doesn't understand, says not to be so silly, there are no letters like that. But on this night, just this once, when Robin asks for the letters, Jenny opens the locked cabinet and takes out the shoebox from under all the piles of wedding linen that they hardly use, and she takes out the old thin letters.

Dear Robin, she reads, *a war goes on electric there are very flies in here I mean a man no girl no what is this sound I have under my wing.* Jenny's tears fall on the scratchy crow ink, melting the thin paper completely away in the worn patches where Robin once held it in his finger and thumb. *You carry it on your back under water meadow grass fear no sky this sky is no good now why are you still flying.* These aren't their letters any longer, the spells have worn off them now, leaving behind the faded inky crow words without any magic left in them. Just nonsense. Jenny wants to put the letters away, but Robin holds her wrist, tells her to carry on. He closes his eyes, waits for the words again. *This boat is sailing swimming birds swim under the water fish fly in the sky the horse comes be on the horse you horses swimming away.*

When the letters are finally finished, Jenny feels empty, but Robin is full up. He doesn't notice Jenny's tears, but he says to her: "Remember how cold you were, little Jenny? And I said, stop if it hurts, Jenny. Tell me if it hurts, love."

In the night, Jenny wakes up in a silent bed, next to a cold husband. He has come undone at last: he is dead. Jenny lays her head on his chest and weeps on his blue cotton pyjamas until they are wet and transparent, and Jenny's face is stone cold all on one side.

Savage Citytatters spreads out her collection of rubbish on the earth. Of all the cigarette ends, she picks out the special one, and this she puts in a little pocket under her soft downy wing. Of the other things she puts the apple cores in for the stew, and the paper scraps are good for thickening soup, and everything else she sweeps into the fire. Again she feels her heart beating its wings inside her chest, and she thinks of her father's grim beak. This is her first secret from him, the way her heart begins to spread its wings, and it is a dreadful bloody one at that.

Savage has never wanted anything before except to curl up under her father's wing and sail into sleep on his dark voice, telling the crow stories into her dreams. She cannot understand why the small watching woman has power, or why Savage must keep it secret, but nonetheless there is an electric thrill in waiting for her father to fall to sleep deep inside the nest, so she can conjure magic in the secretive dark.

When she is sure that the crow sleeps soundly, Savage opens her pocket and takes out the cigarette end. She puts it on her tongue, tasting the vile burning poison in it, and sits next to the hearth, slowly chewing, and spitting the juices into her hand. When she is done, she mixes the juices with a little ash from their fire and puts it on the jelly of her eyes, inside her ears, her nose, her mouth, her anus, and her vagina. It stings and scorches, splitting her open in agony, but then the road appears, and Savage's wings open new and black, spread full out and lift her into the sky above the City, flying the Crow Road into the past.

Savage swoops above the tarpaulin house, above the bridge. She lands on the pale yellow lozenge-topped lamppost, and waits, and watches. She feels the buzz of the light under her claws, the vertiginous afterglow of flight, the viscous heat of magic inside her, and she sees the woman hurrying over the grass, down towards the river. She looks younger, and she is heavy, too, but Savage knows it is the same woman who comes to the City, the one who watches.

Then the Crow Road speaks to Savage, with a voice that uncurls itself from her insides, that speaks inside her mind. *This is a crow story, too, the oldest one we have,* says the Crow Road.

Jenny is getting big, but she runs as best she can over the coarse grass down to the side of the river, where Mortimer Citytatters is waiting in the gloaming. She is coming for her letter. This is the last one, Jenny thinks. She is sure the war will be over soon, sure that Robin will be safe home again. She is glowing with the knowledge of her baby inside her, and imagining Robin's face when he sees, and making a family.

Mortimer Citytatters doesn't have a letter for Jenny today. Instead he shows Jenny his cruel beak, and she tries to run away, slipping up the river bank. Of course it is not hard to catch her, to hold her down on her back on the wet grass. Here is your bill, child, now we always pay our bills, don't we? We got to keep these bargains nicely, see? *Jenny screams but it is not enough, it can never be enough, even if she screams the fish out of the water, the birds out of the trees. Mortimer Citytatters digs into her big warm belly with his razor beak, ripping the stretched flesh apart in jagged tears. He puts his hands inside and pulls out the tiny baby, and it is too soon for her to come out, but it doesn't matter because it is done.* I can see your insides, Jenny, all your secrets. *The crow bites into the umbilical cord, and then all three mouths are full of blood. Mortimer Citytatters tucks the baby under his wing and flies quickly away, leaving Jenny empty on the muddy grass bank.*

Savage Citytatters finds that she knows this story, too. *This is the hour of your birth.* She watches her mother spill her secrets onto the grass, her father ransacking her insides. The Crow Road speaks this to her, shows this to her, cracks her open like an egg, and Savage screams.

Mortimer Citytatters, triumphant father, looks up when he

hears the crow cry, and sees the crow looking down on him. He shakes his head and hurries on, pushing the stolen baby deep into his feathers.

When her father glares up at her, Savage feels the magic in her turn to stone and pull her down. She cannot move her wings. Her claws skitter, she loses her grip and her balance, and she falls, hard, dropping out of the sky.

Savage falls off the crow road, and lands on the earth, in her own home, under the bridge. Her father is asleep in the nest. He has caught her stealing crow magic and when he wakes up he may punish her or praise her, she cannot guess.

Savage lies still for a long while, listening to the quiet earth, telling the crow road story over and over to herself. Sometime before dawn Savage at last sits up, crouches by the dying embers of the fire and reaches for a warm apple core. She is tired and thinks of crawling into the nest with her father. But her heart flutters wildly and longs to fly to her mother's side.

Night turns to morning, and Jenny wakes up next to her dead husband, but her tears are for her stolen child. She imagines the girl's hand warm inside her own. *Time to come home now love,* Jenny whispers.

Mortimer Citytatters is awake. His beak is pushed under his black wing. One beady eye watches Savage crouching by the fire, chewing an apple core. There is crow in the girl already, he can see. So much. She has flown the crow road and seen the fact of her birth, and now, finally, Mortimer Citytatters can smell the human in her.

He watches her chewing her dirty fruit. Savage doesn't

remember that she is any bit human at all, thinks she is full crow, but now she has flown the crow road she has woken up the secret of her human past. Now that Savage can find the human inside herself, now she can feel it and say where it is, in her belly or her eyes or her tongue or her womb or her heart, Mortimer Citytatters will pin her down and cut it out of her with his iron beak, and then she will be fully crow forever.

This is how the spells are passed, from daughter to father, from son to mother. And yes, Mortimer Citytatters was once a boy, though no one can remember, for a long time ago his mother cut out his heart for black-crow magic. This is the crow way.

Mortimer Citytatters calls to his daughter. *Darkling vane, your wings grow so black.*

Savage does not have to decide. It is natural for her to creep under her father's wing, into his humid embrace. It is love.

Now tell me where it hurts, croaks her father, in his velvet voodoo song.

THE QUEEN OF KNIVES

———————◉———————

Mother tied the crimson school tie at Eva's throat, and turned her to face the hallway mirror.

"There," she said. She patted Eva's shoulders. "Ready for big school."

The mirror was too grand for the apartment: tall enough to reach the ceiling, and framed in tarnished gold. Eva knew she must be careful not to smear the glass or chip the frame, as it had been passed down her family, from Mother to Daughter; and so it would belong to her one day. It reflected the bland hallway and Mother's diffident, thin body; the scarlet and gold rug peeling from the floorboards; and everything else, faithful as a mirror should be. But it did not reflect Eva. In her place was someone else, someone who called herself the Other. The Other *what*, Eva did not know. The Other Eva, she supposed. So alike they were, almost identical. But the Other was not Eva. Around her form, a silver aura sparked and glinted with many shards of metal, and the flash of silver blades. There was metal in her eyes, too. *She* had no intention of going quietly to school dressed in that stiff uniform, to sit in a row with her hands folded and recite from a boring book of letters. She would think of something better for Eva to do.

"You look very smart," said Mother, not quite managing a smile. "Shall we take a picture for Daddy?"

The Other smirked at Eva. They both knew Mother was pretending, playing at Happy Families. Father had not been home for days—the last time he had been there, he and Mother had screamed at one another for hours. Eva didn't miss him. She barely thought of him at all, except to remember his penknife with the mother-of-pearl handle; the penknife he had let her play with once. Only once, and then never again. But she had made good use of it, made her first cut.

"Let's take a picture of *you*, Mummy," said Eva.

Eva watched her Mother flinch and turn away from the mirror. Mother didn't like to look at herself anymore. Her pretty scar shone white; it had grown whiter, Eva noticed. It pulled the skin of her cheek tightly around it, dragging the eyelid down: a gouge from eye to lip.

The Other said, *She's scared.*

Eva replied, "Mother is the Queen of Knives."

"Oh no, Eva. We are *not* having this crap! You're starting big school today! It's a new start." Mother pulled Eva away from the mirror, turned her bodily in the direction of the front door. "Let's go."

Mother kept a whole world hidden away from Eva. The Other knew it, and taunted Eva about it often.

Don't you want to know about blood? The Other said.

But Mother had hidden all the knives and locked them away in a secret box, and she wore the key to the box around her neck all the time, even while she slept.

School was not interesting. Eva had wondered what it would be like, had guessed something much like this, and when it turned out she was right, she was immediately bored. Apparently she was expected to endure this for the next several years. Some of the other children cried when their mothers left them at the school gate, and some of the mothers cried too, and waited outside the railings, putting their faces against the bars to watch the children line up by the door. But Eva and her Mother had parted casually, like a pair of acquaintances leaving a party at the same time, and when Eva turned around to wave at her, Mother had already driven away.

It might have been interesting, had there been something for Eva to do. She could read and write perfectly well, but there were no proper books in her classroom, only letters and pictures. There wasn't anything to do at school, Eva quickly realised, except sit quietly and try not to pee your pants. That was the main thing the teachers talked about: how you had to raise your hand if you needed the toilet, not to hold on until it was too late. Probably the teachers were always cleaning up pee. Two children in her class wet themselves that morning.

At lunchtime, Eva sat alone. The dinner lady tried to coax her, telling her not to be shy, but Eva explained that she would rather sit by herself. Then she took a shiny green apple from her bag and, ever so politely, asked the dinner lady for a sharp knife with which to cut it.

The dinner lady laughed. "Daft child. What are your teeth for? Bite it!"

"But my teeth aren't sharp enough," said Eva, and she looked so sad that the dinner lady laughed again.

Eva made sure to sit at the back for all her classes. Because she was quiet and continent, it was easy to escape teacherly attention. Late in the afternoon, she finally managed to prise out the blade from her pencil sharpener, and used it to carve her name in her forearm. The best bit was the crimson blood beading on the silver edge, before it ran free. She cut lines down her chest too, and the teacher didn't notice until it was time to go home and Eva stood up with the others, her school shirt ragged and red.

The Other said blood was her mother tongue. Eva wanted to learn. Every day, she sat in front of the mirror in the hallway, crossed her legs, and tried to understand what the Other was saying.

The Other said, *But how can you understand without a knife?*

Eva's Mother should never have tried to hide the secret of the blood. She should not have locked away the knives, the blades, the razors. But Mother was so careful now, since Father had given Eva the penknife. It had been just the one time. ("Once was enough," Mother had screamed at Father, and Father had screamed back, "It was an accident! She's just a little girl!")

Mother never forgot to put the knives away and lock the box. She never took the key from around her neck, and although Eva watched and waited with great patience, Mother was more vigilant than she.

I'll tell you the stories. But their true telling is in blood. You must have a blade if you want to speak the language.

"Tell me anyway," said Eva.

Father came home but it wasn't for good. He came for his clothes and books, which he threw carelessly all together into one big suitcase on the floor. Eva stood in the doorway of her parents' bedroom to watch. Mother sat on the bed, straining towards him, as if she wanted to grab him but was holding herself back. Her scar glowed white in the lamplight.

"You'll come and live with me," Father said to Eva. "As soon as I've got the place ready. There's a bedroom for you. You can help me paint it. And we'll visit Mummy a lot. If you want to."

Mother said, "She can't live with you. You're not safe with her. You're not responsible."

"Don't start on this again. She's just a child. A little girl, for God's sake." Father threw some shirts into the suitcase.

Mother twisted her hands in her lap. "Let's not have this conversation now."

"Let's not have it at all." He flipped the suitcase lid over, and zipped it all around. "I'm done."

"Take her, then," said Mother, quietly. "Don't leave me with her."

He looked at her face, and flinched. (It was the scar, Eva thought. He didn't like it.) "God. You really are messed up, aren't you?" He opened his mouth to say more, then closed it again. He looked at Eva.

Eva lowered her eyes and said, "Daddy, where are you going?"

Father ruffled Eva's hair. "It's just for a couple of days, sweetheart."

That didn't answer her question, but Eva knew better than to act smart in front of her Father. Her Father, who had once handed over the mother-of-pearl knife with its sharp, gleaming blade.

She started to cry. "I don't want you to go Daddy." He leaned down to her and she flung her arms around his neck and said, "Can I have your penknife, Daddy? I need it so I won't forget you."

"You see?" Mother said. She rose up from the bed and pushed past them, into the hallway. "You see?"

Apparently the other children had been very upset. There had been phone calls to the school, and phone calls to Mother and Father, too. Instead of going back to school, Eva stayed at home with her Mother. Mostly, Mother stayed in her bedroom, watching television and talking on the phone. Sometimes she raised her voice, and then Eva knew she was talking to her Father, or to the school. "Take her," she would say. "You have to take her." After the shouting, she would cry.

Eva sat in front of the hallway mirror.

"Tell me a story," she said.

The Queen of Knives had many fine scars.

Eva pulled at the scabs on her arms and chest. Would they become fine scars?

The Queen of Knives had so many scars that her skin was *shiny. She even had scars on her tongue, lots of them, all criss-crossed, because her words themselves were razor sharp. She knew everything about blood, and her own blood was full of stories. If you spilled her blood, you would know all the stories too.*

A thin red trickle oozed from one of Eva's scabs. "What about the princess?"

The princess doesn't know anything yet. She won't know anything until she is the Queen. It passes from Mother to Daughter, in the blood.

There were many stories. Eva began to sit in the hallway all day, from morning until night, and even to sleep there. The first time she lay down to sleep on the rug, she knew that she would wake up in her own bed in the morning. She could almost feel her Mother's arms lifting her, and carrying her to bed in the middle of the night. But the next morning she woke, cold and stiff, in the hallway.

After that, Eva ignored her Mother completely. Mother told her to move, to dress, to get up and wash and go out to play, but Eva simply would not obey. Mother seemed more nervous now that Father was gone. She would stand at the end of the hallway, watching Eva, holding the key around her neck and twisting it round and round, so much so that Eva would look up and wait for the key to twist right off its chain and into her hands, though it never did.

Father didn't come back. He called Eva, explained it was better if she stayed with Mother for now. Too much change would be difficult for both of them.

He means you'll find the knives in his apartment. He's scared.

"I don't care anyway," Eva said. But she did care about the knives at her Father's apartment, and wondered if she would ever get to see them. She wished she could live with her Father. He would let her have the knives, like he let her have his penknife, that one time.

Mother stayed in her bedroom every day. When Eva pressed her ear to the door, she heard nothing. She might have wanted to go in and put a hand on her Mother's face, to comfort her—but since the scar, she was not allowed to touch Mother at all. Before, there had even been kisses sometimes, Eva remembered, but she didn't miss those so much. She just wished she could touch the scar, even once, to trace the cut she'd made.

The Other was contemptuous.

She is a weak Queen. Weak, blunt, and bloodless. A Queen ought to be strong. A Queen ought to be like a steel blade.

"Am I weak?"

Almost as useless as your Mother.

"How can I be strong, like a steel blade?"

Blood makes you strong.

"Mother is really the Queen?"

Mother has forgotten what it is to be Queen.

Eva knew it was true, because she had heard the singing in her own blood. Blood was power, and it made you strong. Mother had forgotten, and she was weak.

Make her remember.

But how could she remember without a knife?

Mother must not have heard the mirror break, because when Eva crept into her bedroom, she was still asleep on the bed, curled up like a baby.

173

Everything was in the blood. The past, the future, the Queen's power: all secrets of the blood. Even love was there, a mother's love, vibrant as a jewel. Eva saw it, pulsing under Mother's skin; saw it, and speared it with the glittering point of mirror shard. She pushed her small fingers into the wound in Mother's neck, and scooped out trails of scarlet. Like her Mother had done before her, and her Mother before that, and on and on, through time: she painted a crown of blood over her head.

Eva held up the shard of mirror, and for the first time she saw herself reflected as she truly was. Around her form, a silver aura sparked and glinted with metal, and the flash of silver blades. There was metal in her eyes, too. She wore a cloak of blood, and her hair stood high and stiff, and red like rubies.

Long live the Queen.

THE ART OF FLYING

---◉---

Maggie flies in the night. It's like swimming a breaststroke through the air. She can see for miles around, see her truck parked in the bay and the motorway winding in a charcoal line to the horizon. She loves the purple sweet heather, the peach-red sunrise. Currents of air buoy her, lift her, wave upon wave. When the sky lets go, she falls like a feather, and lands in the dew-wet grass.

She's barefoot, dressed in jeans and a jumper. There is nothing to be scared of, she tells herself. This is the sort of thing that might happen in a dream. So she climbs the hill, digging her toes into the grass and soil. On the other side of the hill she sees her truck, and beyond that the mountains with their jagged tops of snow. Yesterday there had been eagles riding the air near the mountain peaks. Maggie had stopped on the hard shoulder to watch their gliding. She had the stereo on at full volume, playing canticles written by Hildegard von Bingen nearly a thousand years before.

I, the fiery life of divine wisdom, I ignite the beauty of the plains, I sparkle the waters, I burn in the sun, and the moon, and the stars.

The bleak morning pulls the day open and pale light falls across the hills. Maggie wishes the dream would pick her up and move her swiftly to her destination. Her body is stiff, and gets stiffer with every step. But when she reaches the truck, it's locked up and heavy blackout curtains are drawn all around the cab windows. Only now does she start to feel panicky constrictions in her heart and stomach. She tells herself *wake up*. Slaps her face with stinging hands.

She has the keys in her hand, but her fingers are too cold and clumsy to open the cab door. She's afraid she might find herself lying there in the back, asleep. Dreaming. Or dead. After some minutes of worrying at the lock, the door springs open. When she climbs into the cab, it is empty, of course.

She doesn't sleep the next night. The cargo has to get to Rakovski, a long haul down the Trakia Highway. She picks up her load of pallets, making sure to check the contents carefully against the paperwork. The supervisor leans back against the cab, slowly smoking a cigarette and watching her through narrowed eyes.

When she can't drive any more, she parks in a bay and straps herself into the driver's seat. She slides the photograph of her daughter from under the mirror, and presses it to her heart, then props it up on the dashboard, next to the figurine of a man with the head of a dog. That is Saint Christopher, the patron saint of truckers.

She works on the problem of her night flight in little parcels of lucidity. Maybe she sleepwalked, hit her head, was concussed, amnesiac. An epileptic seizure. Perhaps the cancer has come back, has spread to her brain. A myriad explanations present themselves for judgment, but none of them convince her. Perhaps it is a gift from God.

Perhaps it is a miracle.

The Church of the Highway holds a service under a large blue tarpaulin, rigged from the top of the bridge down to the grass verge at the side of the road. Under the tarpaulin are hundreds of wax candles, burning gold. The candle flames flicker and blur into teary shapes falling down the insides of Maggie's eyelids when she closes her eyes.

"Maggie," a voice says softly, into her ear.

Maggie jumps and turns towards the voice, fear spiking her blood. But it is only Gabriel, the church pastor.

"Are you okay?" He puts a hand on her shoulder. "I heard what happened."

"I'm okay," Maggie says. How else can she answer? No one speaks of her husband directly. As if to merely speak of him will cause the bruises to bloom on her skin, will cause her bones to break.

Gabriel leads her to a seat at the front of the church. He has to get ready for the service. Maggie sits on her hands, and shivers, perhaps with cold. She wishes her seat were a bit more comfortable, but knows that she would probably fall asleep if it was. There is a feeling of pressure in the back of her head, and her skull makes popping, creaking sounds, like it's contracting in the cold.

About twenty people are gathered under the tarpaulin. In the blue and gold space, with the rumble of traffic overhead, and the cold breaths of wind that sometimes blow around them, the churchgoers become quiet and still. When Gabriel reappears, dressed in a white robe with an orange sunburst sash across his breast, he is transformed by ritual into something other than a man. He's the keeper of the mysteries. Light falls from his hands.

Gabriel speaks, welcoming everybody, and his voice seems to swell and fill all of the space. It bursts from his chest, a wound of blinding light. It rises to the roof and breaks out like it's prickled with stars, exploding over the heads of the congregation. The voice rains fire on Maggie. She puts her hands over her head in frantic prayer, and the voice speaks to her and says, *I burn in the sun, and the moon, and the stars.*

She feels herself rising out of her chair. First her hair rises, then her arms, pointing up to the tarpaulin roof. A hot snake of power muscles its way through her body. It pushes her up out of her chair, up above the congregation who are breathing heavy into the night. The voice is the breath. The voice is the fire. Maggie looks down and sees herself amongst the churchgoers, her body rigidly leaning forward. She is awash with tender pity for herself and in that moment of feeling, she is pulled back and lands inside herself with a jolt. She falls from her chair onto the ground.

"You need sleep," says Gabriel. "That's all. Nothing's wrong with you."

Maggie sips cold water from a plastic cup. It's too dark to see very clearly. They're sitting in Gabriel's cab. The Church is packed up in the back, and everyone else has gone home or driven on to their resting place or their next destination.

"I'm so tired. I'm losing my mind."

"No," says Gabriel. "Don't think that way. It's the breakup. It's stress. You work hard, you miss your daughter. You have a bad dream, and maybe you can't sleep well anymore, it's normal."

"I have to stop driving."

"Yes, of course. If you aren't sleeping."

"But is it from God? Is it a test? Does He want something from me?"

"I don't know, Maggie. But God gives comfort. Don't be afraid of sleeping. I will pray for you."

Maggie's body is a ruined country where everything lovely has been bombed out. Her chest is marked with a ragged white burn scar that pulls the flesh tight in ridges and craters. Her thighs are skinny, hollow at the top, and her hip bones jut out like shark fins. There is nowhere to touch Maggie's body that does not have some painful history. The doctor draws in a breath when she lifts Maggie's shirt up to press her stomach.

"It's come back, hasn't it?" Maggie tenses, and her stomach goes rigid.

"Breathe!" The doctor tells her, pushing on her belly. "There's nothing wrong with you. You're fine. Just a bit thin."

Dr Lesley is the company doctor; an elegant woman with short, manicured nails and grey hair cut like a man's. It was Dr Lesley who helped Maggie gather the strength to leave her husband. It was she who took her to the hospital after he beat her bloody.

"I've brought you something," says Maggie, after the examination, when they are sitting either side of Dr Lesley's desk. She reaches into the pocket of her leather jacket and pulls out a little wooden figurine: a man with the head of a dog.

Dr Lesley takes the figurine and smiles. Saint Christopher, the patron saint of truckers, is also the patron saint of those who suffer from toothache. Maggie and Dr Lesley know all the saints, on account of them both having had a Catholic schooling, and Saint Christopher is their favourite.

"Please don't worry," says Dr Lesley. "Just take care of yourself."

She signs the certificate that says Maggie is fit to work.

There is a convent at Ebstorf, and the nuns there watch over a map. It's a map of two worlds: a portrait of their faith, and a geographical picture. The original map burned in 1943, says the sign, but the nuns made a very detailed and faithful copy. Maggie is allowed to stand for an hour in front of it. The colours swim before her, red and blue and black, and the images seem to move. Creatures rear up on their hind legs, villages crumble to dust, rivers flow in wavy blue lines; and Christ encompasses everything in an infinite embrace. His steely gaze falls on Maggie and ignites her skin. The white scar on her chest flames and burns.

I am so afraid. She prays for something, she's not sure what. Some comfort.

Her cargo is bound for Munich, and she cannot stay for much longer. It is cold and snow is forecast. As she stands to leave, one of the nuns enters the room. She is old, Maggie sees. Her face is a map of lines.

"We are closing the viewing, I'm sorry," she says. Her voice is soft and tremulous.

"I'm sorry," says Maggie. "It's so beautiful."

"Yes." The nun smiles. "It is so very interesting, I think. Are you a Catholic?"

Maggie nods, and the nun smiles again. When they walk out of the room, the nun guides her, holding gently on to her elbow, as if Maggie is the elderly one.

"It is a wonderful thing," says the nun.

Maggie says, "I'm dying, you see." Why did she say that? She is embarrassed and wishes she hadn't blurted it out, but the nun appears to consider her statement carefully.

"Death is just one more thing," she says. "I will pray for you."

Maggie walks back to her cab, her hips aching from the cold. What a thing it is to be so old at forty-two, she thinks. And she wonders if dying is like flying in the night.

Her daughter calls while Maggie is eating her sandwiches in a lay-by near Bad Bevensen. It has already started to snow. She has the heaters on full blast, and is wearing her jacket that feels like being wrapped up in a sleeping bag.

"He's out," says Cara. "Out on bail. Fuck's sake."

Maggie flinches at Cara's bad language, or is it at the bad news? She's not sure.

"Mum, I think you should come home."

"Maybe." It's not safe anywhere now. Not back in England, not with Cara, not on the road. But he doesn't know the rigs like she does. He was only ever a small-timer in the business, never even drove an eighteen-wheeler. He won't get very far if he comes looking for her. Truckers look after their own.

"If he comes here, I'm going to kill him," says Cara.

"Cara. Don't say that. He's probably not even allowed to be in the same city."

"I fucking mean it. I'm serious. And if he lays a hand on you." She doesn't finish her sentence.

"Don't swear, love. He's not going to get anywhere near me, or you, so stop worrying. I don't want you to worry."

"Please come home, Mum," Cara says. She sounds so heartbreakingly young that Maggie has to fight back tears.

"I will, darling, I will come home soon. I'll be home before you know it."

After the phone call, Maggie starts up the engine. The snow is coming thick and fast now. She drives carefully, unable to see far ahead, feeling like a giant in the massive rig, high above the rest of the traffic.

She dreams that Saint Christopher is running beside her, his tongue hanging from his jaws, his long nose pushed up in the air.

Good boy, good…

A struggle to get her breath, and she yanks herself upright. *Where am I?* The cocooning whiteness of snow… But she is warm, dry. She changes focus: she is in the cab, she's safe.

The windscreen is shrouded in snow, obscuring any view. She rolls down the window. Four other rigs are pulled up nearby, but she doesn't recognise any of them. She leans out to knock snow off her windscreen. From across the lay-by, she hears music.

Gabriel's little truck is almost hidden behind a massive articulated lorry. It looks like a sliver of Christmas, lit up in gold and blue, red and silver. Maggie puts coffee, chocolates, and cigarettes into her pockets, and trudges through the deep snow.

"I can't believe it," she says, hugging Gabriel. "I heard the music and I knew it must be you."

"Been here all night. I don't like to drive in bad weather. You too, it's dangerous driving in the snow."

"Maybe. I'll give it a couple of hours, anyway. We can visit."

They sit in the truck. Maggie tries to eat the chocolates, nibbling away at the edges, but they don't taste of anything.

Gabriel leans in so she can hear him over the whirr of the heater. "I'm worried for you. I heard he's out of prison."

"You heard already? Has he been looking for me?"

"Don't think so. He has some friends on the road still. A few. What are you thinking?"

Maggie is staring at her hands. They are shaking. After a minute she says, "I'm sick, Gabe. I shouldn't be driving. I can't drive anymore, I really can't. But I don't know what else to do."

Gabriel takes her hands in his. "The cancer?"

"The doctor said no, she said it's gone. She said I'm fine. But I can feel it inside me. I'm dying, Gabriel. I know I am."

"Oh, Maggie," he says. His hand tightens around hers.

They pray together all morning, until Maggie sees the colours rising from Gabriel, blue and gold, red and silver, and the fiery words burn over her. She lets him massage her hands, which are stiff and cold. Her fingers warm under his gentle ministrations, and she feels them grow soft and strong, young again.

"There are so many miracles," she whispers, and the Pastor cries and kisses her fingers.

They hear about him in Gdansk; a trucker there radios Maggie to let her know. He's driving a baby rig around for one of his old friends; he never could handle a big wheeler. *Let him come*, thinks Maggie. *Let him come and it will all be over.*

She turns in her last cargo in Varna and drives back to Germany. She wants to get to Ebstorf if she can, to see the map again and drink in its strange beauty. It's cold everywhere, but she hardly feels it now. She has stopped sleeping, stopped eating. Sometimes, when she's driving, she loses her body, and her consciousness drifts into the engine of the rig. Her wheels turn, and her gears change up and down, smooth and flowing like breathing in and out.

At a rest stop near Munich, she telephones Cara and tells her she's coming home to England. She'll be back very soon, she says.

"Has he found you?" Cara asks. "Does he know where you are?"

"I won't let him get anywhere near me."

"I'm scared for you," says Cara.

"I love you," says Maggie. "You're my wonderful daughter. I'm so proud of you. And I'm so sorry for everything."

"Don't be daft, Mum," says Cara. "I can't wait for you to come back."

Maggie winds down her window, and throws her cab keys out into the ditch. No more of that. No more. Saint

Christopher barks once from the back of the cab, and she smiles, and draws the blackout curtains all around. She climbs over onto the thin mattress, and curls up next to him. His soft ears flicker against her face. She clutches her wooden rosary and her photograph of her daughter, which she kisses before she closes her eyes.

The air is so cold that when she flies through the clear night, it shatters and falls to the ground in a tinkling rush. Below her, the whole world is spread out in vivid red and blue and black. The world is made of soft vellum, sewn together, embroidered with bold threads. Creatures rear up and canter through the landscapes: a monster with the head of a snake and the body of a lorry charges towards a village made of wheels. A gold and blue church rises luminous on a white plain. The moon burns with white fire and bursts with beams of light, and the voice of the world takes her breath, *I, I, yes, I, the fiery life of divine wisdom, I ignite the beauty of the plains, I sparkle the waters, I burn in the sun, and the moon, and the stars.*

A dog barks, rhythmically yapping into the night. Maggie soars into the sparkling darkness, flying home at last.

LITTLE HEART

T his woman liked to break things. She'd always liked breaking things, ever since she was a child. Breaking, unmaking, unfolding, undoing, prising off, detaching, violently abstracting, dropping, smashing, crushing, agitating, neglecting, disconnecting. Whatever it took. She liked to break things with precision. She liked the moment of breakage, the moment when the broken thing came into existence and the thing it was before ceased to exist. She said, "Only when something breaks can you finally understand its true function and character. It's a process of physical deduction. It's graphic." She explained how she would pull the transistors out of radios, cut off her dolls' hands with scissors, slice worms in half with a penknife. "But it's unpredictable. Like splitting the atom. Such a tiny thing. What a big surprise inside!" She would say this sort of thing in classes and her students would take note. They hung off her words. She would see them in the bargain shop on Saturday afternoons, buying cheap crockery for smashing. "Break plates," she told them. "Break everything in the house."

Plates were one thing. But what this woman—let's call her Anna—what Anna really wanted to break were mirrors. And not just mirrors. She wanted to break windows. She wanted to break a house in half. Tear it apart in her hands. Just like tearing dough, except it would be floorboards and shingles and furniture stretching and breaking, and people falling out. She wanted to break noses. She wanted to break things made of glass and things made of bone. She had a passion for it.

Passion ran in her family.

Her mother had been passionate. She'd been an actress, briefly, and she'd starred in a film that had been popular for a while the year Anna turned seven. It was a black and white film, because in those days, they were all black and white. Her mother won an award for acting in it, a silver twist of metal on a wooden plinth—it was given pride of place in their sitting room, placed high up on a shelf. Anna was forbidden from touching it, of course. She'd been taken to see the film in a picture house, but her father had removed her when she became *disturbed and agitated* (as the doctor said later, pulling on his nose in an unpleasant manner).

The film's themes and images were certainly too adult for a small child to appreciate, even one as precocious as Anna. Perhaps her parents hadn't realised how inappropriate it was to take her to the picture house that night. Anna was over-sensitive, liable to make a drama over the littlest thing.

Anna remembered that evening as a fulcrum upon which the world balanced. From that point it tipped and swung between two dimensions. There was the real world that she had relied upon. And then there was a horrible new dimension. It was the sight of her mother on screen that had precipitated the breakdown. The woman looked like her mother—her exact, identical twin. But Anna saw she was wrong. It was not her mother. She saw that her mother had disappeared, been forced out by someone else—someone who inhabited her completely, and drove her to terrible extremes. There was one scene in particular—a celebrated scene—that had terrified Anna beyond her ability to endure, beyond the possibilities of her father's presence to console. In fact, it was then Anna realised she was alone in the world.

Early on in the film, the wrong mother is seen standing

alone in a dining room. She is newly married. She wears a long black nightdress, sheer lace and silk trailing about her bare feet. Her lips and nails are painted red, but on film they look black. There is the sound of breaking glass. The camera pulls back to take her in. She's dropping wine glasses onto the stone floor. A piece of glass skims the top of her foot and a black wet seam opens. A ball of blood runs down between her toes. She doesn't react. She keeps dropping glasses onto the floor until there are shards and splinters and chunks of broken glass glinting all around her. Her feet are cut and bloodied. The camera shows us her hands, crossed with scars and wet with blood. But it's her face that arrests the viewer: her eyes. Her pupils are dark liquid haloed by ice. And the expression in them—she is lost inside herself, her madness.

When Anna saw this she knew she'd been wrong about everything. No one could now be trusted. Her mother could not even be trusted to remain housed in her own body! Anna guessed it was then, at the height of her distress in the picture house, that her long, confusing estrangement from her mother had begun. It had budded out from that moment, finally fruiting when Anna left home at seventeen, and then hardening as the years went by and drew the two women further and further apart. When Anna's mother died, Anna realised that she remembered the facsimile, the creepy ersatz mother, more vividly and powerfully than the real thing.

Anna thought she was nothing like her mother. On the other hand, she wasn't completely sure. She sometimes wondered if she was the rightful inhabitant of her body or whether another person was simply putting her on and off like a coat. It seemed to her that it was impossible to know. She could be a character in a film, like her mother had been. Celluloid and ink instead of flesh and blood. Of course, Anna would prefer a beautiful film, like the one with all the thin, good-looking sad people having a party, while a massive asteroid hurtles towards the earth. If she died that way, would she know? Would there be time, in the moment of death, to see exactly what had made her tick with life? She hoped it would be a big surprise. She hoped when death came, she would be able to leave the machine of her body and enter the soft machine of the sky. She worried she would grieve for her body, not that it was a remarkable or beautiful body. If anything, she loathed it for its ugliness. But there was no knowing if you could do anything worthwhile without a body: it seemed like you probably needed one. Then again, what if she were just like her mother: a collection of images layered over one another, one over another to create the illusion of moving and talking. Then her ugly body might last forever. Like her mother's body was still, always, walking around an old haunted house, wearing strange old-fashioned clothes and speaking in an odd, pretty voice.

Anna had recently seen her mother's dead body in a casket, her face waxy and coated in make-up. She had once again put on a different body, only this one looked nothing like her. It seemed to have nothing to do with her, at all.

Anna's mother had been found half-naked on the kitchen floor, surrounded by broken glass. The death certificate said natural causes. The doctor told Anna she'd had a stroke, a massive one. She said it would have killed her instantly.

Her funeral attracted quite a crowd—mostly extended family, some of whom had flown in from Israel and claimed to remember meeting Anna as a young girl. They spoke to her in Hebrew and Anna shook her head. "But you used to be absolutely fluent!" They prompted her with words and sayings, trying to coax the little girl out of her. It was impossible—they remembered a different child altogether. Anna was quite sure that none of these people had ever sung to her, dandled her on their laps, or listened enraptured to her childish recitations of poems and songs in their language. Those things had never happened. (However, when pressed, Anna admitted she remembered nothing much of her childhood before the trauma of the picture house. Everything that came before then had been erased from her mind.) She guessed her family were disappointed to see she had not lived up to her mother's beauty.

No one mentioned Anna's father. No one ever spoke of him, not since the day he'd left. Anna wondered if he'd be at the funeral, but she wouldn't have recognised him even if he had been. She couldn't remember what he looked like. Only his handsome, serious eyes, and the gloss of his hair.

The family were kind and made a fuss over Anna, but she was embarrassed by their sympathy. She didn't want it. They thought she must be broken-hearted, but what she had felt most in the few days after her mother's death was a strange heady kind of freedom. The doctor called it shock. She felt herself expanding, growing taller. She walked faster, feeling that the range of her legs and arms had increased, that there was energy powering through her. She grew in strength and stature. She decided her mother's death was the best thing that had ever happened to her, and rather than sympathy, she wanted a celebration.

Of course, someone spoke of the film. Although it had been mostly forgotten by the rest of the world, the family still thought it wonderful that one of theirs had been famous and celebrated. Anna avoided those conversations, but was prompted to recall she still had a copy of the film on videotape. She couldn't think why she'd kept it all these years. She'd kept it even after the video player became obsolete, and she'd thrown all her other tapes away. But she'd never even taken it from the back of the shelf where it was hidden. She wasn't afraid to watch it—it was just irrelevant, of no interest. It couldn't hurt her, break her, psychically dislocate her, force her out of her body and into her previous incarnation… a child screaming in the cinema, wetting her pants, her father pinning her arms behind her back. Of course not. The past was over and there was nothing to be frightened of. And Anna had made her peace, more or less, with her own self now. Despite all her failures, she'd survived nearly sixty years of life. She made art, she was good at it, and validated for it, and paid. Now her mother was finally gone, leaving behind a space for Anna to stretch out into. Why should she put herself through the experience of watching the film? She decided she never would. She would find it and throw it away. Better still, she would smash the casing and unspool the tape and set it on fire.

But that is not what happened.

The wrong mother breaks a mirror and her face is fractured into a thousand pieces. The screen is full of pieces, a cacophony of faces. ("Perhaps the film was too grown up for you," Anna's father said. "You embarrassed your mother. You embarrassed me. Everyone was looking at you." Anna associated this memory with the taste of raspberries, and remembered her father crushing up tablets into red syrup, using the back of a spoon. For a while afterwards, a long time, she felt she was breathing underwater; everyone's voices streamed in distorted bubbles towards a surface she could not break.)

The wrong mother wakes up in the middle of the night. She lights a candle. Her husband is nowhere to be seen. As she casts the candle around, it sheds light and definition on the faces in the wallpaper, and the faces in the crumpled sheets, and the faces in the grain of the wood on the door. She walks, barefoot as always, through the house, holding her candle bravely in front of her. She is looking for him. She whispers his name. Down the staircase and then across the great hall and into the kitchen, where a fire still glows in the range. But where is he? She opens the door to the cellar. Darkness. The candle sputters but the light holds, enough for the wrong mother to pick her way down the stairs. Halfway down she almost slips. She clutches at the banister. It's velvety with moss. There's water lapping at her feet. Then her candle is blown out.

When the light next comes, she is walking through water up to her waist, wading out onto a small sandy beach, beyond which another house stands. It is identical to her own house, there are lights on in all the windows. She's wearing the black lace nightdress again, only now it is soaked through and clinging to her frozen skin. There is a sudden black flapping of wings and the screen is full of birds, pecking and hopping, their eyes glinting cruelly, until somehow they resolve themselves into the shape of a man.

Anna's father had been nothing like that man. Of this Anna was quite certain—but she watched him closely all the same. Anna's father was handsome, and smelled like the inside of his briefcase. Paper and ink. He wore a heavy watch that had to be wound twice a day. He gave Anna books on her birthday and at Christmas. He called her 'little heart' and 'little thing' and said she was pretty when she knew she was not. When she told him she planned to become an artist, he didn't laugh. But after the incident in the picture house, he was different. He was a photograph fading, a memory of a father. He began to remind Anna of the man in the film, the feathered man with his cruel beak. It was silly, really. Just the way he looked at her sometimes.

Since Anna was under sedation, she didn't keep regular waking and sleeping hours. She moved through the days in a syrupy fugue, not quite knowing if it was time for breakfast or time to go to bed. When she woke up in the middle of the night, she thought it could just as easily be the middle of the day. Her perspective was distorted. She would spend long hours sitting in front of a mirror, in a low light, watching as her face became a stranger's face. She watched her father's face just as intently, every time she had a chance. She sometimes thought she saw her father's eye glint glossy-black, and the dull sheen of his beak, the tender attachments where smooth beak grew from soft tiny feathers. Even in the daytime, Anna's father grew darker, and bigger, or was it that Anna was growing smaller and lighter. (Like Alice, she was always too big or too small, or too far away or too dissolved into the air, or something.)

Anna woke up in the middle of the night. She was too weak and dizzy to remember her dream. But certain things came back to her: the sound of a door slamming, and the knowledge that *he* was in the house—and that he wanted her for something—that he had broken her mother wide open and now it was Anna's turn. In the dream, she remembered seeing his face looming towards her, his beak about to pierce the flesh of her cheek. His wings were enormous; his feathers were dirty and smelled of trash.

After the dream, Anna was desperate to see her father right away. Just to prove to herself that he *was* her father, and not a terrible bird thing. She would sneak into her parents' room, quickly look upon his handsome sleeping face, and be relieved of the evil dream. But when she had tiptoed across the landing, she saw a light edging the heavy door, and heard what sounded like a whispered argument—they argued all the time in those days. Anna didn't want to see her parents while they were awake. She was afraid of their anger, knowing from experience it could be deflected onto her simply because she was there. But she was far more afraid of the thing her father had been in her dream. She had to see him. So she pushed open the door.

At first, she didn't understand. Then she realised she

wasn't awake after all, and the dream was still inside her, dreaming her out. There was a black cloak of feathers over the bed, lustrous and crawling with lice. Her mother was naked, on all fours facing the door. There was blood on her beautiful face and breasts and arms. Anna's father was behind her mother, rocking back and forth from his hips. It wasn't her father. It was the dream of her father as a bird, as the man-bird from the film. He looked at Anna and his cruel face twisted into a smile. He licked his lips. He pushed her mother's head down into the feathers and rocked faster as he watched Anna watching him. She felt paralysed, unable to breathe, impossible to even close her eyes. She hated his gleeful expression, the noises he was making, the way his claws dug into the back of her mother's head... Anna concentrated on moving just one part of herself, her little finger... if she could do it, she'd wake up. But it wasn't possible. Later, she remembered this moment not as a dream, but as though it were a film stopped in the middle of a scene, the actor immobilised, her face embalmed in its expression of horror—yet her father and mother were the real show, images moving fast enough to blur skin and feathers, blood and tears. Anna was paused in her place. Then suddenly, without warning, the film unstuck. She took a deep breath, clenched her fists, turned, ran.

It was a dream. Her child's imagination running riot, the strong sedatives enveloping her in their heavy weirdness. Even the next afternoon, when she pulled a soft black feather from her thigh, leaving a little bloody hole, Anna could see that this was only because she had mixed up dreams with films and fantasy with reality. She had invented everything, wicked little fantasist that she was. She always believed it was this that had driven her father away. Her ugliness, her madness that night—he had somehow known how disgusting she was. And that is why, the next morning, he was gone.

In the days after the funeral, Anna's new energy wore thin. She talked too much in class, was impatient, accused her students of being intellectually weak, lacking in purpose. She mocked their work, sent them away with her laughter ringing in their ears. Her head of department said she was too harsh, there had been complaints. Anna countered with passion. She just wanted them to find fractures in their protective middle-class veneer. "Find where it hurts and then dig away there with the sharpest thing you can find," she told them. But her students had trouble recognising their own fault lines. They defaulted to physical violence, to accidents. They were always coming to class with bruises and cuts and their arms in slings. One time, she was speaking with a student she hadn't seen for a while. "I had a heart attack," he told her. She wanted to ask him, "And did it work? Did it open you up?" Instead she said, "Show me the scar." He lifted his t-shirt and she let her eyes trace the sore red weal bisecting his chest. She wanted to slide a craft knife along its length and lever him open again.

The head of department told Anna to take some time off. A family bereavement is a serious matter, she said. Perhaps Anna should talk to someone. By *someone* she meant, of course, a therapist of some kind. "You don't seem yourself," she said. Anna said she was fine. Who was she, if not herself? But she didn't want to hear the answer to this question. She thought she already knew the answer. Not that she could prove it, but it seemed to her she was less real every day. She thought her skin had changed, that her eyes had grown darker; at times she noticed her movements were almost imperceptibly jerky, as though she were an image, stuttering on screen. A series of images layered one over the other, one after another to create the illusion of her body.

Just like her mother.

To prove she was really nothing like her mother, Anna knew she would have to watch the film. And once she had taken the tape down from the shelf, Anna realised she had no choice. The tape had a certain weight, an animus that Anna responded to. She was an artist, after all. Maybe it wouldn't be such a frightening thing, to watch this film again, now, as an adult. She'd no doubt laugh at the stupid special effects and wobbly scenery and terrible acting. Perhaps she wouldn't even recognise what had frightened her back then—it was only the irrationality of a child who didn't understand what it means to play act at being someone else. A sick child who couldn't understand the difference between a film, a dream, and the real world.

It was all in the past and there was nothing to be frightened of. In fact, Anna suspected that once enough time has elapsed, the past is erased and collapsed out of existence. Time breaks everything. Time is really just another word for breakage: every hour self-destructs, every second is irretrievably snapped and broken with the ticking of a watch.

Anna had to go into the cellar to find the video player, which was bigger and heavier than she remembered. It took a while to make it work—the drawer mechanism was jammed and she had to unscrew the front of it and put it back together. When she put the tape into the player, she found it had not been rewound, and it began to play from the middle of the film, the part after the wrong mother washes up on the beach, and follows the wrong man to the wrong house. Anna felt quite calm looking at the wrong mother's face. It was the man who frightened Anna now.

The wrong mother has to be punished for leaving her room. There are intimate sacrifices to be made: her tongue, her hair, her eyes. But for now, they are dancing. He is an excellent dancer. He turns her around the floor until she's dizzy, clinging on to his shoulders, falling against him. The film is not explicit. But somehow the scene is erotic. The way he lifts her hair from her neck. She bites her lip. He grips her waist. She looks away. Anna felt afraid for the wrong mother. Something bad would happen. Something bad was happening. She didn't want to watch, but she forced herself to see, through the cracks in her fingers, what happened next.

But no one sees what happens to the wrong mother that night. To her eyes and her tongue and her hair. It all takes place under the cover of his darkness. The humid cloak of his wings, the trap of his beak, all of his sharp dark vicious pecking—there is nothing to see. It is all left to the imagination.

Then later, she sits by her window in the dim, shadowy bedroom. By candlelight, her expression registers pain. She lifts her nightdress to the tops of her thighs. There is a curled black feather on her leg, the shaft piercing the skin. She plucks it out, and a bead of blood plummets down her thigh, dropping onto the floor beneath the chair.

Anna's hands flew to her mouth. She remembered this exact thing happening to *her*—the tiny soft black feather, the welling of her blood—it seemed so real, this memory, it was shocking to see it played out on screen, to realise it wasn't a memory at all, but something that had happened to someone else. Not even that—to realise it had never happened at all, not in reality. Anna had always known that memories couldn't be trusted, but she was shocked all the same. She could still feel the pinch of pain as she plucked the feather from her thigh, she could vividly remember seeing the blood well out of the tiny hole in her skin. But that was a fiction. All the past is a fiction. The past—what she thought of as her childhood—it was only a film she'd watched, a stupid fairy tale that gave her nightmares. It was the dream and the film all tangled together in the soft knots of her brain.

The wrong mother sits before a mirror. She cuts off her hair with a pair of silver scissors. Her hair is black and glossy and falls away from her in silken ropes. She cuts her hair short, leaving just an uneven shock to halo her head. With her hair gone, she is even more beautiful than before. You see the hollows of her cheeks, the darkness under her eyes. When she looks into the mirror again, she sees him standing behind her, and gasps. In her only true act of resistance in the film, she wrenches the mirror away from its stand and throws it across the room to where he should be standing, but suddenly no longer is. The mirror smashes, and a shard of it curves through the air, pierces her skin, slides through her ribcage and stabs her in the heart.

How utterly depressing, Anna thought—the first time she manages to stand up for herself, it kills her. And the man-bird is completely free, untouched by her death. Even when the police come for her body, there is no mention of a man, no mention of a husband at all. It makes you wonder if there was ever such a person, or whether the whole thing was just in her head. This is infuriating, too. Now the viewer doubts her sanity, her recollection of events, her victimhood. Perhaps she was only ever abusing herself, like a Victorian girl putting needles inside her urethra, having hysterics and crying rape.

Anna was infuriated by the ending of the film. It's so stupid, so pointless. She recalled her parents arguing about it—her father saying that the woman had lost her mind, that she was a fantasist and weak-minded and insane. Her mother crying with frustration, insisting the real story is precisely that no one believes her. It's too easy for the husband to drive his wife out of her mind: he can torment her and no one will ever believe it. Anna couldn't recall how the argument had ended. She had an image of her mother sitting in the kitchen, holding her head in her hands. When she came close, her mother said, "Don't come near me. I don't want *you* anywhere near me." But Anna couldn't remember if it happened after this argument, or some other time.

Anna did remember there had been many, many arguments. She remembered the silence after her father had gone. But no one ever spoke to her about her father leaving. After the night of her dream, he was simply no longer there. She gathered the courage to ask her mother if he was coming back. Her mother said, "No. You made sure of that." That was all she ever said on the matter. She turned cold and silent. Some days she wouldn't even look at Anna. Other days, she stared at her, as if inspecting her for signs of something, Anna didn't know what.

For months afterwards, Anna wrote letters to her father, apologising for everything she must have done to drive him away, and promising to be better. She would try to be pretty, she promised to grow up beautiful, she swore she would, even though there were no signs of this being likely. She wrote letters to her mother, too, but ripped them up and threw them in the fire. Anna was sure her father would eventually forgive her and come home. When he didn't, she began to wonder if he had ever been there in the first place. Her memories of him were so few, and now so polluted by her dream images, she realised she had come to think of him as a fiction. Someone she had made up. No more or less real than a character in a film.

Anna stopped the film before the credits and rewound it.

While it was rewinding, she went into the kitchen to pour herself a glass of wine. She opened the kitchen cupboard and took out a glass. She dropped it on the floor. Was it an accident? Let's say it was. But then she took out another glass and dropped that one, too. Deliberately. She liked it and she didn't want to stop. She dropped the glasses on the floor, one after the other, smashing each one to smithereens. She cut her foot, watched a ball of blood roll down between her toes. She stood for a long time, barefoot in the broken glass, and the thought occurred to her that she should be filming this. It would make an excellent piece of film. Maybe she should cut up her mother's film and make something new out of it. Some kind of installation, a new narrative to make sense of the disjointed, disconnected scenes of her childhood.

It was satisfying to break all those glasses, and to know that whatever happened, they could never be put back together again. The glasses had ceased to exist. They were something else now. But she wasn't sure how she would move from the spot in the kitchen. The floor was covered in broken glass, sheer shards of fine crystal, shattered over the tiles. She would cut her feet badly if she tried to step out of there. She'd have to pick out a path, carefully. Perhaps she ought to telephone someone to come and help.

In the other room, the film stopped rewinding and Anna heard it whirr and click and begin to play again. Soft strains of music floated through to the kitchen. It was strange that it started playing by itself. She couldn't remember if that's what videotapes always did. She was thinking about it when she heard footsteps in the hallway.

He was walking slowly, his shoes clicking against the old terracotta tiles. Anna could hear the scrape and swish of his palms running over the wallpaper.

"Is someone there," she said, but the words were choked and strangled in her throat. There was no answer, only the sound of his skin brushing against the walls.

Anna grabbed a large slice of broken glass, held it in her fist like a weapon, cutting her own palm on its edge. There couldn't be anyone in her house. If someone had broken in, she would kill them and no one could blame her. It was self-defence. She heard him stepping into the kitchen, crunching glass under his shoes. She couldn't help it: she closed her eyes.

She didn't believe in ghosts. But she could smell him: trash and blood. She could hear the rustle of his wings.

In the darkness that followed, Anna broke open a pearl of memory. It was a hard stone, lodged in her throat for more than fifty years. It stopped her from eating, from laughing, from speaking. It was a tiny thing she'd kept hidden from herself, inside herself. And now she coughed it up, shining with blood, and caught it in her fist. It was so small. But it was like splitting the atom. Such a tiny thing. What a big surprise inside.

She huddled under the bed covers, her knees pulled up to her chin. The dream had been terrible, but worse now: her father was outside the bedroom door, knocking gently. *Little heart, little heart,* he called out. He sounded like himself, but Anna had seen him in his mask of feathers and bones. She knew when he entered the room that he would smell strange and look strange. And whatever he'd done to Anna's mother, he would do to Anna. He always said he loved her more, despite her ugliness. He always said she was his little heart.

"Come out," he called from the other side of the door. "Do as you're told, child."

Then there was silence, a long empty silence. Anna wasn't sure if he'd gone away. She crept out of bed, silently, and tiptoed to the door. Pressing her ear to the wood, she heard the haunting sounds of music. Carefully, she opened the door. Her father was gone. But the music was a little louder and clearer out on the landing. It was coming from downstairs.

The house was completely dark. She was the lightest thing in it, in her little white nightdress. She tiptoed down the stairs, following the sound of the music. It came from behind the cellar door. Anna wanted to hear the music more: it was beautiful and enchanting, like the sound of a playground or a fair. There was laughter in the music, and children's voices. Anna opened the cellar door and the music swelled up. She switched on the light. It was a bare bulb hanging over the stairs, too dim to illuminate much, but Anna could see wet moss on the stone steps, and water lapping below. She picked her way down the stairs, and when she reached the water's edge, she stepped in, and the music rose up and swallowed her. It washed her up on a dark sand beach, at the top of which was her house. Identical in every way, but very much in the wrong place. So it must be a dream, Anna decided. It's just a dream that feels real, or something real that feels like a dream. Don't be afraid. The music was loud and insistent now. It drew her to her feet and as she stood, he flew close to her, his wings spread out and his beak pushing towards her. *Won't you join the dance*, he said, with his voice like dirt. He enfolded her in the humid embrace of his wings. She couldn't stop him, she was too small to stop him. Besides, she loved him. He tore against her flesh, his beak sliced open her thigh, cutting through the meat right down to the white. Pink and tender flesh clung to the raw bone. He was only celluloid and ink. He was only a memory, a dream of her father. But he was teeming with dead girls under his wings, he had pinned their hair and eyes and tongues to his feathers. He called them all *little heart* as he dug his beak into their soft fleshes.

If it were a dream, she would wake up now. Now. Now!

He was lost in his reverie of feeding. He bent his neck to suck up her blood, and she saw the opportunity of his bare skin under the feathers, skin that was thin and fragile. The slice of glass went in easily, gently to that soft spot. He groaned and spurted blood over her hands and face.

Anna felt the moment coalesce in her hands. She felt the moment when he ceased to exist, and the broken thing came into existence. At the moment of breakage, her father was graphically reduced to his core: a broken, bloodied, ugly, feathered thing, a little heart that spewed blood until it finally ran dry. She watched him fold into himself like black-winged origami and disappear.

Now.

In the precise moment of breakage, Anna experienced beauty. She experienced it as a child, breaking her father's heart. She relived it now, as herself, bursting open to the knowledge of herself, tearing down the trash-winged ugly celluloid shape of her father, slicing the film into thousands of plasticky pieces. Her own beauty erupted from her hands, struck like lightning, rained broken glass on the floor. A bright glitter of rain, crashing against the stone. It was a big surprise to see all that beauty. She wished she had known it was there inside her all along, waiting for its moment to live.

THE ART LOVERS

---◉---

The museums of Europe have on display many artworks extolling the virtues and sins of women. Women painted, sculpted, sketched and carved. Women as goddesses, whores and animals. Women as all the things women are.

Paul spent his twenty-first summer looking at women. Leaving London, he had kept a souvenir of his first train ticket stamped with the date: May, 1972. Later, he discarded the ticket in case it somehow became evidence against him. He travelled from one European city to another on an Inter-rail card and what remained of his student grant, sometimes supplementing his income with "Greek" tricks he'd learned at prep school. There was no shame in it, at least not for him. He ate in cheap restaurants where the locals would sometimes take offence at his scruffy clothes, but just as often would spot him a meal or a glass of wine. It was true he had his looks, and that made everything easier. Sometimes he would get a room in a hostel, but most nights he slept rough, on trains or in train stations, or in the doorways of the museums where he spent his days. He would rest his head on the canvas rucksack that contained nothing but his few clothes, sketchpads and pencils. No one bothered him. He felt accepted for what he was: a man, an artist, living freely as himself. He didn't give a thought to what he would do with the rest of his life. Let come what may; that was his philosophy.

He sent his parents postcards of the Eiffel Tower, the

Coliseum, various cathedrals—but these places made little impression on him. It was only the women he noticed. Their varieties of flesh, their eyes, the way they turned against him or stared back from their gilt frames. They rested on their haunches, their bottoms and thighs softening against a rose-coloured divan or settling on vivid grass. Goddesses, virgins, with shy, trembling stomachs. They were attended by symbols and omens, clues as to their virtues and intentions. Their familiars were children, animals, flowers, all of nature, it seemed. They were succubae, devils at their breasts; they were cadaverous witches; they were voluptuous whores. Paul walked through room after room teeming with their bare bodies, their provocative mouths— and was disturbed. In Italy, it was especially bad. He left the museums each day jagged with anxiety, and spent the evenings compulsively seeking relief from his feelings. But there was no relief to be had. And the next day, there were still more paintings to see.

He grew sick of it. He felt weakened, enervated. And there was the question of money. He was in Rome when it ran out, and couldn't afford to leave. He took to spending his afternoons in the Café Rosati, smiling at the men who passed by in their white linen suits and hats. But his looks must have been affected by his sickness; he must have been too pallid and soft-looking for the gentlemen, and he had no luck.

One torrid afternoon, his head hanging over a café table, and his hand wrapped around a tiny cup of espresso which he had no money to pay for, he felt a cool current of air slice by him. He looked up to see a tall, thin man, dressed in an ivory summer suit, joining his table. His arms and legs were so long and spindly that he practically had to fold himself up like an instrument to get seated. He didn't introduce himself, but he smiled, a sort of half-smile really, giving little away. Then he took out his sketchbook and pencil, and began to draw. His eyes flickered between

Paul's face and the sketchbook: he was clearly drawing a picture of Paul. And yet there was no acknowledgement of this. Perhaps a cultural matter, Paul thought, or personal rudeness. When the waiter came, the man ordered coffee for himself and his "friend". Are we friends? Paul wondered. What would such a friendship entail? But the man didn't want to talk, only to draw. Paul felt the outline of himself etched in pencil on the sketchbook. He felt himself being translated into grey lines, and didn't quite like it.

He thought he should say something, but couldn't think what. Perhaps the man was seeking a liaison, but Paul could not bring himself to make the usual signs. It was a relief, then, when he heard behind him loud English voices. He made to leave the table. The man glanced up, shook his head and smiled, sly as moonlight. But the other voices were calling out, and Paul recognised them, and turned towards them, leaving the man to his devices.

The voices happened to belong to some others from his university, some dullards reading *History of Art*. He knew them, vaguely, and roused himself to make conversation. They were on the same tourist trail as him; they were leaving that day for Naples, and Paul said he would travel with them. He was glad to go. The others had money and were stupid with it: they threw it away on wine and hashish, and took day trips to Amalfi to sunbathe on the beach. They talked, incessantly, about how Italy was perfect and London was unspeakable. Paul kept himself apart. He slept on the sofa in their rented apartment, making it into a kind of island, strewing his clothes, pencils, and sketchbooks around it. For a time he thought he preferred staying on his island to traipsing across Naples looking at baroque paintings or the frescoes of Pompeii. He had been brought low, exhausted by the heat and the punishing light. His thoughts turned often to the man in the café: he had felt intruded upon, somehow exploited, and these feelings worsened his torpor. Sleep came fitfully, feverishly. At first, the others took turns to lay a hand across his forehead, but soon they left him alone, which was better.

After some days he rose out of his state, bathed, and picked up his sketchbooks. His drawings were pale imitations of the masters he had admired: lukewarm copies of Giorgione's *Venus*, sleeping with her fingers tucked between her legs, and Raphael's mistress, *La Fornarina*, caressing her own small breasts. Dissatisfied with himself, he threw the unfinished sketches on the floor, where his friends found them and made filthy jokes about the figures. Paul learned to keep his art more private. On an evening when the apartment was quiet, Paul began a new drawing of his own invention It was a woman, clothed, her dress pulled tight and low around her chest. She had a wicked aspect to her face, and he saw he had drawn a whore. His skill at drawing her surprised him. She had the look of someone thoroughly degraded, and yet driven by her sickness to go on and on, abasing herself with whomever would pay her price. A worthless whore. He ripped the sketch up and threw it away.

On his last night in the apartment, he was woken by laughter. At first he thought he was dreaming, but he waited a while and then he understood. The others had brought some American girls back with them. They had all been drinking, the girls as well. Paul pretended to be asleep, but the females shoved him and laughed at him until he got up. One of them sat close, her thigh pressed against his. She spoke in an awful, brash American voice, and the others laughed at the low things she said, her swearing and references to sex. All the girls were flirts, relishing their power over the men, but she was the worst. Her dress was very short, showing the tops of her thighs. Paul thought she had something of the whore about her. He could see that the others all wanted her, and he did too, but of course she didn't choose him, and when they all paired off, he was left with a chubby, quiet girl that the others had ignored.

She sat beside him on the sofa, her knees pointed primly away. He leant over to kiss her neck. He was gentle but she didn't respond. She refused even to turn her face to his so that they could kiss, and her knees and thighs were clamped shut against his hands. During his attempt, she stood up and walked away from him to the other side of the room. He saw her glance down at his crotch, and was embarrassed. But the girl laughed. I didn't think you were that way inclined, she said. He hated her for that, but it was how women were. They led you on, danced you over moral precipices, and afterwards, left you broken.

Early the next morning, Paul left the apartment and caught a train to the southern coast, where he boarded a boat to Greece. He paid for the journey with money he had stolen from his friends' wallets. They had riches to spare, his friends. Or perhaps he should call them his patrons. In a sense, that was the true way to understand it. Where there is genuine art, morality does not matter, only the need to service the art, to do whatever is necessary to bring it into being.

He was glad to be going to a new place, and felt inspired again, and free. He took his sketchbook to the ferry's railings and leaned over the churning sea. When he swung back onto his feet, he looked left, and thought he saw someone he knew. It was no more than a glimpse of ivory-suited leg, rounding a corner, but something about the thinness of the movement reminded him of the tall man. He put the thought aside. It unnerved him, and to distract himself, he opened his sketchbook and began a new study. He was idly sketching at first, but by the time the ferry disembarked in Patras, he had that strange, rare sense of a picture beginning to form under his hands. It wanted to be brought out. It only needed his presence, his guidance, to give it life. Clutching the sketchbook to his chest, he made his way through the shaded streets until he found a guest house where he secured a room for the night. A fat woman with a faint dark moustache sat at a table in the front of the house. A bitch: she fixed him with a contemptuous glare when he spoke to her in English. She wrote the price of the room on a piece of paper, and Paul handed over the amount in drachma. It was ridiculously overpriced—a tiny white room with a window overlooking the alley and a mean, stiff bed that creaked when he sat down. But he was satisfied with it all. He only wanted to continue his sketch.

It was a woman, of course. She was dark-haired, young, slender but still fleshy. Paul drew her with large, round breasts, then rubbed them out and drew them again, smaller. She had a little pubic hair, a few wisps, so that Paul did not have to attempt to draw what lay hidden there. Her face was clear, strong-featured, almost peasant-like with its blooming cheeks and freckles. But there was something fragile in her features, a delicate parting of the lips that bespoke shyness, modesty. Her expression was a little stupid—or was she simply innocent, unaware of her beauty?

It was only a study for a painting, and he would normally have tucked it at the back of his sketchbook, to save for when he had time and paints to complete it. But this drawing felt different. It felt complete: there was energy in the lines, a sense of striving, as though the figure were trapped in the paper. He wanted to make the same image over and over, even to draw on top of the lines, but he was scared to spoil it.

He hung the sketch from a nail on the back of the door and studied the woman. Drawing her had been a sensual experience; he became aware that he was in a state of rigid excitement. His thoughts flashed on the woman downstairs, and for a moment he was assaulted with the image of her monstrous breasts flopping about as she was taken. Not that he desired her. She would be grateful, no doubt, and it wouldn't take much... But it would somehow defile *her*, the one he had drawn, to abase himself with the other.

She brought him back to his senses. The excitement did not subside, but Paul began to experience it as a spiritual longing rather than lust. It was a desire to be connected to art itself. Of course, Paul thought. That was why he had been so overwhelmed in the Italian museums. Not lust for women, but love of art was what had assailed him there. He touched himself, looking at the picture, and immediately he was relieved. It didn't feel sordid, but like a pure flowing-out of his essence. Still, he wished that the stuff itself wasn't so messy.

In the following weeks, Paul toured the islands. He found beaches, and coves where one could sunbathe naked. The men in the villages sometimes wandered down to these places in the evenings, bringing cigarettes and retsina. Paul kept away from them, defensively rude when they approached. He still had money from his rich friends and he felt a new sense of ease. His intense feelings were now all directed towards the image of the woman. He frequently took out his sketchbook and studied her, her figure, her maddening perfection. He wished he could touch her. But looking at her strengthened his resolve to live and love only through art.

He came to Crete in August, when the island was full of tourists and the heat and crowds were intolerable. He travelled by bus to Heraklion and took a taxi to the archae-ological museum, intending to see the Minoan statues and the Snake Goddess. On stepping into the chilled air inside the museum, he felt drenched in sweat. His shirt clung to his back, and even his rucksack was damp with it. He wished he had not come. A group of schoolchildren were being led around the museum by their teacher—a tall man in an ivory suit: the sight of him caused Paul a momentary rush of adrenalin, which made his irritation with the children more pronounced. He thought about skipping the exhibits in favour of a cool drink and a cigarette in the shade. But he was here now, and might as well see what he had come for.

He found the Snake Goddess soon enough, but she seemed a joke, with her bare breasts and a snake in each fist, like the cover of a bad novel. There were other sculptures that caught his eye—figures of naked women kneeling, standing. Some had lost their limbs, as statues eventually do. All of them were headless. He wanted to look more closely at a bust of Aphrodite, but a girl was standing directly in front of him, obstructing his view. Annoyed, he fantasised about pushing her out of his way.

But the girl turned. She smiled briefly, apologetically. Paul stepped back, shocked at her appearance. In every respect she looked like the woman he had drawn, whom he had made perfect in his art. She walked out of the room, towards the entrance hall, her low heels tapping on the stone floor. She wore a short, light summer dress and around her shoulders she had draped a scarf that didn't match the rest of her outfit.

He recognised her by her looks, of course, but also by the strong feelings that awakened in him at that moment. He had always suspected that the world could do this—place sudden magic in his hands. His friends would say that was nonsense, of course. They would not understand. But that didn't matter. He had never wasted time on fools or conventional thinkers.

He followed the girl to the entrance, touched her arm to make her turn. Again, he felt the excitement of recognition. Her face was so exactly like the one he had imagined. She looked at him with a mildly questioning expression. He blurted out an invitation. Tea? A drink? When she agreed, Paul thought perhaps she recognised him also, maybe on the deep, unspoken level of her emotions. What other reason could she possibly have to go for a drink with a young man she had only just met?

She told him her name was Miri, short for Miriam. She was from Nottingham, in Crete for a brief holiday with her family before going up to the university in Manchester to study history. She explained all this over glasses of lemonade in a café on the seafront. She had let the scarf fall to the ground beneath her seat, and was sunning her arms. Paul wished that she wouldn't get too brown. His Miri was creamy and rosy, not tan. But that was circumstantial, he told himself. He was brown as a nut, where he had been pasty and milk-complexioned only months before. A tan would fade, in time.

She talked too much, but perhaps that was nerves. All the while she spoke about the wonderful holiday she was having, Paul was watching her lips move, marvelling at the fineness of her features, and the finesse with which he had wrought them. Even her teeth were perfectly small and white. He felt himself growing impatient with her talking, and interrupted her to suggest a walk to the caves. They had to climb down some rough steps to get onto the beach. He dared himself to take her hand as she stepped from the stone onto the sand, and to his delight she did not pull away. Her fingers were pleasingly small and cool, though perhaps a little too delicate, as once she complained he was holding too tightly and hurting her. But for the most part, once they left the café, she shut up and let Paul speak.

He felt that they had known one another for ever. It was fate that had brought them together, the intercession of the gods, natural law. They would marry, of course. She didn't have to go to university, not if she didn't want to, that was. There was nothing much to appeal to him in Manchester, but she might transfer to London, where he had promise of digs. She was his muse. He would paint her. They would be rich, eventually, after a necessary period of struggle. In time, they might decide to live in Italy or France. Their future happiness was assured, he told her. You are made for me.

But when they came to the caves, and stood in the shade of a lip of rock looking out over the sea, Paul was nervous. He had not thought what he would do next. He became distractingly aware of the smell and stiffness of his shirt, drenched in his sweat then dried in the heat. But Miri seemed not to mind. She smiled and stepped towards him. She was terribly thin, Paul realised, and too tall for a girl, taller than he. But he couldn't avoid it now. She moved towards him and he recoiled. Her mouth on his felt slimy. Their teeth knocked together, which embarrassed him. He closed his eyes and tried to bring her back as she had been before, before this had started. When she had been perfect. But when he opened her eyes, her face was changed. It had a masculine cast to it, a mocking expression that reminded him of men he had known. Furious with her, he tried to rip her dress away, but it wouldn't come off. She cried out and made to run away, but he gripped her arms and squeezed until she hushed. She was so thin, so slight. He didn't know his own strength. He flung her from him toward the mouth of the cave. There was a wet crack of skin and bone as her head hit the rock.

Her shoes lay askew on the sand, empty now, and that made him laugh. But it was hollow laughter. He knew he had made a mistake, that he had failed his own promise. He had meant to save himself for the perfect woman, the woman who was the embodiment of his art—not the first dirty little bitch who came his way. He stood over her, watching as the blood leaked from the back of her head. She might still be breathing, he thought, and so he knelt upon her chest, pushed down and heard the weak feminine sternum break. He arranged her on her side, and noted that she resembled Bernini's sleeping nude, recumbent on a marble mattress in the Louvre, though from another angle, the resemblance would fail. She was stone and yet somehow generous, still inviting, still giving.

He left Crete that same day and made his way to Cyprus, arriving in Paphos in time for the festival of Aphrodite. There was a parade, women dancing, their costumes pretty and exotic. Watching them, he thought every other woman was Miri. His thoughts turned often to her face, the way she had looked before he'd broken her. He came upon her doppelgänger in Sardinia, in a small fishing village where she was helping her mother mend nets by the harbour. That girl had to be dragged into the sea, trailing blood behind her. It didn't matter: she was everywhere in Europe, taunting him, tearing into him with her red mouth, dark eyes, long hair, the curve of her waist and swell of her breast. She came towards him and receded, like the tide, pulling him down into his own depths. It was like sinking, drowning. He woke in the nights, gasping for his breath. It was then he threw out his train ticket, his other souvenirs, tried to cover his tracks, grew a moustache on his lip as a disguise.

He made his way north again, seeking her or fleeing her—he couldn't say which. In Paris, by bad luck and bad timing, he ran into his university friends. They took what was left of their money and gave him a beating, stopping when he cried and refused to fight back. Then he had to telephone his parents and ask them to send him the fare to London. He was glad of it, though. In London, no one would be looking for him.

But in London he couldn't be satisfied. Women did not satisfy him. Their faces were fleeting, their features always betraying them. He painted one or two, he altered their beauty, but they stubbornly resisted the transformations. As though they could not give up their own flawed faces, their ugliness always bled through, under the thicknesses of paint. Yet, he painted. Nothing would sell, and he saw he had little of that greatness he had encountered on his travels in Europe. He had so quickly met the limits of his genius. He thought often of Miri, of the other girls: the first drafts of his work, the failed incarnations. Yet he admitted in some part of himself that he had not come close to his vision.

When winter came, he was hopeless with it all. He

gave up painting and took to sleeping late, spending his afternoons in a tiny café near his room. One wet early evening, he was seated in his usual place, sipping milky coffee, when the bell over the door rang. He looked up. The man entering the café was tall, very tall and thin, so tall that he had to stoop to get through the doorway. Paul recognised him at once, but did not speak, and the man, for his part, only smiled his old sly smile. He sat at Paul's table, although the café was mostly empty. He could have sat anywhere and had a table to himself, but of course that was not wanted. The man spoke, and said, I think we're alike, you and I.

Do I recognise you from somewhere?, Paul asked.

The man said not. I would remember, he said.

There was some awkward talk and Paul at last said, my studio is very close by. You might come and have a look at some of my work.

It would be an honour, said the man.

In the tiny, cold studio, with Paul's bed suggestively jutting out into the room, the man circled. He was slow, like a hawk moving in the currents of air. Paul wanted it over with, but the man had his own sense of time. Sit on the bed, the man said. The sheets were mottled with iron, rust stains. The man said, please sit still. He took out his set of tools. A brush. A chisel. A knife.

The man said, don't resist. Allow your face to show its beauty. I know that it's inside you.

The instinct was there to fight, but there was another current within him which pushed the instinct down and blunted it. A strange satisfaction came from the knowledge that he had been pursued all this way, across continents no less. He felt wounded by the man's genius; felt sympathy for his endeavour, also. When it was time for the knife, of course he fought, he raged and swore and hit out with his fists and feet. But deep down he felt it was all an act, that he too wanted the strange beauty of him to be carved out.

In the breathless silence of his room, in the throes of the wordless struggle, he felt again and again the pure passion of an artist, drawing beauty from under his hands. It was all there was. It was enough. And very soon, it was over.

THE SEAS OF THE MOON

The first card she turned. The drowned sailor.

Those are pearls that were his eyes.

Buried treasure. Secrets to be divined.

That moment when the tide ran back, revealing the bodies caught out in the treacherous cove. Drowned mouths all open and full of sand.

The soft slide and tang of an oyster as she swallowed. Tasting the sea. Seasick, sliding around in her guts. She wrapped the cards in a square of soft green silk and put them away in her pocket. Looked out over the calm water, beyond the rocky shore. The slosh of sea in the bowl of her stomach.

Under the ocean, all of the drowned. All of the dead souls glittered with nacre, growing a hard pearly sheen.

A ferry from one shore to another. No choice. Everything broken now, like a crack across the top of her head.

They'd never forgive her.

Getting into trouble. Getting out of it again. They'd never forgive her either way.

The rain started up, hard and heavy, a rain of stones and gravel, bullets and nails. She ran to the covered seating area and listened to the rain bouncing off the deck of the ferry. Couldn't see much through the grey blur, the wet broken lights moving about her in psychedelic blobs of colour. The shadowy sea storming under black clouds.

She'd slipped out in the middle of the night, taking nothing but her passport, her cards, a packet of her dad's cigarettes, and her granny's pearls. They're worth something, her gran had whispered. Knowing that she wouldn't go back, she felt she had no right to take anything else. She left her phone, so they couldn't track her that way. Maybe they wouldn't notice she was gone, for a while at least. Maybe even long enough to lose herself on the other side on the ocean. Would they really bother coming after her, all this way? After this, there was no going back, even if she wanted to. No going back to her Dad with his belt, and the priest with his fat mouth, or her Mam with her hard unforgiving silence, and her brothers with their mocking cries of *witch, witch, bitch*. No going back to Conor. Slight and serious, innocent Conor. He would say she'd broken his heart. He'd cry and call her cruel, evil and unnatural. She was, she was all those things, and she was so, so sorry — but then. If she went back. Then, all possible futures would collapse into one predictable dull layer of drudgery and routine. Teeth at her breasts. Sticky fingers in her hair. No, no she didn't want any of that. Pathetic as it might be, small and pointless as everyone said it was. Still. Whatever. She wanted her life for herself.

For all its ugly bulk, the ferry seemed high and fragile, hanging over tumultuous waters. The sea snapping from below, foaming mouth and hands and teeth—Siobhan couldn't shake the idea that she was to be punished. One way or another. How much did she even believe in that place, anyway? A place of no judgement, where she'd be cut free from that tiny clump of cells growing to a heavy iron ball and chain. Could it really be so simple? But don't think about that. Think too much and you won't have the courage.

The rain and sea spray smashed against the side of the boat; water sluiced over the deck. She felt sick again, and ran to the railings to lean over and spit bile into the ocean. Her granny's pearls hanging from her neck. The wind lashed and caught them, and they split from their fragile thread and fell, one by one, away into the sea.

She watched for lightning and counted the seconds until the thunder. Miles away! Inside the house was cold, the fire small and the floors bare. The boys were out in the storm, drawn to the smash and drama of the cliffs. Siobhan was inside, dandling a sleepy baby on her hip. The child was exhausted from crying but it wouldn't sleep; it woke itself up every few seconds to mewl and pet.

Quiet yourself down, snapped Siobhan. Her mind was elsewhere, watching the garden through the window. The garden was sodden, mud-ridden, a drenched green blur. Something pale moved under the bushes, something soft like a little white baby. Siobhan pressed her forehead to the glass and tried to focus. Something small and whitish was curled under the woody rhododendron bush. But when she blinked she lost focus and couldn't see it anymore; maybe it was rubbish, washed away by the rain.

A new wave of thunder broke over the sky, and lightning followed a few moments later. Close by, now. It rained harder, rain bounced off the window, bored holes into the mud of the garden, drummed up worms. Another roll of thunder came barrelling in, this one shaking the sky, cracking open the earth, and bringing its own nuclear flash of light. The trees blared green for a second, the black sky making a negative of itself. The baby screamed and Siobhan jiggled it up and down on her hip. For a second she thought she saw its bones through the pale illuminated flesh. Little skeleton.

Where were the boys? Oh, gone down to the beach. Don't tell Conor she'd let them go out in this weather.

They'd come back cold, with sand in their hair and lashes, and skin chapped by the storm, their hands full of pebbles and clams and crabs. Bloodied knees. Walking mud all over her clean floors.

Distant tower blocks looked like ships bobbing up and down on the slate-grey churning sea. Siobhan smoked two cigarettes, lighting the second from the end of the first. Stubbed them out under her foot and went back to her bed on the ward.

The doctor had been to see her earlier that day. Grand news, we were able to save the baby. His smile like a thin pecking beak. He'd patted her hand. Come along, there's nothing to worry about.

The ward was quiet now. Siobhan spread her cards across the bed and picked one at random. The Emperor. Seated on his throne, with his staff and his orb. The whole world was his. She always turned that card lately, feeling guilty for the rules she'd broken, the order she'd defied. It was Dad, in his Sunday best, quoting from the bible. He whipped her with his belt but took no pleasure in it. He did what must be done, upright and rigid and placid as stone. She'd say this card was God Himself, the holy patriarch. Except no, God was wild and furious. The terror. He was out to get her, to drag his claws over her and haul her back into his cave.

He'd come for her on the boat. He was a shape at first, a slow emergence, pushing under the water. And then he was a bear, a huge bear, ten times bigger than the boat. Bigger than the sky. His fur snagged with green strands and globules of seaweed. His teeth dripped saltwater from jagged yellow points. He took the boat in his two great paws and lifted it high. Siobhan clinging to the railings, screaming, scrabbling as her feet slid away from under her. Couldn't hold on any longer. She felt herself falling, the boat smashed to pieces around her, and then she was submerged in shocking cold, fighting back the sea that touched with teeth and stinging flesh, and clinging weeds and scraping metal ruins. Deep breath of sea in her lungs, and she sank down, down, under the weight of water. Bear tasted her on the sea's tongue and hooked her with his claw. And her blood ballooned around her, a shining bell of crimson, a teardrop, raining to red mist. And with it a sound, a slow deep boom, the thrumming pulse of her body bursting. Bloodshimmer in the water, bloodshimmer and bloodshine.

Deep under the sea, deep and deeper, the sea that buzzed and crushed her like a muscle, the sea all haunted with roars and gulls. Under the sea, the moon wobbled like a fat white lump of flesh. And the bear devoured the boat and its passengers. He swam in circles, blood bubbling from his enormous nostrils, lashing out with his powerful limbs. Snagging the moon on his claw. The last thing Siobhan remembered before waking in the hospital: the moon hanging on the bear's claw, his sharp-toothed smile shining with pearls.

When the rain eased up, Siobhan put the baby down and went into the back garden. She searched under the rhododendron bush for the small soft white thing she'd seen. There was nothing there, nothing but leaf litter and mud, little black beetles, thin transparent worms, fat flies.

It was foolish to look, foolish to hope. Something she'd sworn she'd given up. After all the treatments, the medications, the bible study and the prayer. Why look now for something more? Because the cards told her to look? But that was no reason. She'd promised Conor that she'd burned the cards, she'd sworn up and down and on the lives of her children. She'd knelt with him and prayed for forgiveness. But it had been a lie, one of many. All an illusion.

The cards—yes, she should have burned them like she'd sworn she would. The cards were evil, Conor was right. They'd taught her to look for another life, a life she'd lost at sea, or so she dreamed. She knew it was wrong, it was foolish. But she couldn't stop herself from looking.

It was the Moon she loved. Over and over it was the Moon. Ever since the time in the hospital, ever since they held her down and those babies had come tearing out of her. It was the Moon, calling and beguiling.

She'd seen it in the garden in the rain. The Moon, its madness, resting under the rhododendron bush like a big white grub. The Moon dragging a tide of blood back and forth through her body. The Moon with all its seas; she knew them off by heart and recited them in her mind: *the Sea of Bears, the Sea of Hands, the Sea of Witches, the Sea of Ghosts, the Sea of Smoke, the Sea of Blood, the Sea of Lies, the Sea of Tears, the Sea of Absence, the Sea of Murders, the Sea of Pearls, the Sea of Forgetting…*

But there was no moon under the rhododendron bush. There was nothing in the garden but mud and green. It began to rain again, and the baby's wailing started up from inside the house. After a while the sound became almost soothing, a repetitive loop, like the cry of a bird swooping high over the waves.

How could you, how could you? The devil must've been in you.

Aye, the devil alright. Squirming and gestating. Pushing out her flesh in a distorted lump, feeding from her blood. Parasitic, hungry little devil.

Towards the end she was exhausted. She knew of course the child would be a boy, another male to square off at the prison door. They would all be boys, all her children. And when it came, the pain of labour was unimaginable. Annihilating. Worse than the bear's mouth. Worse than anything. This was a tearing open of her centre, her intimate self split and turned inside out. Blood, an ocean of it. So much they had to pump her full of it again, over and over. But the child was strong. Robust and demanding.

The lungs of him! Her mother said, cradling him to her bosom.

Keep him, Siobhan said. I don't want him. But no one heard her over the sound of her baby's screams. Only the moon, peering in through the window. Only the moon seemed strange, seemed hopeful. But perhaps that was an illusion too. They gave her medicine, a lot of different medicine, and at times it drove the illusion away. But always it came back, the insistent sly thought that this wasn't real at all. That this was a dream. And her real life—that was elsewhere, happening without her.

How long had she been standing out there in the rain? She'd lost track of herself for a time. Now all at once she was aware of the silence beneath the downpour. The baby—it had stopped crying. Siobhan was drenched, her clothes heavy with rainwater, rain dragging at her skin. Her hair like rivulets of blood running from her scalp. How long had she been standing there? She couldn't tell. Where were the boys? Down at the beach, playing their daredevil games on the rocks. She'd go and call them back, get them inside before Conor came home.

She ran her hands through her soaked hair, squeezed out rivers of water. Went quickly out the back gate and down the narrow hedged-in path to the beach. I've left the baby crying, Siobhan thought. Have I? But the thought was distant, a whisper in the back of her mind. She stumbled down to the rocky cove where the boys always played. Something different there. Something not right. The boys weren't there, she couldn't even hear their voices.

Something dead on the beach.

Dead things washed up in the cove all the time. Driftwood and dead things. Shells with intricate inner staircases. Bits of broken shell and sea glass and bloated drowned things brought by the tide.

But the bear's head was bigger than all that.

Big as a church. Bigger. His neck torn away and trailing broken spine and gobbets of flesh and pouring blood into the ocean. Eyes like two black voids in the wet fur of his face. Jaws wide, a mouth ribbed like a cathedral, teeth yellow and dripping with seaweed. It was a mountain of fur and flesh and bone. Dead. Washed up. Here of all places.

Down, down the rocks, over the sand and shingle, she scraped and staggered. Down towards the great wide jaws of the bear's head. Feeling tiny, minuscule, dwarfed by his giant eyes. Bigger even than she remembered, bigger than in her dreams. The teeth she remembered well, would never forget. Razor sharp and merciless. But he was pitiful now, wasn't he? His head ripped away from his body. His powers all gone.

She saw herself approaching, reflected in his black unseeing eyes. She looked vague and ghostlike as a dream. Watched herself crouch low, hands trailing the sand and blood and surf at her feet. Felt with her fingers, dug and felt around until she found those soft little faces with their eyes and mouths and noses full of wet sand. Their small bodies crushed under the bear's weight.

And there. Nubs of ivory nestled in the weeds between its horrible teeth. Those are pearls that were her eyes. Her eyes, her bones, her heart, her life.

The sea smashed into the side of the ferry. Its voice hard with fury. Snatching at the sky.

It was only sheer luck that she caught the pearls falling from her neck, caught them in her hands and gathered them to her throat. She pulled back from the railings, let the pearls fall into her palms.

Behind her, under the shelter, children played. Climbing over the seats, hitting each other on the arms and legs. A strange feeling passed over her then. Something lost and broken. The sound of small boys playing, voices caught on the wind; it stirred something in her, some unfathomable feeling. But it passed. She stuffed the broken string of pearls into her pocket. Soon, soon, the land came into view.

WHITE RABBIT

———◉———

When Sarah Little dies, the crows in the garden raise their wings and take to the sky in a black, flapping murder. They hurtle upwards towards the noontime sun, a flock of feathers. It is a dog day, the peak of summer.

At the moment of his wife's death, Alec Little is startled by the movement of the crows. He's in the garden, not reading or sleeping, only resting his face in the bowl of the sun. The green of the garden and the blue of the sky lie flat against each other like a child's painting. A book is splayed open on Alec's chest: *The Mathematics of Wonder*. The book is complicated, obtuse. He finds himself, at times, staring at the print, taking in nothing. At times, the words detach themselves from their meanings, and turn into spiders' legs, scuttling off the page. It's the highest day of summer, and the green of the leaves and the grasses, and the cloudless blue of the sky, seem bright enough to ignite. The summer is about to turn, to burn away, to fire the trees in flares of red and gold. Already, the dry grass is turning to yellow and brown. Already, patches of bare earth can be seen on the lawn, dusty grey scrapes in the green.

A few moments to feel the sun on his face. A few moments to spend outside, in the wide skies and in the air. He stands now, letting the book fall from him onto the lawn. He places his bare feet on the prickly summer grass, and walks back to the house, stepping through the French windows onto the cool tiled floor. The shade in the house makes his head spin a little. His vision takes a moment to adjust to the interior.

He knows she's dead before he steps inside the room, or perhaps he knows a moment before then. Already it seems he always knew. He knew when he was sitting in the garden, when the crows flew from the oak tree. Or somehow he knew long before that: an hour before, when the nurse left. He thinks of the nurse's soft smile as he let her out the front door. She's sleeping, the nurse had said. You should try to get some rest yourself.

In the room, the windows are closed. Sarah's body, still and emptied of breath, is cocooned in woollen blankets and silken quilts. There's music in the room, coming from the record player on the dresser. The record's stuck. A phrase repeats. The volume is turned so low, he almost wouldn't know there was music at all.

Alec opens the window to let out the last of her breath. He lifts the needle from the record and turns off the player. Then he lies down beside Sarah on the bed, curving his body around hers, to warm her, or cool himself. He thinks about how her last breaths have already dissolved into the air. He thinks about how they shared the same air all these years, fifty-eight years of marriage. He thinks that the air is made from the breath of birds, from the breath of cats, from his own breath, and that of his wife. He realises that he has not known the sound or the taste of her last breath. His heart creaks painfully in his chest, and he thinks, I cannot survive this.

I can't
survive
can't bear it
can't bear

the shrill cry of the telephone in the hallway. They should know better than to keep calling here. They know his name and say it to him through the echoing empty telephone cables. Alec, they say. Only that. Only his name. But it's the way they say it. It's that they know it.

When he slams down the receiver, the telephone shakes. It shakes with increasing violence and the hard Bakelite bobbles up and sprouts legs, jointed and glossy as a spider's. The telephone clambers down from the little table. It clatters at speed along the tiled floor of the hallway, and swerves around the corner, down into the cellar, its wires slithering behind. Alec can hear it tumble down the stone steps, cracking, breaking open with little trilling cries, little bells spilling out. He scrambles after it into the cellar, and when he catches it he stamps on the broken pieces of telephone. His knees hurt and he stops his angry dance, still breathing hard. How did this come about? The cellar's damp and they've never kept anything in it; it's cold and smells of wet brick, and he doesn't want to be down here.

He tries to retrace his steps but there's some part missing, some moments. It's not safe or wise to contemplate the mechanisms responsible for these missing parts. He's a clock, springing his clockwork, stuffing it all inside again and listening for the *tick tick tick*. As long as he keeps ticking, no one need know there was ever any dropped time. Now he listens, and he hears music from somewhere, and the music stitches the world back together, reminds him that he is standing in the cold, damp cellar, and that there is a whole house sitting above him, a warm, well-fed house, stuffed with books. The music is lilting and slow, as from a music box. Sarah loved music, all kinds of music. He used to love music too, but he's forgotten. He hasn't heard any for a long time.

He walks upstairs, holding tight to the railing so as not to lose his footing on the uneven steps, and closes the cellar door behind him. In the kitchen, he takes a pill for his blood pressure, and one for his heart, and another for his sorrow. He can't tell if the pills do anything. When he was young, there were pills that made him beautiful and pills that made him fast and smart. (Sarah had such long lovely hair back in their wild days, raven-haired they called her, but Alec always thought of it as velvety black. It was the first thing he'd noticed about her. He'd accused her of witchcraft, with that hair, just to get her attention.) Now he takes pills that give him small headaches on the left side, and he takes pills that stop him crying all day long. He doesn't know what to do with the time, since he stopped crying all day long.

He takes his pills. He takes a second of the pills that alleviate his sorrow. A third. He finds that he is hungry for the pills and he pours them into his cupped palm, picks them up with the flat of his tongue. The pills are delicious, each a small taste of nothing. Little white voids.

First his tongue becomes numb, then his teeth. His whole mouth turns to nothing, and the nothing spreads through him like a stain spreading through cloth. He sinks to the floor. The floor becomes numb, becomes rubbery with numbness. The kitchen is bleached of all feeling: the wood in the counter top is blank and cannot remember its treeness. A delicate China tea set falls silent, and the toaster turns to cold stone. All that remains is the singing of the birds in the garden. If only he could get into the garden. But he's so empty now, the sound of bird song can fill him entirely. He is stuffed with birds, their beaks and wings and feathers. They squirm and writhe and peck under his skin. They break through the cage of his ribs and squawk their yellow beaks wide, like blackbirds baked in a pie. Then

nothing

bird song

and

the girls visit, bringing their children, and their children's children who run up and down the lawn, playing tag. Alec is a safe zone, where they can't be touched. He watches the children play while the grown-ups are in the house. He notices *The Mathematics of Wonder* has been kicked into a flower bed, its leaves splayed out and ruined. He ought to pick it up, but he won't; he doesn't want to touch it. When the rain starts, he comes back to the house, weighed down with children; they cling to his arms and legs as he walks. Later, he finds his two daughters in the bedroom, going through Sarah's things. Both of them are crying, they are always crying these days. Isabel says she feels her mother's presence quite strongly in the room. The silk scarves Sarah used to wear, floating through Isabel's fingers. Both girls look like Sarah: they are two aspects of her, two expressions. He doesn't see himself in them at all.

Emily puts her arms around Alec and says, Oh Dad. Please will you come and live with us, just for a while? We've got so much room. I hate leaving you alone here. But Alec says he wouldn't feel right, leaving the house. He might go back to work soon, he says, and Emily and Isabel glance at one another as if they know something he doesn't.

He won't let them take any of Sarah's vinyl. He says they don't appreciate vinyl anyway, they have everything digital these days. He and Sarah hated that. They loved the sound of the needle floating in the grooves of a record. Some evenings, they would put the record player near the window, and sit outside on the bench looking for stars, while Mahler played out, or Erik Satie, or the Beatles. Sometimes, before Sarah got sick, they would even dance. Pink Floyd. Fleetwood Mac. Philip Glass. Alec knows the scratches in the records, the places where they jump. Every object has its animus, its story.

Isabel says it's alright, they don't want the records. She holds Alec's hand in hers and he squeezes it. Isabel is still the baby. She made them worry and laugh, and Sarah called her my crazy curly girl. Emily was the sensible one, the one who could be trusted. She was the one Sarah telephoned first, when they heard about the cancer. And then Sarah cried, and said, we gave her all the responsibility, we should have let her be more free. But it's Emily who is crying hard angry tears now, and saying Dad, let us look after you.

You can have the records when I go. Emily wipes tears from her face, shakes her head. What was that record we liked, he tries to remember. It shouldn't have gone out of his head like that. Of all things, this is what he needs to remember. The least I can do is remember. The record has a scratch so it always sticks near the end, and they sing feed your head... feed your head... feed your head... feed your head... feed your head... feed your head... feed your head... feed your head... feed your head... feed your

Dad. Isabel shakes his shoulder. Hush. You didn't let her down.

head... feed your head... feed your head...feed

Dad, do you want to lie down for a while. The girls fold him up onto the bed, and slip off his shoes. They cover him with a blanket that smells of white lavender. They kiss the top of his head. Isabel is sobbing now, but Emily has stopped. When one of the granddaughters bursts into the room, they shush her, and take her away, so the room is

your head... feed your head... feed until one of them got up and lifted the needle off the record. And that was usually him, after listening as long as he could stand, because Sarah liked that bit, where the record skipped. That's my favourite part of the song, she would say. And if it ever came on the radio or television, she would sing along, and wait for her favourite part, forgetting that it was never going to come.

But this other Sarah. This other Sarah is made of feathers and vinyl and knives. She follows Alec around the house, clanking her sides together, complaining about his housekeeping, eating the furniture. She's hungry for the wood and the velvet of the sofa in the front room. She eats the books page by page. You're not my wife, Alec says, and she says, how can you tell? Maybe it's the other way around. Maybe you're not my husband. Did you ever think of that. She chews the edge of the table, spitting out splinters onto the carpet. Her teeth are very strong, they are made of rocks.

He thinks this has happened because he wasn't in the room when she died. He only left her for a few minutes, but that was all she'd needed. The house made new doors for her to walk through when he wasn't looking.

The mobile phone is kept hidden from the other Sarah, kept in his pocket. The girls gave it to him so they could call him any time. They call him twice a day. He thinks they've got a rota, taking turns to keep an eye on him. When it's Emily's turn, she asks has he taken his pills and has he eaten, and what does he plan to do with the day, and she reminds him that the nurse is coming and the cleaner that she's hired for him, and she says, this would be so much easier if you'd come and live with us. But when Isabel phones, she calls him Daddy, and she tells him stories about when she was little and he was big, when he scooped her up, and plaited her hair, and carried her on his shoulders all the way down the road to the sea. She tells him about summers in the garden and on the beach, how they made him the judge of their cartwheel competitions and their races. How they would bring everything to him: all their finds of shell and stone and starfish. How when it rained, they would watch the drops racing down the window, and count the seconds between thunder and lightning. Mummy would play the piano, and the girls would dance, and he would applaud and throw flowers at the three of them.

He tries to tell Isabel that there is A Something in the house. He wants to tell her, he thinks she will know what to do. But he doesn't know how to explain what he means. The words come out wrong. There's another house in this house, he says. I'd never realised before. There's another house inside this house, and I think I'm living in the other house now. Isabel thinks this is a metaphor. Isabel says, oh Daddy, do you remember that time the picture fell off the wall? And Mummy said, it's a ghost, and Emily thought it happened because she'd gotten really angry about something. She thought she'd made it happen with her mind. And for weeks, we practised moving things with our minds, but we couldn't do it at all.

These conversations with Isabel are good but tiring, like time travel must be tiring. When they are over and he's back in the present, he feels weak and hungry. He thinks he'll eat an egg, so he goes to the kitchen which the girls keep well stocked for him. The eggs are hen eggs from Emily's own hens, who live in her own garden. Clever Emily. Very sensible. The eggs are white and heavy globes. He breaks one against the side of a metal bowl, and the egg cracks, like porcelain. It shatters into pieces, into fine shards and rough surfaces and dust.

Oh dear, he says.

The other Sarah says, all the king's horses and all the king's men won't be able to put *that* together again.

He cannot look at the other Sarah directly; she hides. She makes herself look like white tiles and counter tops and wooden blinds and a pot of flowers. He can see, or he thinks he can see, her outline, a fine edge where the pieces don't quite meet. He can tell she's there, hiding in things. But only when he turns away does she step out from her camouflage. Her teeth clack and crunch, and her tongue is made of thick leather like a belt strap, so when she speaks, it's like a whip cracking over rocks. She eats the eggs, pulverising them to dust with her powerful jaws.

Alec is still hungry. There's a little café at the bottom of the road which sells bacon sandwiches, and the table in the window has a view of the sea. Suddenly he wants a bacon sandwich and a sea view more than anything. Crisp bacon oozing grease into the white bread,

a squeeze of ketchup, a

cup of tea, and

the woman in the café says, did you not bring any money out with you, love? She's very kind, the woman. She reminds him of someone, someone plump and middle-aged he might have known when he was a boy. Maybe his mother. He says, take my watch, take my watch, but when he holds out his wrist, it's bare. He rolls up the sleeves of his dressing gown, checks his pockets. I'm good for the money, he says. I really am. The woman brings him a bacon sandwich and a cup of tea, and she says, there, don't you wander off now. When you've had that, I'll take you home. Where would he go, he wonders, maybe to

the beach

tiny sea snails. Closer to the water, there are jellyfish washed up. He knows better than to touch them, knows that they sting. But they're strange, so passive and patient. Carried around by the water, no muscles to swim against the tide. It's good to be out in the open air, but where are the girls, he should warn them about the jellyfish. He can't remember if they know about jellyfish. He can't remember how big the girls are. He thinks they must be very little because he can't see them at all. It's frightening that they are so small he cannot even see them, they are small enough to be washed out to sea. He looks for them under stones and inside shells. He kicks over the sand with his feet. When the girls find him, they are too big to be his girls, and for a little while he fights them off; he says, I have to find my daughters, they're only little, I have to find them or they'll be washed out to sea.

Here we are, says Emily. Here I am and here is

Isabel

confuses him. She lives in her old bedroom, but she's big now. He wants her to be small again, and so every evening, she sits at the side of his bed and talks to him until she has become five or six years old, with her hair in pigtails, in a pinafore dress and white socks falling down around her ankles, and black shoes with the strap across. She says those kind of shoes are called Mary Janes. He goes to sleep early and wakes in the middle of the night. There is a glass of water on the bedside table, and his tablets set out beside it. He takes the tablets, drinks the water. He doesn't want to lie in bed, awake, until the morning, so he gets up. Puts his slippers on and his dressing gown, and a woolly hat because his ears get cold.

The house is awake too, and wants to play.

What games, what rules?

He's standing with his hands on the dresser, hearing music from somewhere, that lilting music again. He puts an ear to the wood, and his nose touches a box of matches. When he opens the box, there's a deafening blast of music. When he slides the box shut, it goes quiet. He puts the closed box to his ear and hears the music faintly. When he opens the box again, it blares out again: an entire orchestra of sound. The matchbox is heavy because of all the music inside it; it weighs down his dressing gown pocket. Why does he have matches, he wonders, but then forgets to answer his own question.

There are two black shoes dancing at the bedroom door, two Mary Janes, kicking impatiently at the wood. Like two small dogs with lolling straps and buckles. Alec opens the door for them and they squeeze out. He follows them down the stairs, and down through the whole house, into the cellar. They can only get halfway down the stairs, because the cellar is full of salt water. Luminous jellyfish drift near the surface, lighting the space in soft colours. The other Sarah is floating on the water in the guise of drifting vegetable matter and foam. When she floats near the stairs she assembles herself into a Sarah-shape, lashing her rafts together tightly until they become her arms and legs. The Mary Janes slither onto her feet and buckle themselves up.

She has her hands on the walls either side of Alec's head, and although he cannot know for sure that she is there, he can see her outlines in the air and against the bricks. His heart flutters hard in his throat. He turns and stumbles up the stairs and into the kitchen, hearing the clacking coming behind him and the slap of shoes on stone. He wants to get out into the garden, to breathe fresh air, but the back door is locked and he doesn't know where to find the key.

On the kitchen counter is a large, shallow Tupperware box of fairy cakes. He takes off the lid and picks the cakes out one by one, to throw at the other Sarah. He hurls the cakes at her and they turn into little stones and clatter to the floor. He can't tell if she's gone, but he can't hear her anymore, and when he looks into the Tupperware box, he can see the back-door key through the plastic bottom of it. Emily probably hid it there, he thinks. She's always hiding things from him, always telling him to do this and do that. She was always the bossy one, he thinks, but somehow these thoughts slide away from him too soon to make anything of them.

In the glass of the back door, he sees his own face. It's very strange to him now. The lines around his eyes are deep, and the lines on his cheeks, like furrows, where the skin has sagged and loosened, and is rough with stubble. Sarah always complained if he hadn't shaved. Because I like to kiss you, my darling, but I don't like to graze my face. The cells in his skin are aging, drying up, like cells in a leaf. The pattern of lines on his face are like the patterns of river branches in the Amazon basin, like the roots of a tree, like paths in a forest. Everything the same; everything different. He is comforted by the idea of order, of symmetry, of repetition at the heart of the inexplicable and wild.

The Mathematics of Wonder is still lying in the garden, sunk down into the soil, sucked on by ants and mites, bitten by beetles, shat on by birds. It is mouldering, soaking up the dew at midnight, sending up stalks of itself towards the moon. Alec sits under one of its great paper leaves, watching as a caterpillar munches a hole through the inky words. It speaks to him, a mutter of regurgitated letters. No wisdom. The only wisdom he has is pointless, unpunctual. He should never have left the room, should not have left Sarah's side as she was dying. She needed his protection and he was not there. He was meant to take her inside himself and hold her there, and instead the house took her inside itself and wouldn't let her go. He can hear the other Sarah in the kitchen, clanking and clacking the sides of herself together. Fragments of paper leaf fall around Alec. He reads the word *dormouse*, then puts the paper in his mouth, sucks it until the ink has spread over his tongue. The caterpillar spits punctuation marks from its jaws, and they scurry away, over the grass. Alec follows an ellipsis...

...

Isabel tells him the name, over and over, but he forgets. Don't only remember me, she says. Remember Emily, too. She tells him about Emily, how she was the clever one, the sensible one. How she took care of Sarah all those years, coming to the house twice a day, reading her favourite books over and over. Poems and stories and novels, and the newspaper. Emily has hens in her back garden, and three grown up children, and three grandchildren who are still small enough to carry on her hip. Emily is a teacher because she always wanted to be a teacher. We used to play schools, Isabel says, and Em was always the teacher and I was always naughty and so were the dolls. We put our dolls in a row, sitting up, with their backs against the wall, and Emily told them off, one by one, for their terrible penmanship and for not knowing their times tables. Oh yes Emily, says Alec. I hadn't forgotten at all.

Then a strange woman comes to the house and tries to hold his hand. It might be an aunt, she smells like his aunt, his father's sister who was very religious and always asked him to pray with her. Lavender and peony. She doesn't seem to be religious anymore, but when he pulls his hands away from hers, she says oh god, and she cries. She's angry with Isabel, but Isabel hugs her, says, he can't help it. It was always Mum who held us together. Losing her has made everything come loose. It's broken him.

Alec tries to tell her no, it's the house doing this. It's that the other house has taken over. Sarah has slipped through the egg-skin-thin membrane between worlds, through the door that shifted slightly to the left, and is lost in there, somewhere. Alec needs to drive the other house away. He tells the girls that he needs things, he can't say what the things are, he won't know until he sees them. You're not making sense, he tells Isabel. You're not making any sense to me anymore. She clings onto his arm, says, Oh Daddy, but you're

tired now, very tired, because he's awake again, playing the game with the house. This time he thinks he can win it, win her. He wakes the dolls, sitting with their backs straight against the wall, and they stand with jerky slanted motions, eyes rolling in their heads, eyelids snapping shut as their heads fall forwards. They have cupid mouths and lacy collars on their dresses, and look like tiny fat women whose heads are full inside of coiled hair, shiny plastic hair. Too stupid to say anything to him, to try to stop him. They don't even know their times tables. But they like to sing, they sing through their closed or slightly parted rosebud lips, a song of hair and blue eyes that loll and roll. They sing for their mother, the other Sarah, who comes for them with her clanking arms, who crunches them in her teeth, chews until her teeth are covered in yellow scabs of plastic.

When she speaks she is terrible, she has no music in her voice.

Not Sarah.

You can't tell the difference, she says. I look like her. I speak like her. My name is the same as hers, and I live in this house, with you.

Not Sarah.

You don't know what happened when I died. You don't know me in death. This is my death. It looks nice on me, don't you think.

She turns around slowly, all the way, and the walls shudder and the carpet swells and the doors slam shut.

Not Sarah. Sarah liked music.

I like music. Delicious. So refreshing. She clinks her tongue and spits plastic from her teeth. She turns to Alec and holds out her hand for the music.

White rabbit, he says,

white rabbit

remembers

her fingers are cracks in the wall, curling towards him. He hands her the box of matches. A blaze of sound explodes from the matchbox and she shudders, and the door booms out of its frame. The music splinters her jaw and the skirting board. It cracks her spine and the stair bannisters. It turns her bones and the bookshelves to charcoal. She dances like a balloon, darting from one side of the room to the other, her feet blackening and curling, her leather tongue bubbling and unrolling down to the metal buckle, that glows red like a pitchfork.

The music pours into the room, pours into his own chest and pounds his ears. There is music blaring from the walls and the curtains, too much

music

comes from the air, a wheeling siren, a percussion of

sound

heard somehow in his fingers and the skin of his face, his lips, his

heart

and

your head… feed your head… feed your head… feed your head… feed your head… feed your head… feed your head… feed your head… feed you

pure air siphoned into his chest, pushing and pushing, trying to dislodge the black ash that sticks to the sponge of his lungs

r head… feed your

air as fresh and feathery as skies, there's sun on his face, there's the weight of a book resting on his chest. Oh Daddy,

says Isabel, my Daddy, my
    head… feed
    my
    white rabbit
    you didn't let me down, Dad, you didn't let any of us
    your head… feed your head… feed your love, the
record's stuck.

But that's my favourite part, she whispers. He can't tell
if she has spoken aloud or inside his head. He gets out of
the bed, carefully, so as not to hurt or jolt her, and he tiptoes
to the record player, picks up the needle and places it at the
start of the record. The volume is very low, so that he can
hear her breath and her heartbeats.

Through the closed window he sees the crows in the
garden, a crowd of black wings in the tree. The blue of the
sky and the green grass lie against each other like a child's
painting. The green of the leaves and the grasses, and the
cloudless blue of the sky, seem bright enough to ignite. It is
a dog day, the peak of summer.

He slips back into the bed, feels his wife gently rest
against his arm, his shoulder. It's my favourite part too, my
love, he says. It's always been my favourite. Maybe he only
thinks it, maybe he doesn't say it aloud.

They're alone together for a moment, then one goes.

ACKNOWLEDGEMENTS

My heartfelt thanks go first to Mike and Carolyn for taking on this collection, and for being such kind, wonderful people to work with. Thanks to Catrin Welz-Stein for the incredible cover art. I'm seriously indebted to Vince Haig, a genius in several dimensions, for his inspired graphic design.

Many of the stories in this collection were previously published in magazines and anthologies, for which fact I am endlessly thankful. Thanks especially to editors Andy Cox, Mike Allen, Steve Berman, and Mike Kelly (again); and thanks to Vince Haig (again) for his wonderful illustrations of my stories in *Interzone* and *Black Static*.

I'm grateful to every writer who has befriended or pen-friended me over the years. I'd especially like to thank Henry Szabranski for sticking with me through a decade or more of stories. Many thanks also to the former Self-Forging Fragments, Neil Williamson and Ilan Lerman, and of course to the amazing Priya Sharma. Priya, you kept me writing through some terrible times. Thank you for your friendship, patience and kindness. To Penny Jones, Cate Gardner and Simon Bestwick, thank you for the last-minute critiques and your unfailing kindness. My thanks go to Lynda Rucker and Erica Satifka for their life-saving sanity. I will never forget Katrina Leno's cool brilliance in the face of unbelievable idiocy, or the light shone by Rob Shearman in a dark time. I'd like to acknowledge and thank James Knight for encouraging the spread of literary weirdness like some sort of macabre virus. Thank you to Kate Mascarenhas for generously printing and binding my first ever novel. Sincere thanks to Kerry Hadley-Pryce, Aliya Whiteley, Des Lewis, Charlie Hill, S.P. Miskowski, Helen Marshall, Julie Travis, Lee Harrison (and his sticky tables), Victoria Leslie, Tracy Fahey, James Everington, Maura McHugh, and pretty much every member of Fantasycon, Birmingham Writers Group, the Online Writers Workshop and the Almond Aligners. A special thank you to Jim Mcleod, for taking all the blame.

Endless love and gratitude to my Lovely Dads who have made so many things possible for their wayward daughter. Thanks to my family in general, you bunch of dafties. Thanks also to my pals in various workrooms at BMET and Edinburgh Colleges, for making me laugh in the midst of madness. To my friends Louise Knight, Laura Gavin, Kat Wilkinson and Eve Waterside: my thanks and love.

And to you, dear reader, an infinitude of hearts.

ABOUT THE AUTHOR

---◉---

Georgina Bruce is a writer and teacher currently living in Edinburgh. Her short stories have been widely published in magazines and anthologies, and have been longlisted for the Bridport and Mslexia short story prizes. In 2017, her story White Rabbit won the British Fantasy Award for Short Fiction. This is her first collection.

www.georginabruce.com

twitter.com/monster_soup

CPSIA information can be obtained
at www.ICGtesting.com
Printed in the USA
LVHW111728280419
615867LV00003B/25/P